Floyd Patterson

Floyd Patterson

A Boxer and a Gentleman

ALAN H. LEVY

McFarland & Company, Inc., Publishers
Jefferson, North Carolina, and London

LIBRARY OF CONGRESS CATALOGUING-IN-PUBLICATION DATA

Levy, Alan Howard.
    Floyd Patterson : a boxer and a gentleman / Alan H. Levy.
       p.   cm.
    Includes bibliographical references and index.

    ISBN 978-0-7864-3950-8
    softcover : 50# alkaline paper ∞

    1. Patterson, Floyd.   2. Boxers (Sports) — United States — Biography.
    3. African Americans — Civil rights — History — 20th century.
    4. African Americans — Social conditions —1964–1975.   I. Title.
    GV1132.P3L48 2008
    796.83092 — dc22
    [B]   2008032250

British Library cataloguing data are available

On the cover: Floyd Patterson in Elgin, Illinois, September 23, 1962
(AP Photo)

Manufactured in the United States of America

*McFarland & Company, Inc., Publishers
  Box 611, Jefferson, North Carolina 28640
   www.mcfarlandpub.com*

To the memory of my friend
Dave Dixon
(1954–2008)

Contents

Introduction

To any fan of the sport of boxing, Floyd Patterson is anything but an unknown figure. Yet there has been no biography of his full life. Patterson (1935–2006) was once the world's heavyweight champion. When he won the crown, he was then the youngest ever to do so. He was also the first heavyweight champion, after many others had famously failed, to regain the championship after losing it. Muhammad Ali fought Patterson on two occasions and said that Patterson possessed more boxing skills than any other fighter he ever faced. Patterson was a formidable competitor in every respect. When he was a rising young middleweight–light heavyweight, some of the opposition arranged for him appeared to some in the press to be a bit lackluster. But here one legitimate contender revealed a major factor in this when he exclaimed to a reporter a thought shared among many boxers of the day: "Me fight Patterson. What do you think I am — crazy?" Doubtlessly no one would name Patterson as one of the top boxing champions of all time. Still, he was a great talent, and he was twice the champion, no mean achievement by any yardstick.

Much about Patterson's life is also significant in regard to matters that his career encompassed beyond the ring. Tracing his career just up to the point of his twice becoming champion, Patterson's life represents a most ennobling example of the Horatio Alger–American dream mythology. He grew up in the poorest, meanest surroundings imaginable, plagued as well by some severe emotional disturbances. Yet he appeared to overcome all and, in doing so, gained the adulation of many, and not merely in the world of boxing and sports. During his championship days, Patterson could cite as acquaintances and fans such luminaries as John F. Kennedy, Richard Nixon, and Eleanor Roosevelt; later there would be fans and friends among such New

1

York politicians as Ed Koch, Hugh Carey, Mario Cuomo, and George Pataki. Many sports heroes have received phone calls from the president at their moments of triumph. The night Patterson regained the heavyweight crown in 1960, President Eisenhower did not call him. Eisenhower was a fan, and he was kept abreast of the fight on Air Force One while flying back from East Asia. The night Patterson re-won the title, he did better than a phone call from the President; he received a telegram of congratulations from Pope John XXIII.

Patterson was a most appealing figure, a true gentleman in every sense of the word, and while he was champion that gentlemanly, devotedly Christian nature of his gained an extraordinary level of attention and praise. He appeared to embody all the noble human traits commonly drawn from the Bible or from the Boy Scout Manual. He was an appealing example to all who believed in the principle that each of us, at our best, can not only make a finer place for ourselves but for the world. This imagery was especially poignant and grew to have added dimensions amidst the emerging political battles of the United States in the 1960s. In the early part of that heady decade, Floyd Patterson was active in many civil rights causes and represented a most hopeful symbol for liberal America. His example engendered nothing in the way of fear. It presented everything of which to be proud and implied that the road ahead, but for the loutish resistance of such wretched entities as the Ku Klux Klan and their reprehensible confreres, could and would be a smooth one of steady progress. In the mid– and late–1960s, that optimistic world would suffer numerous jolts, to say the very least, and Patterson's career would reflect much of this.

At this apex in his boxing career, Patterson dictated a type of self-examination and autobiography entitled *Victory Over Myself*. It won praise from reporters, from critics, and from such literati as poet Marianne Moore. At that time, a short pocket paperback biography by the *Sport Magazine* writer Jack Newcombe also appeared. Newcombe's little book and Patterson's autobiography each end at the time of Patterson's triumphs as the champion. The issues, troubles, and victories of these early years tell part of the story of what makes the life of the man significant, both as a boxer and as a human being. But so much that Patterson's life encompassed, for better and worse, came after his triumphant times. And it was especially in these years of his boxing career, 1962 to 1972, that Patterson's life was immersed in the flow of so many terribly significant, not altogether happy events, and not just in boxing.

Various sports, including boxing, have often cast significant reflections of and been actors within broader social and political contexts in American and world history. In the early twentieth-century nadir of race relations in post-slavery America, for example, the fearsome career of boxer Jack Johnson was a grim symbol of so much of those shameful times. When Patterson was growing up on the streets of Brooklyn in the 1940s, some of the earliest breakthroughs in racial segregation occurred, and the example of Jackie Robinson's integration of major league baseball at Ebbets Field, just down the street from Patterson's grim Bedford-Stuyvesant neighborhood, was as significant a symbolic event in this process as any. Patterson would later join Jackie Robinson in many civil rights struggles. The ongoing battles of the civil rights movement that continued through the 1950s and reached various peaks of intensity in the 1960s were also influential upon, as well as influenced by, events and people in sports. Here boxing would indeed prove to be as significant as any sport in the broader social and political currents of 1960s America. A major reason for this can be explained by the presence of one man — Muhammad Ali. Ali was undeniably the most significant sports figure in the 1960s and early 1970s, and, as his career concerned so much more than mere pugilism, other athletes touched by Ali's career were also pushed onto stages that were much broader than those to which mere boxers are normally accustomed. The lives and careers of Sonny Liston, Joe Frazier, Ernie Terrell, and, later, George Foreman were all significantly affected by the whirlwinds of political and social events that centered around Muhammad Ali. Floyd Patterson was another such greatly affected figure. In the years before Ali became famous, Patterson had shown political activism in the area of civil rights. His quiet work here received some notoriety, but the intersection of his career with that of Muhammad Ali would cast him into a new role that proved much more noteworthy, often sadder, and at times actually pitiful.

The images of the men that Ali faced, like Patterson, were indeed greatly affected by the hazy rhetoric and politics of the day, tinged especially by the special light that was Muhammad Ali and the force of his unique personality, athletic gifts, and starkly new outlooks. To some degree, Joe Frazier and George Foreman were each able to carve a public niche for themselves independent of that which emerged amidst their crossings with Muhammad Ali. Still, the shadow of Ali was enormous, undeniable, and understandable. For Ali was indeed, as he always famously said, "the greatest"— at the very least of his own day. Whether he is the greatest of all time is a matter of endless debate, although few experts would name anyone but Ali or Joe Louis as the greatest heavyweight. Independent of the statures of boxers within their ultimate rankings, the political legacies of the era of the 1960s are also matters of intense debate. Where those debates intersect with boxing, the legacy of Ali's influence has been strong, and perhaps a trifle unfair. Are the politics of a given sports figure right by virtue of the undeniable greatness he happened to possess as an athlete? There is hardly any logic in such an assertion, yet in the context of the whirligigs of '60s politics, Ali gained certain levels of political weight very much because of his greatness in the ring. If he hadn't been so great a boxer, who would have paid much regard to him elsewhere? Some of the legacies of his views have lingered for many decades. A gentleman like Patterson contrasted markedly with much of what appealed about a man like Ali, especially to the nation's youth, a contrast which was magnified enormously by the outcomes of their matches in the ring. Much of that contrasting imagery has remained in the general historical memory.

While arguments about who is the greatest fighter of all are often intense, equally if not more intense have been controversies as to the utility and strengths of various views, activities, people, ideologies, and attitudes of the turbulent times of the 1960s. Resolutions to so many of the arguments have never come forth, nor will they to any great extent, at least so long as many of the participants are still alive, and likely longer. Perhaps the best book, and certainly one of the best books, on the decade and its meaning, *The Sixties*, by Todd Gitlin, neatly outlines at least a great deal of the tonalities of the time with its subtitle — *Years of Hope, Days of Rage*. And, indeed, the varying levels of legitimacy, of naïveté, of righteousness, of egocentrism, of narcissism which various historians and commentators attach to the elements of hope and rage that tinted the politics of the decade encompass much of the debate as to the era's essences and meanings. The legacy of Muhammad Ali's (and his political allies') stands on racial issues and the Vietnam War remain components of these historical debates. Those who opposed him in the ring, like Patterson, grew to be perceived enemies on the political front as well, often in ways that distorted their actual record of work.

Ali freely admitted that much of the imagery he successfully cast upon his various opponents was driven by a simple, logical desire for hype and for the dollars such hype would bring. As Muhammad Ali was so seminal a figure during these years, the pall he cast over his opponents has lingered, not just about them as fighters but about the relative soundness of their views and sensibilities, both then and since. One of many significant strains of '60s thought and sensibility concerned the degree to which it was hep, and most desirable, to be considered a radical, as, for a time, it was uncool even to be a mere liberal. This desired imagery had its serious sides, as shown by the degrees to which many were drawn into acts of violence and terrorism, and it had its trivial sides — what the writer Tom Wolfe famously termed "Radical Chic." Within the mix of these serious or frivolous strains of radicalism such a figure as Muhammad Ali held a great presence. Ali's famous rejections of traditional politics, traditional race relations, traditional religion, and his traditional name ennobled many, while, especially at first, dumbfounding and scaring many more. He was of singular importance in the growing appeal of new and seemingly radical alternatives to the traditional choices in the politics of race relations. It is no overstatement to say that the rise of the Nation of Islam among African Americans in the 1960s owes as much of its power, significance, and appeal to Muhammad Ali as to anyone else. In the mid–

1960s, few mainstream Americans knew much about, or had even heard of, the Black Muslims but for Ali. While many did not know for what the Nation of Islam stood, there was nonetheless a certain air of coolness that Ali represented especially to the nation's youth, white and black. As Ali was undeniably the best boxer, it was cool to associate oneself, however vicariously, with various forms of radicalism or nonconformity. This grew ever more so as the decade of the '60s progressed and Ali's opposition to the Vietnam War became an ever-more popular stand. Those that stood outside the circle, the whirlpool, that was Ali and so much that he encompassed, gained public identities driven strictly by their relationship to "the greatest," and here various boxers against whom Ali fought, including Floyd Patterson, were as affected as any.

Since the heated times of the late 1960s, some of the day's perspectives have altered. Yet the images and attitudes toward various people and events of the time has left a kind of palimpsest, an intellectual tracing which remains very much alive in common historical memory, especially in regard to areas of popular concern like sports. How so much of this cultural history evolved is very much wrapped up in the life and career of a man like Floyd Patterson. Through the many twists and turns of the unfolding issues and ideologies of the nation in the 1960s and beyond, Patterson was a participant, observer, victim, bystander, and commentator, at times a kind of Everyman or a Forrest Gump, present at so much activity, with decided tinges of naïveté and victimization throughout.

Amidst it all, Patterson was of course a boxer, the lives of whom often stir the imagination of readers. Boxing has always been a subject of fascination for people, as its nature goes to some of the most primal elements of human nature, good and bad. As the behavior of great apes still shows, since human beings first evolved there has been a need for capability in the struggles for such basic elements as food, water, and territory. A prowess in displaying such capability has then been a desirable attribute since the time humans began to think and reason. The validation in such recognized prowess remains desirable among children at play, among adults, and among competing organizations. Human civilizations may have greatly altered the ways that such prowess can be sought and displayed, but they have done anything but eliminate them or the basic desires that drive them. The means and the venues all change, but not the essential desires.

The one-on-one nature of combat in boxing adds to the sport's elemental appeal. And those who are willing to make the extreme sacrifices to engage effectively in the prominent forms of such combat hold a deep level of social respect. The nature of the sport certainly contains elements that involve rigorous levels of organizational work, politics, planning, and training, but the actual event of combat conveys a "thing in itself" essentiality which declares that whatever went into the coming of the fight, it is now secondary to the struggle that is at hand. Boxing is hardly the only sport or activity that embodies this, but it appears to do so at least as well and often better and more poignantly than any other. A point of proof here lies in how the sport fascinates so many in other fields. Actors, musicians, stars of other sports and other such performers, for example, have often commented on their attraction to boxing as an embodiment of a most stark version of what they do. While all preparations and other such work may be terribly important, they are all prologue to the moment of truth when the actual execution of the particular art occurs, and moment of truth is more than cliché here, as the moment has a truthfulness about it that is undeniable. As Joyce Carol Oates observed, in contrast to other sports, "boxing is life and hardly a mere game."

The primal appeal of boxing has drawn a host of literary giants, both to watch as well as to write about it. Whether their goals are to convey something of their chosen literary and cultural settings, or to explore the struggles of given characters, boxing has more than dotted the world's literary landscape, perhaps at more profound levels than any other sporting activity. Alexander Pope, Jonathan Swift, Henry Fielding, Daniel Defoe, Lord Byron, Jack London, Ring Lardner, and Ernest Hemingway have all written about boxing, as have others of more recent times like Norman Mailer, George Plimpton, James Baldwin, and Joyce Carol Oates. A few boxers like George Garrett and José Torres have themselves become reasonably successful writers, with their ring experience serving beyond their expressed thoughts as a basis for their recognized authority and appeal. Oates herself comments about "the habitual attraction of serious writers to boxing," arguing that the attraction lies in the appeal of "the sport's systematic cultivation of pain ... into its polar opposite: ... pain now but control, and therefore triumph later." The sacrifices of those who fought for land and water for their families and communities and the sacrifices of nations against evil forces are all based on the same basic notion — that struggle and pain are often necessary in just causes and that one has to be prepared to engage in it.

Critics of boxing often raise compelling points as to the needless brutality of the sport and the horrible effects it has had on many otherwise decent institutions, as well as on many of the combatants, but the linkage of boxing to the sad but apparently necessary struggles and conflicts in the sweep of human activity are not easy to dismiss. Parallels with cockfighting and bullfighting can be and are drawn to support abolition, but the issue of voluntarism remains with boxing. The chickens and bulls have no choice, and their abuse was (and is) unconscionable, much like antebellum slave owners' forced uses of slaves in fights to the death for the mere sake of entertainment and wagering. Modern boxers can certainly be seen as victims, but the issue of consent and choice here is not the same as with mere defenseless animals or with the institution of slavery. And while some can ascribe nobility to the bull in the ring, the same ascription is vastly more poignant with boxers.

The debates that (and which will continue to) rise and fall about the legitimacy of boxing form another political conflict that has surrounded boxers like Floyd Patterson and Muhammad Ali. For years, an example which boxing abolitionists (as they have called themselves) have begrudgingly acknowledged to be an ennobling point against their charges about the brutality, dehumanization, and criminality of the sport was, indeed, Mr. Floyd Patterson. The sadnesses that would eventually encircle the last years of Patterson's life spoke in a different direction, all underscoring the links which his life had to so many significant social and political issues as well as to the sport that, with its undeniable primal character, so many both love and hate.

Patterson's life encompassed much. Like the culture of African America of which he was a part, it was a life filled with pain, one which showed enormous courage, attained great success, humbly brought its successes into significant service of others, was felled amidst competition that was both fair and unfair, maintained a steady dignity amidst pathos, and spoke (and speaks) poignantly to all who witnessed it.

I

I Never Seemed Not Scared

The Depression era was the cruelest of times. For African American families in the rural South, the economic pain of the decade marked yet another unendurable burden on top of the racial fears and violence all around them. The Patterson family of Waco, North Carolina, was one of many of the shack-dwelling poor who eked out a marginal life in the South. They lived in the country of Cleveland County, forty miles west of Charlotte. Jobs were few. Any redress to economic or political woes was non-existent, and, as in most of the South, in Cleveland County there lurked the ever-present threat of racial violence from the Klan and its many comrades. It was in this world that Thomas and Anabelle Patterson attempted to raise and provide for a family. Thomas Patterson worked as an odd-job laborer for the Seaboard Railroad Company. His mother took work when she could get it as a domestic. The pay was meager, and Mr. Patterson's chances for advancement were nil. This was the life of grinding poverty, insecurity, anguish, and terror into which the Patterson's third son, Floyd, was born on January 4, 1935.

Less than a year after Floyd was born, feeling he had nothing to lose, and with word of some job prospects to the North, Thomas Patterson moved his family to New York City. Unfortunately, life there did not prove much better. The family settled in Brooklyn, although settled may be too concrete a word for what the Pattersons did. Brooklyn was home, but the family's life was never but a slight step above vagrancy. As rents and other expenses bore in, the Pattersons would move, and did so quite often. Floyd Patterson said he recalled "six or seven of the flats in which we lived, but," he added, "maybe there were more" — Lexington Avenue, St. Andrews Place, Macon St., Howard Avenue. The constancy in the Pattersons' world was hardship. The apartments were always dirty and inadequate, "too hot in the summer, too cold

9

in the winter, and never big enough," never with any hot running water. For most of his youth, Patterson shared one bed with his two older brothers, Frank and William. There were eleven children in all.[1]

Thomas Patterson worked hard to support his family, but it was never enough. Construction gangs, dock work, garbage pickups, delivery truck driving at the Fulton Fish market — he did everything, working days and often nights and Sundays whenever there was opportunity, but the family always teetered on the brink of financial failure and often had to pack up and move when financial troubles loomed. Floyd Patterson recalled how his father would often come home "so tired and so frustrated that sometimes he wouldn't even eat. He'd lay down ... and fall asleep in his clothes." Some days he fell asleep as Mrs. Patterson was making something for him to eat. He was that tired. "Next day he'd get up and do it all again. I felt so bad," Patterson remembered, "because here I was, not going to school, doing nothing, just watching my father come home."[2]

In Brooklyn, the Pattersons lived mostly in the section known as Bedford-Stuyvesant. It was "the kind of place," Floyd Patterson grimly mused, "writers mean when they speak of an asphalt jungle." Growing up in such a state, the young Patterson had quickly to learn all the vicious ways of the streets that smacked him as soon as he stepped outside his door. If his mother sent him to the store with merely a little loose change to buy something, he would encounter gangs of kids like the Bishops who would try to steal his money or his food, and for young African Americans in Bed-Sty the notion of police protection was a joke. As a boy, recalled Patterson, "I never seemed not scared." And on the street that would easily invite predators.[3]

The effects of mean streets were felt by millions of inner city youths. Patterson's youth had other special torments besides. Young Floyd sensed the family's financial hardships so keenly that he "began to feel ashamed, even at [an] early age, of eating there. I felt," he said, "like a freeloader." Psychologically, a forbidding rather than inclusive aura may have been present in the Patterson family, one that caused a sensitive child like young Floyd to internalize feelings of being unwelcome and that the hardships and lack of solutions were in some way his fault. Without realizing it, families with extremely tight finances can readily convey to a sensitive child that their money issues are more important than the family's love. "As a child," Patterson recalled, "I was never at ease at home.... I was embarrassed most of the time, shamed at other times, smothered in a feeling of inadequacy." The family had a picture of young Floyd (then two years old) and his older brothers on the bedroom wall. Floyd regularly told his mother, pointing to himself in the photograph, "I don't like that boy." He even attempted to X out the likeness. Feeling inexplicable pressures, young Floyd would sleepwalk. (Many years later, when he once fell asleep on the New York Subway, he awoke and found everyone staring at him, as he had been throwing punches in his sleep.) Amidst such difficult psychological dynamics, by the time he was eight, Floyd Patterson began to stay away from home.[4]

Patterson made a little money shining shoes at the corner of Fulton and Kingston avenues. He gave most of the earnings to his mother. Otherwise, little in his behavior was the slightest bit positive or functional. School, P.S. 93, was doing him no good. Patterson recalled having it drummed into his head that he had to attend school, but the point was that going to school was more of a way to stay out of trouble than it was to learn and improve himself. At school, he felt embarrassed and ashamed there: "No matter what I did everybody was always laughing at me ... — the dirt on my face, the torn, shabby ... clothes I wore, and the way I couldn't read or write or answer a question." "Lots of times in school," he recalled, "I'd know the answer and say to myself 'Raise your hand, you dope, you know it.' But I couldn't." He missed school incessantly, and never knew or cared whether he was promoted or left back. "I felt like even if I tried I would fail. There was just no use in it. I couldn't see success in anything." Seeing no hope in school, and often facing street gangs on route if he went, Patterson simply stopped going. He could have, albeit with difficulty, joined one gang, the Fulton Street Bishops. They were a heavy presence in Bed-Sty. Instead, however, Patterson simply stayed away from everyone as well as from school. "It seemed so easy to do." Instead, he would walk the streets aimlessly. If he had any loose change, he would ride the New York subways, never going to any special destination in the city (like a public library; but, of course, Floyd could barely read, and during weekdays this would have further exposed his truancy), just staying underground, riding to the end of the line and then going back.

At certain subway stations like the stop at 8th Avenue and High Street in Brooklyn, he discovered some of the dingy little tool storage rooms, up a ladder, beyond the boarding areas. There he would often just sit for hours, sometimes even for days! In such little holes, young Floyd would somehow find some sort of heart's ease. With all the shame of his father's losing battle with finances and his felt failure to contribute, he needed "to run and hide." The roar of the trains was not scary; somehow it was peaceful. It meant he was undetectable to anyone. There was comfort in that. He could sleep, untouched. "It became my cave, my hideaway — a safe hole in the wall away from the bitterness of the world. I'd spread papers on the floor, and I'd go to sleep and find peace.... The days would come and go and I'd feel myself safe." Of course, the feelings of peace and safety were illusory. In January 1962, when heavyweight champion, Patterson revisited the IND subway stop, climbed up the ladder and spent a few minutes up in "his room." He found a wallet, not his, and came down covered in soot. "I'm really glad I went up," he acknowledged. "Now I can get it off my mind."[5]

Patterson knew at some level that his mother had to be worrying about him, but, on the other hand, he kept thinking that he was giving her one less mouth to feed. Mrs. Patterson, meanwhile, had all the other children to preoccupy her. She also worked as a domestic and in a local bottling plant. While hiding in the subway, Patterson would dream about somebody giving him a tremendous amount of money and going home and giving it to his mother. By 1945, the family had seven children. With such a conflict haunting him, he would sometimes return home with some food, almost always stolen of course. While he knew stealing was wrong, and he later recalled that he never stole money, he was driven by the notion that he had to do something to help his family. Stealing repeatedly, Patterson was inevitably caught and arrested. One time he stole a mound of dresses for his mother, so many that he piled them on his head and attempted to walk home on the street with them at 2:00 A.M., actually thinking he would not be caught. In the era of World War II and the Cold War, no-nonsense sensibilities among officers of the New York Police Department were dominant. The police were in anything but a generous mood in regard to any child stealing, let alone if he did so habitually. The fact that he was African American, of course, made matters even worse. The children's psychological and economic conditions and contexts were irrelevant. By the time Floyd Patterson was but ten years old he had accumulated a long list of violations — breaking and entering, running away from home, stealing, truancy. Some of the arrests may have been invalid, but not all. "I was forever getting picked up," he said. "[It] seems to me that I lived in court and should have had a room there." Patterson recalled being in court thirty to forty times. He was knocked around by the police. Some beatings he received from policemen were undoubtedly unfair, but the fact was that Floyd Patterson was a deeply troubled youngster, and in September of 1945 his parents accepted the idea that he should be sent away to some sort of reform school. "I know, Judge," Mrs. Patterson acknowledged. "I know something's got to be done."[6]

The Wiltwyck School for Boys in Esopus, N.Y., was different from many of the traditional Marine Corps style, Dickensian reform factories of prior times. Many stories exist of young people being sent away, with the parents, convinced by half-attentive judges and lawyers with bulging dockets and case loads, convincing them it was all for the best, only to find the child even further neglected, abused, and brutalized by a pathetically inhumane set of institutions and pseudo-concerned social workers. Patterson's experience at Wiltwyck was a happy exception. "Every time I think of Wiltwyck the joy bubbles up inside me and I can't wait to say the good things about the place."[7] The Wiltwyck School was a school for emotionally disturbed boys, established during the New Deal through the direct efforts of First Lady Eleanor Roosevelt. The Depression era and the popularity of films like *Wild Boys of the Road* had prompted some revisions in popular social attitudes about juvenile delinquency. Boys were not regarded as innately bad; they had been compelled to do bad things by hard times and bad environments, hence the right kind of environment and care could turn them into productive citizens.

There had been a summer shelter in the town of Esopus, and it lay on a former Payne Whitney estate just across the Hudson River from the Roosevelts' home in Hyde Park. It was this proximity that drew the interest of Mrs. Roosevelt and led to the location of the new styled reform school there, one that would support itself with private funds and by funds from New York State and New York City. Naturally, Patterson was scared about the prospects of going far away to the Wiltwyck School. His family was seemingly abandoning him, even though he felt he had been trying to help provide for them. He was thinking of the school as a jail, "bars on the windows and guards with guns." As it turned out, Wiltwyck had no barred windows, no iron fences, and no armed guards. Instead, Patterson found "a place where I learned how to live." He worked in the school barn, helping take care of cows and chickens. He learned to swim and fish in the nearby lake. He studied, and he worked out in the gymnasium. The boys' ages ranged from eight to twelve, and through elected student councils and committees concerning subjects like the dining hall, sports, and jobs, the boys were encouraged to work out issues and problems among themselves. "Punishment," declared the Wiltwyck principal Ernst Papanek, later a professor of education at Queens College, teaches the child only how to punish. Scolding teaches him how to scold. By showing him that we understand, we teach him to understand. By helping him, we teach him to help. He learns cooperation by cooperating." For young Floyd, the environment gave him senses both of belonging and of fairness. Especially important, as he recalled, were the racial issues, more specifically their absence. From policemen and from the streets of Brooklyn, he had already felt the sting of racial slurs. At Wiltwyck there was, he recalled, "no preference at all." Differences of religion also had no significance at the school. "There were arguments and fights, sure," Patterson remembered, "but never with a vulgar word about a boy's color, never the way it had been in Brooklyn.... For the first time in my life, perhaps the only time in my life, it seemed color didn't make any difference.... That's what helped to bring me out of the shell in which I had been living."[8]

In schooling, a now gradually more confident Floyd Patterson began to make significant strides. Having missed so much school before Wiltwyck, he was basically illiterate when he arrived there. Unlike the financially strapped New York Public School System, class size at Wiltwyck was kept small, very small — seven or eight boys per class. That was critical. Small classes gave the students the individual attention they sorely needed, something that can never come in a larger setting. Students felt the fact, and not the mere act, of someone actually caring about them individually. Patterson recalled his teacher, Miss Vivian Costen, with great respect and affection. "Miss Costen made me feel I was important. She refused to believe that I couldn't learn to read or write. She bought me clothes and gave me little gifts. I had to return that to her in some way, and the only way I knew or was able to was to be what she wanted me to be." Patterson began to work hard. He was still reticent in class until one particular day. When Miss Costen asked a question, Patterson recalled,

> I still didn't dare raise my hand to answer. One day she asked a question of all the kids. She went around the room asking this one and that one. Everybody answered but me. I said I didn't know the answer. Then she told us the answer. Everybody in the class had been wrong, but the answer I had in my mind was correct, and I had not had nerve enough to say it out loud.
>
> That made me furious. I just stood up and ran right out of that room and down the hall. I could hear footsteps after me, but I didn't care. It was Miss Costen. She took me by the shoulder and lifted my head to look into my eyes. There were tears shame and anger in them.
>
> "I knew you knew the answer, Floyd," she said. "That's why you're crying. This should prove to you that if you have an idea speak it out."

No one had ever stopped Patterson from running away from home and hiding in the subway when the problems of life pressed down upon him. No one could have. But at Wiltwyck such an intervention could work. It changed him utterly. "I began to catch on," Patterson remembered. "I was learning to read. I even liked school."[9]

The breakthroughs made at Wiltwyck with Patterson's pre-adolescent troubles occurred just as he was physically growing much stronger. As Patterson was then growing spiritually and physically at Wiltwyck, he discovered other things. He became fascinated with snakes. As a boxer he would later remain enamored of their swiftness and sharpness and kept some as pets. The executive director of Wiltwyck, Walter Johnson (no relation to the famous baseball pitcher), encouraged sports, as most such schools tend to do. Patterson played the usual baseball, football, and basketball. There were horses on the farm, and students learned to ride. They also learned to swim, something few inner city youths of the day had ever had the opportunity to master. At regular intervals, Mr. Johnson also organized boxing matches. Miss Costen encouraged it too. At first, Patterson was reluctant to box, but once Johnson, Miss Costen, and some of the boys persuaded him, something clicked. In his first fight at Wiltwyck, Patterson fought someone who was much bigger, and Patterson felt it was impossible to beat him. "The strangest thing," he remembered, "is that when we put the gloves on he didn't seem to be even as big as I was." Whatever the complex of anger, fear, anxiety, inferiority, dread, and confusion, it all seemed to diminish or find some common purpose. In the ring was a bit of the solitude to which he so often tried to escape in the Brooklyn streets, yet here there was anything but a shameful sense of running away; just the opposite. Whatever the risks, they were completely acceptable, and success here was as liberating as was the new success in the classroom. In the fight with the larger boy, Floyd bloodied the kid's nose. As is usual with bouts between children, no one was badly hurt or knocked out, but when it was over Patterson's bigger opponent "was so mad ... because he couldn't do with me what he wanted to do." Feeling a sense of liberation in the ring, Patterson acted with more and more abandon. His antics would not have met with the approval of any professional fight manager, but at that time and place they were fun as well as psychologically beneficial. The other kids laughed at Patterson's ring antics. Elsewhere he was painfully sensitive to such taunts, but here he found himself anything but self-conscious. "What made me feel so good was when they laughed at me in the ring I didn't feel ashamed at all like I used to." Sometimes Patterson would excitedly leap in the air to throw a punch. This was anything but text-book form, but later he would actually use this as a professional fighter. "The book" may have said "no," but the maneuver was a fully integrated part of Patterson's ring personality. At the time it was something essential to his growth, his development, and his resolving, at least for the moment, of the many deep conflicts of his childhood.[10]

In 1947, Patterson left the Wiltwyck School a changed boy. In 1961 he wrote gratefully to the Wiltwyck School Board of Directors: "When I went to Wiltwyck at 11 years old, I was mixed up and angry at the world. I was given encouragement, affection, understanding, and direction. I was helped to understand my problems and to channel my energies constructively. I am quite sure that I would not have gone on to ... be the World's Heavyweight Champion if I had not been given my chance at Wiltwyck." Returning to New York, he was now twelve years old, more literate and confident. "I never had trouble again, ... the nightmares stopped and I never walked in my sleep any more." Boxing was in his blood too. For this, and for so many other reasons, he happily acknowledged, and would always acknowledge, how he owed the Wiltwyck School a great deal. The only bad legacy from Wiltwyck was that while there Patterson had taken up smoking cigarettes. ("Camels," were his brand; he later called them "a fighting man's cigarette.") In 1961, when Patterson was the reigning heavyweight boxing champion, he had the pleasure of meeting Eleanor Roosevelt. Mrs. Roosevelt did not know he had attended the school near her home in Hyde Park that she had helped establish back during the Depression. Patterson told her of all the good the Wiltwyck School did for him, and she was absolutely delighted.[11]

II

I Didn't Know Where
I Was or What I Was Doing

At the end of the summer of 1947, Patterson had left the Wiltwyck School and returned to Brooklyn to live with has family. The new school year was about to begin, and Patterson was enrolled in New York Public School #614 at 113 East Fourth Street. The city then maintained two 600 schools. (There have since been many more of them.) The 600 schools were special ones for boys with problematic records. The Wiltwyck years had taught Patterson well, however, and he would never again be guilty of truancy or of any other infraction. At 614, some of the same principles used at Wiltwyck were on hand. Boys were given authority. Kids formerly with no regard for law and order were now enforcing law and order. Patterson recognized the value of this. "You've got to really appreciate what that would mean to somebody like me," he noted. "I had been the receiver. Now I wanted to be the giver." Patterson gave to the school and to his studies. He finished the eighth-grade level exams, and he won an award for being the member of his class who showed the best sportsmanship. Patterson would hold P.S. 614 with as much affection as he had for Wiltwyck. He regularly went back there, especially for graduation ceremonies, to show support for and give encouragement to the boys.[1]

From 614, Patterson attended Alexander Hamilton Vocational High School for one year. Again, he was a well-behaved student. There were some minor incidents. Floyd was still small, and some larger boys would naturally test him. One bully tried to steal an ashtray he'd made in wood shop. "He hit me with a right," Patterson fondly recalled, "I leapt and hit him with a left hook, which was my best punch at the time, and poo-foosh, his head hit the

16

concrete." Having boxed at Wiltwyck, indeed, Patterson was more intent here than with any academic or vocational subject. His brother Frank won an amateur title, the New York Golden Gloves, in 1949. Floyd wanted to continue with boxing, and this began to occupy his mind completely. Frank and his other older brother, Billy, were in training at a local YMCA gymnasium, and Floyd was able to tag along with them every day after school. "I figured I could hit," he said, remembering the kid who had tried to steal the ashtray he had made in the wood-working shop. At the YMCA, Floyd found a gym that was utterly primitive. There was no boxing ring, just lines drawn on an old basketball court. One speed bag hung in a corner, and everyone took turns with it. Otherwise, people skipped rope, shadow boxed, and paired off and sparred. The Patterson boys worked with an amateur trainer, a U.S. Customs House employee named Frank Lavelle. Mr. Lavelle soon worked out arrangements for the talented Patterson boys to go to a better installation in lower Manhattan near Irving Place at 114 East 14th Street. The installation, then unknown but later famous, was called the Gramercy Park Gym.[2]

Outwardly, the Gramercy Gym was but slightly less unappealing than the old YMCA. Patterson remembered:

> The paint had long since peeled off the walls. There were two creaking flights of wooden stairs up past a couple of garbage cans. In the front door there was a square hole covered by chicken wire, and through this hole a vicious police dog would snarl at the first sound coming up the stairs.... The windows were always closed, the air always hot inside. It smelled of sweat, and the smell seemed to cling to the dirty walls.... [The manager] lived in the back of that gym with that dog as his only companion at night.

While noticeably rank, the Gramercy Gym did, nonetheless, have a regulation-sized boxing ring and some light and heavy bags. There were the needed mirrors on the walls, but they were all cracked of course. Most importantly, the Gramercy Gym had a grimly-living, bumptious, somewhat paranoid manager who knew the fight game inside and out. He would prove to be very important to Patterson. (As a result of Patterson, and another future champion, José Torres, training at Gramercy, the gym would indeed gain legendary status among boxing enthusiasts. Seeking to imbibe some of this aura, for example, writer and boxing enthusiast Norman Mailer worked out there. Actor Robert De Niro also took training there when preparing for his title role in the movie *Raging Bull*, even though the N.Y. boxer Jake LaMotta, whose life is the subject of the movie, never actually trained there.)[3]

As a young teenager in the gym, Patterson did not generate much attention at first, and he continued to train with Frank Lavelle. He stuck with the regimen and continued dutifully to attend school. His waking thoughts were increasingly on boxing, however, and every day after school ended he ran the ten blocks up to the gym. More and more, Patterson recalled, "I found it difficult going to school and concentrating on boxing, too. So finally, ... I decided to quit and devote all of my energies to the prize ring." His mother did not get mad at him, but she did tell him that he would some day regret never finishing his education. That day never came, but Patterson would later take every opportunity to counsel young people to stay in school.

A boxing life is full of troubles and setbacks. Earlier in his life, especially before the Wiltwyck days, any setbacks would lead Patterson to curl into a shell. Now at the Gramercy Gym, any setback would only deepen his determination to get back, fight more, and overcome any fear. With his steady work in the gym, Patterson's physique also began to fill out impressively. The gym's manager took note of the young Patterson's emerging size, his ability, and his determination. One savvy part of the gym manager's agreement with Frank Lavelle was his right to take over the management of any kid he had allowed to train there. Patterson began to look ever more like he was worth an investment of time, so one day he suddenly learned he had a new manager. The man who ran the show at Gramercy Park Gym was named Constantine D'Amato. Everyone called him "Cus," or among the boys, "Mr. Cus." Floyd Patterson found himself with new boxing trunks, better shoes and socks, a foul protector, and a T-shirt, plus a manager who could teach him for real. Managers can often run afoul of taking on fighters, devoting much time and resources to them, only to have them leave for another manager at a moment's notice. At the time he took on Patterson, D'Amato had a conversation with Miss Costen of the Wiltwyck School. She told him of the time that she gave him some candy for his help in cleaning the room after class. He refused it, telling her that he had made an agreement with a friend to share everything they were given. Miss Costen told Floyd he could keep the candy and share it as he pleased. With that little story, D'Amato never worried about losing Floyd after that; "God," he later nodded, "only made one Floyd Patterson." D'Amato promised Patterson's parents that he would keep Floyd away from all the street problems to which New York teenagers were susceptible. D'Amato lived an intensely focused life. He had no family, never married, and devoted himself inflexibly and exclusively to boxing.* He promised to keep Floyd straight and make his parents proud of him.[4]

Cus D'Amato, as well as Frank Lavelle, worked hard with the promising young Patterson, engrossing him in all the fundamentals. He learned well. In January of 1950, as Patterson's boxing skills and physique grew, D'Amato entered him in the *New York Daily News* Golden Gloves tournament. Patterson had just turned fifteen, and he was fighting at 147 pounds in the sub-

---

*The Gramercy Gym was razed in 1993 to make room for a 14th Street housing project. D'Amato had passed on by then, and on the occasion of the razing, Patterson and José Torres participated in a ceremony renaming that section of 14th Street "Cus D'Amato Way."

novice division. His first scheduled opponent in the tournament failed to show for the fight, so Patterson advanced to the next round by default. His next bout, hence his first real fight, was to take place at no less a site than New York's prestigious Downtown Athletic Club. His opponent, Edward W. Wallace, was a Navy sailor, older and slightly heavier. D'Amato, Lavelle, and Patterson's brother Nick were in the corner with him. Patterson felt nothing but nervousness. There was a reasonable crowd there, and Patterson painfully remembered his acute anxieties: "I didn't know where I was or what I was doing." In such a jumpy state Patterson returned to a more purely street-level fighting pose. For the entire first round he just flailed away madly, looking every bit the raw amateur that he indeed was. In the corner after the first round D'Amato and Lavelle tried to talk (shout) some sense into him and get him to focus on some of the boxing fundamentals they had taught him, but Patterson's nervousness was such that he would not, could not listen to them. "Every time the guy came near me I started throwing punches, not knowing where they were going or even caring." In the second round, it was much the same. Patterson mindlessly swung away at his opponent. Any experienced fighter would dance and taunt such a clearly inexperienced opponent, let him tire himself out, and then move in for the kill. Wallace may have felt this young, seemingly untutored Patterson kid would be so easy that he let himself get a bit careless. Bemusedly, Patterson recalled that, amidst his wild swinging, "an astonishing thing happened. My right hand landed on his jaw and down he went." Patterson could hardly believe it. Remembering hundreds of cowboy fights from the movies, with people being hit with tables and chairs, he fully expected the man to get up, as "it seemed to me I had just tapped this fellow on the chin." Wallace did not get up, however, and young Patterson found himself with a KO to his credit, thirty-seven seconds into the second round — not a bad beginning for a fight career. In his next fight of the tournament, however, Patterson lost, bringing the elation of his first victory to an abrupt end. The following afternoon, he simply went back to the Gramercy Gym and began training ever harder. With no school in the summer, and after dropping out, Patterson also worked, delivering groceries and turning all his pay over to his mother.[5]

The following year, 1951, at the age of sixteen, Patterson reentered the N.Y. Golden Gloves. No longer a novice, he was now in the Open Division, fighting at 160 pounds. He fought with some of the same nervousness and panic of the year before. He later recalled:

> I was petrified. It was all I could do to cross the ring. And then he [opponent Julius Griffin] came at me, and moved close to me ... and from then on I don't know anything. I have no idea what happened. Only thing I know is, I saw him on the floor. And later somebody said, "Man, I never saw anything like it. You just jumped in the air and threw thirty different punches."

Patterson won the New York championship. Two of his teachers from P.S. 614 came to Madison Square Garden to watch.[6] From there he entered the Eastern Golden Gloves in New Jersey. He won again and traveled out to Chicago, up to then the longest trip of his life, to fight the winner of the Western Golden Gloves. He won there too, giving him the prestigious Inter-City title. He also won several New York tournaments that winter and spring.[7] Later that year, and next year too, he won the National Amateur Athletic Union Championship in Boston. Back in the Gramercy Gym, Patterson continued to work very hard. Over the next year he fought nineteen amateur bouts. He won one fight on a default, four on decisions, and knocked out the other fourteen (and all amateur bouts were only three rounders). At the 1952 A.A.U.s in Boston, Patterson was named the outstanding boxer of the tournament.[8] He began to think about turning pro, thinking of how much more he could then do for his family. Cus D'Amato had another idea, however, and young Floyd always listened to Cus.

Patterson's life was certainly turning out a lot better than anyone could have predicted had they seen the emotionally disturbed nine-year-old hiding out in the dingy, squalid supply rooms of end-of-the-line New York subway stops. Nothing was by any means easy. The family was still very poor. When not boxing, Patterson continued to work delivering groceries and took some construction jobs as well. He was making about $17.50 a week, and all of it went straight to his mother. His mother gave him some money back, and occasionally he got a delivery tip and kept it. At this time through one of his school friends he met a girl named Sandra Elizabeth Hicks. She turned out to be only thirteen, but her parents let Floyd see her, and they kept everything proper. Her parents were never far away. They were strict Catholics. Floyd liked her very much; she was not like other girls he dated. He once took another girl to the Apollo Theater in Harlem. A popular doo-wop group known as the Orioles was performing. When the lead singer wiped his face with his handkerchief and tossed it from the stage, Floyd's date was among the girls who eagerly ran for the offering. "My girl was third in the race for that handkerchief," Floyd remembered, adding, "But you know what was even more extraordinary? When she got back to her seat I wasn't there." Sandra seemed different, unimpressed with the frivolities that captivated so many young girls. This must have impressed Floyd, and while he was on the one hand so self-confident as to leave one girl in a theater, he was so nervous at first around Sandra that he would sometimes bring a fast-talking friend along to fill in the awkward, silent spots.[9]

Aside from the gym, the main thing that ever kept Floyd from going to see Sandra was a lack of money. He always wanted to buy her little presents, and when he could not do it, he felt ashamed and stayed away. He even stayed away one Christmas because he had nothing to give her. Sandra was not happy when he did not come by and repeatedly told him it was OK if he did not bring a present. (The following Christmas, Floyd took extra work on the New York docks so he could afford presents for Sandra and her family.) They continued to see each other, and their relationship gained ever firmer footing. Sandra also persuaded Floyd to come to church with her. She introduced Floyd to her priest, and Floyd, ever eager to please Sandra, soon agreed to take religious instruction from him. He wondered how it would be received — his wanting religious instruction while simultaneously wanting to be a professional fighter. The resolution here was easy, for, like many New Yorkers, the good Irish priest, Archibald McLeese, was also a big fight fan. He steadied young Patterson's apprehensions.[10]

Patterson asked D'Amato about turning professional. Cus said "no," and Patterson was perplexed. He asked D'Amato if he thought he was not good enough. D'Amato explained that he was certainly good enough and that there were plenty of professionals he could beat. But then he added two points. One was that he was still too young; the other, which he added off-handedly, was that he wanted Floyd to take a shot at making the U.S. Olympic boxing team![11]

Patterson had little direct knowledge of or concern for the Olympics. As a boy, the Berlin Olympics (1936) had occurred when he was barely a year old. After that, there were no Games during the war. He had just left Wiltwyck when the first post-war games were held, and rather hastily, in London in 1948. The games had no American TV coverage, and the Pattersons did not own a television anyway. (The London Games were a ramshackle affair, with many athletes living in nearby military barracks and some housed in huts in the city's Hyde Park. The BBC covered the games locally. They used all of nine cameras for the entire enterprise and paid the International Olympic Committee all of £1500 for the coverage rights.)[12] Patterson also seldom read a newspaper, so the Olympics simply held no significance or allure for him. "You couldn't eat medals," he recalled thinking, "and you couldn't pawn them for much to buy food or clothes, ... [and] my big interest was still making some money." For much of the generation born in the 1930s, the Olympics held no great aura. The Nazi games of 1936 had greatly politicized them, and with no games during World War II, the entire movement seemed to some all but dead. In 1952, the Soviets made their first appearance in the Olympics since their revolution, and this added new East-West energy and rivalry to the games that was sorely needed.

No matter the immediate background, D'Amato wanted to pursue the Olympic angle. His instincts proved good, as the '52 Helsinki Games would be a great success in both the quality and quantity of the world competition, as well as in the general fan interest in the United States. For Patterson, the timing was right too. In early 1952, he had left school. He was ready to go to work to help his family and had actually begun working with his father as a longshoreman and as a garbage truck driver at the Fulton Fish Market. His mother persuaded him to stay in some metal working classes at Alexander Hamilton Vocational High School so he could learn a trade. But boxing was still his passion, and a friend and boxing enthusiast, Charles Schwefel, landed him a better job working maintenance and housekeeping at the Gramercy Park Hotel on East 20th St. The pay was better than the garbage or dock work, and there was the added benefit that he was now working only six blocks from Cus D'Amato and the Gramercy Park Gym. Now he could focus on boxing ever more fully. He trained even harder, winning every amateur bout D'Amato arranged for him that spring and summer. In April, he won the National A.A.U. boxing championship in Boston. Then in June he went to Kansas City and won the Olympic tryout competition, beating a tough competitor named Harvey Lammers. Lammers knocked Patterson down twice in the bout. Patterson won a split decision, and Lammers was greatly distressed. As late as 1989, he was still rueful, but he did graciously acknowledge: Patterson "could hit like hell, tear your head off with a punch, and he was strong." Lammers' protests notwithstanding, Patterson was off to the Olympics.[13]

The 1952 Olympics took place in Helsinki, Finland. Having been but to tournaments in Chicago, Boston, and Kansas City, and otherwise having rarely been far away from New York, the excursion to Helsinki was quite an eye-opener for young Patterson, and in a most positive way. More than most of the other athletes on the U.S. Olympic team, Patterson and the other American boxers ended up seeing quite a bit of Helsinki and its people. Most of the American athletes could remain in the Olympic Village throughout the games, and, until they were finished competing, many did. There they trained, ate, socialized, and competed. But there was no boxing facility in the Olympic Village, so every morning the fourteen American boxers took a local bus to downtown Helsinki where they trained in the gymnasium of a workingman's club in a blue-collar section of the city — Häkäniemi. The gym was in a ponderous, solid granite building known as The People's House. A people's house in a proletariat section of a European city had a not-so-slightly Marxist ring to it, and this was quite consciously the case in Helsinki, lying as did on the edge of the Soviet Union, still ruled by the aging Joseph Stalin.[14]

The term "Finlandization" was already in diplomatic use, and the Finns were indeed inculcating themselves with an array of self-rationalizing euphemisms to the effect that the neighboring Soviet world was a system with which they needed to and could reconcile and compromise. Connected here was a willingness then to hear propaganda to the effect that the United States was a nation that held much that was evil, with one of its worst features being its history of racism — "the Land of Lynching," as Soviet propagandists were regularly casting it. Having learned so much such historical fact and fiction, the appearance in working class Helsinki of fourteen American boxers, eleven of whom were black, lent a liberating reality check for at least a few hundred Finns who rode the busses and lived in and about Häkäniemi. One reporter noted, indeed, that the boxers' excursions into downtown Helsinki "made excellent counter-propaganda." For nearly a month, amidst the pre-games training and even more during the games themselves, the American boxers became mini-celebrities in their little Helsinki enclave. The repressed knowledge of the truth about Stalinism found some release when the Finns found a group of Americans, black and white, not in some sort of chain-gang situation, but hanging about together on busses on the way to the gym, freely talking with one another as well as with any of the few often laconic Finns who could or would speak any English. Like working class people everywhere, the Finns of Häkäniemi also loved their boxing and treated fighters with great admiration. Patterson and the rest of the boxers also dressed sharply in some of the latest American sports clothing, and this made an added impression on the still spartan Finns who in 1952 had little access even to Macy's-level clothing. Apparently the Finnish girls were especially taken with the Americans. (Nine months later, some reportedly had babies; none was attributed to Patterson, however.)[15]

For the boxers, too, the Finns' genuine friendliness and fascination was an eye-opener. Patterson's only problem in Finland was that he had trouble sleeping with the endless summer daylight. "I slept with the shutters on [the windows]," he recalled. On the streets of Helsinki, with some of the boxers having grown up amidst Jim Crow laws and customs, the busses themselves marked quite a decidedly different experience as it did not matter where or with whom they sat. For many, this was the first time they had experienced an environment truly devoid of racial tension. The only racially based sensations they received from the Finns lay in the fact that few of the Finns had ever actually seen a black person. But this was not fear or prejudice; it was largely a fascination that brought only smiles. Every day as the American boxers arrived at the People's House, they would be greeted and applauded by an admiring group of young Finnish boys and girls, many of whom would wait for them to finish their morning training and cheer them again as they hopped the bus back to the Olympic Village. Patterson greatly enjoyed the lightness of being here. This marked a stark contrast to what Patterson saw when he witnessed the Soviet boxers training. He watched as they all lined up together like members of an army unit. One shouted command, and they all jabbed in unison; the instructor motioned to throw a right, and they all threw a right. There was indeed little freedom in their ways, and, among many other things, that did not necessarily make for good boxing. "After that," Patterson chuckled, "I stopped worrying, at least about the Russians." He even bartered clothing with some of the Soviet fighters and came home with a Soviet-monogrammed sweatshirt and pants.[16]

The chief U.S. Olympic Boxing coach was a short, balding, congenial New Yorker named Pete Mello, then the head coach of the Catholic Youth Organization boxing team of New York. Mello had a strong squad of established NCAA and amateur stars, and he brazenly predicted, correctly as it turned out, that the American boxers would take as many as five gold medals. Even within the context of such a strong team, Mello further bragged to reporters that the surest winner of all the Americans was his seventeen-year-old middleweight, Floyd Patterson.[17]

There were sixteen middleweights entered in the Olympic boxing tournament, so Patterson would have to win four bouts to secure the gold medal. In preparation, during the training down at the People's House, Pete Mello had Patterson fight the Americans in the two weight classes above him — heavyweight Ed Sanders and light-heavyweight Norvel Lee. Nobody else could handle him. Ed Sanders was a huge, hulking ex-football player from Idaho State University. Patterson went a few rounds with him and sharpened his quickness and defensive skills, staying away from Sanders' considerable power. Sanders would win the gold medal, defeating a Swedish heavyweight, Ingemar Johansson, in the medal round. In the heavyweight finals, which Patterson witnessed, Johansson seemed to be afraid of Sanders and stayed on his bicycle so much that the referee ultimately disqualified him for inaction. After the fight, Johansson confessed to reporters, only half-jokingly, that it suddenly occurred to him that he could be killed in there. Sanders took the medal, while Johansson took a lot of jeering from the many Swedish fans and press who had ferried over from Stockholm to root for him. It would take Johansson several years to repair the bad image his Olympic performance left among the Swedes, but repair it he would.

Sanders proved too big for Patterson to spar with, so his main opponent in training was the light-heavyweight, Norvel Lee. Lee still had twenty pounds on Patterson as well as a lot more experience. He was twenty-eight years old, a law student about to enter service in the F.B.I. He had won over a dozen amateur titles and was about as experienced and savvy as any amateur boxer of his time. He and Patterson fought regularly, and, according to one observer, with all his weight advantage and ring experience, Lee "couldn't quite hold Patterson even."[18]

Norvel Lee proved the toughest opponent Patterson faced in Finland. In the opening bout of the tournament, Patterson easily decisioned an Algerian-French fighter named Omar Tebakka. "I could have stopped the fellow in the first one," Patterson recalled somewhat bemusedly, "if he hadn't got scared and covered up and run."[19] Next he faced the Dutch middleweight, Leonardus Jansen. Jansen actually caught Patterson with one good right to the chin that Patterson later admitted shook him up. But he gathered himself and scored a knockout in the first round. Reporters noted how he landed several hooks while leaping in the air. They did not know how far back this extended into Patterson's days at Wiltwyck. To them it looked like someone trying to get into a New York subway car just before the doors slammed shut. Still, the technique worked in Finland, at least in the ring. When he knocked out Jansen, one reporter said "they could have counted to 100 over the loser." By the time of Patterson's third Olympic fight, ticket sales at the Games' boxing matches had begun to rise.[20] In the semi-finals he faced a Swedish fighter named Stig Sjolin. The first round was close. Then in the second, Patterson knocked Sjolin down three times. Sjolin began grabbing and holding, hoping to survive the round, and the referee soon disqualified him. The win was officially a disqualification but, in effect, it was a TKO. The victory set up a final for Patterson with a fighter from Rumania named Vasile Tita. Here Patterson and Mello were a trifle worried about cold war politics entering the ring, as they faced not only a Rumanian opponent but a Polish referee.[21] With the peculiar nature of Finnish-Soviet relations, fears and rumors of collusion ran widely.

Patterson had already gained a reputation as one of if not the best fighter in the Olympics, and it seemed that Tita was a bit unnerved by it. Sensing Tita's anxiety, and perhaps remembering his first Golden Gloves fight in 1950, Patterson appeared to clown a bit as the bout began. Patterson missed with a left hook, and as he did Tita grabbed him into a quick clinch. Patterson responded by whirling his opponent around. It looked a bit like a comical dance, and some boos erupted from the crowd. The referee issued a warning, and Mello grew a little edgy. With that, Patterson settled down to work. His very next punch was a right uppercut that landed smack on the point of Tita's Roman chin. Tita went down, and he never got up. From the bell, to the missed hook, to the clinch, to the playful whirl, to the boos, to the warning, to the right uppercut, to the knockdown count — the entire fight lasted twenty seconds! One American fan at the Games went up to Patterson after the fight and complained: "I like to see you fight, but you never fight long enough."[22]

Patterson had won the Gold Medal. With his inglorious defeat of Ingemar Johansson, Ed Sanders had won the heavyweight medal. Norvel Lee took the light-heavyweight title. Two other Americans, Nate Brooks and Charley Adkins also won gold, respectively in the flyweight and light-welterweight divisions. The team lived up to all expectations, as did Floyd Patterson, for whom the expectations were highest. Beyond Leonardus Jansen's shot to his chin and sleeping with the midnight sun, the chief obstacle Patterson encountered at the Olympics came at the medal ceremony. He had no idea what to do. No one had taught him anything about protocols. At the medal ceremony a girl in Finnish national costume presented him with a bouquet of flowers. Standing with them awkwardly, Patterson suddenly remembered having seen old movies about boys in dancing school. So when the gold medal

Floyd Patterson, 1952, standing with four of his American Olympic boxing team-mates. From left to right are Nate Brooks, flyweight; Charley Adkins, light-welter-weight; Patterson; Norvel Lee, light-heavyweight; and Ed Sanders, heavyweight. All won gold medals at the Helsinki Games, Patterson taking the middleweight crown. The gold medal would launch Patterson's professional boxing career. In three years he would be the heavyweight champion. ©Bettmann/CORBIS.

was placed around his neck, Patterson awkwardly placed his flowers and left hand behind his back. Then he put his right hand over his stomach and bowed nervously from the waist. The band played *The Star-Spangled Banner.* (No one danced.)[23]

In early August, Patterson returned to New York. The Olympics had certainly given him some notoriety. Red Smith of the *New York Herald Tribune* described Patterson as having "faster paws than a subway pickpocket." He went on to praise Patterson for how he "confuses his opponents with his impetuous style.... He doesn't mind if he miss[es with a punch]," laughed Smith, "because he has six or seven other hands to follow up." One reporter excitedly called him "another Ray Robinson," and in 1952 to be mentioned in the same sentence as Sugar Ray was as good as it could get.[24]

Patterson was eager to turn pro. He told his parents: "There's nothing more to gain as an amateur. If you'll let me turn pro I can make money and help. Mr. Cus will see to it. And if I don't show any promise as a pro, I promise you I'll quit and forget all about it." D'Amato's trust in Patterson was confirmed at this point. Like all Olympic champions, Patterson was besieged with offers to switch managers. He did not give them a second of thought. He was Cus's man, and Frank Lavelle was his trainer. Strains would come to the team but not then. On August 8, the day after he returned from Helsinki, Patterson went right back to the Gramercy Park Gym, but when he arrived

Cus D'Amato told him he should not come there any more. Patterson was perplexed for an instant. Then D'Amato explained that while he would continue to manage him, he wanted Patterson at a bigger gym. Floyd Patterson was now to train at Stillman's Gymnasium. Stillman's Gym was further uptown on West 54th Street. Before it was replaced by a hotel in 1961, Stillman's was *the* gym where some of the giants of the fight game trained — Joe Walcott, Ezzard Charles, Sugar Ray Robinson, Jake LaMotta, Rocky Graziano, Joey Giardello, Carmen Basilio. Entering into that world, Floyd's gold medal did not seem so grand any more. Now he was turning pro, and it was a whole new game.[25]

III

He'll Be the Champ

As Floyd Patterson entered the world of New York professional boxing, he could not help but feel awestruck. His Olympic medal may have gotten a nod or a smile from a few pundits, managers, and opponents. Nevertheless they all basically saw it as mere amateur boxing, and with all fights going three rounds or less, that was indeed all it was. Patterson recognized this right away and acknowledged it without a hint of defensiveness. The gap separating amateur and professional boxing was psychological as well as physical, and at both levels it was considerable. Amateur boxing, Patterson reflected, "is like a sprint race. You go all out because you know you don't have to go far. The other is like a distance race — you have to pace yourself and look out that your opponent doesn't have too much for you at the finish." Patterson was indeed an ex-sprinter now entering training for marathon racing. He knew Cus D'Amato was serious. D'Amato hired a new trainer, Dan Florio, to help in the preparations. Florio had trained many great fighters, including featherweight champion Tony Canzoneri and, recently and most notably, heavyweight champion Jersey Joe Walcott. This was the big time, and Patterson knew that nothing less than total dedication was absolutely necessary.[1]

Within a month, D'Amato had Patterson set for his first professional fight, September 12, 1952. Some reporters chortled that Cus had carefully chosen young Patterson's first professional opponent, "a sacrificial lamb," snorted one, implying that it would not signify too much if Patterson won, and a great deal if he lost. Such is standard, and often valid, journalistic fare when a celebrated amateur boxer makes his professional debut. While some reporters may have been taking Patterson's first fight lightly, the debut certainly meant a great deal to Floyd. The morning of the fight, as he left his family's Brooklyn apartment, his parents were quite solemn. His father actu-

28

ally stayed home from work for a few hours so he could be there to say good-bye. His brothers and sisters were all there too. "They made me feel," Patterson later nodded, "as thought it was my first day going off to school." The fight was to take place that night at the St. Nicholas Arena, a large hall on the West Side of Mid-Town Manhattan on 66th Street, just off Columbus Avenue. Throughout the autumn and winter, St. Nick's regularly held boxing matches. They were hardly Friday night Madison Square Garden–level fights, but they were genuine professional venues which, most importantly, held the visibility that came with a New York City identity. New York had always been the absolute center of the world's fight game, and the post World War II decades marked one of the city's boxing heydays, as it did for so much of the sports and entertainment industry.

Because of Patterson's Olympic notoriety, a good number of boxing reporters made a point of being present at his first pro fight, as did Bob Christenberry, then the New York State boxing commissioner. In the early afternoon before the bout, Christenberry and some reporters spoke with Patterson as he stayed with D'Amato at the Gramercy Gym. Patterson emphasized that the bout was scheduled for six rounds, a distance he had never gone as an amateur fighter. He was not saying it merely for the sake of hype. He was very much in earnest. Generally, D'Amato did not like such pre-fight press attention and talk. He worried it would make his fighter more nervous. He always sweated such details. When the press had finished, D'Amato had Patterson eat a steak lunch and then take a nap at the Gramercy Hotel. Steak before a fight was another of D'Amato's rules. Patterson had always preferred to eat pork chops and sweet potatoes on a fight day, but Cus insisted on steak. D'Amato knew to monitor this, because Patterson's eating habits were not always disciplined. Indeed at home that morning he had eaten only a chocolate bar for breakfast. After his afternoon nap, Patterson went back to the Gramercy Gym and met with D'Amato and Frank Lavelle. Together they took the subway up to St. Nick's.[2]

At the arena, Patterson dressed, tried to relax, and waited for the call. When it came he walked out to the ring wearing his white Olympic robe with "USA" proudly on his back. He was proud of his Olympic achievement; besides, why shell out precious, hard-earned money for a new robe? His opponent that night was a journeyman middleweight named Eddie Godbold. To that point, Godbold's record was 3-12-1, hence some of the writers' guffawing about "a sacrificial lamb." In the fight, Patterson showed some of amateurish nervousness — overly aggressive, arms flailing. D'Amato expected this. Patterson leaped at Godbold a few times, swung wildly, and did not pace himself. Nevertheless, he "flooded his game opponent's face with flashy combinations." Patterson floored Godbold in both the second and third rounds. In the fourth, he hit Godbold with "a right and left to the jaw [that] sent

Godbold sprawling half way out on the ring apron." Patterson knocked God-bold out at 2:39 of the fourth round. One reporter called victory "an easy, breezy cuffing." Such pooh-poohings of the quality of Patterson's opponent may have been on the mark, but Cus D'Amato knew best how to bring along a young talent. At this point, he certainly preferred an easy victory over push-ing his fighter along too fast. Patterson's victory earned him $300.[3]

For the next two years, Patterson fought a series of bouts, mostly in Brooklyn at the Eastern Parkway Arena. The arena's manager, Teddy Bren-ner, and chief promoter, Emil Lence, created a kind of lower-profile addi-tion to the city's big-time venue of Madison Square Garden. St. Nicholas Arena served similarly. Lence and Brenner figured New York could accom-modate other boxing centers. The density of fan support was certainly there, and now, even more importantly, they had secured a tidy financial contract with a New York area television station, Channel Five, which regularly broad-cast professional fights on Monday night. Television coverage was a key to Lence and Brenner's success at Eastern Parkway. American television was then in its burgeoning state. By 1952 most of the nation's major cities had but three stations affiliated with the three major networks, ABC, CBS, and NBC. Only a few of the largest metropolitan areas had any other stations. Of course, New York was one that did, and the city's independent Channel Five, then called WABD, was quite successful. They developed their own program line with local shows, and they presented lots of old movies and reruns. In their evening listings they especially targeted the city's working class populations, focusing on local sports including baseball, basketball, football, and hockey, as well as on working class entertainment sports like pro wrestling and roller derby. One of Channel Five's most successful venues here was boxing, and the Monday Night Boxing from the Eastern Parkway Arena was one of the station's popular weeklies. All over the New York area, especially in the city's 100,000s of bars and clubs, working folks, as well as many others, sat around and drank beer while watching the fights. New York, especially Brooklyn, was the center of boxing fandom in the 1950s. Fans were everywhere. "You had fights every night," Patterson later recalled. "You had Monday nights at East-ern Parkway. Wednesdays were the St. Nicholas Arena. Every Friday night the fights were televised, sponsored by Gillette Blue Blades." Channel Five's marketing strategy worked extremely well. Ratings were good, so the station could make money selling advertising spots to razor blade makers, as well as to breweries and cigarette and cigar manufacturers, all of whom obviously knew their best customers were watching. Among the fighters, Patterson was a regular on these Eastern Parkway bouts. Indeed he became their biggest star. From October of 1952 to January of 1955, he fought no fewer than twelve Monday night bouts at the Eastern Parkway Arena.[4]

As Patterson's career as a professional boxer unfolded, Cus D'Amato chose his opponents well. Opponents ranged from beginners who never amounted to much like Lester Johnson, Sammy Brown, Don Grant and Jacques Royer-Crecy to journeymen like Godbold, Sammy Walker, Earl Sabotin, Esau Ferdinand, and Alvin Williams. D'Amato would say directly, "You try to vary the style of opponents, punchers, fancy boxers, counter punchers." Some reporters and pundits criticized the level of some of D'Amato's choices, feeling their stature and ability were not always strong. To the extent this may have been true, it was not always D'Amato's fault. Several fighters of the day frankly told reporters: "Me fight Patterson! What do you think I am — crazy?"[5] Generally, each fight took young Floyd a step up in difficulty. Sammy Walker, his next opponent a month after Godbold, was out on a technical knockout only 47 seconds into the second round. Four weeks later, in a fight on the undercard of the prestigious Friday night venue at Madison Square Garden, Patterson disposed of another rookie, Lester Johnson. It was a TKO in the third round. The Garden aficionados were impressed with Patterson's punching power. Earl "Lalu" Sabotin cane next, and he was the first fighter Patterson faced who had a decent record to that point, 21–6. Sabotin was a respected boxer, and a generally good athlete. (Indeed, he would later win the Ohio State Amateur Golf Championship, and Ohioans take their golf seriously.) Patterson was also giving away eight pounds to Sabotin, who fought at 175. Patterson's quickness would win out, as he stopped Sabotin with a TKO in the fifth round. Reporters noted the fight to have been "far from exciting," as one reporter put it, and the 3000 at the Eastern Parkway did jeer a bit. But the respect for Patterson did not fade, and his victory over Sabotin yielded Patterson his first sports headline in the *New York Times*. As the fight came at the end of December, the closing of the year prompted one writer to note that Patterson was a reasonable candidate for "Rookie of the Year" in professional boxing. He actually could not be considered, as he had been a professional only since the Summer Olympics.[6]

In January of 1953, D'Amato took Patterson out to Chicago, where a national television broadcast audience saw Patterson fight a man whom the *New York Daily News* described as a "rough and ready Chicagoan" named Chester Mieszala. Patterson was to receive $1000 plus expenses to and from Chicago for himself and his entourage of three. This was a new level of wealth for him. Mieszala was the hometowners' favorite, not just because he was from Chicago but even more because he was Polish. It was the first time Patterson fought before a crowd clearly disposed to his opponent, and it did not appear to bother him one bit. Patterson even showed a bit of arrogance, something most fight pundits think to be a plus. When he had the opportunity to watch Mieszala spar at Chicago's Midtown Gym, he begged off, saying, with a smirk, it would be unfair. Dubbed by the press "a speed merchant," Patterson showed the Chicago and TV viewers his lightning quick hands.

Mieszala appeared "confused much of the time." Again, it was a clear victory for Patterson. He knocked Mieszala down in the first and third rounds. At one point in the fight, Patterson knocked out Mieszala's mouthpiece. Mieszala immediately dropped to his knees to look for it. To D'Amato's (and much of the crowd's) chagrin, Patterson did not hit him at that vulnerable point. Amateur rules dictate that when an opponent has any part of his body but his feet on the floor he cannot be hit. Patterson allowed himself to be chivalrous, turning away until Mieszala was ready again. Various writers would later note this as part of the unusually gentlemanly composite that was Patterson's nature. D'Amato lamented: "Floyd showed he was a good sport. He turned his back. That's saying to the other guy, 'You're a good sport too.' But you turn your back, the other guy'll apologize all right, and you'll hear him — when you wake up. You can't be too good a sport; you gotta take care." The question of killer instinct would come back at Patterson at various times in his career. People recalled how heavyweight Jack Sharkey had once appealed a matter to the referee and took his eye off Jack Dempsey for one fatal second. That night in Chicago in January 1953, Patterson's good sportsmanship proved no problem. The referee picked up Mieszala's mouthpiece and stuck it in the fighter's mouth. Patterson then resumed pummeling him. Patterson appeared ready to floor Mieszala again in the fifth round, but the referee intervened, stopping the fight and giving Patterson a TKO. Mieszala protested, but even the partisan Chicago crowd agreed with the referee. A respected reporter from an African American paper, the *Pittsburgh Courier*, Wendell Smith was in Chicago for the fight. He noted Patterson's great promise. Patterson told Smith how he was rapidly gaining weight and would "be a light-heavyweight before long," adding, "I hope I grow big enough to be a heavyweight." That was where the big money lay.[7]

While some of Patterson's early fights took him to Chicago, to Oakland, California, and to Washington, D.C., the steady fare remained in New York and at the Eastern Parkway Arena. The Channel Five link made these fights financially worthwhile. With the TV station making good advertising money, they were willing to pay a good fee to the arena, which in turn paid the boxers well. Patterson made no less than $2900 for each appearance there. Television was indeed a blessing both to Patterson and to D'Amato. Other than a few highly touted heavyweights, few new professional boxers had ever made such money right out of the amateur chute. In his year out of the Olympics, Patterson had been working at the Gramercy Park Hotel for $44 a week (with $25 always going to his mother). He soon did not need to work there. With ten fights in 1954, for example, five of which were at the Eastern Parkway Arena, Patterson netted $37,901. The following year he topped $40,000. Aside from a few baseball stars of the day like Ted Williams and Mickey Mantle, there were not many athletes, and certainly no blue collar workers in America, making that kind of money. D'Amato took his manager's cut of one-third, but it left Patterson far more cash for himself and for his family than they had ever seen. With all his deeply ingrained history of inadequacy in regard to supporting his family, Patterson felt very, very good about this. He took care of his family, of course. He also bought himself a nice car. Patterson had once bought a $35 used Oldsmobile which, he laughingly recalled, "wound up an abandoned car on the street just six hours after it had become mine." Now that he was making good money, he bought himself a new Cadillac. And he was no longer ill at ease about ever spending time with his girlfriend, Sandra.[8]

While Patterson had piqued D'Amato's concern over his display of chivalry towards Chester Mieszala in their Chicago bout, on other occasions, he showed the opposite sort of mentality, one that D'Amato doubtlessly preferred. There was the incident in Chicago when Floyd refused when D'Amato wanted him to watch Mieszala train and pick up some ideas on how to fight him. Patterson had calmly replied: "I think that would be taking an unfair advantage.... I don't want to watch him until I get into the ring with him." D'Amato may have been taken aback here, but he liked that sort of attitude and confidence in his fighter. On another occasion, in November 1954, Patterson fought Jimmy Slade. Slade was a fighter with whom Patterson had shared a training camp, and there the two became good friends. A reporter asked Patterson, then still but nineteen, how he felt fighting a friend. Patterson responded emphatically: "Let me tell you now so you'll understand. Jimmy Slade is my friend, but when I get in the ring I don't even know who I'm fightin.' They just become another body." D'Amato applauded. His man was confident and relaxed. Patterson went to the locker room before the bout and slept soundly for nearly a half hour. D'Amato woke him up, and Patterson calmly went out and won a unanimous decision over Slade. A year later he gave Slade a return bout and knocked him out in seven. "If you can't understand how one fighter can have affection and sympathy for another and still fight him as hard and as fiercely as he can, it can't be helped. We're a strange breed, we are men who make our living with our fists." From July 1954 through April 1956, Patterson fought and beat sixteen opponents. Three he won by unanimous decisions. One opponent would not come out for the sixth round. All the rest were knockouts.[9] Cus D'Amato was smiling broadly.

A particularly hard fight for Patterson came in April of 1953, a few months after the Mieszala bout. Patterson squared off on a Brooklyn Monday nighter against an experienced middleweight named Dick Wagner. Up to then, Patterson had stopped five fighters in a row. Wagner was another a New Yorker, and he also trained at Stillman's Gym. As with regard to Mieszala, Patterson broke off all training at Stillman's while preparing for Wagner, again claiming he did not want to take unfair advantage. The featherweight champion of an earlier era, Abe Attell, once commented: "I never seen a good fighter who wasn't a conceited son of a bitch," and Patterson always had a bit of that in him, although many would say not enough.[10] With his sportsmanship and his conceit, Patterson was displaying a complex psychological arsenal which was another key ingredient of being a good fighter. How this arrogance and vanity inherent in his words and actions *vis* à *vis* Slade and Wagner merged with the sportsmanship he showed against Mieszala went to the unsettled (possibly schizophrenic levels in extreme cases, such as Mike Tyson) elements that also lie in varying forms in many great fighters.

Dick Wagner proved to be Patterson's first really tough opponent. He was the first opponent that went the distance, and he tested Patterson in ways he had never experienced before. His strategy was to tire Patterson with body punches, corner and pummel him, maul him in clinches, tire the kid out with body blows, then knock him out. Amateurs and novice pros are seldom accustomed to such in-fighting tactics and may not know how to react. In the fourth round particularly, Wagner was able to corner Patterson and wail away at him with some body blows, "beating my belly like a drum," Patterson remembered. Some of the crowd were yelling that Patterson was "out on his feet!" "How I survived that beating," Patterson sighed, "I'll never know." After the fourth round, D'Amato yelled at him: "You want to be a champion? Well, start fighting like one!" Wagner continued to do some damage, but Patterson danced well, darting in and out, landing enough punches to maintain a slight edge with the judges. The fight went the distance, with Patterson finishing strongly. Wagner was left with a big dent in his nose and his left eye was closed. Patterson was hurt too, but the judges gave him the fight on a split decision, the first time any judge had ruled against him as a professional. Patterson would later admit that Wagner was the first fighter he faced who genuinely hurt him with the punches he landed. "He beat my body so bad," Patterson later recalled, "I was urinating blood for days."[11]

Both Patterson and Wagner were eager for a rematch, but Wagner had hurt his ankle, so the bout had to be postponed. Meanwhile, D'Amato did not waste any time. Two months after the Wagner fight, Patterson scored a three-round TKO over Gordon Wallace. This marked another significant step, as Wallace had been the Canadian light-heavyweight champion. Wallace thus had undeniable stature, and he was from a higher weight class. D'Amato was working Patterson heavily with weights (and steaks) and moving his fight level up steadily. He wanted him to grow into the heavyweight division — where the big money lay.

Patterson may have remembered Wagner hurting him, but reporters said another opponent in October of 1953 hurt him even more. Wes Bascom of East St. Louis, Illinois, who outweighed Patterson by nine pounds, apparently "battered [Patterson] into bloodiness." By the third round, Patterson had cuts around each eye. In the fourth round, he was blinking through blood; then Bascom drew blood from Patterson's nose with an uppercut. Bascom's punches were hard, but Patterson's, while often lighter, were more numerous. He piled up points, and finally staggered Bascom with a left to the jaw in the seventh round. He won an unanimous decision and after the fight went immediately to a doctor.[12]

Two months later, December 14, 1953, Patterson finally had his rematch with Dick Wagner. D'Amato had known that Wagner was a body puncher, and in the first fight he had instructed Patterson to box and win by building up points, with the idea being that Patterson needed to learn to absorb body punches and go the distance. It had worked, barely. This time, at Patterson's insistence, D'Amato let Patterson be more aggressive. This worked better, as Wagner was unable to maneuver Patterson into the corners. Patterson stopped Wagner with a technical knockout in the fifth round, but it was another tough fight, one which significantly increased his reputation. New York reporters noted, with some hyperbole, that "the big guy who gave Floyd Patterson trouble last April was [this time] a lead-pipe cinch," with Patterson "in complete command." The young novelist Norman Mailer was in attendance that night at the Eastern Parkway Arena. He later reflected that, while he indeed knew little about boxing at that point in his life, when watching the Patterson-Wagner bout something caught his novice eye. Patterson, he said, "knocked out a rugged fighter named Dick Wagner in five rounds, and there had been something about the way he did it which cut into my ignorance. I knew he was good. It was like seeing one's first bullfight; at last one knows what everybody has been talking about." The N.Y. boxing press's conclusion was that Patterson had "vastly improved." "They said I couldn't take a punch," Patterson recalled. "Then I fought Dick Wagner. He gave me a good beating and I managed to survive that." Wagner himself retired from the fight game after the bout. Patterson nodded respectfully, "I'll always remember Dick as a game, tough fighter." They would meet again, in Portland, Oregon, in 1971, when they shared Thanksgiving dinner at Wagner's house.[13]

Patterson's opponents would only get tougher, but he was certainly not going to shy away from anyone. Such dangers were part of the fight game. Besides, he was undefeated, and, given the reflections of people like Norman Mailer, his reputation was growing in ways he did not fully realize. In January of 1954, the Boxing Writers Association voted Patterson the James P. Dawson Memorial Trophy as the fight game's Rookie of the Year. At a ceremony held at the Astor Hotel in New York, Patterson received his award. On hand were such notables as former Postmaster General James A. Farley, New York's Mayor Robert Wagner, and fellow boxer Kid Gavilan, then the world welterweight champion. For Patterson, however, the biggest thrill of the evening was that the man who officially presented him the Dawson Trophy was none other than his boxing idol, Joe Louis.[14] The praise was growing. Beyond the plaudits, Patterson also had a family to support, and he was still seeing Sandra. So there could be no lingering on the good feelings. It was immediately back to Cus and to Stillman's Gym to train for the next fight.

Another important, and somewhat touchy matter for Floyd Patterson occurred in January 1954 that could have posed a serious problem for his career. On January 4, he turned nineteen. The New York State Athletic Commission required a boxer be nineteen before he could fight longer than six rounds. In 1953, Patterson had fought Wagner (twice), Wallace, and Bascom in scheduled eight-rounders at but the age of eighteen, going the distance in two of the matches. He had gotten away with this because he, and D'Amato, had been falsely claiming his birth date to have been March 27, 1933. (Patterson had actually first lied to D'Amato when he first met him in late 1949, telling him he was fifteen.) The records of the United States Olympic Committee revealed Patterson's true birth date. On December 18, 1953, just four days after the second Wagner fight, the State Athletic Commission announced that, because of the infraction, Patterson would be inactive for an unspecified time. The commission could have been tough about suspending Patterson for a lengthy time over this matter, conceivably for as many days as he had been falsely listing his age. He had first signed to fight Wagner back in March of '53, hence the particular date, March 27, which D'Amato and Patterson had invented. Patterson could thus have been kept out of N.Y. boxing for nine months, or even more, and such a length of inactivity could have critically affected his development. But the Commission chose to be lenient. Perhaps his notoriety as Rookie of the Year made the potential financial gains of many boxing and television people something not easily pushed aside with a stringent enforcement of commission rules. So the infraction was allowed to pass, and by mid–February, Patterson had another bout at Eastern Parkway.[15]

The February '54 fight was against a former Canadian middleweight and light-heavyweight champion Yvon Durelle. Pointedly, the papers were explicit in stating that the fight was limited to eight rounds because Patterson was under twenty years of age, a clear indication of how everyone wanted to emphasize how the i's and t's were now being dotted and crossed. Durelle was a tough fighter, although at this point not yet known to most New York pundits. A few years later, in 1957, he would give a very rough, gallant fight to then light-heavyweight champion Archie Moore, knocking him down three times in the first round. He was an awkward fighter, "a spoiler," hard to hit, and with a heavy punch himself, "the most complicated fighter I'd ever fought up to then," Patterson recalled. On February 15, no one in New York had any sense of this when Patterson stepped into the ring against him. One reporter wrote that "Durelle was supposed to be an easy mark," after which he emphasized: "He *wasn't.*" It would indeed be a tough fight. It went the distance, and

Patterson won a unanimous decision. But the unanimity was misleading. The three judges' cards read 5–3, 5–3, and 4-3-1, and "Durelle shook Patterson up repeatedly with right uppercuts and more than once set Floyd back on his heels." Still, the toughness of the fight only added to Patterson's growing reputation, the *New York Daily News* dubbing him "Brooklyn's nineteen-year-old battering ram." D'Amato's training and steak diet were working. Patterson was already turning into a light heavyweight.[16]

The following month D'Amato slated a bout for Patterson in Washington, D.C., against an opponent named Sammy Brown. Patterson's reputation among fight people had now grown considerably, and the Washington boxing press was eager to see Patterson for themselves. Folks in the Maryland countryside outside Washington were less hospitable, however, as on route to D.C., Patterson was refused service by racists at a roadside restaurant. Patterson could only shake his head. "When is this stupidity going to stop?" he asked D'Amato. Back in Washington, reporters were upbeat. Plugging the fight at Washington's Turner's Arena on the afternoon of the fight, one local paper described Patterson as "one of those rare fighters who apparently has everything — speed, punch, boxing skill, and ability take a punch." D'Amato was adding to the hype as much as he could. Cus loved to hold forth to the press, and the Washington papers were willing to give him plenty of space. D'Amato laid it on thick. He called Patterson "a wonder boy.... When he hits you, it's like Louis. When he hurts you he follows up immediately like Louis did. And when he has to box he does it like Sugar Ray used to do." Patterson, meanwhile, showed Washington fans a certain modesty. Noting that Brown, recently out of the Army, had won eight straight pro bouts, all Patterson humbly noted was, "I hope he doesn't make it nine," adding, "I just hope the people in Washington like me. I'd like to come back here and fight some more." Washington was a more Southern city than Brooklyn, although definitely less Southern than the Maryland countryside nearby, and such humility resonated well in such a culture. The events of the fight sat well with Patterson's fans too. In the first round, he dropped Brown to his knees twice. The referee soon stopped the fight, giving Patterson a TKO in the second round.[17]

Light-heavyweight champion Archie Moore was seated in the crowd, and he obviously knew that this Patterson kid was fast becoming a contender. "That boy can sure hit hard.... He looks good and fast to me." D'Amato added to the sense of momentum here, noting that Floyd was "still a growing boy. His parents," he noted, "are both big people, and his brothers are also big." Patterson, he concluded, is "going to grow into a solid heavyweight." He was now ranked fifth in the light-heavyweight division. D'Amato opined: "In about three years look for him as heavyweight champion of the world."[18]

Two more fights went well for Patterson that April and May at Eastern

Parkway. Alvin Williams gave Patterson some trouble with his "clumsy but sturdy" defense and staggered Patterson with a right to he jaw in the fourth round. Still, only two judges gave Williams even one round of eight, with the other judge awarding Patterson a shutout. In May the same lopsided numbers came from the judges when Patterson beat Jesse Turner. Patterson was already an established contender, ready for something more substantial, but the Turner bout was Patterson's 13th as a pro, and the ever-superstitious D'Amato was taking no chances. A big fight would have to wait for the fateful #13 to pass.[19]

After defeating Williams and Turner, D'Amato then signed his undefeated prodigy to a genuinely big fight. On June 7, 1954, Patterson would fight his tenth Monday night bout at the Eastern Parkway Arena, his fourteenth fight overall. This time it was not merely Channel Five but New York's ABC affiliate that agreed to pick up the fight for a television broadcast. Patterson would get a new high for his work — $5000. His opponent was to be Joey Maxim, a former world light-heavyweight champion. Patterson was still only 19. Maxim was 32 and had fought over 100 professional bouts. Boxing pundits had been talking about this possible match-up for over a year, but D'Amato was not to be rushed. Maxim came into the ring nine pounds heavier than his young opponent, but he was not the heavier puncher. Rather, Maxim was a "cutie," someone who could slip punches beautifully and fend off 'most any kind of attack. He was, as one reporter put it, "one of the cleverest" boxers in the game. Indeed, Maxim was to that point the only man ever to knock out Sugar Ray Robinson.[20] As Maxim was a Cleveland native, the Eastern Parkway Arena crowd was decidedly pro–Patterson. Maxim was also white, and this may have added to the decidedness of the battle lines, although not many white working class New Yorkers were likely thinking about race as they rooted for their Brooklynite Patterson that evening.

At the outset of the fight, the Brooklyn partisans cheered Patterson mightily, as in the very first round he connected with some good left hooks and rights to Maxim's jaw. Maxim fought better in the second round, connecting with several left jabs and rights. But Patterson returned fire, and he opened a cut over Maxim's right eye. According to the reporters on hand, this remained the pattern in the early rounds. In the sixth, Patterson continued to land good combinations, with Maxim appearing to tire. The same sequence held in the seventh round, although Maxim rallied gamely in the eighth to make the ending appear close. With the fight going the eight-round distance, the outcome was in the hands of the three fight judges. The crowd and the ringside reporters were sure of a Patterson victory. Then the judges' cards were read to the crowd — 5–3, 4-3-1, and 7–1, all for Maxim! The crowd was stunned, and angry. Boos echoed everywhere. Eleven boxing reporters were on hand to cover the fight, and all eleven had scored the fight for

After turning pro, Patterson was on the way up in the boxing rankings. Here he is in 1954, connecting with a right to the face of former light-heavyweight champion Joey Maxim. Every reporter covering the bout scored the fight for Patterson. The judges gave it to Maxim, however; the crowd booed vociferously. It was Patterson's only loss on his route to becoming heavyweight champion. ©Bettmann/CORBIS.

Patterson.* "If Floyd Patterson didn't have the better of Joey Maxim at Eastern Parkway Arena on Monday night," scoffed one, "[then] Independence Day doesn't fall on July 4th." "What impressed me," wrote another, "was that Maxim couldn't make Patterson look foolish except at infrequent intervals, and then only for a second or two." "Patterson," simply sighed another, "had been robbed." Maxim admitted Patterson "had my tail dragging after the fourth." Patterson certainly felt he won the fight but later reflected more generously. Maxim, he said, "was the first fighter who never hurt me at all in the whole bout, but as time has gone by I've developed more and more respect for the way he handled me."[21]

An old adage has it that the only thing that is ever square about boxing is the shape of the ring. Patterson certainly seemed to have been a victim of something that was at least stupid, and possibly fishy. The loss, his first as a professional, was not easy to take. D'Amato tried to put a good face on it to reporters: "I wanted to see how he'd go against a seasoned campaigner who knew all the tricks, and I think he went very well." At the same time he was irked and promised Patterson he would file a formal protest with Robert

*The New York Daily News *reported 11 of 11 writers gave the fight to Patterson. Patterson, likely relying on D'Amato's word, said it was 11 of 12. In either case, the journalistic sense was overwhelming.*

Christenberry, chairman of the New York State Athletic Commission. He did, and nothing came of it. Some wondered whether there was some sort of fix in the works, possibly to give an added slap for Patterson's falsehood about his age that came out earlier in the year. That was speculation; no one ever produced any evidence on this point. There would be other tough breaks for Patterson in his career, breaks that would actually hurt more. This time the loss, while painful, did not hurt Patterson's status as a contender, for the controversy surrounding the Maxim decision was not the least bit lost among New York's boxing pundits. Patterson's reputation did not even significantly diminish. In early July, the National Boxing Association listed Patterson as the number four contender for the light-heavyweight title, then held by Archie Moore. (Maxim was number two.) Patterson had gone toe to toe with a one-time champion, from a markedly higher weight level no less. Thus he remained a highly-touted up-and-comer. Once the immediate disappointment of the loss had worn off, Patterson himself was not bitter: "The fight," he later reflected, "convinced me that someday I would be a champion. Maxim showed me nothing in the ring I couldn't learn to handle. And he had been a champion." Patterson very much wanted a rematch, but Maxim never gave him one.[22]

A month later, Patterson was back to his winning ways. At St. Nicholas Arena on July 12, he beat the French middleweight champion Jacques Royer-Crecy. It was another eight rounder for the nineteen-year-old, but Patterson won it on a TKO in seven. On the three judges' cards to that point, Patterson had lost only one round. Royer-Crecy had knocked Patterson down, however. He was the first man to do so. (Many more would follow.) The knockdown came in the first round. While working out of a corner clinch, the Frenchman caught Patterson with hook to the chin. Patterson immediately dropped to one knee. D'Amato eagerly claimed it was a mere slip (it wasn't). Patterson was up instantly and showed no ill effect. He won the rest of the rounds and twice cut the Frenchman. Then in the seventh round, Patterson caught Royer-Crecy's right eye with a left hook. Royer-Crecy began to bleed profusely, so badly indeed that he had trouble seeing. After the round, the ring physician examined the cut eye and immediately stopped the bout.[23]

In August, Patterson returned to the Eastern Parkway Arena, now as the main event. Here he stopped a highly regarded Los Angeles light-heavy named Tommy Harrison. "Harrison," wrote one boxing scribe, "should have given him a good fight." Patterson, however, easily stopped him with a technical knockout at 1:29 of the very first round. "He didn't land a single punch on me," Patterson gloated. At the bell he was on Harrison, knocking him into the ropes in the first ten seconds. Over the next minute Patterson knocked Harrison down twice. The crowd was screaming, and all the New York ring experts were duly impressed. Patterson had known Harrison from Stillman's, and he did not want to hurt him. After the second knockdown, the referee stopped the fight fearing worse injury to Harrison. Patterson said he was grateful. After the fight Harrison's manager thanked him for not hurting Harrison any more than was necessary.[24]

With his defeat of Harrison, Patterson very much wanted a rematch with Joey Maxim. Instead, in October, just eleven days after another St. Nicholas Arena fight, came a unanimous (7–1) decision over another journeyman, Esau Ferdinand. D'Amato subsequently signed Patterson for his next big night. Patterson was to be in the main event on the Friday night card at Madison Square Garden. D'Amato felt the managers of the Garden had been slighting his fighter and not giving him a Garden date sooner than they did. It was one of many irritations D'Amato would have with the boxing establishment, but the victory over Ferdinand forced matters ahead.[25] Back in October of 1952, Patterson, in only his third pro outing, had squared off against another professional rookie named Lester Johnson. That fight was buried on the undercard of the Madison Square Garden's Friday night fight venue. That was Patterson's first appearance at the fight game's mecca. Now he was to be the main event. The "Old" Madison Square Garden was indeed *the* boxing showplace, not just of New York but of the entire boxing world. The arena was certainly used for other major sports like basketball and hockey, as well as for circuses and rodeos, but boxing was truly what the arena was all about. The IBC, the International Boxing Club, kept its headquarters there. Many boxers have reflected that the other major arenas of boxing, then and since, including the new MSQ on 33rd Street have never created the same mystique for boxing as did the Old Madison Square Garden. (The old Madison Square Garden on 78th Street and Eighth Avenue, replaced by the new garden on 33rd Street and Seventh Avenue, had actually been the second Garden. The original, hence the real old Madison Square Garden was built at the corner of Broadway, 23rd Street, and Madison Avenue, on Madison Square, hence the name. Beyond this history, the second old Madison Square Garden was the center of the boxing world, and every great boxer of the 1940s and 1950s passed through there with reverence.) By October of 1954, Patterson had seventeen fights under his belt, and his only loss was the debatable decision to Joey Maxim. He had indeed earned his way onto the main event on a Friday Night fight at the Garden. The night came on October 22, 1954. Patterson would make $4000 for the night's work. New York's NBC affiliate, along with the NBC stations of many other cities, broadcast the fight live at 10:00 P.M. that evening.[26]

Floyd Patterson's opponent at the Garden was Joe Gannon. It was originally to have been a ranked light heavyweight named Willie Troy, but Troy hurt his shoulder ten days before the fight date. The Garden's managers substituted Gannon. Gannon was hardly a contender in the class of Floyd

Patterson. He was, however, under the same management as the heavyweight champion of the time, Rocky Marciano. He had been one of Marciano's sparring partners when Rocky was preparing for his two title fights with Ezzard Charles and had fought on the undercards of those two bouts in June and September of 1954. Back in 1944, Gannon had been the National Amateur Athletic Union welterweight champion. From that point he had dropped out of the fight game for a time to serve in the army and then become a Washington, D.C., policeman. He was now twenty-seven years old and considered, as one reporter put it, to be "a pretty good conventional boxer," not as good as some of Patterson's previous opponents like Joey Maxim but by no means a "chump." In the fight, Gannon showed skeptics that he could take punches, as Patterson did not first seem able to hurt him. Patterson was landing three punches for every one of Gannon's, and the points built up. He put on a boxing clinic, nailing Gannon with flurries of punches, all thrown with text-book form. There was no single, big punch landed in the early rounds, but the combinations were taking their toll. By the fifth round, Patterson was well ahead on all cards. In the seventh, Gannon did land one good right, and this appeared to anger Patterson a bit. From this point Patterson appeared to be "punching for keeps," as one reporter noted. The crowd was cheering Gannon, not for any dislike of Patterson, but because they wanted the fight to go the distance and felt Gannon needed the encouragement. In the eighth, Patterson nailed Gannon with a left hook. Gannon staggered across the ring. Patterson quickly pursued, landing five more punches. Towards the end of the eighth, a Patterson right to Gannon's face knocked him through the ring ropes, landing him flat on his back on the ring apron. Gannon was out, although within seconds the bell rang, ending the fight. Technically, then, there was no knockout, but there was absolutely no doubt in the Garden as to who won the fight. "If there had been a ninth round," opined one scribe, "the other fellow wouldn't have been able to come out for it." Prior to the fight, there had been skeptics who wondered if Patterson's amateurish ways, jumping with hooks and the like, had been supplanted by solid boxing technique. There were also pundits who wondered if Patterson could hit hard and bore in for the kill when given the opportunity. In the crucible of a Friday night feature at the Garden, Patterson appeared to have answered all the questions.[27]

A month later, Patterson won a unanimous decision over his old friend Jimmy Slade in another Madison Square Garden fight. Again, Patterson and D'Amato had been trying to set a match with Willie Troy, but he was unavailable. Slade had a decent record and seemed a worthy opponent. He had been ranked as high as fourth among the light-heavyweight contenders. Oddsmakers actually had Slade the slight favorite. The fight, however, proved to be so one-sided that the Garden fans were jeering Slade. Patterson had scored knockdowns in each of the first three rounds. By the third, Patterson's effectiveness prompted Slade to begin running, avoiding all contact he could. The crowd soon began singing "Let Me Call You Sweetheart." One reporter panned that at least Slade "was smart enough to run after the beating he took in the first three rounds." Patterson knocked him down again in the seventh and the eighth rounds. The decision was a complete "shutout;" the fight judges had awarded Patterson every round. The lopsidedness of the fight was so enormous that the New York State Athletic Commission temporarily retained Slade's fight purse of $5821, pending an investigation as to whether he had "laid down" for Patterson. (Patterson grossed $7500, netting $6,185.) Slade's handlers pointed out to the NYAC that prior to the Patterson fight, they were anticipating a victory and angling for a bout with champion Archie Moore. Obviously, they were not going to cast such a chance away for any smaller gains they could garner throwing such a lower-level bout as this one. (And if he was throwing the fight he would have likely been less evasive and simply taken a dive amidst the beating of the early rounds.) Slade was cleared and got his money. All the suspicions ultimately underscored the point of just how good young Patterson was. Given Slade's prior ranking as high as fourth among light-heavyweight contenders, the *New York Times* coyly concluded that "a change is now in order."[28]

After the Slade fight, the Christmas holidays were approaching, but Patterson and D'Amato stuck with their training regimen. Floyd was training hard every day. "I can't be home for Christmas," he told his mother, "but I want you to know that me and Mr. Cus have been figuring up my money and soon we will have that house in the country we've been dreaming about for so long. And you can have a garden and chickens and a cow; I promise you!" D'Amato was figuring Floyd for a future shot at the championship. At the end of the year, Patterson was ranked fourth among the light-heavyweight contenders. But D'Amato had more in mind than Archie Moore's light-heavyweight crown. Patterson was still young and had more growth in him. D'Amato was insisting on a steady diet of steaks and milk (three quarts a day). He expected Floyd to put on about ten pounds of muscle in a year. His eye was still fixed on pushing Patterson into the heavyweight division and the big money.[29]

On January 7, 1955, just three days after his (truly) twentieth birthday, Patterson scored another Madison Square Garden triumph, at last getting to fight Willie Troy, with a fifth round technical knockout. The fight had a certain amount of hype. Patterson's growing fame was part of what made for the publicity surrounding the fight with Troy, of course. Troy, as well, was an accomplished young boxer. His record to that point was 30 and 2, with 23 of his 30 victories coming via knockouts. (Patterson's ratio here was only 10 of 18.) Patterson actually came down in weight, to 166, to fight Troy in the middleweight division. He and D'Amato had agreed to fight Troy as a middleweight, but he had to struggle to make the weight. Some speculated that Patterson could be a trifle weaker at such a level. Troy had also been bragging that he would test Patterson with close range in-fighting. He should not have bragged so much. Troy indeed intentionally stood at close range against Patterson, and Patterson teed off with incessant punches to the head. With the barrage, Troy was never able to mount any offense. Patterson piled up points in every round, winning them all and leaving Troy with a huge welt over his left eye. The referee stopped the fight after the fifth round. No one disagreed with the decision.[30] The Troy victory was the start of an impressive run of nine KOs and TKOs in one year. A scant ten days later came another TKO in the fifth, this time over Don Grant, theretofore 16 and 1 as a pro. Cus D'Amato later said that Patterson's victory over Grant was, by any technical yardstick, his best fight. D'Amato said it was even better than Floyd's subsequent victory over Archie Moore. Doubtlessly hyperbolic, but D'Amato claimed here that "the Patterson of the Grant fight would beat even [upcoming heavyweight Sonny] Liston." Patterson was now twenty years old, hence his fights could go ten rounds. Most of the fights that had been slated for fewer rounds in order to protect the young man never got to that point. Now that he was twenty, the round limit was still proving no issue. The Grant win would be his last Monday nighter at the Eastern Parkway Arena. Indeed he took the Grant fight as a favor to Emil Lence, the arena's promoter, who needed a named fighter to maintain a TV contract. Patterson had graduated from the Brooklyn arena as well as from the eight-round limit. He was a bona-fide contender. D'Amato said he could beat anyone. One reporter for the prestigious *New Yorker* was now calling him a "*Wunderkind*."[31]

The boxing world now fully saw Patterson as a top contender. "Patterson is not as fast as Ray Robinson," wrote one scribe, "but his blend of smartness and punching is hard to beat." The fact that someone would put him in the same sentence as Sugar Ray spoke volumes. At the time of the Gannon fight, Patterson was six feet in height, weighed 166 pounds, and was still growing. He had fought several bouts against bigger men, giving away as much as ten pounds. As he continued to train, his musculature continued to fill out his growing frame, the very thing D'Amato was expecting and pursuing with all those steaks and milk. D'Amato reflected: "Floyd's brother, he's a heavyweight, and he started like Floyd, a middleweight. He's the kind [that] matures late. So's Floyd. Give him two years, he'll be a heavy. Give him four, he'll be the champ." *Time Magazine* agreed. In a brief article in February 1956 it declared that Patterson's "future seems delightful." *Time* openly proclaimed him with a headline, "The Next Champ."[32]

IV

Champ

Through the year 1955, Patterson continued to win, and as the wins piled up his status as a contender grew ever brighter. Early in the year, Patterson hurt a knuckle while training, so after the Donald Grant fight of January 17, he did not fight for two months, the longest layoff of his career to that point. D'Amato had scheduled a return bout with Esau Ferdinand, against whom Patterson had fought back in October. The bout had to be postponed until March 17. Patterson flew out to Oakland, California, for the fight, his first appearance out West. His reputation had well preceded him. No one was betting on Ferdinand, and ticket sales lagged. As the fight day approached, D'Amato tried to perk up the gate, claiming, "Esau gave the twenty-year-old sensation his hardest fight outside of his lone loss to Joey Maxim." D'Amato was not just blowing smoke here. Ferdinand had indeed given Patterson a rough time. Still, few Californians bought what appeared to be mere hype from Patterson's manager, and they were proven right. The Western reporters were impressed with Patterson's "lightning fast hands," as he won round after round and floored Ferdinand in the seventh. In their first fight, Ferdinand had bullied Patterson in the clinches. Patterson had then proven a trifle weaker on the "inside," preferring to dance and jab. Ferdinand's bullying tactics were effective, and he had been able to prevent Patterson from staying outside. While in the clinches in the first fight, Ferdinand had also taunted Patterson, saying "Why don't you punch me? Why don't you punch me?" Even though he had won the first Ferdinand bout, these unsettling events in the fight had left Patterson determined to make amends. He decided this time he would beat Ferdinand on the inside. As the fight commenced and he began to go inside, D'Amato yelled at him to stay outside and box, but after the first round Patterson yelled back: "[I] want to beat him *his* way." D'Amato relented, and

Patterson succeeded. Patterson later recalled that Ferdinand "didn't say any-thing to me in the second fight, [and] in the tenth round I said something to him, 'Why don't you punch me?' He didn't say anything." In that final round, Patterson connected with a right to Ferdinand's head that sent him through the ropes and onto the ring apron. He did not survive the count, with the fight ending just as the count was getting to ten. Three months later he won a TKO in another rematch, this time with the Canadian light-heavy-weight Yvon Durelle. After the fifth round, Durelle called it quits, not answer-ing the bell for the sixth.[1]

In both the Ferdinand and Durelle fights, Patterson had gone up in weight. He was now fighting at 170 to 175 pounds, just at the edge of the heavyweight division. That was where D'Amato knew there was big money to be made. As Patterson was steadily building himself into a top contender, stories were circulating that heavyweight champion Rocky Marciano was soon to retire. Marciano had beaten every major boxer in the division. There was no one left to challenge him. When *Time Magazine* declared Patterson "the next champ," they asked Patterson for his thoughts on Marciano. In an obvi-ous posture that *Time* wanted to promote controversy, Patterson declared that Marciano "looks sloppy in the ring." Recognizing that "they say Marciano is the fighter who can't be hurt," Patterson speculated that "if you want to beat him you have to fight him and make him back up." Patterson confessed, "I think of Rocky Marciano a lot," and he wondered, "Maybe Rocky Marciano thinks of me." (Apparently he did not.) Considering any possible future fights for Marciano, one writer, Arthur Daley of the *New York Times*, mentioned Mr. Floyd Patterson but emphasized that such a match lay "over the distant horizon." Patterson, Daley pointed out, is still "a couple of years away, and it would be idiotic and suicidal to rush him." D'Amato may have agreed, but he would never cast the situation of his meal ticket in so negative a light. As far as he was concerned, Patterson was going to be the champion. Indeed D'Amato had raised the idea of fighting Marciano in 1955. At the time of the Durelle fight Patterson was ranked number three among the light-heavy-weight contenders. The fact that Patterson was still only twenty needed no emphasis, except as another point at which to marvel and recognize the young man's room for growth. Talk of soon contending for Marciano's crown was thus at least a trifle less than purely idle.[2]

Patterson's next fight on July 5 came against no great boxing figure. His opponent was named Archie McBride. McBride had a respectable record of 20–9, but what was significant for Patterson and his reputation was that McBride was a bona fide heavyweight. He weighed 187. Patterson came into the fight at 170. This was the heaviest fight weight Patterson ever carried, but he was obviously still giving away a lot of heft. At this point, D'Amato and Patterson were saying to the game's pundits that this man should be considered a heavyweight. Here they intended to prove it, albeit against a middling-level opponent. The fight was yet another main event on a Friday night Madison Square Garden venue and was broadcast nationally by ABC television. Reporters wrote of Patterson's "invasion of the heavyweight division." The issue of Patterson's speed had long been answered. Throughout his three years as a professional, his power seemed to be the slightly lesser of his assets. Such alleged limits, some feared, would be greatly magnified among the heavies, as, of course, would the question of how well he could take a heavy punch. In the bout with McBride, Patterson seemed to answer those questions. McBride was the aggressor through the early rounds, moving steadily forward with Patterson dancing and fending off blows with jabs and footwork. In the fourth round, McBride appeared to connect well with a right lead that caught Patterson above the left eye. There was no question that the blow hurt Patterson, but he continued to fight well. Otherwise, it was Patterson who was inflicting most of the punishment. After the fifth round, Cus urged Floyd to pour it on. In the sixth round, he floored McBride. Patterson and Cus were full of confidence after that, and in the seventh, Floyd knocked McBride down twice. With the second knockdown, McBride did not get up.[3]

Patterson's invasion of the heavyweight division was a decided success. In September he ventured up to Canada for a minor bout with Alvin Williams, a man he had beaten back in April of '54. D'Amato then took Patterson out to the West Coast for a succession of bouts. In September he easily knocked out Dave Whitlock in the third round. D'Amato expressed disappointment with Whitlock, contending, doubtlessly with an intentional pomposity, that Patterson needed better opponents. D'Amato's posture of concern for quality here may have been a way of diverting public attention from some New York State Athletic Commission inquiries into potential collusions among fight managers, something which, at the very least, gave an untidy appearance as to the objectivity and fairness of the fight game. This was a concern that was as old as the sport itself, and the leaders of the fight game would often go to great lengths to give the public the impression that they were policing themselves rigorously. The New York State Athletic Commission had the power to suspend or even revoke D'Amato's license to manage in the state's fight game, so this inquiry was nothing to take lightly. D'Amato may have gone out West to avoid the heat of the inquiry and hope some pressures would abate while he was there. Right after the Whitlock fight, D'Amato stood before the press in San Francisco and promised that, after returning from California, he would testify before the New York A.C. Then he solemnly proclaimed that, meanwhile, "my first obligation is to my fighter." That fall the commission's inquiries came to no major finding requiring the disciplining of D'Amato or any other fight manager in New York. There would be trouble for D'Amato, but it would come later.[4]

In October, Patterson reappeared in California for a Los Angeles bout against a novice named Calvin Brad. Brad had only fought thirteen fights and had lost five of them. Local bookies set Patterson as a 4:1 favorite. This proved an underestimation, as Brad was out for the count in the very first round. Patterson was scarcely breathing hard. The *Los Angeles Times* proclaimed Patterson to be "the finest piece of boxing property to step forth in years." It is "a good bet," they chortled, that "Los Angeles boxing fans saw the next heavyweight champion of the world." In another Los Angeles appearance in December, Patterson had a rematch with Jimmy Slade. Thirteen months before, Slade had been embarrassed when he fought Patterson and ran so much that the Madison Square Garden crowd hooted him, and the N.Y. Athletic Commission threatened to withhold his purse. Here he had the opportunity to gain back some of his reputation, one which had been strong before the earlier fight. He failed to reclaim it. Patterson stopped him with a TKO in the seventh. The Los Angeles papers snickered, describing Slade as "a punching bag." Having stopped the fight in the seventh, the referee was even more explicit: "Slade just wouldn't fight. I kept telling him to get in there and look good even if he was losing, but I guess he felt that he was too outclassed." Unlike the sarcastic New Yorkers in 1954, the Los Angeles fans and press were not so much critical of Slade as they were praising of Patterson. One reporter beamed: "Marciano need look no further."[5]

There was no doubt that by the end of 1955, "the spectacular young Floyd Patterson," as the *New York Times* dubbed him, was in almost every boxing enthusiast's thoughts as a future opponent of champion Rocky Marciano. He was becoming a known sports figure. While in California, even though his training regimen was generally strict, Patterson began to make a few rounds among and be accepted in the circles of movie celebrities. He met several of Hollywood's stars, including Frank Sinatra and Kim Novak. His family and friends back in New York were absolutely amazed. The talk of him being "a couple of years away" had passed. In January 1956, he had turned just twenty-one, but he was now one of boxing's top guns. That month, *Sports Illustrated* ran an article about Patterson with the chesty headline to their readers: "Meet the Next Heavyweight Champion." D'Amato bragged that if Patterson and Marciano fought that fall, his man would be too much for the then 33-year-old Marciano. Patterson's trainer, veteran Dan Florio, chortled even more over the prospect of taking on what he saw as an aging Marciano:

> It'd be no contest. Patterson is just too fast. I've trained a lot of old guys. I trained Joe Walcott. They get tired, and if you get tired in there against Patterson, then God help you. I'd hate to be the guy. [In] a year, he'll be ready for anybody. I've trained 500–600 fighters, and I've never seen anything like this boy.

An easy second round knockout of James Walls that March in Connecticut, and another KO of prior victim Alvin Williams in April added to Patterson's growing luster. Walls never landed a single punch against Patterson; his performance was so weak that the Connecticut State Athletic Commission permanently suspended him from fighting there. As for Williams, he was not only knocked out, his handlers had to pick him up and carry him to the corner well after the ten-count.[6]

While Patterson trained and traveled, he kept in constant touch with Sandra. Frank Lavelle may have wanted to keep her away from the training camp, but Patterson's commitment was too strong, and he could accept the possibility of Lavelle leaving him rather than not see Sandra. Patterson shared all his Hollywood excitement with her. Phone calls were constant, and he thrilled her with autographs of the many stars he had met. After Patterson returned from his Los Angeles fight with Jimmy Slade in December of 1955, he asked Sandra to marry him. She agreed, provided her mother approved. With all the parents' consent, Floyd and Sandra were married in a civil ceremony in Connecticut on February 11, 1956. Five months, and three bouts, later, they had a church wedding on July 13. Patterson had her name tattooed on his left forearm. There would be no honeymoon; Patterson had to go right back to training.[7]

Cus D'Amato attended Patterson's wedding, of course, but his mind remained fixed on the idea of his prodigy becoming the champion. Fighting champion Rocky Marciano was indeed not a far-fetched possibility. When Patterson celebrated his twenty-first birthday (which meant he could now officially fight ten- and fifteen-round bouts), D'Amato boasted "we are ready and willing to meet anybody." When a reporter asked if that included Marciano, D'Amato snapped, "Anybody means anybody.... We're after his crown." Given Marciano's unblemished and awesome record, such a fight may have proven too much for the young Patterson, but no one will ever know what may have happened, for on April 27, 1956, Marciano announced his retirement as heavyweight champion. In the previous September, he had fought his last fight, knocking out the veteran and light-heavyweight champion Archie Moore. Marciano's record as a professional boxer then stood at 49-0-0. No other heavyweight champion, then or since, completed an entire professional boxing career undefeated, untied. Marciano had beaten everybody worthy of stepping into the ring with him, and many others besides. Now there seemed to be no other challengers, and there was nothing more to prove. Some fans wanted Marciano to continue fighting, but few intelligent people could find fault with a man stepping away from the fight game, with his health and finances in good order and having soundly defeated everyone he possibly could. Archie Moore tried a bit of psychological warfare, chortling that Marciano would be back as he was too much in love with the money that boxing brought him. Moore was wrong. Marciano proved quite content to walk away and never seriously look back.[8] With the title vacant, the question was how to determine a new champion. Former champions Ezzard Charles and Jersey Joe Walcott had left the game. There were only a few other contenders. Archie Moore was one, and as the top ranked challenger at that point, despite his loss to the champion, he was regarded at least as the man someone would have to beat in order to be recognized as the new champion.

There were two young heavyweight contenders considered worthy challengers to Moore, either one of whom could thus acceptably fight him with the winner justly gaining the crown. The two were Floyd Patterson and Thomas "Hurricane" Jackson. What the situation called for was then utterly obvious — have Patterson fight Jackson with the winner to face Archie Moore for the title. On May 9, D'Amato struck a deal. Patterson would fight Jackson. Once more, the venue would be Madison Square Garden, Friday night, 10:00 P.M. — Fight of the Week on national television. Every major boxing venue in the United States recognized the legitimacy of the fight with respect to the finding of a logical successor to Rocky Marciano. All the major boxing organizations of Europe recognized it too. Each fighter was to receive a minimum guarantee of $40,000, half from radio and television money, the rest from the gate receipts. (Ticket prices ranged from $2 balcony to $12 ringside.) Forty thousand dollars was a higher figure than Patterson had ever made in a year. Reflecting the snake-pit that was the fight game, the International Boxing Commission and Madison Square Garden first offered D'Amato and Patterson all of $4000 for the fight. D'Amato was disdainful, of course, and negotiated Patterson a good deal. Patterson certainly needed the money. His parents and ten siblings were still anything but well off. Now he had Sandra and her family too. The money from the Jackson fight would help begin the solving of a lot of problems. A victory over Jackson could, moreover, lead to a huge pot of money.[9]

Thomas "Hurricane" Jackson seemed a formidable fighter, as well as an unusual one. He was an odd character; he had never learned to read or write, and this was symbolic of a certain primitive quality that pervaded his boxing style. Jackson's record to that point stood at an impressive 77-4-1. His nickname stemmed from his unorthodox fighting style. From the outset of a fight, he would swarm an opponent and punch wildly, often swinging his fists in windmill fashion. A few times he actually hit his opponent with both fists at the same time. According to one boxing analyst, "Fighting Jackson is akin to fighting a swarm of bees." To another it was "like fighting a handful of ashes in a high wind." Jackson was a flurry of energy in the ring, and he seldom tired, even in late rounds. This made him particularly dangerous. His swarming style could puzzle many, and his remarkable stamina could (and many times did) lead him to overwhelm a tiring opponent in the late rounds.

Jackson's weakness was that his punches were rarely very hard, "feather-duster punches," as one writer described them. Still, his many blows coming so incessantly from any sort of angle surprised many. The dozens of little pops could also pile up points with the judges, and Jackson won many fight decisions just that way. Indeed, he twice beat former heavyweight champion Ezzard Charles, the man who had succeeded Joe Louis to the crown. In February 1956, he had just beaten the third-ranked heavyweight contender, Bob Baker. Charles was a bit past his peak when he fought Jackson, but Jackson's two victories were nonetheless noteworthy, as was his defeat of Baker. Given all this, Patterson was certainly not taking Jackson lightly. He trained especially to build his stamina — three miles of running and six rounds of sparring every day, plus work with the light and heavy bags. While hitting the bag, he broke a bone in the pinkie finger of his right hand, the fourth metacarpal. He didn't know it was broken. He just thought it was sore, but rather than risk the cancellation of the big pay day, Patterson told no one, not even D'Amato.[10]

Patterson hoped for an early KO but recognized that he may have to stay with the tirelessly flurrying Jackson for a gruelingly long fight. New York odds-makers figured a skilled boxing artist would not be thrown awry by Jackson, and they gave Patterson a 2–1 edge. Jackson had a reputation for sometimes being a slow starter, so Patterson went into the bout with the idea of being aggressive from the outset, hoping to knock Jackson out early before he was warm and loose. Jackson, however, anticipated this strategy and began the fight hotter than usual. He swarmed Patterson with his famed wild ways, and as he held a weight and reach advantages of fifteen pounds and nine inches, the pressure forced Patterson onto the defensive. Patterson was prepared, however, and was able nimbly to switch tactics and fight with more finesse and speed. Reporters were impressed with the ring-intelligence Patterson showed that evening, adjusting his strategy as he did. As Patterson could not get his desired early knockout, the fight became one of attrition. This could have played into Jackson's hands, as he was not the harder puncher but could outlast almost anyone. But that night it was Patterson who out-boxed Jackson, landing the far greater number of punches, at least that was how most reporters saw it. In the late rounds especially it was Patterson who carried the fight. Several times Jackson looked as though he would soon fall, and twice he staggered back to his corner at the bell. The fight went the full twelve rounds, a length over which some reporters had harbored doubts with Patterson. Patterson knew of the doubters, so he was explicit afterward: "I proved I could stand up and punch with Jackson for twelve rounds."[11]

The two judges and most of the reporters gave the fight to Patterson. The two judges' cards read 7–5 and 8–4. The referee, Harry Kessler, voted 6-5-1 for Jackson, however. This greatly surprised many ring experts, save for the fact, as one reporter put it, that Kessler was known for "bad decisions."

The *New York Times* called Kessler's judgment "incomprehensible." People also chided Kessler *ad hominem* for being independently wealthy, presuming with a kind of reverse snobbery that someone from the good side of the tracks cannot appreciate the true nature of boxing and will make bad judgments given the opportunity. Such swipes were fun for sports journalists who often like to posture themselves to be one with the working class and who enjoy using any excuse to get back at a referee or umpire who possesses an authority that they may secretly, or even overtly, covet. Still, Kessler's may have been a bad judgment, but likely not because of his financial security. As with the Patterson-Maxim fight, such decisions are the vagaries of any sport when victory is left in the hands of judges. Patterson would see more of this, but for the moment he had his victory and attained the status of leading contender in the heavyweight division.[12]

With the big fight money he had amassed, Patterson bought himself a new Cadillac Eldorado, *the* status car of the day for athletes, especially for fighters. In August he bought a ten-room house on the corner of Fifth Street and Tenth Avenue in lower Manhattan. He bought a house in Mt. Vernon, New York, for his mother and father and his five youngest brothers and sisters. Patterson and his new wife moved into the Mt. Vernon house with everyone until they were able to buy their own house on Long Island. He also bought a Long Island house for Sandra's mother. Patterson said that he later saw the movie *A Raisin in the Sun.* The movie involved an African American family moving out of the slums and into a suburban home with trees and a nice lawn. The movie made Patterson cry unashamedly. Getting his loved ones out of the streets of Brooklyn meant everything.

It was a month after the Jackson bout that Patterson completed his religious studies and was baptized a Catholic. This was something Sandra had wanted very much. At that point, they married a second time in a church. Sandra was then five and one-half months pregnant. Floyd had obviously been breaking from D'Amato's training demands, but he was usually dutiful here. In the few times he was neither with Sandra nor training with D'Amato, Patterson was occasionally making the scene in the Harlem night life. Here, of course, with the depth to which people in the African American communities of the inner cities always followed the fight game, Patterson was the new boxing hero. Thus in Harlem he was a genuine celebrity, the equal of any other athlete, political figure, or entertainer. At the Apollo Theater the manager regularly gave him the best seats in the house on the house, and the crowd at the Apollo would always wildly cheer his presence. Patterson was a star. The Jackson fight had indeed aroused enormous interest, and not just in the inner city. The national TV audience was strong. Vice President Richard Nixon was also reported to have inquired about the outcome amidst some evening activities at the White House. Nixon lamented that his busy schedule in politics now prevented him from getting "to see the fights," but he was still a fan, and Floyd Patterson was one for whom he, and millions of others, now rooted enthusiastically.[13]

Amidst all the hoopla over the victory, Patterson had a big problem beyond three house payments and a baby on the way. After the fight when Patterson's seconds were unwrapping his hands, Dr. Alexander Schiff of the New York State Athletic Commission was on hand. Such supervision was part of the rules of boxing to protect against any foul play, such as "something in the gloves" that could be revealed during the unwrapping. Examining Patterson's hands, Dr. Schiff immediately discovered Patterson had indeed fractured the fourth metacarpal bone of his right hand. Patterson never let on that the finger was already broken. Still, with the injury, the plans (and the big money) which had been assumed to be completely in motion in regard to a championship fight with Archie Moore were now in abeyance and possibly in doubt.[14]

The post–Jackson fight with Archie Moore had tentatively been planned for Yankee Stadium in September. Now everything depended on how Patterson's hand healed and when the doctors pronounced him fit to fight. D'Amato was assuring the press that the big fight would still come off as planned. "The doctors told me Floyd had youth and good health on his side and that these factors may bring about a more rapid healing." A medical report did reassure fans that no surgery was needed, but the question of time remained, D'Amato's buoyant blather notwithstanding. Patterson could stay in shape with road work and shadow boxing, but any bag work or sparring was out of the question. This, of course, added to concerns as to how sharp he would be when, or if, the bout with Moore would occur. In these uncomfortable months, Patterson actually refereed a bout between two lesser heavyweights — Jimmy Riggins and Randy Brevard. Riggins won unanimously; Patterson's officiating was without controversy.[15]

In mid–July, one doctor (orthopedic surgeon H. Leslie Wenger) pronounced Patterson fit to fight as of September. Dr. Wenger did not speak for the New York State Athletic Commission, or for any other such organization, but it was reassuring to many fans. By August, however, Patterson still had not received an official go ahead from the NYAC. Some of Moore's handlers were posturing that Patterson was dodging the showdown. Further trouble lay in the fact that Archie Moore, in cognizance of Patterson's condition and the likely delay of their fight, had slated another bout in late July. (He had also fought in London on the same day that Patterson beat Jackson.) On July 25, he fought a Canadian journeyman named James J. Parker. Moore easily defeated Parker and pocketed $40,000 for his evening's work. Few could fault Moore for picking up such easy cash, but the scheduled bout had held the possibility of Moore losing or getting hurt. The result was more fretting and delays about the big fight. Amidst the on-off negotiations came debates over the fight site. The hopes for a venue of Yankee Stadium in September were fading. Time was simply pressing too much, and any fight date after September made an outdoor stadium site in the Northeast too risky with respect to the weather. The result then was even more to discuss and negotiate. By August, Patterson had still not received the NYAC's OK about his injury, and some were actually talking about Moore fighting Hurricane Jackson. Finally on October 15, the Moore and Patterson people came to an agreement. The heavyweight championship would be settled in a fight between Archie Moore and Floyd Patterson on November 30 in an indoor arena, the Chicago Stadium. Late November was obviously going to be too cold for any outdoor venue. The Chicago Stadium, the city's main indoor arena where the professional hockey and basketball teams (Black Hawks and Zephyrs) played, was a good site. When Patterson went out to Chicago to train, he set up headquarters at a horse racing track, Sportsman's Park. It was rather drafty, and he learned just how cold and windy Chicago could be.[16]

NBC radio and television won the rights to broadcast the fight, 9:00 P.M. Chicago time, hence the usual Friday night Fight of the Week at 10:00 P.M. in the East. This was the biggest such fight ever broadcast live on that or any other television venue. The television rights went for an unprecedented $200,000. NBC expected easily to make that money back from the Gillette Safety Razor Company who contracted for most of the between-rounds advertising. With ticket prices ranging from $5 to $30, a sold out Chicago Stadium would yield a gate of $471,000. With the television money and the gate minus the expenses, the net for the International Boxing Club would be in the neighborhood of $500,000. Each fighter was then expected to get $150,000, the biggest payday either had ever seen. (Patterson would actually make $114,257.) Beyond the obvious excitement over the fact that the fight was going to determine the new heavyweight champion, the Moore-Patterson matchup intrigued many pundits. At least one superlative was going to result from the fight no matter who won. If Patterson won the fight, he would be the youngest man ever to be heavyweight champion. He was twenty-one; Joe Louis had been twenty-three when he defeated Jim Braddock for the crown in 1937. If Moore won, he would be the oldest ever to be the champion. Moore *said* he was thirty-nine. His ex-wife said he was forty-three. In any case, Joe Walcott was thirty-seven in 1951 when he won the crown from Ezzard Charles. Some reporters joked here that Moore was thirty-nine going on forty-three. As of the day Patterson was born in 1935, Moore had already fought several professional fights. To that point in his career he had fought a staggering 156 times, and won 131 of them. For reporters to say he was a crafty old veteran was to state the utterly obvious. While Patterson had compiled an impressive 30 and 1 record, he was so comparatively inexperienced and young that some wondered how he would react to the pressure of the situation.

People joked about how Moore would flatten Patterson if he tried one of his leaping "gazelle punches" that reporters recalled from the Olympics a mere four years before. Reporters noted the trouble that Hurricane Jackson and Joey Maxim had given him, adding that Maxim was the very fighter Moore had defeated to take the light-heavyweight crown. Moore was confident. "They tell me that Patterson is a fine young prospect," he condescendingly chortled, "If he'd asked me, I would have been glad to take him in the gym and give him the benefits of my twenty years as a professional." Then he feigned a touch of anger: "But that's out now. The lesson I [will] give him when we get together will not be conducive to furthering his fistic education." Redonning his condescending voice, Moore concluded: "[Al]though I'm offended by Patterson's lack of respect and expect to punish him for it, I am not without pity for the boy." Moore was always known as a pitchman, and here he was being his usual loquacious self. Patterson said comparatively little: "If Moore can knock me out, more power to him," he deadpanned. He confessed that Moore's taunts had irritated him, and the irritation did lead him to wisecrack about the experience question: "Maybe I learned as much in four years as it took him to learn in twenty." Patterson would later show considerable irritation at other opponents who appeared to brag a lot. For the moment he was generally quiet, content to let Cus do most of the talking. D'Amato and others in his camp made statements to the effect that Hurricane Jackson was more problematic in their eyes than Archie Moore. The press and the fight fans knew, of course, that this was all part of the build-up to a big fight. Amidst all the posturing and conjectures, the pundits had Moore as the slight favorite.[17]

Just before the fight, each boxer received some pressing news. On November 28, Moore received official word that he was being sued by a woman in Cleveland who claimed that he had broken a promise to marry her and that he had raped her twelve-year-old daughter! Patterson's news was much better, but certainly nerve-wracking in its own way. On the day of the fight, Patterson's wife, Sandra, gave birth to a six pound, two ounce daughter. Wisely or not, D'Amato helped see to it that Patterson received minimal news before the fight — only that there was word about the baby from New York and that the news was good. Patterson, D'Amato felt, needed to know little else before the fight. D'Amato was in a highly controlling mood, even by his standards. Out of fear of the Mob, D'Amato had been sleeping for the previous month on a cot in the hallway in front of Floyd's bedroom door at their training camp. No thing and nobody was going to get to his fighter. Patterson stayed cool. Upon arrival at the Stadium, he was able to get his usual rest. With the championship in the offing, he stretched out on the rubbing table and took a long, quiet nap.[18]

One of the most remarkable figures in the history of boxing, Archie Moore fought an astonishing 229 professional bouts in his long career. He was already fighting professionally in the year Floyd Patterson was born. Moore had held the light-heavyweight title, and in 1956 he and Patterson were top heavyweight contenders when champion Rocky Marciano retired undefeated. After beating another contender, Thomas "Hurricane" Jackson, Patterson then squared off against Moore for the vacant crown. Oddsmakers predicted the venerable Archie would beat the 21-year-old Patterson, but Patterson whipped Moore decisively, becoming then the youngest man ever to hold the heavyweight title. © *The Ring*.

The fight itself proved a fairly simple one. Patterson was giving away just over five pounds; he came into the fight 182½ pounds with Moore weighing 187¾. At round one there was a false start, as the two began to fight upon hearing the stadium buzzer. The referee held them apart until the actual bell. Moore then stabbed at Patterson's head repeatedly. A few punches connected; many did not. Several Patterson lefts connected with Moore's head. By the third round, Moore had a noticeable cut over his left eye, but he jolted Patterson with several rights, one landing squarely on Patterson's jaw. When a hard right from Patterson connected, Patterson, the reporters, and others at ring side all heard a distinct and loud groan out of Moore. Apparently it was more than a groan that came out of Moore at that juncture, as from then on, Moore appeared decidedly slower and weaker. Patterson was ever more the aggressor. In the fifth round, Patterson drew more blood above Moore's eye. With a minute to go in the round Patterson caught Moore with a hard left hook. Moore went down, but he was up at the count of nine and appeared clear. At once, Patterson was on Moore and quickly floored him again. Moore again got up at nine, but this time the referee stopped the fight. "I never saw the punch," Moore later admitted. "They tell me it was a left.... I got up from that one, but there wasn't anything left when he put me down the second time." Patterson had a TKO and was thus the undisputed heavyweight champion of the world. He was then the youngest ever to win the crown.[19]

After the loss, Moore alibied a bit but was generally gracious toward Patterson. "I just couldn't get up the steam to hold him off," he shrugged. But then he added of Patterson: "He's a great kid, and I think he'll go for a long time. He's the fastest thing of his weight I've seen to many a moon." Moore did not use the lawsuit and rape charges as an excuse, but some reporters speculated they may have affected him. Others commented how he looked a little heavy around the midsection and a bit sluggish in his legs. Moore was emphatic: "I wouldn't say anything to take away the glory from Patterson. Let's just say that the better man — the much better man — won out there tonight." Patterson was also courteous, but he showed no false modesty: "I know that tonight I was opposed by one of the smartest boxers and sharpest punchers in the business," he conceded, "but I never had any doubt about what I could do to him. Frankly, I didn't expect to win so early. But the opening for the left came and I took it. Moore walloped me with authority several times but never in a real[ly] vulnerable spot. I was able to head-slip his real heavy punches or block them."[20]

Patterson was now over $114,000 richer. After he'd left the ring, waded through the Chicago throng, and gotten to the locker room, he learned the details of Sandra's giving birth to a daughter. Both were doing fine. He did not stay around to celebrate with anyone. With no sleep, he immediately drove all the way back to New York to be with Sandra and his new daughter. Her baptized name was Seneca; they called her Jeannie. Heavyweight champion and a new father in one day; matters had certainly come a long way in the mere ten years since being consigned to the Wiltwyck School.

V

Frustrations on Top

When Patterson assumed the heavyweight championship, great ballyhoo rose over his being the youngest ever to win the title. He was named Fighter of the Year, and he came in second in the voting among Associated Press sportswriters as the nation's overall Athlete of the Year. Baseball's Mickey Mantle won the award. Mantle's winning the triple crown and leading the Yankees to a World Series victory made him impossible to deny. Patterson was actually the only athlete besides Mantle to get any first place votes. (Mantle received sixty-six votes; Patterson seven.) Patterson did win an award as the "Catholic Athlete of the Year," something that hardly held the status of the AP's Athlete of the Year, but it meant a great deal to Floyd and Sandra.[1]

Amidst the cheers for Patterson's securing the crown there was little national ado, at least overtly, about the issue of Patterson's race. Marciano was white, and doubtlessly this had pleased many racist boxing fans of the time. But Patterson's gaining of the crown came amidst some changing times; unjustly slow changes certainly, but changes nonetheless. There had been a number of African American heavyweight champions before Patterson. Jack Johnson was the first, and the sheer terror which had surrounded his reign as heavyweight king was at this point nearly a half century old. The political landscape had altered somewhat, at least within the boxing and sports world. Joe Louis had earlier been champion, of course, as had Ezzard Charles and Joe Walcott, and in other weight divisions fighters like Archie Moore, Henry Armstrong, and Sugar Ray Robinson had also gained the respect and admiration of virtually everyone. Meanwhile such African Americans as Jackie Robinson, Willie Mays, and Marion Motley had also begun to dent the long-established racial barriers in the nation's other major sports. Even some of the most begrudging racists had to respect these athletes. Outside the sports world, however, matters were still quite problematic to say the least. Patterson's championship came about in a nation that was just beginning, and quite reluctantly in many if not most cases, to extricate itself from the clutches of Jim Crow. Patterson would never have to contend with the sheer terror that surrounded Jack Johnson, but he would have to contend with the many manifestations of a nation beginning to wrestle with the legacies of Jim Crow.

With the money from his championship and previous fights, Patterson had moved his family (his mother, father, eight brothers, and a sister) out of Queens and Brooklyn and bought them a house in Mt. Vernon, N.Y., in Westchester County, just north of the Bronx and Yonkers. Floyd and Sandra would live with them for a short time and then move to the town of Rockville Centre on Long Island. Later they settled in Mt. Vernon too. Outwardly, the Westchester County township's residents appeared happy with its new, famous family. On December 18, the town of Mt. Vernon even staged a parade in honor of their champion. The mayor, Joseph P. Vaccarella, was himself a former boxer, and at a ceremony that evening in the town's Wood Auditorium he presented Floyd with a gold watch and an official proclamation of town citizenship.[2] Despite these outward plaudits, some of the Pattersons' immediate neighbors were nervous about the new residents on their street. A few may have veiled their misgivings along the lines of there being not just Floyd, Sandy, and their children but an entire extended family of children, brothers, sisters, parents, and grandparents in the house. But there was really only one reason they were concerned about the appearance of the Pattersons, and it was not because he was a mere boxer living with his extended family. If it was Rocky Marciano or Billy Conn who had moved in with his family, the townspeople would have been delighted. With a black family the reactions were quite different. Several years later, one of Patterson's Westchester County neighbors would actually construct a high fence along their adjoining property line. Patterson eventually responded by building one of his own.

The many pressures of race, subtle and otherwise, would bear upon Patterson continuously. But he maintained a steady, firm, dignified course against them. At a confectioner shop in Indianapolis, Patterson was refused service when he asked for an ice cream. Patterson left in disgust. Some who were with him wanted to yell at the shopkeeper that "this is the champ you're denying." Patterson, however, refused to make an issue of the matter on the basis of his championship. "I won't always be champ," he noted intently, "but I will always be a man. I don't want to go into a place where other Negroes can't go." This humanistic conviction would always guide Patterson, and it would contrast markedly with the self-absorbed braggadocio that drove many other fighters of his time. Which was the wiser approach to such social-political issues or to boxing would always be a matter of debate.

Within a year after becoming champion, Patterson gave several boxing exhibitions in the Midwest. In Kansas City, Missouri, when strolling near their hotel, Patterson and his sparring partners found themselves victims of verbal abuse from passing drivers. They were also unable to find a restaurant that would serve them. Ironically in their hotel they ran into none other than Jersey Joe Walcott, who had gone into pro wrestling since leaving boxing and happened also to be in Kansas City for an exhibition. He could not get served either, so they all relaxed together in Walcott's hotel room over milk and bags of cookies. Patterson always tried to respond with a quiet dignity that would stamp his personality. "I have an obligation," he wrote, "to those who may look up to me." There were ways in which this bearing would serve him quite well. There would also be ways in which it would cause him great anguish and pain, and not solely from white racists and reactionaries. Most of these complex political crossfires lay in his future. For now, amidst such indignities, Patterson's boxing future was full of pulls and tugs too.

During Patterson's tour of the Midwest there was at least a break in the repeated racial indignities. A priest from the Little Rock, Arkansas, diocese, Father Samuel J. Delaney, witnessed Patterson and his entourage meeting verbal slurs and hostility as they were getting off the train in the town of Fort Smith. Delaney stepped through the crowd and offered his hand in friendship. His priest's garb helped quiet the crowd a bit. Delaney escorted Patterson from the station without incident, took him around town in his car, and had him avoid the indignity of a segregated hotel by staying in his church rectory. Patterson gladly and humbly accepted the good priest's hospitality. His feelings about Southern racism did not abate, but his belief in the goodness of some and the value of such an institution as that of his own adopted faith were all greatly strengthened. Later, as the civil rights movement fully unfolded and a range of stances presented themselves to African Americans — from the quietly conservative, to the non-violently liberal, to various forms of radicalism — Patterson would always choose the liberal path. His deep religious faith and his life experiences all steadily made this course abundantly clear.[3]

In the months immediately after winning the crown, Patterson made the rounds on television programs and at various clubs, dinner engagements, and athletic venues. This was obviously part of the fight game, and everyone expected and accepted it. The dignified tone that Patterson always brought to his activities was one that recalled Joe Louis far more than Jack Johnson, so all the racists looking for excuses upon which to pounce could find nothing.[4] The main thing for which the mainstream boxing press and fans were wondering concerned who Patterson's next opponent would be for the crown.

Soon after Patterson's championship, many boxing pundits hoped that Rocky Marciano would come out of retirement and fight the young Patterson. Such a fight could have certainly given each man a great pay day, far more than even the $100,000 that Patterson received from his victory over Archie Moore. In an obvious attempt to goad Marciano out of retirement, Cus D'Amato chortled that his man could beat Rocky. Marciano, however, proved quietly firm in his commitment to stay out of the ring. He had made enough money and wanted no further fighting. Eventually, as everyone recognized that Marciano's decision was final, the pressure would fade.[5]

With Patterson's victory, Cus D'Amato was also on top of the world. Simultaneous to Patterson becoming Fighter of the Year, D'Amato was named Manager of the Year.[6] For many years he had been a respected figure in the fight game, but he had always kept himself a discreet distance from some of the game's power loops. He had done this out of what was for him an altogether legitimate fear of the criminal elements that always plagued the fight game. To many, however, there always seemed an additional element of almost raging paranoia that laced D'Amato's actions and attitudes. The International Boxing Club (the IBC) had dominated the fight game since 1949. Two men, Truman K. Gibson and James D. Norris, had formed an organization that bought out the Twentieth-Century Sporting Club of New York, previously owned and operated by boxing enthusiast Mike Jacobs. This gave them an in with respect to the major boxing venues and events of New York City and beyond. Gibson was a suave, handsome lawyer and an extremely shrewd executive. In 1949 he had befriended Joe Louis. Together they persuaded the wealthy Norris to bankroll a fight between those Louis picked to square off for his title upon his retirement. And it was indeed the Norris-Gibson organization that sponsored the Ezzard Charles–Joe Walcott bout of June 22, 1949, which Charles won, thus succeeding Louis as champion. The subsequent buyout of Jacobs' Sporting Club created the IBC, and under Norris's crafty control it thrived spectacularly. Gibson was always able to pay as much or more than other promoters, and thus he held control over the major fights of the 1950s, including those of Charles, Walcott, and Rocky Marciano. Envy, fear, and distrust, of course, grew as a result of the control Norris exercised. The fact that he was African American, indeed the first man of color to hold such a position of responsibility in sports or entertainment, may have been a major part of the grudges and the sniping.

Cus D'Amato was one of many who had always hoped that the IBC's grip on the fight game could be broken. He had played ball with them to some degree, as they had control over the title fight between Patterson and Moore. Now that he was managing the top fighter in the game, D'Amato thought he had the leverage to beat them, even if it meant bypassing some financial rewards in the process.[7] This would lead to a great conflict between Cus and the IBC, one that would ensnare Patterson and come to cloud his credibility as champion, for the nature of the opposition D'Amato began to choose for him would be controversial to say the least. The IBC had control

Constantine "Cus" D'Amato was Patterson's manager from Floyd's amateur days into his championship years. Cus was a brilliant, savvy analyst of every aspect of the fight game. Muhammad Ali called him "a genius." Depending on one's view, D'Amato held a sharp, or paranoid, outlook with regard to his perceived enemies in the fight business. The extremism in D'Amato's fears was rooted in the lurking presence of the Mob throughout boxing. D'Amato was determined to take on the Mob, and when Patterson won the heavyweight championship, D'Amato created a great deal of controversy as he kept Patterson from fighting some of the top heavyweight contenders because of their alleged connections to organized crime. Many felt this avoidance, justifiable or not, unduly limited Patterson's growth and stature as champion. © *The Ring.*

over the careers of most of the top heavyweights, except Patterson. Among their top heavyweights in the late 1950s were Zora Folley, Willie Pastrano, Eddie Machen, and Cleveland Williams. D'Amato made the determined choice to steer clear of them, and Patterson never fought any of them except Machen, and only after he had lost the championship. Cus always feared IBC–Mafia connections, and to many observers, Cus's goal appeared to be more one of taking on the Norris, Gibson, and IBC than it was of boosting Patterson's career.

At first, the issue of Patterson's opposition was reasonably clear. After defeating Archie Moore, Hurricane Jackson seemed the logical choice as the next opponent. In 1957, Jackson was still the number one contender. In late

December of 1956, Jackson had defeated another contender, Julio Mederos of Cuba, in a unanimous decision.[8] His June loss to Patterson had been a split decision, albeit with a debatable call for Jackson on the part of the referee, so giving Jackson the first shot at Patterson's title seemed a move that was both sporting as well as one that would enhance the respect with which Patterson was held as champion. This issue of respect was a more pointed one for Patterson than it had been or would be for most heavyweight champions. Patterson was young, leading some to regard him as less than fully seasoned. Tied to this point was the fact of Marciano having retired undefeated, the only fighter besides Gene Tunney ever to do so. (Tunney had lost once on the way up, but he and Marciano, who had never lost, were never defeated as champions.) Patterson's gaining of a vacant title thus left a slightly less than invincible aura around him. Pundits commented on Patterson's quickness, his good footwork, and his generally sound boxing skills, but the sense still pervaded that somehow the boxing world now had a slightly less than stellar champion, one, according to many in the proverbial barber shops and bars of the nation, who could certainly have never beaten the great Rocky.

Patterson was getting panned. Talk flourished here as well over the point that Patterson had merely won the crown by beating Archie Moore, a *light* heavyweight who had lost convincingly to Marciano and who was approximately forty-one years old when Patterson beat him. Many were also eager to point out the closeness of the earlier decision over Hurricane Jackson. Stories of how Patterson liked to (and could easily) sleep in the dressing room before a fight left some with the impression of a champion whose casualness (Arthur Daley of the *New York Times* dubbed him here "The Sleepwalker") would have left him easily floored by a Dempsey or a Marciano. Former champion Gene Tunney indeed condescendingly opined at this juncture that because Patterson had been rushed to the top so fast, he would prove in time to reveal insufficiently sharpened skills and would likely not last long as champion. Cus D'Amato responded here, claiming that Tunney knew deep down that he could not have beaten Patterson, hence his criticism, aimed at D'Amato as much as at Patterson, involved some projection and insecurity. Tunney offered no comment. Such jabs were being thrown at other fighters of the day besides Patterson, and with Marciano out of the picture, the pundits seemed to enjoy snickering at the perceived mediocre level of the fighters left in the heavyweight division. The venerable seventy-four-year-old Abe Attell, the oldest living champion, featherweight champion in 1901, and a veteran of (and never knocked out in) 365 fights, commented tersely "Outside of Floyd Patterson who have you got now?" At Christmas time in December of 1956, the *New York Times* wished Santa Claus would give Floyd Patterson "a few non-collapsible heavyweights so that he can capitalize on his newly won championship." There may have been more than a tinge of racism in the idolization that fight people were engaging with respect to the retired, white Marciano, especially since the rest of the heavyweight division was now dominated by African Americans. There was obviously only one thing that could put the snickering to rest, and that was for Patterson and D'Amato to get busy and fight the best challengers they could find. In the minds of many boxing fans, this failed to occur.[9]

The frustrations over the lack of respect that the young champion felt echoed in other aspects of his life. One Saturday evening in 1957, Patterson left his training camp and drove down to Brooklyn to see Sandra and take her to the movies. Before arriving home, while driving on Lewis Avenue in Brooklyn, Patterson saw a taxi racing behind him, "blowing his horn like a wild man." Patterson was stopped at a red light, so there seemed nothing to do but wait. The cabbie, however, tried to swing around him and make a right turn. He hit Patterson's car, smashing one of the tail lights. Patterson then pulled over and began pulling his insurance and registration materials from his glove compartment when he noticed the cab driver rushing out of his car and running toward him. "He was a big guy, much larger than I," Patterson recalled. "He reached right through the window and grabbed me by the neck." Unable to get a word of conversation into the situation, Patterson found himself collared as the man "pulled out a small knife and cut me on the [right] hand." The cabbie obviously did not know who he had grabbed, but he found out fast. "I got out of the car, hit him with a left hook and a right." Rather than really inflicting some serious damage on the idiotic and now dazed cab driver, Patterson propped him against a fence and left him there. Patterson elected not to phone the police. He actually felt a bit scared of exposing to Cus D'Amato that he had left training camp without telling him. So he nervously drove back to training camp, and called Sandra to tell her what had happened. Like many athletes, Patterson had imagined that if he ever got to the top, life would be so different. Here he was the heavyweight champion, but the streets of Brooklyn weren't treating him any better than when he was a boy, except now, of course, he could take on most any opponent who tried to pummel him. It was a better feeling, but hardly a good one. On another occasion that year, Floyd was simply walking in Brooklyn when a man came out of a bar and punched him in the mouth. Fearing such headlines as "Patterson KO's defenseless drunk," Patterson refrained from hitting back, although he dearly wanted to. Fame was always a bit perplexing to Patterson. He once asked a friend a conundrum: "What's the most powerful license plate there is?" His friend guessed either one's initials or "No. 1." "No," Floyd replied, "it's no license plate at all." For the rest of his life, a jagged scar from the cab driver's knife remained on a knuckle of Patterson's right hand.[10]

As boxing fans expected, Patterson did eventually square off against Hurricane Jackson. Prior to the bout there was more than the usual jockeying for position and money in regard to the fight. The rumors about D'Amato wanting to take on the International Boxing Club were proving anything but idle. The IBC had recently lost an anti-trust case in federal court, so D'Amato's timing was fortuitous. He was able to avoid the IBC's president Jim Norris and any of the fight promoters tied to him, securing an agreement with Emil Lence, the promoter with whom D'Amato had worked so often back in the days when Patterson fought his many early bouts at Brooklyn's Eastern Parkway Arena. Back in 1955, after Patterson had graduated to higher venues, Lence had lost his television contract for the Eastern Parkway fights. He was anxious to get back in the fight promotion game, so his link-up with D'Amato was mutually beneficial. D'Amato could get a promoter and a venue without the IBC, and Lence could both promote a championship fight and, with such a card, easily land a fat television contract. Jim Norris and all his connections could only grimace.[11]

After the usual wrangling over money, the fight between Floyd Patterson and Hurricane Jackson was set for New York's Polo Grounds on July 29. Patterson's champion's share was a guaranteed $175,000; Jackson was to receive 20 percent of the gate and radio and television fees. Lence sold television advertising rights to General Motors for $175,000, a substantial sum for those days. With tickets running from $5 to $30, the gate was first predicted to yield as much as $750,000; it would fall short, however. As in the build-up to the first Jackson-Patterson fight, the papers were full of stories about Jackson's oddities — that he could not read or write; that he was a "mauler" who sometimes hit with both fists at once, "as zany as he is strong.... It is difficult," noted one reporter, "to probe the workings of his primitive mind." To some this made Jackson a pitiable curiosity; to others such stories enhanced his image as an unpredictable wild man. To racists it confirmed many hateful stereotypes. Jackson was by no means oblivious. At his training camp, a reporter asked him what he like to do in the evenings. When Jackson mentioned playing records, the reporter queried, "What records?" Jackson snarled: "The records upstairs." At the official signing for the fight, Jackson added to his edgy image. He perfunctorily shook hands with Patterson and began to storm out of the room shouting, "No more hand-shaking!" His mother restrained him and persuaded him to go back to the table with Patterson. Jackson did so, but he would not shake hands again. "This time," he raged, in reference to his close but losing effort against Patterson the previous June, "I'll leave my heart [at] home." As to reporters again noting that he and Patterson had once been friends and trained together as young fighters, Jackson tersely sniffed: "Now it's different."[12]

Patterson, meanwhile, came across as urbane, modest, and religious, a solid citizen in every way. His training camp in Greenwood Lake, N.Y., some fifty miles north of New York City, was the site where Joe Louis used to train.

Patterson even slept in the same bed Louis used. At Greenwood Lake, Patterson worked quietly, maintaining no ostentatious entourage like other champions of the day such as Sugar Ray Robinson, who always kept himself in training with a social secretary, a chef, a financial consultant, a barber, a valet, and a golf pro. Women were a regular presence at some champions' camps; never at Patterson's. (He did have a pet monkey, however. Her name was Connie, short for Constantine, Cus's real name.) When in training Patterson would see Sandra but once a month. At camp his only diversions involved the monkey, a little television watching, playing pool, and listening to music. He named saxophonist Stan Kenton as his favorite. In response to the sense that his life was a tad boring, Patterson asked impishly, "What can a guy do at night in Greenwood?" His training life was all business — up every morning at 5:30, healthy eating, running, and ring work. Amidst his rope skipping, calisthenics, bag work, and sparring, Patterson also trained a group of ten-year-old boys from the nearby village. Patterson never forgot his troubled youth, and he always made time for kids. The boys enjoyed it immensely. Some of their parents had misgivings, however. In Joe Louis's day, racists would give begrudging respect to the champion by referring to his solid-citizen credentials with the ugly phrase "a credit to his race." With Patterson, no such backhanded gratuities came forth. He worked hard to earn the respect of the boxing establishment, and his acts of caring were anything but a mere act. Still, not everyone was appreciative.[13]

The Jackson fight proved more one-sided than the first one. Patterson appeared in command the entire way. Afterwards Patterson beamed: "Everything went according to plan." He came out of the fight with not a mark on him. Noting the trouble of his first fight with Jackson, Patterson noted that this time he prepared especially well and found Jackson "wasn't quite so tough this time.... He didn't hit me as hard. I was never hurt." Patterson floored Jackson in the first round and two other times as well. Jackson kept taunting Patterson. "You're a bum," he mumbled repeatedly. He could mount no offense, however. The referee, Ruby Goldstein, stopped the fight in the 10th round, with Patterson well ahead on all cards; on one he had won every round. At the moment in the tenth round when Goldstein intervened, there seemed no single event to cause the TKO. There were a few boos from the crowd at that point, but no reporter or pundit disagreed with the decision. Patterson had actually been urging Goldstein to intervene for fear of Jackson getting seriously hurt. Given the injuries some fighters sustain from excessive beatings, some applauded Goldstein's move; "'Rah for Ruby!" wrote one. Pundits were less sanguine about Patterson's show of sportsmanship here. Goldstein's decision proved a wise one, as Jackson had suffered a bruised kidney that required immediate hospitalization. The next day, Patterson and Sandra went to Meadowbrook Hospital on Long Island to visit him. The two would later appear on the Ed Sullivan Show. Sportsmanship thus tinged the bout, despite some of Jackson's pre-fight antics. It added to Patterson's image as a gentlemanly, soft-spoken champion, but the ease of his victory maintained the critics' sense that he was a lesser champion. The gate for the fight, 18,101, did not turn out as had been optimistically anticipated, and, as a favor to Emil Lence, Patterson accepted a reduction from the $175,000 he had been guaranteed, going home with a gross of $123,859 that netted him personally $46,910. The cost of Patterson's previous nine months of training was just under $120,000, so there was not a lot of profit. As for Jackson, in November he would fight one more bout against the young contender Eddie Machen. Again he lost badly, and the New York State Boxing Commission urged him to retire. After his two losses to Patterson, Jackson was never as cordial to his former friend as he had once been. When Jimmy Slade lost to Patterson, he reacted the same way. Ego, jealousy, envy — they all tend to be wrapped up in a fighter's makeup. Patterson was seldom so affected. Years later, after Jackson was hit by a car, with the injuries from the accident ultimately proving fatal, Patterson made a point of going to see Jackson in the hospital.[14]

While still standing in the ring at the end of the Jackson fight, Patterson took questions from a television commentator who raised to Patterson the point that he was soon to pack himself off to Seattle for another fight. Indeed, Patterson had already agreed to a fight out there, just 25 days after the Jackson fight. In the Polo Grounds locker room, Patterson further responded to the "What now?" questions, shrugging, "I'm going right back to Greenwood Lake." Indeed, he did not skip a beat, stayed right with his training regimen, and flew out to Seattle on August 8. Fighting just a month after a title defense was unusual, although not completely so. In 1941, Joe Louis had fought what some had dubbed "a bum-a-month campaign." What made Patterson's schedule a little curious, if not controversial, concerned his chosen opponent. There had been some discussions about fighting a contender named Willie Pastrano. Instead, however, Patterson was to take the ring against a fighter named Peter Rademacher.[15]

In the late fall of 1956, Pete Rademacher had won the gold medal at the Summer Olympics in Melbourne, Australia,* and in the medal bout, he beat a Soviet fighter, Lev Moukhine. The timing of Rademacher's victory was politically fortuitous, as the American rivalry with the Soviet Union was acute, and an American victory over a Soviet in any visible genre, let alone such a combative one as Olympic boxing, was great copy. The Soviets had participated a bit in the 1952 Olympics, and the games in next-door Finland marked their first appearance. The year 1956 marked the first time that the U.S. team,

---

*With the Southern Hemisphere's "reverse seasons," the Summer Olympics of 1956 were held in the late spring in Melbourne.

and the nation in general, genuinely geared up for a Cold War rematch and showdown with the Soviets in a sports venue. So Rademacher's heavyweight victory was huge. The Soviet Union's launching of the Sputnik I satellite in October of 1957 would put this fever to even greater intensity. Many parts of the nation were going through all sorts of bureaucratic and cultural contortions as the country was trying to come to grips with the challenge before it. In such an increasingly hysterical environment, any American who had countered a Soviet victory was going to be an especially heroic figure to many in the nation. When the pianist Van Cliburn, for example, won the Tchaikovsky Piano Competition in Moscow in 1958, the national acclaim for him vastly eclipsed the attention given to any classical artist in America who had ever won such an international competition. It bordered on the tumult then accorded some rock-and-roll stars.[16] Similarly, Rademacher's taking Olympic gold from the Soviets in the heavyweight division rendered and sustained for him considerable heroic status. The press coverage accorded him was greater than any amateur boxer in the nation had ever received. Patterson's '52 Olympic teammate Ed Sanders, for example, had won the heavyweight gold medal. He won some press plaudits certainly, but they were a trifle compared to what Rademacher received. Of course beyond the Cold War–driven politics, there was one added factor in this contrast — Rademacher was white. D'Amato knew this could yield money.

Accompanying the Cold War hype, Rademacher's personality and general nature proved to be winners with the All-American hero-hungry press as well. Rademacher was a good family man with a broad smile, a farm boy who had grown up in rural America — Washington's Yakima Valley. Attending Washington State University, he had been a football star, and he had subsequently served honorably as a lieutenant in the U.S. Army. While stationed in Fort Benning, Georgia, Rademacher trained for the Olympics and gained lots of notice with local sports fans. Georgian press coverage of his triumph was keen, and after the gold medal, a group of local investors formed. They were led by a sporting goods store owner from Columbus, Georgia, named Mike Jennings, by one of Rademacher's army buddies named Joe Gannon, and by a local television commentator and station manager, Johnny Hughes. They put together a package to make Cus D'Amato and Floyd Patterson the proverbial offer they could not refuse. In April 1957, they offered D'Amato $100,000 for a fight with Rademacher. As always, D'Amato first turned them down. A month later they came up with a better offer. With the hoped-for gate of the Jackson fight, Patterson expected $175,000, yet he received 30 percent less. This time, no matter the gate, no matter the outcome, no matter anything, Patterson was to receive $250,000 for climbing into a ring against Rademacher. Given that the Patterson camp had barely broken even from their bout with Jackson, the offer was irresistible. There were then but a few

people in all of sports making even $100,000 a year. On May 17, D'Amato
accepted. This set up the unprecedented, an amateur being able to fight for
the heavyweight championship in his very first professional fight. It also nicely
facilitated D'Amato's plan of doing no business with Frank Norris and the
IBC.[17]

With this odd Rademacher-Patterson fight in the offing, pundits began
to chortle. A few spoke of Jersey Joe Walcott going into a 1947 fight a 10–1
underdog against Joe Louis and fighting 15 good rounds, nearly taking Louis's
title and losing only on a highly questionable decision. A few others spoke of
Rademacher as potentially another Jimmy Braddock, the "Cinderella Man"
who had taken the heavyweight title from Max Baer in 1937 in a fight no one
thought he had a chance of winning. But this was all silly hype. Virtually all
boxing experts shrugged and giggled at the prospect of an Olympic amateur
fighting for the heavyweight title in his very first professional outing. To serious fight fans, this was not a Cinderella story; it was a fight that simply made
no sense. The only point some could make on Rademacher's behalf was that
he was unlike most Olympians in that he was 28 years old and had a lot of
ring experience. That was true, but the experience was all at the amateur
level. He had never gone beyond three rounds.[18]

Among ring experts, all the pre-fight hype was just not working. Nat
Fleischer, the universally-respected editor of *Ring Magazine*, and never one
given to superlatives, called the Rademacher-Patterson pairing "the greatest
mismatch in the history of boxing." The National Boxing Association's president, Floyd Stevens, said the organization would not sanction the fight as a
title bout. Rumors flew that Patterson had made a deal to carry Rademacher,
as Jennings' consortium was to have rights to the fight's films, and they
allegedly wanted the fight to last so the films would have some value. The
rumors were false, but they were sufficiently widespread that Cus D'Amato
went out of his way to deny them. A Pennsylvania congressman, Hugh Scott,
subsequently a senator, wrote to the governor of the state of Washington,
Albert D. Rosellini, urging him "to take immediate steps to cancel the scheduled Floyd Patterson-Pete Rademacher so-called world championship heavyweight fight." The bout, Scott claimed, "amounts to no more than pre-planned
slaughter and would perpetrate a farce and imposition on boxing fans and
television viewers." Scott urged the governor to act swiftly in order to "save
boxing and elevate television."[19]

While Jennings and the other Georgia contributors never said anything
directly, it was abundantly apparent to many observers that, just a glimmer
away from the hype about Rademacher as an All-American Boy, the fight
contained a huge element of white hope. By the 1950s the white hope theme
had gone through a metamorphosis, however. In 1910, when Jim Jeffries came
out of retirement to fight Jack Johnson (and the radical-racist writer Jack

London coined the phrase "The Great White Hope"), the words were a rallying cry to white Americans who had grown apoplectic over the presence of the "outrageous" Johnson, with his fast cars and womanizing, holding the championship. Now it was different. Floyd Patterson was anything but a Jack Johnson. Indeed one Seattle paper pooh-poohed all the hype about Rademacher, the All-American boy, and openly opined that "Patterson was the better example for the youth." But Patterson was black, and there were still plenty of Americans who wanted the title to rest in the hands of a white man. How many of the fight backers in Mike Jennings's consortium of twenty-two-Southerners were racists is impossible to determine precisely. Certainly, many believed at the very least that the racism around them in the South could prove an economically exploitable sensibility. Rocky Marciano conspicuously agreed to help Rademacher train, and this added to the racial dimensions of the fight. Patterson himself was quoted at the time saying that in New York people "couldn't have raised $250" for the fight; it "couldn't've been raised," he half-chuckled, "in any other place but Georgia or the South." Patterson quickly denied saying he had meant to say anything about race. Years later he confirmed that he had.

The irony throughout the white hope hype, of course, was that among the people who most fully exploited the not-so-closeted racism were D'Amato and, consequently, Patterson. D'Amato realized, whatever the political, sociological, and psychological motives, if people wanted a fight with his champion so badly that they could guarantee the $250,000 purse they did, he would have to be the dumbest fight manager in history to turn it down. Rademacher, too, was hardly a pawn in the whole stunt. Gay Talese of the *New York Times* called him "frightfully glib" and "a phenomenal salesman." Rademacher was indeed anything but a mere soldier and boxer. He "d'aw shucks'ed" his way into a big time fight and was instrumental in promoting it. "Pete," smiled Mike Jennings, "does a mighty fine job of selling himself." One boxing writer called him "The Pug in the Grey Flannel Suit." Rademacher, wrote another, may be "an amateur boxer, but [he is] a professional thinker and a professional operator."[20]

The beat-the-Russians theme, the All-American family man image, the unstated race issue — it all fit together quite well. Still, the hype proved not to resonate with the public nearly as much as the promoters hoped. A Seattle newspaper reported a poll it had taken showed that only 1 percent of the fight fans in the Seattle area felt their local man could win. One paper dubbed the fight a "pro-amateur bout." Another writer referred to Rademacher as "Floyd Patterson's private pigeon." Throughout the weeks prior to the fight, Las Vegas houses would not even make book on the fight, bluntly declaring, "It's no contest." Attendance in Seattle was mediocre, and after paying Patterson's fee, Rademacher's Georgia buddies ended up $100,000 in the red. One of the under card fights had to be cancelled. It involved Esau Ferdinand, Patterson's opponent from 1955. Ferdinand was serving as one of Floyd's sparring partners in Seattle. At fight time, Ferdinand took sick, and the Georgia promoters refused to pay him. Floyd paid Ferdinand the $500 he was due out of his own pocket.

Despite the financial woes among the promoters, the fight came off—such as it was. *New York Times* columnist Arthur Daley had likened the fight to the Mad Hatter's Tea Party in *Alice in Wonderland*, with Rademacher standing as the Knave waiting, hoping, the Queen of Hearts will scream, "Off with his head." Cus D'Amato qualified as the White Rabbit, always in a hurry, off to a very important date, the date being August 22. Alice herself had found the Mad Hatter's party was "the stupidest tea party I ever was at in all my life," and the dreamy Floyd Patterson may have quickly come to that conclusion. The dream was over quickly, as the fight was utterly one-sided. Rademacher had a 15-pound weight advantage; the ring was smaller than normal; the gloves were larger, but with all these edges he could not land much. In the second round, Patterson went down, and the highly partisan Seattle crowd roared over their perception of a knockdown. Some said it was a knockdown, and it was officially deemed to have been one. A few said Patterson was tripped. "I was surprised," Patterson later admitted; "I didn't know he could hit that hard." Other than that one moment, there was little for the Seattle partisans, all 16,961 of them, to cheer about. After the second round, Patterson was completely in control. He knocked Rademacher down seven times. The seventh knockdown came in the sixth round, and mercifully Rademacher did not get up from it. That was the fight, such as it was.[21]

The victory over Rademacher made two utterly lop-sided title defenses for Patterson. To a few this may have been impressive, but Rademacher's virtual amateur standing hardly lent any credibility. Hurricane Jackson, moreover, had been seen as a strong challenge, but the fight was a dud, and Jackson's subsequent loss to Eddie Machen in November made most conclude that he was washed up. Already suffering from invidious comparisons to Marciano, Patterson was holding anything but the high esteem of the boxing world. Questions of worthiness began ever more to circulate in the bars and barber shops. The solution was simple. Patterson had to keep fighting, and do so against the top challengers.

While Patterson may have needed to take on the best, his leaving the selection of opponents and arrangement of fights in the hands of D'Amato meant the issue of D'Amato's ongoing, somewhat paranoid, distrust of the IBC continued to operate. As a result of an anti-trust case that the IBC had lost, the organization was restricted to staging two championship fights per year. Obviously, the IBC leadership wanted those precious two to be of the highest importance. While they could certainly have done well, for example, with a middleweight bout with the likes of Sugar Ray Robinson, they clearly wanted to have a hand in a championship fight in the heavyweight division. Aside from Patterson, the top heavyweights in late 1957 were Eddie Machen, Zora Folley, and Willie Pastrano. The promotions of their fights were all contractually tied to the IBC, and D'Amato would have nothing to do with them. Cus always saw the IBC as nothing but a mob front, and he always stood up to the mob.

As a result of D'Amato's attitude, Patterson appeared to languish. He continued to be the butt of disrespectful jabs from the boxing press, with D'Amato angrily viewing the press jabs as an indication of how much evil influence the IBC had on the boxing world and confirming his determination to resist them at every turn. The press was hardly in the pocket of the IBC, however, and its sniping at Patterson continued. In its "Review of 1957 in the World of Sports," the *New York Times*, for example, panned "the heavyweight ranks, shorn of the flailing fists of Rocky Marciano and suffering from a dearth of 'suitable challengers,' provided nothing spectacular." The *Times* went on then to comment explicitly on Patterson fighting twice in '57, noting "in neither instance could the challenger be described as a battler of note." For Christmas, the *Times* joked that Santa Claus should give Floyd Patterson "an identification tag so that people will know he's the heavyweight champion of the world." In January, addressing directly Cus D'Amato's apparent avoidance of the top heavyweight challengers, the *Times* puckishly predicted for the year 1958: "Floyd Patterson, the heavyweight champion (remember?) is taken to Europe by Manager Cus D'Amato on a tame tiger hunt." The Rademacher fight would remain in many reporters' minds. As late as 1986, when Marvin Hagler's middleweight bout with Ray Leonard proved a dud, one reporter scoffed that "along with Webster's definition of farce, it ranks with the time they matched Pete Rademacher with Floyd Patterson." D'Amato may have had a point about the monopolistic practices of the IBC. His intransigence was hardly helping his fighter, however, and his outlook was not always rational. One night, for example, the young radio reporter Howard Cosell received a phone call from a phone booth on the Merrit Parkway in Connecticut. It was D'Amato. "They're after me," he yelled. "The IBC is after me. They want to kill me. Promise me you'll let people know what happened to me. And promise me you'll take care of my affairs, and watch out for Patterson." (Cosell always liked to brag about any contact he had with anyone famous.) There may have been a great deal of substance in D'Amato's concerns about the mob, and his concern for Patterson was genuine. Still, the point was clear that Cus was setting up Patterson with a bunch of stiffs. "Patterson was an artist," wrote Norman Mailer, "and an artist is no greater than his material." By late January there was talk of Machen fighting Folley, with the obvious point in mind that D'Amato would have to accept the winner as Patterson's next opponent. D'Amato had to be ready to counter.[22]

In the spring and summer of 1958, Pete Rademacher actually exploited the tensions between Cus D'Amato and the IBC. After losing to Patterson, Rademacher did not fight for nearly a year. Despite the lopsided loss, he still schemed to leap into the big time quickly, rather than by sensibly building up his professional standing slowly, starting against lesser opponents. Acting as his own manager, Rademacher got in touch with D'Amato and asked him to "spread a rumor that he was considering giving me a rematch." Rademacher later admitted that he figured "this would force either Eddie Machen or Zora Folley's people to contact me." D'Amato kept his word and told the sports press: "As for Rademacher, we might fight him." Rademacher's ploy worked (and Cus must have chortled), for Folley's camp soon contacted Rademacher, first offering $10,000 and eventually going up to $38,000. Rademacher felt a bit confident, as he had once beaten Folley when they were both amateurs. Folley, however, had grown enormously as a professional, a process for which Rademacher obviously had little feel. He would learn to feel it the hard way: "Folley," Rademacher ruefully reminisced, "gave me the worst beating of my life." Folley knocked Rademacher out in four rounds, and the press certainly did not overlook the fact that this marked two fewer rounds than Patterson required, nor did they forget that this time Rademacher did not knock Folley down. All this hardly helped Patterson's image. After the Folley fight, Rademacher took another year off. Then he adopted a more conventional strategy of building himself up through the ranks. He would fight 21 more bouts, winning 15 of them, including a significant win over Canadian champion George Chuvalo, but he never seriously contended for the crown. Still kidding himself somewhat about his one strange shot at the title, as late as 1987 Rademacher lamented about the huge payday he could have generated with a rematch had he beaten Patterson the first time. Referring to his alleged knockdown of Patterson, Rademacher chuckled, "Getting up was the biggest mistake Floyd ever made. Just think what the rematch would have made." The rematch would likely have made little, and the stature of the title would only have been eroded more. Rademacher could not grasp this. He could only think narrowly as a businessman, where, after boxing, he would do very well, not coincidentally, as a salesman and motivational speaker. The rest of the boxing world, meanwhile, had some sense and concern for the stature of the heavyweight crown.[23]

As for Patterson, the charges of inactivity continued to grow. By February of 1958, several boxing officials were increasingly annoyed at "the unknown champion." Patterson had not shown any signs of fighting a legitimate contender, and since Rademacher he had neither fought anyone nor even signed to fight anyone. He had merely fought a few exhibitions. By January he had been out of training for months and had put on fifteen pounds. He looked like a heavy weight, but not like a champion. By the late winter he was back training, but there was still no fight on the horizon of which anyone knew anything. At a February luncheon of the New York Boxing Writers, Julius Helfand, a man who was both chairman of the New York State Athletic Commission and president of the World Championship Boxing Committee, made a point of mentioning to reporters that the committee has a rule demanding that a champion must defend his title within six months of winning or retaining it. Boxing people likely knew that D'Amato was largely to blame here, but there was only to put pressure upon the situation and let Patterson and D'Amato work out the matter between them. In late February, when two heavyweights, Nino Valdes and Alex Miteff, signed to face one another, papers were quick to mention the importance of the fight, snorting: "The victor will gain considerable stature in the heavyweight ranks, now stymied by Floyd Patterson's inactivity."[24]

While the *New York Times* had joked in their early January prediction about Patterson going to Europe in 1958, in March that year, Patterson did just that. The trip had several oddities about it. There were rumors that Patterson was going to fight British Empire champion John Erskine. As it turned out, Patterson had planned and would fight no official bouts in Great Britain, just a couple of exhibitions. In New York, he had been enjoying some of the good life that comes with being the champion, and he did some of the same on his trip to Great Britain. He had even taken a first class cabin on a ship to London. (First class passengers dined separately, and it was expected that they dress formally. Patterson had and wore a tuxedo, but he felt uncomfortable "in a monkey suit" and ended up taking his meals in his stateroom.) As in New York, no one begrudged Patterson's bits of pleasure, especially since they were so stolid and responsible compared to the likes of Jack Johnson. But like their American counterparts, the British fans still wanted a real fight, and they got none.

The fight game seemed dead in Great Britain, and some hoped that Patterson's presence could revive things. One London weekly, *The Boxing News*, had been openly lamenting the lack of home-grown heavyweight talent. A prominent fight manager, Arthur Boggis, had even taken out an advertisement in the *News*, offering a considerable reward for a good heavyweight. Great Britain always had great fight fans, and they wanted to see the best. The lack of worthy challengers gave some excuse to Patterson's mere exhibitions, but it hardly endeared him to the British, or to the already frustrated boxing press in the U.S. It simply looked like more inexplicable inactivity.

Another top American heavyweight of the day, Cleveland "Big Cat" Williams, was in London at the same time as Patterson, and he got in the ring and easily beat a big Welshman named Dick Richardson. Even if it is against a lesser pug, "Why can't we see Patterson fight?" wondered the rabid British fight fans. Patterson inadvertently angered his British hosts further when he confessed that he had never heard of John Erskine or of another top British heavyweight, Brian London. Meantime, D'Amato's rages against the evils of the IBC continued. In April, D'Amato's nemesis, IBC president Frank Norris, resigned, but D'Amato showed no mollification. An unknown Australian heavyweight named Allen Williams even wrote the *New York Times* an open letter to Patterson, claiming that he was a worthy challenger and that a Sydney syndicate could guarantee the champion $200,000 for a fight with Williams in Australia. D'Amato took no note, and much of the boxing establishment continued to get more and more frustrated.[25]

Amidst D'Amato's no-commerce policy with the IBC and the resulting press pressures over inactivity, Patterson showed some of the stress. He later said that in his relatively inactive year he was hoping that Marciano would come out of retirement and fight him. Reflecting, perhaps, a touch of D'Amato's paranoia, Patterson seemed to feel that the press had it in for him. "If I beat Marciano," he lamented, "they'd all say Marciano was just too old. It seems impossible for me to prove myself as a champion." When asked, then, how good a champion he thought he was, Patterson merely shrugged: "Oh, I'm not a great champion, I'm just a champion." "I need more competition," he suggested, "and open competition which will bring out better fighters. Lots of good fighters get discouraged and quit because they don't see any future ahead of them." Fans and reporters could only return to the obvious point that the competition was there to be fought if only Patterson could extricate himself from the boxing politics that his manager was playing. The boxing public usually has to deal with the colossal egos and brazen braggadocio of its champions. Until Patterson, the heavyweights had never seen such a one-two combination of frustrated, lonely humility and paranoia-driven management at the top of its division. It all gave press and fans more than a little disquietude. Maybe a bit of the disrespect extended from the race issue that lay beneath the fact that Patterson had succeeded the great Rocky Marciano, but the main contenders in the division were also black, so that explanation had its limits. The issue was intramural boxing politics. The press and the fans felt victimized, and in his own way so did Patterson.[26]

Patterson returned from Britain in April, and late that month D'Amato announced, at last, that he had tentatively scheduled Patterson for a title defense. He opponent was to be a man named Roy Harris. Harris was a ranked heavyweight, although not a top one. He had compiled a record of 21–0. While most of his opponents were nobodies, one of the victories had been against the well-regarded Willie Pastrano. Still, Harris was hardly a prime contender. The higher ranked boxers in the heavyweight division like Eddie Machen and Zora Folley still had ties to the IBC, and D'Amato would not budge from his refusal to do business with them. D'Amato tried disingenuously to assert that Harris was "probably the best of the other fighters around to challenge Patterson." When probed about that point, however, D'Amato had to admit that neither he nor Patterson had ever seen Harris fight. The IBC politics were clearly the issue, and D'Amato's clumsy posturing was certainly no help to Patterson's credibility. D'Amato's efforts at circumventing the IBC had also failed in two other basic ways: Patterson was still left looking like he was ducking the top challengers; and the promoters of the Jackson and the Rademacher bouts had each lost money. By setting up a fight with Harris, D'Amato and Patterson would at best get some of the inactivity-sniping off their backs. Even here they were not completely successful. On June 1, the World Boxing Committee conspicuously issued an order to Patterson to defend his crown before the end of September or be compelled to forfeit it, something a heavyweight champion had never been forced to do. When the press attended some of Patterson's training sessions, many of the writers also snidely chuckled that they had come to the camp just to see whether there really was a Patterson. After the usual wranglings, the Harris fight date was set for August 18. The site would be Los Angeles, conspicuously far away from the IBC's New York base.[27]

As with Pete Rademacher, the Roy Harris fight had, just beneath the surface, some elements of white hope. Once again, the opponent was white as well as a recently-discharged Army man. Rademacher's backers were a bunch of Georgia crackers; Harris was the pride of a town called Cut 'n Shoot, Texas. Texas good ole' boys loved the name of their town, and they loved their boy Roy. As the press came down to Texas to check out Harris's background, townspeople made a point of flying Confederate battle flags everywhere, and many smiled about how Roy was going to "whup that n ——-." Sportswriters reported of Harris's exploits wrestling alligators in the swamps around Cut 'n Shoot, of his family living in a log cabin, of his father having formerly been a bare–knuckle heavyweight, and of his cousins named Hominy, Coon, Armadillo, and "Wildman" Woodman. Roy got his name because his father had named him for Roy Tipton, a local criminal of the 1930s who had been part of Machine Gun Kelly's gang. Patterson shook his head and said he felt it was all like reading *Li'l Abner* in the funnies section of the *Daily News*. Like Rademacher, Harris was actually more urbane than many of his staunchest supporters. He was a college graduate, and a school teacher with some credits completed toward a master's degree. But just as Rademacher easily played the "All-American Boy," Harris was certainly willing to play to the hilt the role of a rootin,' tootin,' smilin,' guitar-pickin,' chu'mbacky-spittin' Texan. As he did, the nature of the battle lines was clear, and it was something that D'Amato appeared once again quite happy to exploit.

The press and fans had not completely bought the hype of rookie

Rademacher. With Harris, however, no mater the hillbilly hype, they were looking at a more bona fide contender. Harris's manager and trainer, Bill Gore, emphasized his fighter's courage. Here he laid the Texas blather on thick: "Has Harris got courage, sure he has. They all have in the Harris clan," he drawled. "They gotta have, because down there they drown cowards." This all contrasted to Patterson's soft-spoken manner. Meanwhile, the press pounced on the fact that Patterson was actually knocked down in training by one of his sparring partners, another D'Amato protégé, an up and coming light heavyweight from Puerto Rico named José Torres.[28]

With the press and fan interest in the fight, a few effects were visible. The town of Cut 'n Shoot began receiving such an upsurge of mail that the U.S. Post Office Department OK'd the building of a post office there. Before then, the town's mail had all been handled in nearby Conroe. Elsewhere, the Harris fight was sparking middling interest at best. The promoters, led by a newcomer named Bill Rosensohn, decided to bypass network television coverage. They sold film rights to the fight to United Artists and broadcast rights to a closed circuit theater operation. This closed-circuit method had never before been employed with a heavyweight championship fight. With the financial losses to promoters in the Jackson and Rademacher fights, another approach seemed worth a try. Fans in New York and elsewhere had to buy theater tickets for the fight. Fans in Los Angeles would have no closed-circuit theaters. They would have to buy tickets at the city's Wrigley Field.*

Los Angeles politicians and chamber of commerce leaders were thrilled at having a heavyweight championship in their city. Pro football's Rams in 1946 and the baseball Dodgers and Giants that very spring in 1958 had begun the trend of major sports organizations relocating to the West Coast. Many Californians thus hoped the Patterson-Harris bout would be the first of many such big fights on the coast. To add to the big-time posture, Joe Louis was hired as the fight referee, his first appearance as the third man in a heavyweight championship fight. Attendance at the fight was not great but good — 21,680. It yielded a gate of $234,183, a new record for boxing in California. The closed circuit audience was 196,762, yielding $763,437, more than a network television contract would likely have garnered.[29]

In contrast to the Rademacher pro-am, Las Vegas oddsmakers were at least making book on the Harris fight. They rated Patterson a 5–1 favorite. Some ring pundits observed that Patterson had looked a little sluggish in practice. Otherwise, few could find any basis to give Harris much of a chance.

---

*The Wrigley family, owners of the Chicago Cubs, had for many years owned the Pacific Coast League baseball franchise called the Los Angeles Angels, and the field at which they played was also owned by the Wrigleys, hence the stadium's name. When the Brooklyn Dodgers moved to L.A., in the same year of the Patterson-Harris fight, they first played in the L.A. Coliseum. With the coming of the Dodgers, the PCL Angels were defunct, and their old field was available for other venues in the summer.

In the fight, some repetition of the Rademacher bout occurred. Early in the bout, this time in the second round, Harris tagged Patterson with a left to the head and immediately followed with a right uppercut. Patterson went down. He said he was tripped. He got up quickly, shook off the effects, and from there won every round. He knocked Harris down four times, and at the end of the 12th round, Harris was out for good. One writer smirked that Harris basically "passed out." Harris's seconds, including his father, refused to let him come out for the 13th round ("ain't no use, boy," his father advised), leaving the fight officially a knockout in the 12th round.

Some praised Harris for his courage. Patterson later admitted he was not sharp against Harris — "the worst I have ever been as the champion." He conceded that his lay-off had likely left him a trifle rusty. To reporters he was generous in his praise for Harris. "I have the feeling," he noted, "that if he had taken the title from me that he would have gained enough confidence to become twice as good a fighter as he was tonight, and that would have made him quite a champion." Again, Patterson left some with an uneasy feeling. How often had a champion responded to a victory with thoughts about what would be the case if he had lost? Again, as well, Patterson came out of a title defense with most shrugging that he had not been severely challenged. The fact that both Harris and Rademacher had floored the champion also made some wonder about his susceptibility. Did he have a glass jaw, and if he did, what would happen if he *finally* stepped into the ring and had to face the heavy punch of a genuine contender, assuming Cus D'Amato would ever let that occur.[30]

Within weeks after the Harris fight, boxing writers returned to their usual refrain: "Who's next for Patterson?" And there was a decided undertone of sarcastic wonder as to whether his next opponent would at last be a true contender. In September, the New York State Athletic Commission, with obvious self-interest at heart, was putting out press statements expressing "hope" that before the year was out a heavyweight championship fight would be held in Madison Square Garden. The Cuban fighter Nino Valdes's name was coming up as a possibility. Meanwhile, some new faces entered the circle of contenders. Willie Pastrano had already lost to Harris, and in September he lost to the British heavyweight, Brian London. Meanwhile, heavyweight Eddie Machen, one of the chief contenders of 1958 and one of the IBC-connected fighters with whom D'Amato had refused to do business, was ranked as high as the number two contender. On September 14, he went to the Swedish city of Goteberg. There he fought a local heavyweight, Ingemar Johansson. Johansson was already a known fighter in Europe. He had fought at the 1952 Olympics. He had defeated the British champion John Erskine and had been ranked in the top ten in the heavyweight division. To the surprise of all pundits, and to the enormous joy of all the fans in Sweden, Johansson knocked out Machen, and he did it in the first round no less. Immediately after the fight, Johansson rejected the idea of a rematch with Machen. "There's no money in it," he scoffed. "I want Patterson."

Secretly, Johansson had cut a deal with Bill Rosensohn, the Harris fight promoter. If Rosensohn could get Patterson to agree to a bout with Johansson within forty days, Johansson would accept the fight, accept Rosensohn as the fight's promoter, and, win or lose, accept Rosensohn as the promoter of a rematch. If Rosensohn failed to get Patterson in forty days, he would have to pay Johansson $10,000. Rosensohn did not have to pay.[31]

VI

Ingemar

By the autumn of 1958, the memories, such as they were, of Patterson's August bout with Roy Harris had faded, and back rolled the questions of when, at last, he was going to fight a real contender. Reviewing the sports year of 1958, the *New York Times* was again sarcastic. "Floyd," they shrugged, "has been spoon-fed a diet of pap in recent years." Considering his previous twelve months, they apparently saw no need even to mention the Rademacher bout, and as for the Harris fight the *Times* summarized that the challenger "patently did not have the armament or experience ... [but he] surprised by sending Patterson to the floor." Later in January, they sniffed at Patterson as "the relatively unknown and inactive heavyweight champion." When the Associated Press named Archie Moore, still light-heavyweight champion, Fighter of the Year for 1958, Patterson conspicuously received no votes. Phrases like "failed to fulfill early promises of greatness" began to dot sports section commentaries. One writer wrote a satirical piece in the *Times* in which he depicted the D'Amato-led heavyweight division as an unfolding play called "*The Great Heavyweight Mystery: A Farce in One Act*." The "play" was being staged at "D'Amato's Little Theatre." Cus D'Amato had the role of "Guardian of the Crown," and Patterson was assigned the role of the "Phantom Champion." Aside from the behemoth Primo Carnera, a champion in the 1930s, who had been laughed at as a bumbling 260-pound oaf owned by the mafia, few other heavyweight champions had ever been subjected to such ridicule as Patterson received.[1]

Even Patterson's new boxing style added to the consternation. It was known as the Peek-a-boo Style. D'Amato had taught it, and Patterson did as instructed. By the end of 1958, it was all that Patterson was using — gloves glued to the cheeks, elbows clamped to the body. No one had seen a cham-

pion fight like that. From John L. Sullivan to Jersey Joe Walcott, many champions had audaciously stood in the ring often with right hand cocked and left
hand extended, sometimes with their hands practically at their sides. They
seemed to be announcing defiantly "Hit me if you can; meanwhile I'm
gonna...." Even the more scientific stances and styles of Joe Louis and Gene
Tunney never seemed to lack aggression. "Peek-a-boo" Patterson, on the other
hand, seemed so purely defensive. D'Amato was candid about it: "Every boy
knows fear," he adamantly asserted,

> but he won't admit it, even to himself. So I explain fear to him. Fear is your
> friend, not your enemy ... it's the control of it that counts. To stop that fear,
> you gotta be protected — not part of the time, not most of the time, but all of
> the time. You can't gamble by using the open stance. Because every time you
> gamble and lose you get hurt. And when a fighter gets hurt, he's intimidated, he
> thinks he's tired, pooped. He covers up. Now in my style you cover up from the
> start. You never gamble. The right arm is always protecting the liver, the left
> the solar plexus. The hands are protecting the chin. When you flick out with
> your left, the arm works like a piston. When you move, you move like an owl.
> Then suddenly you're not being hit and that means you're not being hurt. And
> when you're not being hurt is when boxing becomes fun. As soon as it's fun for
> a fighter, nothing's going to stop him.

The logic was there, but how well did it resonate among fight fans when they
read of a fighter being driven by fear? How did they react when they heard
phrases like "cover up" and "never gamble?" In contrast to a bull or a tiger,
when was a heavyweight champion ever associated with an owl? For some the
sense was certainly that such a modern fighter as Patterson had a style that
eclipsed the dull, oafish ways of the heavyweight sluggers of yore. But in an
age when people were being trained to "duck and cover" in case of a nuclear
attack from the Soviet Union, there was something depressing about the idea
the nation could be attacked. Maybe many were living in forms of denial, or
maybe a few saw through the absurdity of it all, but a lot of Americans were
uncomfortable with the idea of preparing defensively and fearfully for a
nuclear attack from such an opponent as the Soviets. This was somehow not
what true Americans ever did. While many could debate the political and
philosophical questions at stake here, even among those who were comfortable with the need for defensiveness, the heavyweight boxing championship
was about the last place such a seemingly timid mentality should manifest
itself. Yet there was Patterson, peek-a-booing and boxing out of a self-imposed
shelter. It may have been an advancement over the loutish slugger style of a
John L. Sullivan, but it all served further to note a heavyweight apparently
devoted to not being hit rather than to hitting, hence a champion more concerned about not losing than with winning. The peek-a-boo style was actually quite effective, and many fighters would subsequently copy it with success.

But for the time, much of the boxing world felt it was saddled with a heavy-weight champion whose temperament and style seemed hardly to stack up to the legacy he inherited from the likes of Jim Jeffries, Jack Dempsey, Joe Louis, and Rocky Marciano. Patterson may have been a bit more scientific, but was he the killer that was supposed to symbolize what a heavyweight champion truly was?[2]

Patterson was fairly quiet amidst the grousing about his inactivity and less-than-stellar opponents. He was certainly aware of the complaints, but he saw little point in trying to grapple with it all on a verbal level. To one reporter he tried to explain: "The killer instinct can be harmful. Most fighters are more dangerous when they're hurt. He has nothing to lose, he figures, so he throws everything he has. I try to think cautiously when I have my man in trouble. I try to place my punches." Reporters and pundits were not impressed, at least not until Patterson beat a genuine contender. At best, such explanations smacked of a high-percentage hitting shortstop rather than a towering-home run hitting slugger. One morning, in the presence of a friendly reporter, he was glancing through the sports pages of a morning paper and threw it down in disgust. With a decided anger and frustration, he turned to the reporter and orated: "Do you solemnly swear to condemn and criticize a man you've never seen?" Presuming such a swearing, he then mocked: "Today, you are a reporter." To the criticism of his unworthiness he would be a philo-sophical though a touch bitter.

> Golden Gloves; Olympics; Who am I to complain? I became the heavyweight champion. It makes you happy to know that you're on their [journalists'] minds. I'm gracious and proud to accept it ... even if I never become good or great. I never thought I'd have that chance. I'm not a great champion. It's not that I haven't had sufficient fights. I haven't had *the* sufficient fight [emphasis added]. Even if I do I won't be accepted. There's always going to be an excuse. I have to live with it and I'm satisfied. There'll always be something in the way.[3]

Immediately after their ho-hum summary of Patterson's year, the *New York Times* also made the point of mentioning that 1958 was also a rare year for boxing in that "no fight of any consequence was held in this state." Some of this may have amounted to mere pouting from notoriously provincial, excessively self-entitled Manhattanites, but the political maneuvers of D'Amato doubtlessly came to mind among many New Yorkers who read the *Times'* words. Legitimate challengers to Patterson's title loomed, and New Yorkers not only wanted some real heavyweight fights, they wanted to be in on the action. In late 1958, Zora Folley was a strong figure for D'Amato's consideration. In October, Folley had gone to Great Britain and defeated a rising English heavyweight, Henry Cooper. A month later, still in Britain, Folley knocked out another though less significant British fighter named Joe Bygraves. Nonetheless, Cus D'Amato's position with regard to the International Boxing Club was steadfast, so the connected Folley was still not going to get a shot at Patterson. D'Amato had control over the heavyweight champ. He also had José Torres, a rising young light-heavyweight. With such a stable, he felt he could wait out the IBC and not be bent to their will.

Events would fall D'Amato's way. In 1958 the IBC had lost an anti-trust suit in the state of New York. Their monopoly in jeopardy, they appealed the decision, and in January, 1959, their appeal was denied. The IBC was thus a lame duck, so there was no reason for D'Amato to yield even one inch to them, and he did not. D'Amato had won the war, but with the non-commerce with the IBC's top contenders, he had done damage to his own champion. "He has artfully contrived to manage Patterson into obscurity," one sportswriter sardonically nipped. By late November in 1958, clearly wanting to show the boxing world that his champion was not ducking a challenge, D'Amato began making noises about the possibility of fighting Ingemar Johansson. There was some talk of another bout with Archie Moore and of a fight with Henry Cooper, but D'Amato began to fixate on Johansson. The momentum here would continue in early 1959, and the press was interested. That winter, the New *York Times* cast another "play," "*The Great Heavyweight Mystery.*" Johansson's manager, Edwin Ahlquist, was playing the role of "A Swedish Visitor," and Johansson was cast as "An Aspiring Hero." (Archie Moore was the "Ancient Gladiator.")[4]

Ingemar Johansson was a charismatic figure. By 1959, he was immensely popular in his native Sweden, of course, and well-liked everywhere else. He had actually started his boxing career on a sour note with his fellow Swedes. He was the heavyweight on Sweden's Olympic boxing team at the Helsinki Games of 1952, the same Olympics where Patterson won the gold medal as a middleweight. In the heavyweight competition Johansson had made it to the finals, there facing the big American, Ed Sanders. He employed a strategy of staying away, hoping Sanders would rush him, tire himself out, and be vulnerable by the third round. Sanders would not accommodate him. He slowly stalked Johansson, with Johansson steadily retreating. As Sanders was his friend and teammate, Patterson watched the bout, and he recalled: "I had never in my life seen a man so scared in the ring as Johansson was in that fight against Sanders. I, like so many others, may have done Johansson an injustice, but first impressions are lasting and that was mine." Johansson may have hoped that Sanders would tire by the third round, but he never got the chance to implement the strategy. In the first two rounds, the referee issued several warnings to Johansson for non-engagement. Towards the end of the second round, with the crowd booing, he disqualified Johansson for his inactivity. Many Swedes who had hopped over to Helsinki and given Johansson virtual home-boy status were greatly embarrassed. They felt Johansson had disgraced the country. (As neutral Sweden had allowed the Nazis to march through their country and take Norway, which did resist, historical memory accentuated acute senses of shame and cowardice here.) Johansson was actually denied the silver medal because of the disqualification and was only later awarded one in 1982.

As of 1952, Johansson's reputation back in Sweden was terrible. This would change, however, as Johansson turned professional and proceeded to beat everyone he faced. He won fourteen bouts in a row, and after his fifteenth bout, a victory against the Italian champion, Franco Cavicchi, he was the European heavyweight champion. He went on to beat several British fighters including Henry Cooper and Joe Erskine. Then in September 1958, he faced the tough American contender Eddie Machen, his first bout against a world class fighter. Johansson shocked the boxing world by knocking out Machen in the very first round. His record then stood at 21–0, and he now he had a reputation throughout the boxing world, including the United States. On January 29, through the determined work of promoter Bill Rosensohn, Patterson and Johansson tentatively agreed to fight one another.[5]

With the clear sense that, at last, Patterson was going to fight a real contender for the crown, the question of the fight's site came under a great deal of pressure. With the significant Scandinavian element of their region in mind, some sports promoters in Minneapolis made a bid. Chicago did too, guaranteeing $500,000 to the two sides. There was talk of another fight in Los Angeles, and, with the summer as the expected fight time, the town of Colorado Springs received some consideration. New Yorkers, however, were in earnest about bringing the heavyweight championship venue back to the city, no matter that the NYC–based IBC was in steady decline. New York's mayor, Robert Wagner, made a personal effort on behalf of securing the fight for the city, and he succeeded. The fight would take place on June 25 in Yankee Stadium. (The Yankees would be on the road from June 21 to July 3.)[6]

As the fight date loomed, a few complications arose. Eddie Machen claimed he had contractual rights to a rematch with Johansson. He was threatening a civil suit, and his attorneys claimed that they could stop the Johansson-Patterson match. The efforts would fail. Meanwhile, seemingly as an afterthought, D'Amato actually slated a fight for Patterson before the Johansson bout was to occur. In May he was to fight the stocky British pug, Brian London.

If the Johansson fight was not already in the offing, Patterson and D'Amato contracting to fight Brian London would have led to another round of guffaws from the boxing public and press. Even accepting London as a preliminary fight for Patterson in his preparations for Johansson (otherwise he would have been going into the Johansson bout with no fights for ten months), many were still shaking their heads. London "threw his right hand like a girl," giggled Wendell Smith of the *Pittsburgh Courier*. "For Floyd," snorted the

New York Times' Arthur Daley, "this is merely a tune-up for his June bout....
It sure will add matchless luster to a record that already shows knockouts of
such tigers as Hurricane Jackson, Pete Rademacher and Roy (Cut 'n Shoot)
Harris." British reporters were joking that London was on his back so often
that his handlers were selling advertising on the soles of his shoes.

Within the context of the existing heavyweight ranks, London was basically a journeyman. He had once beaten the American heavyweight Willie
Pastrano, but on January 13, 1959, he had just lost to the British Empire title
holder Henry Cooper. In March the British Boxing Board of Control declared
London unfit for a title fight with Patterson, refused to give his effort their
official imprimatur, and actually fined London for his impertinence. British
bookmakers set odds at 10–1 in favor of Patterson, and no one felt any urge
then to point out that those were the odds James Braddock received before
his victory over Max Baer. With the build-up of his fight with Patterson
already churning in the world press, Johansson ridiculed London: "My little
sister could beat him," he scoffed. "He won't last one round unless Paterson
decides to carry him for the sake of the crowd."[7]

One suspicion that was circulating concerned D'Amato's motives for
staging the bout. After his successful battles with the IBC, many boxing insid-
ers were sore at D'Amato's power. Rumors now flew that it was D'Amato who
was the one with mob connections, hence the London bout was supposedly
a payoff to them. At this point, indeed, the *Times* referred to D'Amato as "the
suspicious proprietor of the titleholder." The London bout was originally set
to take place in the mob's flourishing gambling mecca, Las Vegas. It was to
be Las Vegas's first heavyweight championship fight, a venue which the connected casino operators obviously knew would draw more crowds to their slot
machines, crap games, and card tables. With the gambling and mafia rumors
flying, D'Amato suddenly announced on April 6 that the fight was being
moved to Indianapolis, Indiana. D'Amato was not in anyone's pocket, but
he knew it was best to remove unnecessary clouds, especially since he had
already created so many. Amidst all the hubbub, Patterson, to whom some
reporters actually began to pay some attention, appeared a trifle bewildered
by it all. He said the move to Indianapolis "didn't concern" him, just so the
fight occurred. Patterson confessed that he had thought he would be fighting
Henry Cooper and not Brian London. Since Cooper was the British champion, many boxing fans thought much the same thing. Cooper had actually
been tough in negotiations, and D'Amato, thinking mainly about Johansson,
simply chose to sign the cheaper of the two British opponents. Yes, it was a
mere tune-up for Johansson (indeed, Johansson flew to New York and signed
the final contract for the Patterson bout just five days before the London
fight), but the tune-up could have carried more prestige. Patterson's confessions hardly added much hype.[8]

With the same odd self-effacement, Patterson answered the charges of those who chided the stature of his title holding, given that he had won a vacated crown and then fought only three lesser lights. Doubtlessly he was a trifle preoccupied amidst some of the wranglings. He had always tried to ignore gossipy matters, letting the loquacious Cus handle it all. At this point, as well, Sandra had just given birth to their second daughter, Trina. When pressed on the issues of worthiness, Patterson admitted later that he "came to feel that there was some truth in what the detractors said, that my championship was almost one of default for lack of a challenger of stature." Even amidst the preparations for London, he actually acknowledged: "I am not a great champion. Many people may not look upon me as a good champion, much less a great champion." Then he did confirm, "but I am the champion and that can only be taken away from me in the ring." He went on to emphasize: "My feelings are rather delicate. You can say something and hurt me very much." Once again, pundits were left a trifle dumbfounded. What champion ever claimed he was not great, much less spoke of his "delicate" feelings? In the annals of American culture, the apotheosizing of the quiche-eating, sensitive male was decades off, and boxing's heavyweight champion was certainly the most inauspicious place for its premature appearance. Former light-heavyweight contender Billy Conn mentioned to a reporter in disbelief that he had heard of Patterson saying that when he gets an opponent in trouble he lays off hitting him in the eye because it would be like pouring salt in a cut. When the reporter confirmed to Conn that Patterson was truly that sort of person, Conn shook his head: "Then he's got no business being a fighter."[9]

No matter the perceptions of Patterson as champion, out in Indianapolis most folks were delighted at the city hosting its first heavyweight championship fight, and promoters worked hard to create any sort of build up they could. (The enthusiasm notwithstanding, Patterson and some of his sparring partners were refused service by a racist coffee shop manager. When the manager realized to whom he was refusing service, he apologized, but Patterson then rejected him, as he had others in such situations. "I may not always be heavyweight champion," he admonished, "but I'll always be a man.") If the Patterson-London match held little glory, the timing of the bout was at least fortuitous for the city's sports-hyping efforts. Every year in late April and throughout May, the city would always gear up its commercial enterprises for "the race" at the end of May. The race, of course, was the Indianapolis 500. The Indianapolis 500 Speedway would always open for its first racing practice on May 1, so the staging of a fight on or around that day would capitalize on and perhaps enhance the crowds that were just beginning to form. A few people even tried to hype the actual fight. One young trainer, Angelo Dundee, who had already trained heavyweight contender Willie Pastrano,

praised London as "a big rough man who climbs into you like a heavy haul-
ing truck. I know," Dundee puffed, "London can hit harder than Roy Harris." Given Harris's performance against Patterson, some may have thought
Dundee to be damning by faint praise. Still, Harris, and Rademacher, had
knocked Patterson down, so Indianapolis papers were trumpeting the point
that London could win since Patterson could obviously be hit. One even
explained that Patterson had "small feet and thin legs" and was, thus, "top
heavy and when tagged can go down." Here many added the point that London did hold a 24-pound weight advantage.[10]

Despite the hyping, interest and ticket sales lagged. The 10–1 betting line
held. The fight's original promoter, Cecil Rhodes, quit two weeks before the
fight. Bill Rosensohn, the promoter of the Johansson fight, took over the
work. Financial hopes did not pan out. NBC agreed to televise the bout, but
when the venue shifted from Las Vegas to Indianapolis, they reduced their
offer from $225,000 to $200,000, and then down to $175,000. Originally
promised $75,000, London had to settle for $60,000. Patterson also had to
take big cut in his anticipated fee. He first expected a guarantee of $175,000,
but he ended up accepting a guarantee of a mere $75,000 against the possi-
bility of 60 percent of the gate and TV. Attendance would be a non-capac-
ity crowd of 10,088, grossing a gate of $122,800 (resulting net: $103,111).
Patterson and D'Amato thus wound up with a mere $168,000.[11]

The negatives were everywhere, and the London fight lived up to its list-
less reputation. Patterson admitted that he "missed punches a lot," but London posed absolutely no threat. Throughout the fight he held his big red
gloves high and appeared to cower behind them. "You don't feel right beating up a man like that," Patterson later said. "Any man that's a human being
feels sorry for someone that offers no opposition." With World War II still a
powerful memory for many, several reporters clacked out the phrase "The
Bombing of London" on their typewriters. Patterson dropped London in the
tenth round and knocked him out in the eleventh. "As an offensive fighter?"
chortled one observer about London, "the Britisher was offensive period." "A
high-grade clinker," snorted another. With the pounding he took, London
looked "lobster pink" by the third round. From London, reporters watching
the fight on TV among British fans reported "stiff upper lips all around." The
judges declared one round a draw; Patterson won all the others. It was a
slaughter. At several points, the crowd actually booed. After the fight, reporters
asked London about his future plans. He responded: "I am coming back to
the States and learn to fight." Always gracious, Patterson praised London as
his "gamest challenger." Such good manners notwithstanding, nothing could
put much of a decent face on the London fight. Patterson later confessed: "I
was terribly embarrassed by that fight and all the circumstances surrounding
it."[12]

The London bout only added to the persistent carping among reporters that Patterson was not a worthy champion. Still, with the upcoming bout with Johansson just eight weeks away, much of the boxing world's attention immediately turned to Ingemar. Johansson came to Indianapolis for the London fight. There, as well as in New York, the press was all agog at his attractive Swedish secretary and his even more alluring Swedish fiancé. Reporters noted that he came to the U.S., not with just a boxing retinue, but with his family (his mother did all the camp cooking) and golf clubs, setting up training with the full intention of getting in some golf during his weeks in America; "strangely gay training methods," noted one writer. Johansson and his fiancé conspicuously saw all the major sites of New York City. He had hoped to do all his fight training in Central Park and first tried to set up his camp on a 51st Street parking lot next to Toots Shor's Restaurant. Unfortunately, a wilting heat wave hit New York that spring. This combined with the city's putrid air and some balking by city officials about the training in Central Park to send Johansson packing up to the posh Grossinger's Resort in the Catskill Mountains. There he trained and rode horses, swam, and played golf. One reporter smirked, "a millionaire priming himself for a yacht race couldn't ask for more sumptuous quarters." Even Patterson noted how Johansson "lived like a king while preparing to become one." All this vitality and panache from the Johansson camp marked quite a contrast to the ascetic, spartan life that Patterson had always led. Patterson trained in Summit, New Jersey, in what one reporter dubbed "a barn-like camp." Patterson himself described it as "only a couple of nails above a squatter's shack." As always, Patterson stayed completely away from Sandra throughout his training too.[13]

A few expressed concerns about Johansson's fun and games, including the boxing guru Nat Fleischer, who penned some articles for the Stockholm paper *Expressen*, which issued a front-page two column article: "Is Inge dancing away his chances?" A.J. Liebling of *The New Yorker* cast a similar concern when he jauntily referred to Johansson as "an autodidact [who] scorned the precepts of the scholastics." Still, given the raised eyebrows Patterson's dull two-and-one-half year championship reign had engendered, the presentation of Johansson's contrasting animation, fun loving, and pretty girls largely prompted cheers. Thoughts rose of a new champion who would excite the public and provide the press with good copy. From Europe came reports of easily positive contrasts with Brian London which all pointed to same conclusion — Ingemar Johansson was a genuine challenger; Patterson was finally in for a real fight. Yes, it was against another non–IBC connected white man, but, wrote one English journalist, "Johansson is infinitely more dangerous. He's a truly fine hitter, sharp and crisp. London had all the intentions, but he doesn't know how to fight. Johansson does."[14]

There was no question that Johansson had a big punch; "The Hammer of Thor," he said of his big right hand; "Toonder," proclaimed his manager Edwin Ahlquist. But Johansson charmed the press and public with more than his boxing skills. In the late 20th century, the word "charisma" would grow to be overused with sports and entertainment figures, but Johansson certainly had it. He was good looking, charming, educated, and pleasantly articulate in several languages. If Patterson's peek-a-boo style symbolized a rigid, fearful stance with which the public was uncomfortable amidst the pressures of the Cold War, Johansson embodied the *savoir faire* that, like agent 007 in Ian Fleming's James Bond spy novels, conveyed a type of reassurance to the effect that the nuances and subtleties in the handling of the world's key issues were those over which the best of the West had such command as to make the other side look humorously bumbling in comparison.

The boxing public loved to read about Johansson, and the press was more than happy to provide copy. Johansson accepted an offer from *Life Magazine* to fly out to Indianapolis to watch the Patterson-London fight and write an article about his impressions. As *Life*'s editors expected, Johansson used the writing as an opportunity to do a little breast-beating in regard to his upcoming bout with Patterson. In his article, Johansson quickly dispatched Brian London as an utter mediocrity. Believing that he could knock out London very quickly if he had him in the ring, Johansson smirked, since London was "still up" in the sixth round, "I am not very much afraid of the way Patterson is fighting." From this he smiled: "If Patterson does not fight any better against me than he did against London, I do not worry." Johansson went on to chortle that he was faster than Patterson, that he hit harder than Patterson, and that he would be in better shape than Patterson. Johansson conceded that, like himself, Patterson was a thinking boxer, but he added that "there are times when he [Patterson] stops thinking; he gets over-anxious and doesn't look close enough."

Above all, Johansson bragged about his big right hand. With a clear level of self-luxuriation, he wrote effusively:

> There is something strange about my right hand, something very hard to explain. It is almost as if it was not part of me at all. I never know when it is coming. The arm works by itself. It is faster than the eye, and I cannot see it. Without my telling it to, the right goes and when it hits, there is a good feeling all down my arm and down through my body. It is a wonderful feeling. Something right has just been done.... It is something almost mystic.... All I have to say to the Champion Floyd Patterson is one thing, watch out!

"Nobody sees my right hand when it comes," he embellished to the *New York Times*. "Even the films miss it." Reporters, of course, questioned Johansson's braggadocio as mere hype. Many wondered when they might see an example of it in his training. Ingemar smiled at them, explaining, "I don't want to hurt my sparring partners." Elsewhere, in the *Saturday Evening Post*, Johansson thundered: "I must destroy Patterson." All this was naturally calculated to irritate Patterson, promote the upcoming fight, and sell magazines for *Life* and others. It did.[15]

Johansson may have been shooting his mouth off, but it worked at several levels. One result was the simple fact that reporters and fans were ever more keen about the man's punching power. He had shown that when he knocked out Eddie Machen, and several reporters noted that indeed Johansson had a lethal, one-punch right. Another result involved the fact that boxing people were more comfortable with such confidence among champion boxers. To many that was the mark of a champion, and it was something Patterson had never shown. Modesty may have been a more noble trait for almost every other profession, but it was out of place in the fight game. Given the menu of mediocrities D'Amato had served up for almost three years, many could wise-crack *à la* Oscar Wilde that Patterson had, indeed, a lot to be modest about. Several times Patterson mentioned how, if he lost, he would "go back to the beginning and fight my way up again." Hearing such words, Joe Louis shook his head. "A fighter can't think that way," he declared, "and he can't talk that way."[16] Amidst all the cross-fires there was the underlying contentment that, finally, the boxing world *and* New York City were going to see a real heavyweight bout.

As Cus D'Amato was heavily involved in the management and financial details of the fight, the negotiations over the bout were sticky even by boxing standards. Patterson was generally oblivious about such business issues, and as Cus was not stealing from him, there was at least no classic boxing rip-off tragedy at work here. Some speculated that D'Amato was stealing, however, and this added to tensions around Patterson. While Patterson was usually passive in contractual matters, Johansson would actually involve himself in the contract's particulars, and he fought hard against some efforts of managers to sneak extra percentages for themselves. The additional legal complication of Eddie Machen's claim that he had a "return bout" promise from Johansson after their fight arose at this point. Johansson also wrenched his back a month prior to the fight. He had to take a few days off training and see a chiropractor. Patterson was squeamish too. At church on the Sunday before, the priest asked Patterson to help pass around the collection basket. Patterson agreed, but he suddenly saw himself "passing the basket and hitting an elderly lady in the face, and spilling the money all over the floor." Patterson then begged off helping with further passing. He may have later recognized that should have done it.[17]

Promoter Bill Rosensohn grew emotionally spent as the fight date approached and complications kept coming. Among the worst things that happened was that it rained (actually, it poured) on the original fight date (Thursday, June 25), and the bout had to be rescheduled for the following

ing. "My luck is consistent," shrugged Rosensohn. "It's all bad." Patterson took no note; perhaps he should have. Friday the 26th was clear; then it rained in the early evening, killing off most last-minute ticket sales. Those that could not use their tickets because of the 24-hour rain delay could not get refunds.[18]

The fight came off on June 26. Johansson weighed in at 196; Patterson was but 182. ABC provided television coverage. (The television producers tried a new angle for its viewers, as they hired not just a blow-by-blow commentator but also had a young New York journalist named Howard Cosell give bits of color commentary between the rounds.) All the hype had worked but not as well as Rosensohn and others had hoped. With its boxing set up of field seats, Yankee Stadium has a capacity of nearly 80,000. Attendance that evening came to only 21,961. It was the smallest outdoor gathering for a heavyweight championship bout since Jess Willard and the World War I era. Patterson recalled, "there was almost a feeling of desolation." Among the crowd, however, were some 4000 loud, enthusiastic Swedes who came over to root for Ingemar. A few European reporters had said that Johansson, with that supposedly big right hand, *could* win. Still, most of the ring experts picked Patterson. In the week before the fight, the betting line generally ran at 4:1 and 7:2.

The fight began normally, as each tested the other with jabs. In the first, Patterson threw one of his famous and amateurish "leaping rights" that missed. Each fighter connected with jabs and with a few hard rights, but no apparent damage was done. The referee and one judge awarded both rounds to Patterson; the other judge gave Johansson the first and Patterson the second. When the second round was over, Johansson said that "Patterson gave me a bad eye [look]. It's not nice to do that," he nodded, adding, "I thought I could do something about that; so I try to punch harder." In the two rounds, Patterson had come out in his peek-a-boo style. Noting this, Jack Dempsey said to a friend, "He'll get murdered if he sticks to that style." Patterson, meanwhile, had decided that he was going to move in closer in the third round. He had not been impressed with Johansson's jabs. "They tell me," Patterson recalled, "that in the first round Ingemar flicked out his left had 96 times and 107 times in the second, but I can honestly say I never felt one of them." As the jabs seemed more irritating than dangerous, Patterson figured there was little to lose. There was a touch of arrogance in his thinking, hence the scowl that Johansson saw.[19]

With Johansson determined "to punch harder" and Patterson ready to move in closer, combustion was inevitable. As the third round opened, Patterson shot two quick jabs at Johansson's head. With Patterson's left extended, Johansson connected with his vaunted right. The punch was all everyone had said it was, and it sent Patterson to the floor. At the count of nine Patterson

Ingemar Johansson, knocking out Patterson and taking the title from him in their 1959 Yankee Stadium bout. The next year, with equal decisiveness, Patterson would knock out Johansson, becoming the first man to regain the heavyweight title. In 1961 he beat Johansson a second time. Thereafter, the two maintained a warm friendship. ©Bettmann/CORBIS.

was able to wobble to his feet. Johansson immediately swarmed in and dropped Patterson again for nine. No sooner was Patterson on his feet than a series of Johansson lefts put him down, this time for a count of six. He got up and, in but a few seconds, went down for another six count. Now bleeding and groggy, Patterson soon fell again for seven, then once again for nine. Somehow he rose, and Johansson knocked him down once again. At that point the referee, Ruby Goldstein, finally stopped the fight. The time in the third round was 2:03. Seven knockdowns! Taking into account the 46 seconds Patterson had spent on his back that round, it meant that Johansson had floored the champion every 11 seconds. Reporters were reminded of the pasting that Jack Dempsey had given Jess Willard, or the mauling of Primo Carnera by Max Baer. It was as lopsided as those two championships and worse than any other heavyweight victory anyone could remember.[20]

All the previous guffawing about Patterson's less than honorable place among the pantheon of heavyweight champions now seemed to have been quite well taken. As for Patterson, there was little anyone could say. He had been beaten once, by Joey Maxim, and that was a split decision. This was the first time he had been genuinely "whupped." What he went through — the heavy punches, the disorientation — was not something for which he or anyone could prepare in training camp. His main memory was of the fourth knockdown, when he started to rise and found himself looking straight into the eyes of actor John Wayne. He was not imagining. The Duke was at ringside, and he provided no ennoblement. Just the opposite; getting knocked out in front of such a screen idol only added to Patterson's embarrassment. In 1998 one interviewer noted, "Thirty-nine years later, he still cringes at the memory." When Patterson got back to the dressing room, there was Sandra. "She threw her arms around me and embraced me and said something which didn't touch my consciousness at all." Significant was the fact that he could not remember her words. Nothing could reach Patterson at that point. As he confessed: "There was no feeling in me — just a kind of despair and numbness."[21]

VII

It's Never Been Done

As it would be for any fighter, the loss of the championship to Johansson was devastating for Patterson. Some fighters have rhapsodized that a boxer loses some of his soul when he is beaten like that. Patterson reflected this very way. "I was bewildered, ... in a state of shock. Maybe I was even a little bitter.... There was no feeling in me." Not even Sandra could reach him, nor could anyone else — his mother, his friends, "they were so sympathetic," he snarled, and "I hate sympathy." In addition to the fact of the loss came the daily newspapers and the undeniably disrespectful tone they brought to their coverage. "He's got no business being a fighter," scoffed former contender Billy Conn. Before the Johansson fight, many reporters had continued to emphasize Cus D'Amato's excessive control over Patterson's career, with the result being views that Patterson "has yet to gain the acclaim and reputation he undoubtedly deserves." After the loss, the blame no longer fell so squarely upon D'Amato, and phrases like "obviously overrated" began to appear. Former champion Gene Tunney sniffed at Patterson's list of lackluster opponents before Johansson and scornfully lamented: "Because he has no experience [with quality fighters], he's lost his chance at greatness." Even the African American *Pittsburgh Courier* writer Wendell Smith commented in the wake of the Johansson loss that while he had hoped Patterson "would be a stimulant to a rugged, anemic business," he proved to be "one who has added nothing to the fight game whatsoever." Smith gave Patterson a backhanded slap when he consoled his readers upon the occasion of the new year in 1960 that although Patterson had lost the title, "colored American athletes still dominate the boxing rings of the world." "To say that Floyd was a disappointing champion," Smith lamented, "is putting it mildly."

When Patterson defeated Archie Moore in 1956, he had been heralded as the youngest ever to hold the title. Now, two and one half years later, he was noted to be the youngest ever to lose it. An element of nationalism also lay within American journalists' gnashings over the loss. People simply believed, almost axiomatically, that an American should always hold the heavyweight title. While Johansson being a Swede was no issue per se, the fact that the two previous non–American heavyweight champions, Primo Carnera and Max Schmeling, had accompanied Fascist and Nazi regimes made Patterson's loss to a foreigner a trifle more distasteful in some memories. Patterson felt this nationalist sentiment himself: "I'm an American citizen.... Two of my brothers served in the Army. I fought on the U.S. Olympic team. So you can imagine how hurt I was." The crying sense of American boxing fans was that somebody had to bring the title back where it belonged, and Patterson did not seem like the man to do it. Here a few even hoped that Rocky Marciano would come back. Some said that if it were not for the return bout required in the first Patterson-Johansson contract in case of a Johansson victory, Marciano was going to get $1.25 million to face Johansson.[1]

Johansson was the man of the hour, and his dash, good looks, and braggadocio were all good copy for television and the boxing press. He certainly made the most of it. He sang with Dinah Shore on television and acted in a play based on Ernest Hemingway's "The Killers." He went to Hollywood and made a movie about the Korean War called *All The Young Men*. He entertained United Nations troops in the Gaza Strip. He was seen conspicuously with a seemingly endless string of beautiful women (all the while maintaining his engagement to Birgit Lundgren). Through it all, he made a ton of money. Reporters were delighted, noting over and over what a contrast this was to the decade-long dull ways of the heavyweight division.

When Patterson read repeatedly that Johansson holding the crown was the best thing that could happen to boxing, it was impossible for him not to take it personally. Reporter Roger Kahn was brutally blunt here. "Joe Louis," he lamented, "grew fat and bald and plodding.... Ezzard Charles and Joe Walcott were tedious performers, bereft of personality. Then came Rocky Marciano, who missed the real glamour because he took the championship as a monastic calling. Finally," Kahn sighed, "there was Patterson, young, shy, and totally dominated by the strange personality of D'Amato."[2] It was now almost 1960, and it seemed to many that it was time for a new, confident tone in many walks of life from politics to sports. Patterson dropped out of sight, and few reporters showed even a hint of sadness over it.

Patterson went back to his home in Rockville Centre, Long Island. He was occasionally seen mowing his lawn, but otherwise he seemed to be in absolute seclusion for a month. His door was locked; the shutters were closed. Everyone in the house walked and spoke softly. It was, the boxing writer Gay Talese noted, "as if there had been a death in the family." Patterson said he "wasn't ducking anybody," but he admitted, "I didn't want to be bothered with a lot of people." He left his home to have an obligatory medical exam. (Johansson's punches had actually damaged his left eardrum, but it healed.) One night he took Sandy to a drive-in. Otherwise he remained inside except, of course, to go to Sunday Mass. Even then he went late Saturday night to a small church in Brooklyn that offered services at 1:00 A.M., admitting frankly, "there weren't many people there, and that's why I went." He could not sleep well. He would endlessly stare into space, frightening his children to tears. To Talese he ruminated that he "didn't see Johansson's punch coming." Speaking in reassured tones, he reflected, "It was not painful when [Johansson's right] hit me." Nevertheless he conceded that it "was the hardest punch I have ever felt." But, he added, "I felt more hurt pride than anything else. I let so many people down. And I'm not the champion anymore." He noted that "Sandra has been crying all week, and she's asking me to quit."[3]

For Patterson the question of "where do we go from here?" was quite simple. Sandra's desire for him to quit would arise again and again. For the moment, however, Patterson gave it not the slightest thought. "I'm just waiting to get back to camp — in about two weeks." Even amidst the immediate depression after his loss to Johansson, Patterson left no doubt as to his desire to return to the ring. He was also adamant when asked about the possibility of making some changes in his ways. In particular, would he change his controversial peek-a-boo defense? Patterson left no doubt: "My style of fighting won me the title. I'm not going to change. Cus D'Amato's style is the best defense. I was just careless against Johansson." Later he reaffirmed: "Everybody has these stories about changing this, changing that, ... and maybe I should use a different style. Why should I change it. It made me the champion, didn't it?" Patterson was equally firm in response to any questions about D'Amato's alleged mismanagement: "Cus is the greatest, most honest person I know. He's like a father to me. Many sports writers twist around everything that Cus says. But just remember that Cus has no starving fighters; none ... go broke like Joe Louis." Wendell Smith maintained that D'Amato, whom he called "one of the great confidence men of all time," was slickly impoverishing Patterson. This recalled the classic, sad story of so many fighters conned by their managers. Smith put forth no evidence of D'Amato's con game but nonetheless declared Patterson to be "a slave to another man," adding, "why he persists in being so is one of the great mysteries of the age."

Despite such slings and arrows, Patterson was firm in his commitment to D'Amato, and the firmness had a new edge because of the ways that Johansson flaunted his new fame. Others may have delighted in Ingemar's star power, but Patterson seethed. When he saw Johansson smiling on TV and read about him in the newspapers, Patterson reflected, "I sat there and hated him. I had never felt that way before about anybody." Over the next year, Johansson

made repeated statements about his big right hand ("de fist like toonder!").
He claimed that Floyd Patterson never knew what hit him. Of course, Johansson was interested in hyping himself so as to maximize his financial payout from the boxing public. Patterson may have understood that, nevertheless he took it all very personally: "It seemed to me that he went out of his way to disparage me.... He even referred to me once as 'a gymnasium fighter.' All that boasting in public, and his showing off his right-hand punch on television, ... his 'toonder and lightning,' ... I'd be home watching him and *hating* him" (emphasis in the original).[4]

Patterson admitted that the hatred he felt went against his better Christian judgment. "It is a miserable feeling hate. When a man hates, he can't have any peace of mind. And for one solid year I hated him because, after he took everything away from me [and] deprived me of everything I was, he *rubbed it in*" (emphasis his). Patterson's bitterness compounded when, soon after the Johansson loss, some newspapers were reporting that he had been unwilling to give financial support to one of his brothers. It was untrue, and it was genuine salt in the wound as few were as loyal to and supportive of their family as Patterson. Meanwhile, the questions of how Patterson's troubles would resolve were one with his fight future. That future was simple — a rematch with Johansson. Regaining the championship was a tall order. It had never been done. Like many championship fights, the contract for his bout with Johansson contained a rematch clause. Complications arose, however. Some were talking of a rematch as early as September 22 that year, Johansson's birthday. But Johansson had to contend with various government figures angling for his purse money from the first bout, and the legalities took time. Johansson would beat all his opponents here; he would indeed always prove to be a savvy businessman throughout his career. Meanwhile, with everyone expecting a rematch, the questions of when and where remained unresolved. The Johansson-Patterson rematch would certainly be a big money fight. Some said it would be the biggest ever, bigger than any of Jack Dempsey's million dollar gates of the 1920s. With closed circuit television and a good stadium turnout, some predicted a gate of as much as $3 million. Prior to the first fight, promoter Bill Rosensohn had half-jokingly mentioned that a Johansson victory would be great for him as it would set the stage for a big return bout. Rosensohn and his associates got the rematch they desired, but they would not reap the rewards, as a series of investigative battles would affect virtually everyone who had been significantly involved in the first Johansson-Patterson bout.[5]

Through the rest of the year 1959, investigations and legal troubles were endless. New York State Athletic Commissioner Julius Helfand placed Johansson's winning purse of $153,457.17 in escrow. (Johansson would not get his money until June 24, 1960.) Patterson was actually the only major figure not directly affected. Rumors about unsavory characters involved in the promotion of the bout turned into investigations. Fight promoter William Rosensohn hinted that there may have been underworld money involved in the promotion of the Johansson-Patterson fight. Both the New York State Athletic Commission and the Federal District Attorney's office began to investigate. The key person on which both offices fixated concerned one of the chief attorneys involved with Rosensohn's organization, Vincent J. Velella. Velella would eventually own two-thirds of Rosensohn Enterprises, and he had admitted to have had as a client for over ten years one Anthony Salerno, known in boxing circles and in the underworld as "Fat Tony." (The obese character "Clemenza" in the famous 1972 movie *The Godfather* was reportedly modeled on him.) Fat Tony Salerno had a record of 27 arrests, one conviction for grand larceny, for which he served a sentence in Sing Sing Prison, and two indictments for homicide. (He would later die in prison.) His mob ties were unmistakable, and Rosensohn admitted to having accepted a $10,000 loan from him. The boxing world wanted absolutely no appearance of any such underworld ties, as any notions of fixed fights would destroy the credibility of the whole fight game, much as nearly happened to baseball after the 1919 World's Series.

It would be just a few months later, in June of 1960, that the former middleweight champion Jake LaMotta admitted to a U.S. Senate committee that he had purposely lost a fight on November 14, 1947, as a result of mob tampering. With the concurrent investigations into the Patterson-Johansson fight, several important things happened. One was that Rosensohn's organization disbanded. Rosensohn maintained that there was no gambling money behind the staging of the Patterson-Johansson fight. Still his associations were shady to say the least. The papers were full of lines about gangsters invading the heavyweight scene, and Rosensohn lost his license to match and promote fights in New York for three years.[6]

As boxing people scattered with all the inquiries, new promotion enterprises had to form. Amidst the fluidity of the management situation, the question of who could put the best promotion package together led to various locales again vying for the right to host the Johansson-Patterson rematch. Jack Dempsey made some noises about forming a promotion team. Some Los Angeles promoters pushed the idea of the big fight there, with the vast L.A. Coliseum as the venue. With Johansson holding the title, several European promoters made the logical point that the fight should take place on their home turf. (The key was whether they could put together enough money to make it worthwhile for the combatants. As it turned out, they could not.) With all the troubles in America, some European boxing organizers also wanted to forget Patterson for the moment and set a fight for Johansson against the British champion, Henry Cooper. Back in the U.S., non–New York promoters stepped forth. Besides the Los Angeles people, a Philadelphia group made efforts to host the fight, as did another in Miami. Bob Short, then owner of the Minneapolis Lakers basketball team, tried to woo Johansson, playing up the region's Scandinavian ethnicity, even though it was largely Norwegian, not Swedish, with many Norwegians hardly feeling much kinship here. Talk also popped up among American pundits of Johansson fighting not Patterson but Archie Moore or even Rocky Marciano. Marciano himself added to the speculation when he shrugged to reporters: "How can you not listen when people talk about a million and two million dollars."[7]

New Yorkers grew indignant, as well as a bit nervous, about the prospect of the rematch going anywhere else. An old New York fight promoter named Humbert J. (Jack) Fugazy came out of semi-retirement at age 73. He had been known as a friendly, honest organizer, whose only bad pattern in his career involved the fact that it often rained on the nights he staged fights, hence the nickname by which he was fondly known: "Hard Luck" Fugazy. Fugazy would serve as the lead figure in an organization, Feature Sports, Inc., that would be above any of the reproach that brought down Rosensohn and his associates. Feature Sports bought up the remnants of Rosensohn's organization and began work in earnest. The real brains and energy behind Fugazy came from his son, William Fugazy, and from his partner, a young attorney, already known for his work in Washington earlier in the decade, Roy Cohn. Cohn, of course, had been the chief counsel to Senator Joseph Raymond McCarthy during the infamous anti-communist campaigns of the early 1950s. Many have subsequently regarded Cohn to have been nothing but a depraved witch hunter, but in 1960 Cohn's name and reputation were perfect as far as professional boxing people were concerned when it came to their desire to give the fight world a squeaky clean image with the public. (Certain aspects of Cohn's personal life, especially his homosexuality, were simply not discussed.)[8]

Another bit of fallout from the investigations of improper associations and activities in regard to the first Patterson-Johansson fight concerned Cus D'Amato. Investigators looked into any possible impropriety, and they found several points with D'Amato. He had associated with a man named Charles Black, a convicted gambler and a known affiliate of illegal bookmakers. Through D'Amato, Black had become part of the Roy Harris camp when the latter fought Patterson. This smacked of collusion, and, moreover, in a fight of dubious quality from the outset. D'Amato placed another questionable friend, Nick Baffi, in Brian London's corner during the 1959 bout in Indianapolis. D'Amato actually claimed here that he was afraid the International Boxing Club was going to kidnap Brian London! (Many chuckled, sarcastically here, wondering why the mob would ever think of kidnapping such a ridiculously inept pug as London.) All such potential conflicts of interest among ring seconds looked shady. D'Amato had also served as both a matchmaker and participating promoter in the Patterson-Johansson fight; that was explicitly against the NYAC rules. He had tried to foist on Johansson a manager named Harry Davidow and another buddy, Daryl Davidson, a move which if successful (Johansson cagily refused him) would have given D'Amato control over both contestants, thus indicating another attempt at monopolizing. Patterson was not pleased when he learned of D'Amato's conniving here—"'kind of an alarm clock for me," he recalled. D'Amato also failed to file a manager's report within five dates of the bout. And he failed to testify when called before the New York State Athletic Commission.

Taken in isolation, each of these charges may not have come to much. Even collectively, they may have amounted to little were it not for the shady aura and issues that were increasingly surrounding the June '59 bout. The New York State Attorney General's Office also made its own investigations of the events surrounding the June fight. D'Amato was issued a subpoena, and, stupidly (there can be no other word for it), he failed to appear. D'Amato was always a slick talker, one who fully believed in his own street-wise verbal capacity to finesse any situation in which he found himself. But here his famous feistiness was not going to carry the day. He denied any links to Fat Tony Salerno. In regard to other charges like those relating to Davidson, Black and Baffi, he simply, and quite feebly, claimed he did not remember. Rosensohn gave testimony about D'Amato which supported the charges that he had been in restraint of competition with regard to the Johansson fight. In November of 1959, that testimony combined with D'Amato's failure to comply with calls to testify and lead the NYAC to revoke his license to manage or serve as a second for professional fighters in New York. D'Amato's failure to comply with a state attorney general's subpoena got him a 30-day jail sentence, suspended. (If he took up any association with the upcoming Patterson-Johansson fight, however, he would go to jail.) After all his allegedly railings against the evils of the International Boxing Club, D'Amato had certainly lost that saintly aura he had tried so hard to cultivate. One reporter now brazenly dubbed him "a ridiculous manager." He was now out of Patterson's corner, and on the mere margin at his training camp.[9]

Without having to deal with D'Amato, the Fugazy-Cohn syndicate was able to put together a package for the Patterson-Johansson rematch, and they pushed through the legal thickets to hold it in New York. The old Polo Grounds, underutilized since the departure of the baseball Giants in 1957, would be the site. The only conflict in the use of the Polo Grounds concerned a fledgling, and ultimately unsuccessful International Soccer League which had been using the Polo Grounds for its New York games. Its finances paled before the levels of a heavyweight championship fight, and they were easily compensated.[10]

With Cus D'Amato now relegated to the sidelines in the Patterson camp, to many reporters there appeared a kind of liberation for Patterson. He had been through a long, depressive trough of "blackness and despair," but it had passed. Baseball great Jackie Robinson stopped by and assured him that they were friends, no matter what. That meant a lot. A letter from Archie Moore did too. He'd lost big fights, so he could say to Patterson that "he knew how he felt" and have it mean something. Moore was also blunt: "You fought a stupid battle," he wrote, "Look at the film. Evaluate it. Never once did you lead with a jab. All you did was move your feet and try to leap toward him.... If you concentrate on your jab and move around this guy, you will be the first one to regain the crown." Moore's advice confirmed any thoughts that he should remain confident in his basic style. Other things also finally lifted Patterson. "One night," he recalled to reporter Arthur Daley,

> my wife went upstairs and left me watching television. Finally I turned off the set and just sat there alone, thinking again. Suddenly a thought popped into my mind. I don't know where it came from or why. But I thought of the time I visited the wards in a cancer hospital. There was one little girl, maybe 4 or 5 years old. Her arms and legs were no thicker than my finger. She was wasted away.
>
> When I walked out of the room, the doctor said to me, "she won't live twelve hours more." I'd never seen her before but I was heartsick. As I sat at home that night, I thought of the little girl who really knew what trouble was. I jumped to my feet "Who am I to feel sorry for myself?" I said out loud. The next day I walked out of my front door, ready to face people for the first time in a month and a half. I was cured.

The next evening he took Sandy out to a club. He arranged for an exhibition tour of Canada and took it with his family just before Christmas.

In addition to overcoming most of his depression, Patterson was now more fully and personally in charge of his own professional life. With D'Amato's suspension, Patterson could have severed all ties and turned to someone else. Instead he quietly took more personal control. He made no pompous declaration of independence. "I'm not going to change my style of fighting," he declared. "The peek-a-boo style is the best for me. When I drop my hands, I get hit. I pick off too many punches with my gloves to discard it. It brought me to the championship and that is good enough proof for me." As for D'Amato, there was no dramatic pronouncement: "Cus is still my friend," but, he emphasized, "I'm my own manager now." Dan Florio was his chief trainer. He kept an attorney, Julius November, to look after the details of all contracts. "But," Patterson remarked, looking ahead, "if I win the championship again, I intend to call the shots." Johansson had shown himself to be that very sort of self-manager, and Patterson recognized it as the obvious way to proceed. "Eventually," Patterson reflected, "the son grows up." When asked after the Johansson rematch who had been the greatest influence upon him, Patterson answered firmly: "Floyd Patterson."[11]

Few gave much notice to Patterson's maturing. "Patterson will hardly do better," was Wendell Smith's sad prognostication. In the eyes of the pundits in the press, Patterson was still clearly the *former* champion in every respect. Virtually all boxing eyes were on the charismatic champion. Johansson had been better copy, more "affable" and "witty." As before their first fight, the same contrast impressed reporters about the two camps. Patterson trained in spartan conditions in Newtown, Connecticut. One reporter described the camp as "an abandoned road house that was buried in the Connecticut woodlands. Paint was peeling from the walls, plaster was cracked and neglect had taken over." Meanwhile, Johansson again trained hard and luxuriated at Grossinger's. Patterson disdained all frivolity, as well his wife and family. Meanwhile, Johansson's motto was: "Don't let training interfere with living." Reporters delighted in it, and all the time they were largely ignoring Patterson. One day in early 1960, it snowed heavily up in Connecticut, and Patterson and his trainer Dan Florio were snowbound. No one was on hand to help shovel them out. The press and all fair-weather friends were long gone. At the Connecticut training camp, Patterson even had to hang out his own washing. The main thing the press noted from Patterson's training was that one day one of his young sparring partners, José Torres, had knocked him down. (It was a slip.) So many contrasts between the two combatants thus seemed just as the year before, so this time the odds-makers set Johansson an 8–5 favorite.[12]

Conspicuously, former champion Joe Louis came to Patterson's camp to help analyze Johansson's style and give Patterson tactical advice. D'Amato may have objected had he still been present, but he was now playing no role in the preparations. Even over the matter of Joe Louis, however, Johansson again won himself a kudo in the press. Louis said that in helping Patterson prepare, he was going to try to watch Johansson train and joked here about how he may have to sneak into Johansson's camp: "If the United States can send a spy plane to the Soviet Union, why can't I go to the Johansson camp?" Johansson merely smiled graciously: "I have always been an admirer of Joe Louis. He does not have to come here as a spy. He is welcome anytime as a friend." While Johansson was conspicuously magnanimous here, Louis's visits did provide some insights for Patterson. Jack Dempsey thought they would: "Joe's a smart guy. I'm sure he'll make Floyd stop peeking from behind his gloves this time." Louis felt that Patterson had been too flat-footed in his loss to Johansson. He recommended that Patterson try to keep Johansson close, work on his body to bring his guard down, and not let him get set in the middle of the ring. "The only way to beat a puncher," Louis surmised, "is to crowd him. If you give him punching room, he'll beat your brains out." Louis predicted Patterson would need seven to ten rounds to defeat Johansson. After visiting Johansson, Louis revised his prediction — to eleven rounds.[13]

Louis may have picked Patterson, but other former champions were not so supportive, some were downright disrespectful. Max Schmeling scoffed, "Patterson is not a real heavyweight. Johansson is. My guess is Johansson by a knockout. Only a miracle could give Patterson a chance at a knockout — a wild lucky punch." Jack Dempsey, who had predicted a Patterson victory in the first fight, nodded: "I got to go with the puncher, the guy who can end it with one punch. Johansson's right is a helluva punch. Patterson? He's an amateur." Gene Tunney conceded that he previously "took a dim view of Patterson as a champion." His views had not changed. Patterson, he said, "was a novice. I think Johansson will do it again — an early knockout." James Braddock was not so insulting, but he did note that in the first bout "Patterson fought a foolish fight. If he stands in front of Johansson again," Braddock thought, "it'll be quick." Rocky Marciano cited Johansson's right as "the best right I've ever seen." He concluded that Johansson was "too strong and too tough for Patterson," concluding "it could end early." A few champs like Jack Sharkey and Primo Carnera conjectured that Johansson's KO could have been a lucky punch and that Patterson had likely learned not to be so careless. Noting all the high living Johansson had enjoyed while champion, Sharkey worried that Johansson may be overconfident. Aside from Joe Louis, the only other ex-champion who picked Patterson was Jersey Joe Walcott. (As he had never seen Johansson fight, Ezzard Charles offered no opinion.) "At the last fight," affirmed Walcott, "Floyd was stale. He beat himself. He won't do it again."[14] Aside from Jack Sharkey, everyone who picked Patterson was black, and all who picked Johansson were white. Doubtlessly, this was not a completely conscious matter, but the pattern was striking.

While few took notice, Patterson expressed confidence. "I think I was trained too fine for the last fight," he noted to the African American *Pittsburgh Courier*. "I'll be heavier this time. It will cut down on my speed, but I think it will add to my hitting power.... [Last time] I was fooled by his training methods, the reports of his lack of a big punch and by the odds of 6 to 1. I won't be fooled this time." Later he added: "I won't be afraid of Johansson, or his right, when we meet.... This fight is going to be entirely different." For most fighters this sort of bragging is nothing unusual, but it was different for Patterson, perhaps an extension of his new independence from D'Amato. His passive voice phrasing — "I *was trained*" — seemed obviously directed. Even though he was not optimistic about Patterson's chances, the *Courier*'s Wendell Smith chortled here about Cus, not fully recognizing the changes that had come over Patterson: "D'Amato is not a good man for Patterson to have around.... It is strange, indeed," Smith noted, "that Patterson — the man — can't see how ridiculous Cus D'Amato is. Perhaps he will after this return fight ... but it may be too late then. If he loses, which is likely, it really won't matter who manages him." Wendell Smith openly picked Johansson.

"Johansson is too big and too strong.... Floyd has our best wishes, but they won't help him much." Patterson read the press, and he expressly noted the "nasty digs" that came from the likes of Wendell Smith. He shrugged it all off: "A reporter must have something to write about in order to keep the public interested." Another reporter from the *Courier*, Bill Nunn, did note Patterson's quiet confidence. "What I found," he said, "was a man who has undying faith in GOD and in HIMSELF as a fighter" (emphasis his).[15]

The daily blurbs of the papers covered the preparations for the fight. The usual hyping took place, although little was needed, as public interest in the rematch was keen. The unique and compelling factor here which was receiving the largest amount of attention concerned the fact that Patterson was trying to do the unprecedented. No one had ever lost the heavyweight championship and then regained it. The nation's barber shops and bars were full of such talk, and the foreign press was abuzz of it too. (By fight time, 100 foreign press requests had come to Bill Fugazy.) Several of the all-time greats had tried but failed to regain the heavyweight championship. John L. Sullivan could not do it, neither could Jim Corbett. Jim Jeffries had come back from retirement and lost to Jack Johnson in 1910. Jack Dempsey had lost to Gene Tunney in the famous 1927 "long-count" bout. In the late 1940s, Joe Louis failed against Ezzard Charles and Joe Walcott. With such a legacy, there seemed a certain jinx confronting Patterson's quest. Perhaps with a bit of this history in mind, the only fuss Patterson raised before the fight involved his insistence that Ruby Goldstein not serve as the referee. Goldstein had reffed Patterson's first bout with Johansson. The parties agreed, and Arthur Mercante would be the referee this time. Often, Patterson still appeared his usual subdued self, sometimes striking a pose which, to some reporters, continued to seem odd coming from a boxer about to go into the ring. On the one hand, Patterson did snarl: "Johansson's got something that belongs to me and I'm going to get it back." That was what people expected from boxers. Elsewhere, he reflected "I feel I can beat him," he told reporters. "I feel it but I could be wrong." Convinced that he had eclipsed the habits and errors that led to the loss to Johansson, Patterson added with a decidedly modest edge: "If he [Johansson] should win, I want him to know he was in a fight. I don't want it to be easy for him — the way it was last time. I want to come out of the ring like a man."[16]

Ever since Jack Johnson had engendered such rampant racial fears in the nation, black fighters had avoided too much braggadocio. Joe Louis was counseled along these very lines. With Patterson it was more than mere counseling. It was his nature. Still, he was in as angry a mood as he had ever been in his adult life. Ever since the loss to Johansson, he had not looked at the fight film. He just couldn't. Without realizing it, he was being a master psychologist with himself. He let his confidence reemerge; he let his anger build;

he trained hard. Then, just three weeks before the bout, with his mind and body in peak form, he finally watched the fight film. It was not depressing, for it was now like watching another fighter. He analyzed what had gone wrong and made his plans. "How could I be so bad," Patterson wondered confidently. "I knew I could do better on my worst day." Patterson was more intent here than at any time in his career. "I never in my life felt the way I did before the [second Johansson] fight. I wanted to hurt him. I not only wanted to win, I wanted to get *him*. It wasn't his arrogance.... It was what I was reading about me and my chances that made me so mad."[17]

One major difference from the night of the first fight was the fact that on June 20, 1960, the weather cooperated. It did not rain, and the fight came off as planned. Fugazy and Cohn were pleased with the crowd that grew to over 31,892, especially the 4500 who paid $100 apiece for ringside seats. In addition, the closed circuit television audiences totaled 484,894. New York governor Nelson Rockefeller was at ringside, as was former governor Thomas Dewey and former champions Jack Dempsey, Gene Tunney, and Joe Louis. Cus D'Amato sat in the ringside area too. Just before the opening bell, Patterson's trainer, Buster Watson, a usually light-hearted man who could always make Patterson laugh, gave Patterson a serious look and simply said, "This is it, Pat." "Maybe it's because Buster never talks that way. I don't know," Patterson remembered, "but it got me in the right mood at the start of the fight."[18]

As the fight began, Patterson followed Joe Louis's advice, and sought to crowd Johansson. In the first rounds, there was little feeling out, as both knew fully what to expect from the other. Patterson won the first round on all cards, catching Johansson with several stiff left hooks, driving him to the ropes with a strong attack, and opening a cut under Johansson's left eye. Johansson came back and swept the second round on all cards. He hit Patterson with one of his vaunted rights. The crowd gasped, remembering the first bout, but Patterson shook it off. "This time," he noted, "I saw the punch coming; [I] ducked a bit, and the blow landed too high on my head. Momentarily I was stunned, but not enough that I wouldn't know completely what was happening." Patterson had planned to clinch if in trouble. He did and bought himself a little needed time. While in the clinch, Patterson looked at one of the ring commentators, Irving Kahn, and winked at him, letting him know that he was not hurt. After the referee separated them, Patterson back-pedaled. Here, perhaps Johansson should have charged him with complete abandon. Instead, he hesitated ever so slightly. Patterson thus realized that Johansson saw "that he wasn't fighting the same guy who had been so easy for him twelve months earlier.... It was the look of a man who understood that things were going to be different this time." The trouble passed. Patterson's head cleared, and the round ended with Patterson feeling a certain confidence about Johansson's apparent outlook.

The third round was close; referee Arthur Mercante called it even, while the two judges each gave it to Patterson. Patterson appeared to gain an edge in the fourth, landing the greater number of punches, winning the round on all cards. Still, Johansson hit Patterson with a good right just as the round ended, and as they entered the fifth round the bout's outcome still seemed an open question. Then came the fifth. Patterson scored several solid shots to Johansson's face. Johansson countered with one solid shot to the body. Patterson was not fazed, however, and he suddenly landed a right that dropped Johansson for a count of nine. Johansson was up, and so was the crowd. Patterson bore in, landing several shots. Johansson scored one right to the body, but this left him open to Patterson's left. Patterson did not miss the opportunity. He quickly threw a left hook. "I have never tried to throw a harder punch," Patterson recalled. The swing of Patterson's punch took him off his feet, and the blow landed squarely on Johansson's jaw. Johansson went down, and he was out. He lay there on his back motionless, bleeding from the mouth and his left foot twitching eerily. Patterson's blow to the side of Johansson's jaw had violently twisted his head and unleashed a flood of nerve impulses from the reticular activating mechanism of the base of his brain. When this mechanism is suddenly overcharged by nerve signals, the victim can easily lose consciousness immediately (and his feet can twitch). Johansson certainly did. He fell to the canvas. Mercante counted to ten, and Johansson did not move, nor would he for a full ten minutes.[19]

All the carping and moaning about Patterson having been a boring champion all changed, as did all the journalistic delight in the high living and apparent less-than-ascetic training of Johansson. When Patterson decked Johansson, one reporter chuckled how Johansson "went down like a double portion of Swedish pancakes with lingonberries and sour cream." (Johansson did come into the fight heavier, 206½, than any bout he'd previously fought, so the training traditionalists likely had a point. Patterson, at 190, was eight pounds heavier than he had been for the first fight, but his was a lean eight.) The fickle winds of popular and journalistic perception shifted. Patterson had achieved the unprecedented. He had regained the heavyweight crown. He raised his hands in triumph with a euphoria no one had ever seen from him. Yet in the very next moment, Patterson's euphoria ceased. Unnerved by Johansson's convulsive shaking and twitching, Patterson ran over to Johansson and knelt by his head, trying to talk to him and to see if he was OK. The concern was real. "I was scared I had hurt him badly.... I'd never seen anybody shake like that. I was frightened." Back and forth the emotions ran in him, as the ring quickly swelled with officials and well-wishers, all now trying to get near the re-crowned champion. The ecstasy was there, but it had a slightly troubled edge. Patterson would renounce any feelings of hatred after that. As long as he was the champion, fans and sports writers would hold such transcended thoughts in awe and respect. After Patterson later lost, many of the same fans would point to such renunciations with derision. As in military and political matters, in boxing all fame is fickle and fleeting.[20]

Fans all over the Polo Grounds were cheering wildly for Patterson. The nation celebrated, in significant measure because the heavyweight crown was now back in the United States. Cus D'Amato, seated in the sixth row near ringside, was chortling to people, "I told you he could punch." "Floyd, Floyd, I'm over here," he yelled. Patterson could not hear him, however. The crowd noise was too much. Patterson looked into the crowd. He caught the eye of actor James Cagney, and they exchanged smiles. Joe Louis came in the ring and warmly shook Patterson's hand. His smile of congratulations and respect was unmistakably earnest. Johansson did get up. His handlers sat him in the corner. His head cleared, and his manager assured the TV announcers that his fighter was not hurt. That night in New York City, African American communities were rejoicing in ways that recalled nights of some of Joe Louis's triumphs. Elsewhere in New York, the television Emmy awards ceremony was taking place. Dancer Fred Astaire interrupted the proceedings to announce to all that Patterson had won. The crowd went wild there too. Patterson had brought the championship back to the United States. For the historic regaining of the crown, for neighborhoods like Harlem, for the country, he was a hero to everyone. Sandra had agreed to stay away from the Polo Grounds. She was nine months pregnant with their third child (who would be born on July 8). That night she could not stay away, however, and she secretly went to the fight. As the fight celebration grew, she found Cus D'Amato, and he took her to the locker room. Floyd was anything but mad. Only one thing could have made the moment sweeter for them, and it actually came. It was not a phone call from the president, who was returning from a not-so-successful trip to the Far East. President Eisenhower was actually interested in the fight. Indeed, films of the fight were flown to Hawaii especially so he could see them while flying back to Washington. For Patterson, however, even the idea of that the President was a fan paled before something else: he received a telegram of congratulations from Pope John XXIII![21]

VIII

On Top of the Boxing World

With the victory over Ingemar Johansson, Patterson experienced the joy of complete vindication. "Patterson," wrote Wendell Smith, "forced the prognosticators who brushed him off as an imposter to swallow their words." Smith was, himself, among the "swallowers," as he had picked Johansson. "Please pass the crow," Smith graciously conceded. "It's dinner time." Floyd had been utterly depressed after his loss to Johansson, and as he had prepared for the return bout he incessantly endured questions about whether he would crumble at first sight of Johansson's big right hand. The loss and such humiliating questions had motivated him to work extra hard, even by his standards, in preparation for the return bout. The work obviously paid off. Johansson would get a rematch, of course. The site and the usual details would have to be worked out. Meanwhile, Patterson could sit well with the knowledge that he had defeated everything before him.[1] He was on top.

In certain respects, Johansson was almost a minor obstacle among the many victories for Patterson at that moment. He had defeated his detractors who had disrespectfully sniffed at him for being a less-than-worthy champion. He had shown those who speculated that he could do nothing without Cus D'Amato, and he had overcome the image that had grown as a result of the list of nobodies he had fought before Johansson. "Cus was in a big battle with the International Boxing Club," Patterson conceded. "I was the only thing he had to fight with.... I went along with Cus and I don't regret doing it. In going along," he admitted, "I didn't develop as fast as a fighter as I would have otherwise." All that debate and controversy was not behind him, but for the moment it certainly died down, especially in October 1960, when the IBC officially disbanded. Even more deeply, Patterson had overcome his own past — the little kid who hid for days in the subways; the boy who

shoplifted from grocery stores because he felt ashamed he was not contributing to his family's budget. It was at this time that he began his own memoir
about it all. Fittingly he would call it *Victory Over Myself*. He had indeed
beaten his demons; Ingemar Johansson's big right hand was the least of it.
Patterson hoped most deeply that his testimony could serve as inspiration to
other troubled young people.[2]

When Patterson first became champion after beating Archie Moore in
1955, a grocer in his old Brooklyn neighborhood had asked him for an autographed picture. Patterson graciously obliged, and the grocer proudly displayed the picture in his store for all his customers to see. When Patterson
lost to Johansson, the picture suddenly disappeared from the grocer's shop.
Patterson learned of this but never commented. He obviously had many more
important things on his mind. Then when Patterson beat Johansson, the same
grocer had the unmitigated gall to ask if he could have another autographed
picture. Patterson did not oblige. Beyond the fact of it being a bemusing little story, it underscored something Patterson had learned while he did not
hold the championship — how shallow some of his alleged friendships were.
"I lost the title and my phone stopped ringing," he noted. "When I [won it
back] my phone started ringing again. This time I didn't answer it." From
the point when he was no longer completely under the stewardship of Cus
D'Amato, Patterson had learned to consider all friendships in the boxing business with a most decided grain of salt. Even with respect to D'Amato, Patterson once winced: "Cus thinks I'm Superman. Sometimes I have to run away
and shut the door." D'Amato would never be shut out of the picture, but
after his troubles with the NYAC, Cus never again exercised the full command he first held. Patterson was firm in his answer to the critics who had
been complaining that Cus had damaged his career. "Whatever anybody says
about him, I don't think he ever did anything to intentionally hurt me. Right
now I'm not even bound to Cus by a contract. But actually there will never
be any need for a contract. He'll get his share like he's always done and I won't
mind one bit.... People will say I'm crazy for going along with Cus now, but
that is the way I am and I hope I'll never change." Patterson would never fall
into the trap to which the egos of many famous boxers let themselves fall
prey — of letting an expensive and parasitic entourage, complete with its own
lilliputian "palace" politics, build up around him. Sugar Ray Robinson would
be a victim of this, as would Muhammad Ali. At times, especially when he
was down, Patterson's relatively simple organization-coterie was part of what
led reporters to decry about his dullness, but others recognized the wisdom
in his ways — as long as he was winning. Recognizing that Patterson's "habits
have long baffled boxing's epicures [*and*] freeloaders," the *New York Times*'
Gay Talese emphasized how Patterson is simply "an introvert who ... thrives
on solitude and meditation." His diffidence, Talese noted, was not to be con-

fused with a lack of confidence: "He is supremely sure of his talent," a lot more than was a certain grocery store owner in Brooklyn.[3]

Once again, Patterson, the re-crowned champion, was the toast of all. Some wanted to celebrate him; others wanted to use Patterson's celebrity for their own gain. Patterson would be always wary of the mix at play here. A week after the Johansson victory, New York mayor Robert Wagner held an afternoon ceremony for Patterson in front of City Hall, where he gave Patterson the city's Bronze Medallion. Harlem congressman Adam Clayton Powell tried to turn the Patterson hoopla here into a kind of competition, for obvious election-year reasons. He called upon the mayor to do more and hold a Lindbergh-type ticker-tape parade up Broadway in connection with the City Hall ceremony. The parade did not occur, but Powell accomplished what he wanted. He knew Patterson was wildly popular in his Harlem congressional district. By outdoing all and grabbing press notice with his posture of adoration of Patterson, Powell helped himself politically. That fall he easily secured reelection to Congress.

Cus D'Amato, now back in Patterson's corner, bought Floyd a three-pound gold crown, studded with assorted diamonds, rubies, sapphires, and cultured pearls. Its estimated worth was then $35,000. The president of Ghana sent him a ceremonial robe. On and on it went. One touching little gift was an oil painting from a twelve-year-old boy at the Wiltwyck School. With all the celebrating, Patterson held onto his quiet, strong sense of self and the sense of what was worth his time and energy. That June and July, right after his victory over Johansson, he had offers for all sorts of appearances. Incredibly to some reporters, Patterson accepted very few of them. He attended a testimonial dinner, making sure all the proceeds went to Wiltwyck. Another thing he made a point of doing was to attend the graduation exercises of New York P.S. 614. He would never forget his feeling of obligation to help the boys and pay his respects to the teachers at the schools that had helped him so much. There was nothing incredible about this to Patterson. He simply knew his real friends and his true obligations. He had also learned that ultimately he had best to depend only upon himself. After Patterson defeated Johansson, Jackie Robinson went to visit him at his New York hotel. There were parties all over the hotel, as well as all over the city. With jubilation all around him, Robinson entered Patterson's suite and found him "sitting in the room all by himself playing solitaire." The last words in Patterson's autobiography state, with absolutely no lament or regret: "I am alone. Is there any other way?"[4]

There was, of course, the one constant of Sandra. When asked if anything could have given him greater pleasure than beating Johansson, Patterson responded, "I don't believe so." Then he immediately added, "but I couldn't have beaten Ingemar without my wife, Sandra. She goes along with whatever I say. Don't forget that when I go away to live in camp, she's lonely too. I don't think there is any other woman who could have endured the things my wife has." Patterson mused further: "If every fighter was married to a Sandra, I would really have troubles." Sandra would not always go along with Patterson's wishes, but that would come later. For the time being Patterson had the assurance that comes with such total support and love. Given his difficult past, it was more than he could have ever imagined. About the only bad personal mishap that year concerned an attempt by the CBS television show *This is Your Life* to set up a surprise show with Patterson. The plans leaked. The surprise was gone, and the effort had to be scrubbed.[5]

A much more sobering point for Patterson was the fact that there still remained the issues that every African American was facing in the country in 1960. When Johansson knocked out Patterson in 1959, one radio announcer had indeed immediately yelled: "We have a fair-haired champion!" As a youth, Patterson had been stung by many taunts from racists, just like any kid on the streets of a major city. As an adult there was more of the same, no matter his notoriety. There were some genuine liberals who saw Patterson's triumphant regaining of the crown as an example of perseverance in which all could rejoice. "In my own small way," Patterson had noted to the *Pittsburgh Courier*, just before he beat Johansson, "I think I can help us gain a little more stature if I become the first man to ever win back the heavyweight championship. Every bit helps us to the day when there won't be such a thing as race prejudice, when we will all be equal." In June, 1960, however, that day was anything but on hand. Patterson still suffered many stings of racism. As for so very many African Americans, his travels in the South had yielded nasty roadside hostilities at service stations and restaurants. The victory over Johansson led some to speculate that Johansson had to have been drugged or poisoned, with the implicit question being: how else could Patterson have won? (No one besmirched Johansson's victory of the previous year in any such way.) Soon after he defeated Johansson, Patterson's wife, Sandra, made an appointment at a beauty parlor near their home in Rockville Centre, only to find that the parlor manager, upon learning of Mrs. Patterson's race, cancelled her reservation, telling her the salon's schedule was full. Patterson had his lawyer's wife go the same salon, and, sure enough, she got her hair done without an appointment.[6]

When Patterson had been training in Greenwood Lake, N.Y., for the bouts with Pete Rademacher and Hurricane Jackson, he had befriended a number of nine and ten year old boys who had been hanging around his training site. He decided to take them under his wing, let them do road work with him, and teach them some basic boxing skills, with the hopes that his guidance and training discipline would serve as a good example to them as they grew into manhood. "Giving back" like that while disciplining himself to the otherwise often selfish processes of training was always important to

Patterson, and he later reflected: "I don't believe I had ever gotten any more deep-down pleasure than from watching those kids develop." The mother of one of the boys told him that the boxing training had definitely taken her son off a bad and onto a good path in life. After the Jackson and Rademacher fights, Patterson often took time away from his obligations in New York to travel up to Greenwood Lake to visit the boys and give them boxing lessons, and he had always taken the time to check up on their marks in school. Several newsmen gave coverage to Patterson's work here. Some offered Patterson payments for his time in regard to the stories and photo opportunities, and Patterson always told them to put the money into a Christmas fund for the boys. Then suddenly in 1958, after Patterson had taken his tour of Great Britain, he returned to Greenwood Lake. He found the children no longer interested in or allowed to train with him. It did not seem credible that all the boys would move on like that. Patterson indeed learned that some of the locals and parents had spread rumors that Patterson was merely exploiting the children for financial profit and publicity. Patterson was deeply hurt by this poisonous gossiping. "To this day," he later lamented, "I don't understand how any adult could have poisoned a kid's mind like that." If Ingemar Johansson had worked with the same boys, the parents would likely have been delighted. At work here was racial ignorance and hatred, pure and simple (and ugly).[7]

There were other struggles for Patterson too. Within his family he endured troubles with his older brother Billy. Patterson did everything for his parents and siblings. He bought them a house in Westchester County, and they were all grateful and hugely supportive of Floyd — all except Billy. Billy, five years older than Floyd, had been a fighter and a good one. When Floyd first entered the boxing gym, Billy entered the ring against him. Told to take it easy, Billy nonetheless, Patterson recalled, "hit me with a right hand that almost took my head off." Billy happened to develop eye trouble and had to give up the game. Whatever the resentments there or at deeper levels, he always held a grudge. "I've never been able to understand why Billy has always been jealous of me," Floyd mused. "I've never tried to hurt him — ever — but he hasn't returned the favor." He helped Billy with the finances of a restaurant Billy had started in New York. Floyd made repeated appearances there to help the place attract customers. The restaurant venture did not succeed, however, and Billy gave a story to a New York writer that the reason the place went bankrupt was because Floyd refused him a loan. Relations between Floyd and the rest of his family were excellent. With Billy he just had to bear up stoically.[8]

To the public, Patterson may have appeared to feel on top of the world, but he knew it was only of the world of boxing. The struggles of African Americans against segregation and racism were anything but over; indeed they were entering a new chapter at the very time that Patterson reclaimed the championship. The Southern Christian Leadership Conference, the Congress of Racial Equality, and other such organizations were just emerging into significant organizations that would help shape so much of the social and political transformation of the United States in the 1960s, and it was during Patterson's championship years that such groups were developing many of their famous non-violent principles, strategies, and tactics. They had already begun to use boycotts, sit-ins, and demonstrations. Television would give much coverage to their work, as would the participation of many famous people. In the late 1950s and very early 1960s, however, the levels of publicity and general public awareness had a long way to go to be called widespread. There were great risks for those who chose to be involved. With little public and media scrutiny, the reactionary forces of opposition felt more comfortable about using any means they felt necessary to resist change and sustain segregation. Threats of violence were always present. For Patterson, the issues were clear. He did not feel any urge to make himself a focus of the press's attention on the subject. He felt there were others who could speak to the issues far more eloquently than he. He was but a boxer. Not as a boxer but as a man he wanted to do what he could, however. With absolutely no fanfare, in 1961, for example, he traveled to Jackson, Mississippi, for a CORE fund raiser. Local papers like the *Jackson Clarion-Ledger* gave such work as that of CORE no coverage, except for some disapproving editorials. They felt the less said the better other than to brand such people as mere agitators. When Patterson arrived at the Jackson airport, there was but one fan and her son waiting to greet the heavyweight champion and ask for an autograph. Patterson graciously obliged, of course. An athlete of more theatrical bent would have used such occasions to trumpet himself and his activities. Many of the civil rights leaders of the day may have doubtlessly preferred such self-promotion and the extra media coverage and publicity it would generate. Patterson, however, was almost scrupulous in his avoidance of such self-promotion. Others may have wanted it, but it was not in Patterson's nature to behave that way.[9]

While the major social issues of America would occupy much of Patterson's time, he also had to dedicate himself to his next bout. Even here the snares of racism hovered. There was no doubt what was on the horizon — a rematch with Johansson. There were the usual wrangles over the site and over money. Los Angeles made a strong bid, as did Dallas, through the work of oil tycoon Lamar Hunt. The same promotion organization, Feature Sports, Inc., and its two leaders, Bill Fugazy and attorney Roy Cohn, were handling all the details concerning the fight date and location. While Patterson was outwardly content leaving such matters in their hands, he held back on anything that could be considered warmth or friendship. During the negotiations, Roy Cohn noted what sharp business acumen Ingemar Johansson had shown. In contrast, when Patterson's lawyer, Julius November, had asked

Cohn whether Patterson should see any of the preliminary contracts, Cohn sniffed: "Floyd? Can he read?"[10]

Leaving the bickering and unpleasantness of the promotions behind him for a time, Patterson left New York in August, 1960 and toured Europe. Ingemar Johansson and he were both genuine gentlemen. They had come to respect and admire one another, no matter what they did to one another in the ring, and it was Johansson who set up a series of exhibitions for Patterson in Sweden. Patterson earned about $14,000 for his exhibitions. As had occurred back in 1952 when he went to Helsinki for the Olympics, Patterson enjoyed in Europe a world that was so vastly more free of the racial tensions toward African Americans that he regularly encountered in the U.S. Patterson's honest, sincere manner also resonated well with European fans, and his presence certainly prompted more enthusiasm in Sweden than it did in Jackson, Mississippi. Patterson recalled: "When my sparring partners and I landed in Sweden, the interpreter's daughter kissed me on the cheek, and an elderly lady kissed my hand. I was so moved that I kissed her hand and said 'Thank you, thank you.' Everywhere I went in Sweden, I saw there was no color line." The notion that there could be a world devoid of racism, rather than a world of hatreds and counter-hatreds, was an ideal Patterson would never abandon. His disdain for various forms of African American radicalism in the 1960s would be rooted in this hopeful ideal. "I used to think Jesus was a white man," he reflected. "All the pictures I've ever seen of Him showed him white. But I no longer can accept Him as a white man. He is either Jesus of no color, or a Jesus with skin that is all colors."[11]

In several ways Patterson had previously seen hints of the adulation he felt in Sweden and in Europe more generally. After his loss to Johansson, he had actually received hundreds of letters from Sweden, saying that while they had rooted for Johansson, they were sorry Floyd had lost and that they considered him an excellent boxer. Another example came in May, through the United Nations, no less, and it concerned a group of students from a Swedish university (Lund). The students had organized a cravat auction for refugee relief. Through the Swedish U.N. secretary-general Dag Hammarskjöld, the students were able to contact and persuade an array of famous international dignitaries each to donate a necktie which they then sold at auction, the proceeds going to the aid of international refugees. Hammarskjöld's tie sold for 500 Swedish Kroner ($100), as did one from American vice-president Richard Nixon (although during the auctioning of Nixon's tie, several Swedish students were heard jeering and chanting, "We Want [Adlai] Stevenson."*) The

*In May 1960, the American presidential elections were still in their primary phase. Nixon was the clear front-runner in the Republican Party, and the liberal Stevenson was then still regarded as a possible Democratic candidate, apparently generating more enthusiasm among Swedes than Democrats.

only tie to secure a higher bid than Hammarskjöld's was one donated by Floyd Patterson. There was one tinge of hostility in Sweden, but it came from members of a radical Pentecostal religious sect. They protested all boxing as sinful and were against Johansson as much as Patterson. (And in Sweden, to be against Johansson was sinful.) Otherwise, Patterson felt quite comfortable. With a kind of calm, fatalistic shrug he noted: "I do not think I will ever be recognized as a great champion in the states." Thinking of the enormous civil rights struggles back home and the non-issue of race in Sweden, he pointedly added: "I no longer seek recognition in America. I am just happy to go on winning fights, and after each victory I will tour Europe, where I know I am appreciated." Patterson would not tour Europe as often as he had planned, but he would return there often. As with many African Americans, he greatly enjoyed the experience of being in a spot where black-white identity issues simply did not matter at all. "My feelings are rather delicate," he reflected. "You can hit me and I won't think much of it. But you say something and hurt me very much."[12]

While in Europe, Patterson did experience one pressure-filled situation, and it led to a boxing contact that would emerge later in his career. The incident occurred in Rome, where Patterson had traveled, both to visit the Vatican and to watch some of the Summer Olympic games held there that September. Before the terrorist attacks on Israeli athletes at the '72 Munich Games, Olympic venues were easy to visit for any tourist, and one afternoon Patterson sauntered through the Villaggio Olimpico, a dormitory-like row of apartments where the athletes stayed. Patterson arrived at the village wearing normal dress and dark glasses. It was lunch time, and few of the hungry athletes noticed him until he arrived at the section of the village where the American team was staying. There an 18-year-old member of the American boxing team immediately recognized him. Word quickly spread, and within minutes Patterson was besieged by autograph seekers. Police actually had to be called to help extricate Patterson and keep order. Patterson obliged each and every athlete and tourist who wanted his autograph, and after all the signing he felt a trifle weary. As he massaged his signing hand, Patterson joked, "By my book, I lost this bout." "Not you champ," immediately cheered the Olympic boxer who had originally spotted him, "you got a draw at least." Patterson relaxed the rest of the day, and he went out of his way to congratulate the boxer who had spotted him. The night before, that young amateur had just won the gold medal in the light heavyweight division. As Patterson left the Olympic area, the young boxer sang out to him: "So long, Floyd. I'll be seeing you — in about two more years." The young man's name was Cassius Marcellus Clay. They would see one another, but it would take a few more years than young Clay imagined.[13]

The biggest event of the European trip for Patterson occurred in Rome shortly after his encounter with young Cassius Clay. He toured the Vatican and had an audience with Pope John XXIII. As he waited for the Pope, Patterson recalled some of the acute nervousness he had felt back in his elementary school days when he was afraid to raise his hand in class. When the pope came out, Patterson remembered, "I kneeled and kissed his ring. I touched his hand, and I was sweating. I was scared of messing up." Fortunately, Patterson noted, "I didn't mess up with the Pope."[14]

Patterson returned from Europe, ever more content with the nature of his fame in the world, hence with some Americans' opinions assuming an ever smaller perspective. The haggling continued over the site and details of the third Johansson bout. By the end of the fall, matters were basically settled. Miami Beach had outbid Los Angeles and other hopefuls. The fight would be in Florida in early March, when the tourist season from the Northeast would be at its peak. The use of closed circuit telecasting had shown itself to be more profitable than home broadcasting, and that would be the venue for fans everywhere in the country. This meant no advertising, and as a result the closed circuit broadcast team again included the young New York journalist Howard Cosell to give between-round commentary. Purists may have thought it was unnecessary, and some said the broadcast director should at least hire someone expert on boxing, but the wider, less boxing-savvy audience had to be considered.[15]

With his accomplishing of the unprecedented reclaiming of the heavyweight title, Patterson was again named Fighter of the Year by the Boxing Writers Association. He was also the only non–Olympic athlete of 1960 to receive any United Press votes for Athlete of the Year. Reviewing the sports year of 1960, the *New York Times* called Patterson's victory "the outstanding occurrence in boxing through the year."[16] Many of the writers in the association that had named Patterson Fighter of the Year had previously been chiding him as a less than worthy champion. Patterson may have enjoyed a touch of revenge here. He also understood here ever more the old adage that all glory is fleeting.

Despite their awarding of Patterson, talk continued among the boxing press about other worthy challengers. Johansson's loss to Patterson had knocked him down to number 4 among the heavyweight contenders in some rating columns, including that of the acknowledged guru of boxing authorities, *Ring Magazine*'s Nat Fleischer. So even as the hype for the third Johansson bout began to build, the nagging issue of worthiness still remained. The three heavyweight contenders ranked above Johansson after the latter's loss to Patterson were Zora Folley, Eddie Machen (whom Johansson had knocked out in one round), and a rapidly rising heavy puncher named Sonny Liston. Talk also returned of Rocky Marciano attempting a comeback. Marciano had had some business ventures go bad, and he now needed the money. Marciano added to the speculation here, as he actually said that he could give a Patterson or a Liston "a real tough time," adding, "I'm not the boasting type. I don't want to say I could whip them, but then I don't want to lie about it either." Some of Patterson's supporters argued that the ranking of Liston, Machen, and Folley was a contrivance by boxing people because of the battles that went back to the war that Cus D'Amato had waged against the International Boxing Club. Machen, Folley, and Liston were all supposedly connected fighters. Liston's handlers appeared especially "mobbed up," and Liston had a horrible reputation, even among boxers, having spent time in prison for armed robbery and reportedly serving as an enforcer for the mob in Philadelphia. The worthiness question was all part of jostling for power, money, and status in the dirty game that was boxing. There was no escaping it. For the moment, Patterson knew that these pokes and shoves could be largely ignored. He was going to fight Johansson. No one was going to stop that, and the build-up would take whatever twists and turns it would.[17]

In the winter months leading up to the bout, the sports world was in its usual lull. Bob Hope had wanted to take Patterson on his USO Christmas tour to entertain the armed forces, but Patterson had to put his training first. In the years before basketball and hockey were of wide interest beyond a few major cities, and before pro football came up with an extended playoff system to sustain interest beyond December (and before *Sports Illustrated* came up with the concept of a swimsuit issue in the dead of winter to boost lagging newsstand sales), newspaper and magazine sports pages always seemed adrift and empty from the end of the January 1 college football bowl games until baseball became news again. Preparations for a heavyweight championship bout in the winter months, were thus perfect grist for an otherwise dull sports world. The legacies of great pairs of fighters like Graziano-Zale and LaMotta-Robinson, who had each waged a great series of bouts, were all recalled here. The nuances of Patterson's training were subject to heavy scrutiny. The suspicions of Johansson having been doped before his June loss all came out too. Patterson's camp boasted how Floyd had bulked up and would be an even heavier puncher this time. Patterson promised any of his sparring partners a $200 bonus if they could knock him down. Johansson, meanwhile, claimed perfect health. He added to the doping rumors of the second fight by confirming that he did actually lose a full six pounds in the 24 hours before the previous bout. Few mentioned that the loss of a couple of pounds is not unusual for a fighter at the peak of condition, or that a scale could simultaneously malfunction. Johansson said that he had now altered his style, going in lower and moving his legs faster. He dropped one of his sparring partners with his famous right. Young Cassius Clay came to Johansson's camp in February and went a few rounds with him. Several months later Clay told the *New York Times* that he had befuddled Johansson with his speed:

"By the end of the first round I had Johansson pinned against the ropes, all shook up and very mad." Clay claimed that he made the former champion so angry that Johansson's people cancelled further plans to do more sparring. With a hyperbolic flair that would only grow, the always extroverted Clay rhapsodized: "Two fellows came over to me with hats pulled down over their eyes like movie gangsters. 'Cass,' says one out of the corner of his mouth, 'You better watch yourself. You're going to mess up a $4 million gate.'" Johansson's people never behaved this way, but the press was learning how the new kid of the heavyweight division would always be good copy. Meanwhile, Johansson passed on Clay and used other, less speedy sparring partners to prepare for Patterson.[18]

While Patterson stepped away from his activities on behalf of racial justice while training for a fight, at times the two worlds collided anyway. With the Johansson fight slated for Miami Beach, Patterson trained up in New York in January and early February. Then a month before the fight, he moved his training to Florida. He originally planned to set up camp in the South Florida town of Homestead, some forty miles south of Miami. Patterson learned, however, that Homestead, very much a traditional Southern community, maintained and enforced racially segregated housing laws, hence that he and some of his associates would be barred from staying in certain hotels. Miami Beach may have begun to be dominated by Northeasterners, but the rest of Florida remained decidedly retrograde in sensibility. Some authorities in Homestead apparently felt there would be no problem in Patterson's camp splitting themselves racially between two sites. Patterson was not the least bit amused. He moved his camp and entourage to the Deauville Hotel in Miami Beach. Johansson encountered no such prejudice, of course, but he had a problem of his own. The IRS claimed he owed the U.S. government $598,181, and they attached his purse from the upcoming fight.[19]

The Deauville Hotel suited Patterson just fine. Outwardly, it was much more posh than the accommodations he typically preferred. Keeping to his usual spartan training ways, Patterson had all unnecessary ornaments removed from his hotel room. As before, the boxing press still wrote of the contrastingly lavish ways that Johansson lived while training in Miami. Prior to and in the wake of Johansson's 1959 victory, the contrast with Patterson's asceticism had been raised with much gusto and jest. Now that Patterson had reclaimed the crown, the portrayal of contrasts commanded a different tone. (While Patterson's camp had sought the help of Joe Louis before the return bout with Johansson, this time a syndicate, Feature Sports, Inc., tried to induce Louis to go work with Johansson. Louis turned them down.) Writers were quick to emphasize how hard Johansson worked while training even though he lived splendidly in his resting hours. Patterson's ways brought forth the point of most boxing purists that the body and the spirit are best driven together in harsh, unrelenting severity. Whatever the regimen, both appeared to be peaking well. Patterson, many observed, "never looked sharper." He was ten pounds heavier than he was when he first met Johansson, yet he held the extra weight in complete trim and appeared to be faster than ever. The oddsmakers installed him as a 3–1 favorite to keep his title. Amidst the pre-fight hype, there was none of the personal rancor that accompanies many bouts. Indeed, the two actually appeared together on several TV programs hosted by such luminaries as Jack Paar and Jackie Gleason. Gleason's show was especially poignant, as it occurred just two nights before the fight, and Gleason himself ran the show from Miami. (Paar aired from New York and relied on a videotape of the two.) The two fighters showed the world how thoroughly civil they were, an atmosphere boxing had seldom seen and would seldom see again. Some may have felt it was a bit too civil, however, as Miami ticket sales lagged.[20]

As the fight approached, Patterson appeared a trifle nervous. He admitted he was not as edgy and angry as he had been before his second fight with

Patterson training in Miami Beach in 1961 for his third fight with Ingemar Johansson. Florida still imposed strict segregation laws and customs in such places as restaurants and hotels. Patterson always resented and resisted Jim Crow wherever he encountered it, and in Florida that year he switched training camp locations because of one hotel's retrograde practices. © *The Ring*.

Johansson. Previously, Patterson had always prayed before a bout, never for victory, only for neither fighter to be hurt. This was more his mood again. "Kill Johansson?" he asked rhetorically; "I hope not." Hearing the endlessly repeated questions from reporters, he was short, although never rude, and clearly wanted to get into the ring and get to the business at hand. He conveyed a sense of that nervous impatience when he appeared on television with Jackie Gleason. For good luck and publicity, D'Amato had arranged for Patterson to be chauffeured around Miami in a long white Lincoln Continental—the same Lincoln that President Kennedy had used when campaigning in Florida the previous year. The new president's popularity was strong, and D'Amato wanted Patterson to be clearly cast as America's fighter against the foreigner, and to be well-regarded among the chic, well-heeled Miami ringside crowd among whom the Kennedy glamour was already taking hold.

Somewhat against many of the wealthy's wishes, and definitely against many local officials in Florida, Patterson had successfully insisted that none of the seating in the Miami Convention Hall be racially segregated. It always had been, but it would not be this time. The fight's promoters had to post a $10,000 forfeit that would be payable to the NAACP if the Convention Hall was not integrated. It would be integrated, and Patterson donated $10,000 to the NAACP out of his purse. The *Pittsburgh Courier* had occasionally chided Patterson for being a "serf" with respect to the likes of Cus D'Amato, especially in his fight against Truman Gibson, Frank Norris, and the IBC. With his successful challenge to the Miami seating rules, their applause of his "stirring stand" was thunderous. They hoped it would create more distance between Patterson and D'Amato. Even more, activists hoped Patterson's efforts could possibly open up other segregated sports venues in the South, including, most significantly, those of the pre-season Major League Baseball circuit. African American reporters indeed used Patterson's stance to call upon the prominent "'Uncle Toms' among Negro major leaguers who would rather 'leave well enough alone' ... than take a position such as Patterson did.... Patterson's forthrightness demonstrates dramatically what one can contribute toward the fight against bias." At the Miami Convention Hall, meanwhile, the financial capacity to pay for a more or less expensive ticket remained the big seating divider.[21]

On Monday evening, March 13, the fight began at 10:46 P.M., and it began badly for Patterson. After Patterson had reclaimed his title in 1960, some pundits had begun to scoff about Johansson to the effect that he had previously had little competition but Eddie Machen, and that his two significant victories over Machen and Patterson both involved the good fortune of his landing one of his vaunted rights. They were thus saying that Johansson was but an average heavyweight with one big punch. True or not, good fortune appeared to come his away again in the first round in Miami, for after landing a few good lefts to Patterson's head, Johansson landed his famous right to Patterson's jaw. The punch sent Floyd to the floor. Memories of Yankee Stadium, 1959, were returning. Patterson was up at the count of two and took a standing eight count, a mandatory rule in Florida but never before employed in a heavyweight championship bout. Some of Johansson's supporters said that without the standing eight, Patterson would not have survived. After the eight, Johansson was on him immediately, landing another combination that dropped Patterson for the second time. Now the groans of déjà vu were everywhere. Again, Patterson was up quickly and stood for the eight count. This time the action suddenly reversed, however. Johansson bore in and must have thought he had Patterson in a daze, for he got careless about his defense. Patterson landed his own left to Johansson's jaw, and now the Swede went down. He also rose immediately and took a standing eight. After a few more punches the round ended. With his two knockdowns, Johansson won the round on each of the three official cards. The crowd was in a frenzy. Not since Dempsey-Firpo in 1923 had a heavyweight championship fight seen such a rapid exchange of knockdowns. Everyone expected great action from there, and no one expected the fight to last too long.[22]

In the second, Patterson went to the floor again, but it was correctly ruled a slip. Compared to the first round, the fight here was relatively cautious, and basically even. The same went for the third. The referee and the two judges gave the third to Patterson. It was close; indeed some reporters gave it to Johansson. In the fourth, Patterson appeared to be gaining the advantage. He landed more shots, and appeared not at all shaken when one of Johansson's rights landed squarely on his jaw. Patterson kept his edge in the fifth. Up on all cards, Patterson entered the sixth and appeared to be sliding back again. He took several hard blows from Johansson right in the face. He missed wildly with a right to Johansson's head and took another Johansson right in the face. Patterson then went to the body with a left hook. Immediately from there he clubbed Johansson with two solid rights to the head, one big one just under Johansson's ear. Johansson went down. He was anything but out cold as he had been at the Polo Grounds. He was fully conscious and appeared to rise just in time, but referee Billy Regan ruled that Johansson did not get up before the counting of ten. It was a controversial ending, but it left Patterson winner and still champion.[23]

Johansson was simple and blunt about the final knockdown: "They did not count correctly, I think." "I heard 'nine' and he say 'ten' when I was up." Many argued that Johansson's knee was indeed off the canvas before "ten." (It was.) But obviously there could be no recourse in regard to the decision, so Johansson and his fans had to accept the results. "I never argue with the referees," Johansson shrugged, with the clear implication of "what's the point?" Pacifist, anti-boxing elements in Sweden, led again by a group of Pentecostalists, had been imploring for an end to the sport. More pragmatically and nationalistically, many now urged Johansson to leave the ring. ("Ingo, it's time to stop!" said one Swedish newspaper.) Johansson had hinted at one point before the Miami fight, that, win or lose, this bout with Patterson would be his last fight. Always a shrewd businessman, he had made plenty of money, so he did not need to suffer any more blows from the likes of Patterson. He would make noises about staying in contention for the crown and fighting several other leading heavyweights, including Sonny Liston. This would come to naught. He would fight four more inconsequential bouts in Sweden against some lackluster British and Dutch journeymen named Joe Bygraves, Wim Snoek, Dick Richardson, and Brian London. Then he retired. He still had another big fight on his hands, however, as the IRS was still all over him about U.S. taxes from 1959 and 1960. (Comedian Joe E. Lewis had predicted "a taxing fight.") Johansson had been claiming to be a Swiss resident and the sole asset of a holding company called Scannart. He was vague as to who actually owned Scannart; some half-joked that the owners were members of his family. Johansson was not able to leave the country until the end of March, and then only because of the intervention and permission of Attorney General Robert Kennedy. The tax situation was eventually settled, and Johansson returned to Sweden, tanned, healthy, and wealthy, although the Swedish government proved to have as many issues with Johansson's tax situation as had the IRS. Johansson was so frustrated with his continuous tax troubles that he blurted out with uncharacteristic boorishness: "Swedish people mistreat me, the government plunders me, and the damned laws allow Negroes to socialize with Swedish girls." A few members of the American press pounced on him. "Sounds like his mammy and pappy raised him in Mississippi," quipped one. Johansson apologized for his outburst. Floyd held no grudge anyway. He would maintain a life-long friendship with Johansson.[24] For Patterson, meanwhile, questions immediately came forth about who his next opponent would be, and everyone now had one man in mind.

IX

Sonny

As the Miami Beach crowd was cheering Patterson's sixth-round knock-out of Ingemar Johansson, reporters and seconds entered the ring. In contrast to the aftermath of the previous June bout, Johansson was certainly OK this time. He and his entourage complained that he had beaten the count. But that controversy would have simply to pass, as no such decision is ever reversed. While Johansson and his seconds were leaving the ring, the closed-circuit TV commentator Howard Cosell approached Patterson for an interview. After the obligatory congratulations, Cosell turned immediately to the question of Patterson's future. He went right to the heart of the heavyweight picture, asking "What's next for you, Floyd, Sonny Liston?"[1]

Charles "Sonny" Liston was a bruising heavyweight with a record to that point of 32 and 1. In 1958, Roy Harris lasted 12 rounds with Patterson. Less than two years later, Liston easily put Harris away in the first round. Liston possessed solid, some said underrated boxing skills, and he was all too well known and feared for his heavy, heavy punching power. For many boxers, the basic left jab is simply a defense, a starter, and a trivial part of their arsenals in regard to causing damage to an opponent. Liston's left jab, on the other hand, was said to hit like a telephone pole. Some have argued that Liston's jab, the rudimentary punch of all boxing, was the best ever. When Sonny hit you, recalled Marty Marshall, the only man who to that point had ever beaten him, "it hurt all over." (In addition to beating Liston in a 1954 eight-round decision, Marshall then lost to him twice.) Liston hit so hard that many opponents and corner men suspected his handlers were slipping lead into the lining of his gloves. Liston and his people would cheat in bouts, putting skin irritants on his gloves, for example, to sting the eyes of opponents, but no one ever found anything *in* Sonny's gloves, just his huge fists. He was just a punishing puncher with a brute force seldom seen, one that recalled such greats as Rocky Marciano and Jack Dempsey.[2]

When Howard Cosell asked Patterson about fighting Sonny Liston, Patterson's response was another oddly modest statement that was hardly something expected from a man who had just retained the heavyweight crown. Rather than a "Bring 'em on!" snarl, Patterson was reflective. "Well, Howie," he nodded thoughtfully (as Cosell visibly winced, "Howie" being a name he had apparently hated since childhood), "if there is someone out there who can beat me in a fair fight, I'd rather he have the crown than I." As with other instances in his championship career, Patterson's modesty made many people wince besides Howie Cosell. This was the complicated soul of the man with the crown. "An introvert whose way of life confounds the high-spirited chaps of the boxing world," wrote *New York Times* writer Gay Talese. Some were beginning to refer to him as "Freud" Patterson, as they shook their heads in strange disbelief and skepticism. The boxing world always accepted braggarts and boasters, if only for the purpose of hoping to watch their postures be challenged and ultimately defeated. Patterson's outlook may have been more modestly mature, but the heavyweight division of professional boxing continued to seem the absolute last place for it. A few continued to praise Patterson for his gentlemanly, intelligent, modest character. But that was getting old. P. L. Pratis of the *Pittsburgh Courier* lauded Patterson as "a Peace Corps wrapped up in one." The problem was that in 1961 no one could imagine a Peace Corps volunteer taking on such a menacing figure as Sonny Liston.[3]

The third Johansson fight had left more questions. With his two knockdowns in the first round, Patterson again showed that he could obviously be hit. The fight itself, beyond the controversy of the final count that put Johansson out, did not impress the pundits as much as the first two. "Like a bottle of beer, which has been open too long," wrote *Sports Illustrated*'s Gilbert Rogin, "it had an undeniable kick, but to the purists the flavor was faintly stale and flat." Patterson, he declared, had appeared to perform "in what almost amounted to a trance; he was distant and feckless, with heavy, futile legs and arms.... He stood erect as a man treading water.... That fiery particle which had blazed across the Polo Grounds last June had become a cinder." Patterson had said to several newspapermen that he was not so up for the third fight as he had been for the second (so he made it easy for reporters to embellish knowingly here). Patterson admitted, "I looked terrible; I showed no skill." Even in victory, then, reporters and fans expressed concerns about Patterson's future. Some questions were silly. One, for example, actually raised the matter, *à la* Samson, of whether Patterson should have had a haircut the day before the fight. Others were more serious: Why did he look so bad at times? Were there problems with his training? Was he vicious enough in temperament? Patterson and D'Amato had devised a strategy which involved steadily pumping the left jab to force Johansson to keep using his vaunted right defensively. Why was Patterson unable to carry this out? More gravely, what could happen against an opponent like Liston, who was certainly as strong a challenger as Johansson and a lot better than those four pathetic chumps Patterson had fought before.[4]

After leaving the ring in Miami, Patterson received further post-fight questions about facing Liston. Having now had a little time to formulate his thoughts, he raised the critical point — that he would gladly fight Liston provided that Sonny could assure the boxing world that he had cleansed himself of all his crime connections. Sonny Liston had done jail time for armed robbery, and he apparently had mob links. He had allegedly been a thug for the mafia's protection rackets in Philadelphia. In the mean sections of north Philadelphia it was said that if you ran such a mafia controlled establishment as a pool hall and were late on your protection payments, it was Sonny Liston who paid you a visit. (And you definitely paid.) Liston had been in Miami to watch the Johansson fight. He had been introduced to the crowd before the bout (and there were some noticeable boos). Asked afterwards about the fight, Liston chortled that he was impressed with neither boxer and could easily beat either of them. When queried about Patterson's point concerning mafia connections, Liston sniffed that Patterson should not worry about such a matter: "It's up to the boxing commission to investigate this talk about undercover managers. As far as I'm concerned," he chided, "Patterson is just afraid to fight me. That's all, and that's his way of avoiding me." This was the kind of posturing to which the boxing public was accustomed. Simple bragging and controversy — these were the norms of boxing, not complicated introversion and modesty.[5]

Sonny Liston indeed had mafia connections, especially through his manager, Joseph "Pep" Barone, and other associates Frank "Blinky" Palermo and Frankie Carbo. Barone's mob connections had been substantiated by the Kefauver Committee. Soon after the third Patterson-Johansson bout, Liston's links to Palermo and others prompted the California Athletic Commission to bar him from fighting there as of April 1, 1961. The stigma of organized crime's influence in boxing was acute in these years. Exposures of fixed fights threatened to undermine the entire sport. The June 1960 confessions of Jake LaMotta about deliberately losing a nationally televised Madison Square Garden fight with Billy Fox on November 14, 1947, stuck with many fans. (The memory was sufficiently deep that as late as 1980 Hollywood producers felt it was worthwhile to produce a movie about the sordid life of LaMotta — *Raging Bull*.) The immediate shock and anger prompted NBC television and radio executives that very summer to end all their previously popular Friday night *Fight of the Week* broadcasts. ABC would try the venue for a short time but soon dropped it too. Closed-circuit broadcasts could work only in the very biggest championship events. With such disgraces and television losses, the sport felt itself in great financial peril.

In the spring of 1961, the investigations and prosecutions of Vincent Velella and William Rosensohn, the promoters of the first Patterson-Johansson fight, were also coming to a head and receiving press coverage, all adding to boxing's notorious image. Under the new Kennedy administration, the posture of the U.S. Justice Department aimed ever more at organized crime. When previously working under Tennessee senator Estes Kefauver, the new attorney general, Robert Kennedy, had already famously investigated several crime figures. As A.G. his anti-mafia zeal would increase. At the very time Liston was being barred from fighting in California, Sen. Kefauver was also discussing the idea of creating a federal commission exclusively for boxing, possibly to oversee the sport permanently, with a federally appointed and paid commissioner at the rank of assistant attorney general who would have the power to license boxers, managers, promoters, and matchmakers. This not only made crime figures nervous, it disquieted many of the snugly ensconced, handsomely-paid bureaucrats of many state athletic commissions. In the spring of 1961, Senator Kefauver held hearings about the issues over boxing's future and about the ways to demolish the mob's corrosive influence. Here former champion Jack Dempsey testified that unless boxing fell under federal control, the existing mob power would doom the sport. Boxing, Dempsey lamented, "is ready to be buried if something isn't done and done fast." Kefauver was strong in justifying his call for the federalization of boxing, illustrating here his fear with the explicit example that if Sonny Liston won the title from Floyd Patterson, the title would "revert to mob control." Dempsey exemplified the mob problem the same way, directly pointing to what would likely occur if Liston took the title. The anxieties of the mafia's corrosive influence were pronounced, and the fears bore down on no fighter more than Sonny Liston. The notion that *he* could take Patterson's title shook many throughout the sports world.[6]

The luster of Patterson's victories over Johansson was vanishing quickly. While there was hardly anything good about the allegations of Liston's mob ties, at another level they actually lent an aura of evil that underscored the image Sonny held as the most fearsome man around. While thinking people clearly fully understood the wisdom of preventing the control of boxing from falling further into mob hands, the possible prevention of Liston getting a shot at the title once again besmirched Patterson's standing. Patterson became ever more a symbol of the good world, and within the context of the law this all seemed civilized and noble. But the question of who was the best fighter was not and could never be merely a question of morality, of legality, or, certainly, of civility. It was a question that involved a world unto itself that involved a very primal sphere within the human psyche which could not be denied, and to which the boxing world lent an arguably healthy, or at least not altogether unhealthy release. Aside from groups like the Swedish Pente-costalists who wanted boxing banned altogether, those who believed that the sport should exist, or that banning it would be pointless, as it would always occur regardless of legality, were left unable to deny the fact that they did have to respect the boxing skills of a Liston, no matter his illegal connections, and that these skills should not be denied their place in the question of who is the champion fighter of the day.[7]

Most vexing here was the notion that Liston was somehow the better fighter because of his connections to that "dark world" that so many feared. At the same time in the world of jazz, figures like Charlie Parker and Miles Davis held a certain aura over the reputation of a contemporaneous artist like trumpeter Clifford Brown, in no small measure because Brown was com-pletely clean in regard to all matters of drugs and alcohol. Davis's and, even more so, Parker's reputations for drug use lent lurid elements of drama to their work in the minds of many music fans. There was certainly no proof that drugs made for a better musician or that criminal connections made a better boxer, but that very sort of devilish linkage lay in the minds of many fans. The conflict here of base, primal instincts versus legality-morality consti-tuted, and still constitutes, a snare for many fighters, artists, and musicians. The implicit notion here was that the layers of civility somehow limited the baser qualities that a fighter needs to be his best. Patterson seemed especially vulnerable here because of the ways that he had seemingly grafted a layer of civility onto his mean-streets roots and because of the ways this image easily underscored all the previous allegations he had endured about dodging some of his strongest challengers. There existed, then, the deep, if unstated view that if the mob were to be truly driven out of boxing, it needed to be done in the ring and not just through the law. Otherwise the cleansing would be less than fully convincing. This made the call for a Patterson-Liston match all the more compelling.

Would the raising of Liston's mob questions be perceived as Patterson ducking yet another contender? Liston spat out that very point in Miami just after Patterson beat Johansson. Even if every state boxing commission barred Liston, even if Senator Kefauver fully federalized the sport, and even if the federal government banned Liston, the specter of Sonny would continue to loom over Floyd Patterson. After all, it wasn't the mafia that would climb into the ring against Floyd. Some speculated that D'Amato was once again duck-ing the main contenders and looking for bums. Sonny was *the* challenger, and in the spring of 1961 every boxing fan simply wanted to know if Patterson could whip him. In April, Liston offered to sever ties with Pep Barone, Carbo, and Palermo. There were no formal ties with Carbo and Palermo, but Barone was his manager, and Liston himself bought out the contract (still in force for two more years) for $75,000. The April break was hardly full, however, as Liston would take time to pay off Barone. Additionally, a man Liston kept as his attorney, Morton Witkin, had also represented "Blinky" Palermo. Nevertheless, now purporting to stand "clean," Liston renewed his challenge to Patterson to fight him for the title.[8]

Patterson and D'Amato were ready to respond. (D'Amato was back in the picture by this time. While he had lost his New York license to manage Patterson or any other fighter, he had appealed the conviction for allegedly refusing to answer a subpoena, and the New York State Appellate Division had reversed his conviction. He was back working with Patterson, and Patterson still trusted him.) Patterson pointed out that the mere fact that Liston had "ostensibly" purchased his contract from Pep Barone certainly did not mean Sonny had no other mob affiliations. Cus D'Amato was even more contemptuous. "Where did Liston get $75,000?" he asked, implying that other mob connections must still be present. D'Amato told reporters, in his usual fast-talking, bumptious manner, that "plans for Floyd Patterson have already been made, [and that] Liston does not figure in those plans now. I am not interested in Liston at present."[9] Again, the matter of Patterson's title defenses appeared somewhat in abeyance, and the space was there for those predisposed to be disrespectful to claim that Patterson was avoiding his top contenders. The concern for the mob's influence was certainly to be respected. But D'Amato's decrying the mob raised the memory of how he had always been controlling his man unduly and steering him away from the top challengers. Liston was a question Patterson could not avoid, and D'Amato's superficial, fast-talking defensiveness only raised more troubling questions. For most fight fans there was just one simple question: what would happen if Patterson squared off against Liston?

In the spring of 1961, Sonny Liston greatly damaged his own cause, if only temporarily. With the stories of mob connections all about him, he had several run-ins with the law. On May 17, he had an encounter with some Philadelphia policemen and was charged with loitering. A magistrate eventually dismissed the charges. Then just before dawn on June 12, he and a friend eerily represented themselves as policemen as they attempted to stop a female motorist in a remote section of Philadelphia's Fairmont Park. Liston and his friend pulled alongside her. They shone a spotlight into her face, declared themselves policemen, and ordered her to pull over. The woman did pull over, and as Liston and the other man walked toward her car, a real police car approached. Liston and his friend ran back to their car and attempted to drive away. The policeman pursued them, resulting in an an eighty-mile-an-hour car chase. Liston was finally arrested for impersonating an officer, conspiracy, and disorderly conduct. Liston claimed he thought he knew the woman, and that was why he had stopped her car. It certainly seemed a weak argument, nonetheless the charges were dropped. The stopping of the car was ruled an "error of judgment." In the summer, however, Liston was rearrested for the same violations. After an apology to the woman in court, he was ultimately acquitted. The two arrests marked the 18th and 19th times he had been collared by the police.[10]

Liston's volatility and encounters with the law only underscored his sinister image. That very summer he made a show of moving to Denver and accepting the kind offer of a Colorado priest, Edward Murphy, who offered personal and spiritual guidance as well as tutoring on basic reading and writing skills, both of which Liston lacked. For the time being, no matter his new church connections, Liston's various criminal matters put his boxing career on hold. His home state of Pennsylvania was threatening to revoke his license to box there, and that could have led other states to follow suit. Given the pressures of the ongoing Kefauver investigations, the various state commissions appeared quite willing to crack down hard, if only to show that they did not need to have their authority superceded by the federal government, a prospect hardly relished by any status- and salary-conscious state bureaucrats. Fortunately for Liston, after his 1961 acquittals the state bans did not occur. He stayed in Denver and conspicuously visited his good priest on a regular basis.[11]

With Liston out of the heavyweight picture at least temporarily, the questions of Patterson's future plans were still in abeyance. Patterson insisted that he would not fight Liston until he had cleaned his camp of reputed racketeers. Meanwhile, Patterson continued to maintain a focus on and an activism in civil rights causes and other social issues. At the Johansson fight in Miami, for example, Patterson had insisted that there be no segregation in the arena's seating; Liston did not care one whit about that. (How could you make any money pushing an issue like that, Liston disdainfully thought.) On many other occasions Patterson gave his name freely for good causes. Through his efforts, for example, the proceeds from the closed-circuit broadcast of the third Johansson bout at the Audubon Ballroom on Broadway at 166th Street all went to the Wiltwyck School. Also right after the Johansson bout, Patterson and ex-major league ballplayer Jackie Robinson co-chaired a successful NAACP membership drive in New York City. In July, Patterson also put in an appearance for the NAACP's Freedom Rally at Pittsburgh's Forbes Field. "I am not only proud, very proud, of the NAACP," Patterson declared, "but I am also proud to be a member." Patterson had indeed become a hero among politically active African Americans. Up to that point, perhaps only Joe Louis and Jackie Robinson were the only athletes who stood higher. In 1960, when the NAACP held its annual convention, that year in St. Paul, Minnesota, the meetings occurred just when Patterson retook the title from Johansson. The depth of emotion when word of Patterson's victory got around the convention was palpable. Sonny Liston never inspired any such feelings among African Americans. With Patterson's and Robinson's efforts, New York's NAACP membership nearly doubled.

Having been to Jackson, Mississippi, on behalf of CORE in 1961, Patterson returned there in early 1962 to address an NAACP conference. Archie Moore, Jackie Robinson, and a young baseball player, Curt Flood, were there too. (In the summer of 1962, Patterson would also head a committee to honor Jackie Robinson when Robinson was named to the Baseball Hall of Fame.) Reflecting his sense of the significance of mere professional boxing to the struggle for civil rights in America at that time, Patterson was candid when he addressed his audience in Mississippi. He spoke in almost whispered tone, emphasizing how proud he was to be a part of the fight for civil rights. "I feel extremely guilty sitting there in the North, reading and hearing about the things you are going through down here. You people are the ones going through all the danger." Liston never raised a finger on behalf of the cause of civil rights. The relative danger and safety of his labors were matters he never considered. When Patterson spoke with such contrasting sensitivity in Jackson, no one was wincing.[12]

While Patterson may have felt guilty about the greater fight being waged in the South over civil rights, back in New York he did face a few social battles of his own back. He never forgot Sandra having to endure a Long Island beauty salon manager canceling her reservation when she merely wanted to get her hair done. Feeling no great love for Rockville Centre, and with other members of his family already living in a house he had purchased for them in Westchester County, he, Sandra and their children moved to Westchester in June 1961. The home they purchased lay in the very northeastern corner of Yonkers, between the Bronx River Parkway and Troublesome Brook, just at the edge of the previously all-white community of Scarsdale. A sad irony was at play here; Scarsdale had grown in the post–World War II years as a community where Jews, Italians, and other ethnic groups leaving New York City could purchase homes, while some older wealthy Westchester towns like Rye explicitly excluded them. Patterson bought a house on Wyndcliff Road (a ten-room ranch house with a half acre of land *then* worth $140,000). Shortly after he moved there, Patterson encountered one of his neighbors, a dentist named Ondino Morelli, the son of Italian immigrants, who owned the adjacent property. At first, noted Patterson, "their kids used to play with mine, mine with theirs, and everything went nicely." Then Dr. Morelli installed a tall redwood fence separating the ninety feet of their adjoining property. Patterson responded with fence of his own. When Patterson was constructing his fence, Mrs. Morelli called out to him: "Mr. Patterson, I'm surprised at you. My husband welcomed you to this neighborhood." "Yes," replied Patterson, "with a six-foot fence." The Morellis denied they had put up their fence to keep the children apart. "I'm a person that likes a little peace and quiet," Mrs. Morelli huffed. "I think as a human being I have a right to put up a fence. I expect my neighbor to take this as a normal, everyday occurrence." Why Mrs. Morelli did not then go out of her way to explain this to her neighbors in advance so as to head off any misunderstandings, she never said; nor did she explain why she did not, in turn, take it "as a normal, everyday occurrence" when the Pattersons put up their fence. Patterson took the Morellis' move as one of the sadly normal things he and his family had had to endure for years. He had thought it was tougher in Brooklyn or in Jackson, Mississippi, and indeed it was, but Scarsdale was proving no nirvana either.

The day that Patterson was building his fence, Dr. Morelli arrived home and snarled at the fence workers: "Touch on my property, and you better have a court order for it." Patterson glanced at the workers and snarled, "If he touches anything over here, he'd better have an ambulance." This was quite a statement from Patterson. Outside the ring, he seldom expressed himself in such a physically threatening tone. While boxing, he thought of nothing but boxing. Out of the ring, he rarely if ever let it even enter his vocabulary. When it came to matters of family and of race relations, however, he was always in deadly earnest about using any means necessary to protect them. Within a month of the fence face-off, the Morellis sold their property and moved. A month after that, the Patterson's new neighbors, Mr. and Mrs. Arthur Walker, removed their property's fence and the Pattersons had theirs taken down as well.

The Pattersons' fence incident would leave its mark on one of his former neighbors, Arthur Goldstein. Goldstein would later be in a battle with a group of racism-motivated people on New York's Nassau County Board of Supervisors who opposed support for housing for the homeless in the Long Island community of Roslyn Heights and for a home for the mentally ill in New Hyde Park. Goldstein took umbrage at the high-handed presumptuousness of the board members, as though their consent constituted some sort of royal favor or dispensation. "For many years I had Floyd Patterson as my next-door neighbor," Goldstein yelled. "I didn't consent to him moving in, and I didn't consent to him moving out." Racial groups, the poor, the disadvantaged — none of these things should matter, Goldstein argued. He lost his fight with the Nassau County Supervisors, however.[13]

Earlier in 1961, on behalf of another cause dearest to his heart, Patterson found himself working with none other than Mrs. Eleanor Roosevelt. They worked to raise funds for the Wiltwyck School. Patterson had seen to it that boys at the school got to see a closed-circuit broadcast of the Johansson fight from Miami. Patterson waived some of his closed-circuit TV proceeds to Wiltwyck. That January, he and Mrs. Roosevelt raised over $10,000 to help purchase new residences for the Wiltwyck School. When Patterson's autobiography was released in May of 1962, the publisher held a commemorative dinner at Toots Shor's restaurant. Tickets for the dinner cost $50, and all the dinner's proceeds went to the Wiltwyck School. The new Wiltwyck residences were not to be up near Mrs. Roosevelt's home at Hyde Park but in Manhattan, at 208 East 18th St. just off Third Avenue, near the gym where Patterson first learned boxing with Cus D'Amato. The Wiltwyck's Manhattan residence hall would be called The Patterson House. It opened in January 1962. The new house enabled the school to reach more needy youths. Twenty-five boys would be housed there full time, and many more would visit it daily. For many of the boys, Wiltwyck would be their first real home. Mrs. Roosevelt had been thrilled to learn that Patterson had been greatly helped by the school she had worked so hard to establish back in the 1930s. And it was quite a thrill for Patterson to work with such a distinguished person in service to the school that had done him such good. Mrs. Roosevelt would pass away the next autumn, and, training issues notwithstanding, Patterson made a special point of attending her funeral at Hyde Park.[14]

Back in the boxing arena, Patterson was again feeling the pressure to fight a worthy opponent within a reasonable time after the last bout with Johansson. With Liston temporarily on the periphery, the list of heavyweight contenders in 1961 showed several possibilities, but with a lot of confusions. The young Olympic champion Cassius Clay had just turned professional, had easily won several bouts, and was already in the top ten (#9). Everyone knew, however, it was too soon for him to contend seriously for the title. Ingemar Johansson was now #6. He was making noises about a comeback and wanting to fight Liston, but there seemed little point of him fighting Patterson a fourth time, at least not until he'd beaten some other contenders. Near Johansson was the rising British star Henry Cooper (#8) and Cleveland Williams (#7). Other contenders included the Argentinean Alejandro Lavorante (#4), Zora Folley (#3), and Eddie Machen (#2) (Liston was the #1 contender). Folley and Lavorante would fight that spring, with Lavorante winning. *Ring Magazine* had cast Lavorante as "the new heavyweight hope," perhaps because he was white.[15]

Lavorante would be busy that year, actually fighting eleven times, winning ten, although largely against journeymen. The following year he would move up and fight Archie Moore. Moore, however, knocked out Lavorante, and he KO'd him with such force that Lavorante had to be carried out on a stretcher. Then in July of 1962, Lavorante lost decisively to Cassius Clay. (Two months later he faced a lesser heavyweight named John Riggins. Riggins knocked Lavorante out, and Lavorante sustained such head injuries from the bout that he had to retire and died a little over a year later.) In the summer of 1961,

Zora Folley sought to rebound from his loss to Lavorante and began negoti-ations with Cooper. The two would fight one another in December, with Fol-ley winning. The two fighters were obviously hoping a victory would earn the victor a title shot, and there were reports of Patterson being offered $350,000 to meet the winner. The bout's preparations, however, put aside any immediate possibilities of either fighting Patterson in the immediate future. Cleveland Williams loomed as a genuine contender. But he had lost two bouts to Liston in 1959 and 1960. Still, Williams had broken Liston's nose in the 1959 match and lost in 1960 only because Liston's handlers had smeared eye-stinging coagulant on his gloves to impair Williams' vision (a dirty trick he would famously try with Muhammad Ali in 1964). In 1961, Williams was relegated to fighting nobodies down in Texas. Some were grumbling that the hard-hitting Williams was one of the IBC fighters that D'Amato and Patter-son had been ducking. The only other major contender was Eddie Machen, but he had already lost to Johansson in the first round in 1958, and in Sep-tember 1960, Liston beat him, although there again Liston had to put eye-stinging coagulant on his gloves to do it. In April 1961, Machen beat a journeyman named Mike DeJohn and made noises about deserving a shot at Patterson. In July of 1961, however, he lost to a tough 32-year-old Philadel-phia heavyweight named Harold Johnson. Whether they were ducking any-one or whether all the contenders were otherwise engaged, Patterson and D'Amato made what seemed to many boxing fans to be another pointless, low-level choice. In July, they announced that Patterson's next opponent would be an undistinguished Boston-area fighter named Tommy McNeeley.[16]

Grumblings immediately grew about Patterson fighting such an unranked nobody as McNeeley. He seemed another Pete Rademacher. The *Pittsburgh Courier* guffawed, "Floyd Patterson has signed to 'risk' his title against the heavyweight champion of Vassar." More noise grew about D'Amato unduly shielding Patterson and fighting only weak, white opponents. On July 7, the National Boxing Association issued an official warning to Patterson that he must fight a qualified challenger by mid–September or they would withdraw their recognition of him as champion. D'Amato did his usual fast talking in response to the NBA, arguing that Patterson had fought plenty of highly ranked contenders like Johansson, Archie Moore, and Hurricane Jackson. He tried to argue that Roy Harris and Brian London were highly ranked, and that no one of rank was available at the time he fought Rademacher. The argu-ment impressed few pundits. Meanwhile, McNeeley did have a record of 23–0, but it was against a bunch of nobodies. He tried to make the most of the situation, posturing himself as a someone who was mean, tough, and hun-gry and who would surprise the fans and sportswriters. The Boston area's Irish population embraced him as one of their own, of course. Few others bought the hype, and some may have likened the hoopla to what James Joyce called "the Irish romance of failure." The fight was to occur in Boston in late October. Disputes grew over the referee. Massachusetts boxing officials were insisting a state resident get the job. Patterson and his camp would not accept this. This ultimately proved significant enough to force the promoters to move the fight to another location.[17]

The parties eventually agreed upon Toronto, with the fight date postponed until December 4. Former champion Jersey Joe Walcott would be the ref. The National Boxing Association's threats of removal of recognition came to naught, but the fight public appeared anything but impressed with the bout, "bland detachment," being the mood one reporter sensed in Ontario. The rescheduled fight was poorly planned in one major respect — it was to occur the same weekend as the Canadian Football League's Grey Cup final, then a huge event for all Canadian sport fans, and the game was to take place in Toronto on Saturday, December 2. Some hoped the Grey Cup final would reap ancillary benefits for the fight, but it did not happen. The city's sports fans were fixated on the football championship. The fight was an afterthought. Held just two day's later at Toronto's Maple Leaf Gardens, it would only sell to but 50 percent of capacity.

Folks just were not that interested. The idea of Tommy McNeeley as a heavyweight challenger just did not excite anyone. McNeeley would not even leave Boston and come to Toronto to train. The closed-circuit television ticket sellers were also in danger of taking a loss. Here they got a bit of a break, but it was one which actually brought the question of Patterson's fight future into clearer focus. Liston, his troubles with the law in the past for the moment, had been seeking another fight, if only to keep himself sharp. He settled on a lackluster journeyman from Germany named Albert Westphal. Liston and Westphal were to meet in Philadelphia, and the fight's organizers were able to schedule the bout for December 4, the same night that Patterson was to fight McNeeley in Toronto. (Liston's sordid past, and dubious present, did make for some difficulties in his ability to get a license to box from the Pennsylvania Athletic Commission, but in any sport, especially boxing, money overrides all but the most morally outrageous of situations.) American and Canadian closed-circuit theater operators then worked out a deal to televise both bouts in succession and give their audiences two "premier" fights in one evening. The promotion naturally pointed to one obvious conclusion: the winners, presumably Patterson and Liston, should then fight one another.[18]

The usual build-up for the McNeeley fight ensued. McNeeley's manager, Peter Davenport Fuller, provided a nice example for those who remained leery of the mob's influence in boxing. *The New York Times* even ran a *Sunday Magazine* article about him. Fuller was a wealthy, Harvard-educated blueblood, the son of former Massachusetts governor Alvin T. Fuller. It was good publicity for the bout as well as for boxing. Meanwhile, the outgoing McNee-ley also parried well with the press. He proved popular with the Toronto ladies, and like Pete Rademacher, McNeeley was also a former college foot-ball star, in his case at Michigan State. This all sat well with sports fans too. In the end, however, no matter the stature of his retinue and the cleanliness of his ways, McNeeley's boxing skills were the real issue. The bookmakers set Patterson at a whopping 1 to 10 favorite, and the betting was light.

In the fight, by his own admission, Patterson did not box well. Still he won each of the first three rounds easily, knocking McNeeley down over and over. One reporter yawned and dubbed McNeeley a "standing target." McNee-ley knocked Patterson down to one knee in the fourth round. Patterson bounced up immediately. He was not hurt although a trifle surprised. The knockdown also surprised referee Joe Walcott, so much so that he forgot the mandatory eight-count. Walcott later said he had ruled it as a slip. D'Amato always maintained it was a slip too. No eight-count did not matter anyway. Patterson quickly turned and knocked McNeeley down, for the *eighth* time in the bout, and McNeeley did not get up. It was not much of a fight. Mean-while, Liston's bout with Westphal was even more lopsided. The bell rang; Liston jabbed a bit; Westphal backpedaled steadily. After 90 seconds, Liston landed one left-right combination. Westphal was down, and he stayed down well past the count of ten. That was it, a rude first-round KO. Barely sweat-ing, Liston immediately spoke again of his desire to face Patterson. Liston went to his dressing room and watched the Patterson fight. Then, when asked for his thoughts on Patterson, Liston smiled and sniffed: "Tell you what I think? You want me to blow my chances of getting a fight with the guy?"[19]

By all accounts McNeeley had shown strength and courage. He had made for a lively evening, but it was painfully obvious that he did not belong in the same ring with a man of Patterson's skills; "pitifully inept" was one writer's summation of McNeeley. After the glow of the evening had faded (in about two seconds), boxing pundits still felt themselves wondering, as they had so many times before, of what was Floyd Patterson truly capable. "If anyone tells you that Patterson can't hit," noted Tommy McNeeley, "send him to me. He left me numb." Of course, McNeeley was anything but a respected veteran, so his praise convinced no one. D'Amato actually tried to claim after the fight that Patterson would have beaten Joe Louis in his prime! No one was con-vinced, and many were offended. Meanwhile, Liston's 90-second knockout of Westphal left no one doubting his punching power. Watching the fight on television in Toronto, one man in the press section loudly exclaimed: "Wow! Can that guy hit." The exclamation happened to come from none other than Rocky Marciano. That praise certainly stood higher than any words from Tommy McNeeley. After one of his eight knockdowns of McNeeley, how-ever, Patterson actually leaned over and helped McNeeley up from the floor.

This made boxing fans remember the odd time he stopped fighting and helped an opponent pick up his mouthpiece. Noting all this, Arthur Daley of *The New York Times* scratched his head: "Boxing experts ... still can't categorize that baffling puzzle, Floyd Patterson."[20]

Once again the images of "Freud" Patterson were resounding through boxing world. The athletic level of the two-fight night of December 4, noted one reporter, "would not be tolerated as sport in any other field." The ambivalence here over Patterson combined with the contrasting concern about Liston — an undeniably formidable boxer but with a police record and apparent mob connections that could do the sport no good — to make many wonder about the immediate future of the heavyweight division. There was every reason to respect Patterson and revile Liston as human beings, but the comparison of the two purely as fighters left everyone at least a trifle dubious as to who was the worthy champion, and it certainly left no one in doubt as to the way to resolve the question. The day after the McNeeley fight, Zora Folley knocked out Britain's Henry Cooper, and it was a decisive KO in the first round. Now Cooper was no longer as worthy a challenger he had been. Had Cooper won, Cus D'Amato may have likely gone for the idea of fighting him. That would certainly have led to many screaming the same ducking charges they had been spewing for years, but now that option was closed, and the idea of a Liston-Patterson fight seemed ever more a certainty.[21]

No one expected Patterson to jump back in the ring in just two or three months. Still by January some rumors were already flying that a Liston-Patterson bout was a certainty. The issue of Liston's ugly reputation did not abate, however. Indeed Patterson received more pressure about avoiding the mob, and this time the pressure came from quite a source. On January 12, Patterson went to Washington and met President Kennedy at the White House. Kennedy gave Patterson his own tie pin and congratulated him both for his heavyweight championship and for his work on behalf of New York youths through the Wiltwyck School. After the meeting, the press asked Patterson if he had told the president whom he was going to fight next. Patterson coyly told them that indeed he had — and he left it at that, not telling them who he had named. Patterson had told Kennedy of his intent to fight Liston, and Kennedy relayed to Patterson that the Justice Department was indeed concerned about the presence of the mob in the fight game. Patterson respectfully listened to President Kennedy but responded, "I'm sorry, Mr. President, the title is not worth anything if the best fighters can't have a shot at it. And Liston deserves a shot."[22] The mob issue, about which the President, the attorney general, and others were so concerned, was not going to go away, but Patterson had made up his mind, protests from Cus D'Amato or even from President Kennedy notwithstanding. Meanwhile, a visit with the President marked quite a capstone on the long journey of someone who had come from out of the catacombs of the Brooklyn High Street exit of the New York subway. The White House meeting served to reinforce all the positive "only in America" stories about the nation and the promise it holds to anyone who was honest and worked hard. Patterson certainly represented all that was good, and his story not only honored the nation, it served as an example to African Americans and other minorities whose status was then pushing, despite determined resistance, ever more into the mainstream. Meanwhile, as a boxer and as an icon of a very different element of African American culture, there stood before Patterson and the nation the ever-menacing presence of Charles "Sonny" Liston.[23]

X

Sunglasses and Fake Whiskers

The year 1961 was a big one in sports, but it was a notoriety that came with an asterisk. That summer, the New York Yankees' Roger Maris broke one of the most famous records in sports history — Babe Ruth's single season home run mark. Maris eclipsed the Babe, but his achievement earned an asterisk from the baseball commissioner in the game's official record book because he hit his 61 home runs in a season that was nine games longer than the one Ruth played. Had a true star like Willie Mays or Mickey Mantle topped Ruth, many felt the commissioner's asterisk may not have come. But Maris seemed such an improbable hero that he and his record just did not sit well with people. Somehow eager to downplay the less-than-charismatic Maris, many baseball writers were indeed quick to emphasize further that Maris hit only .269 that season. (Indeed, the Yankees used the stat as a basis for an actual cutting of Maris's salary the next season.) In boxing that year, another sort of asterisk would continually hang over champion Floyd Patterson. By the end of 1961, the young Cassius Clay was beginning to make his mark. Sportswriters were impressed not only with his skills but with his outgoing personality and loquacity. Clay knew it, and he was always willing and able to give writers good copy. "Boxing is not as colorful as it was in the past," he spouted, a statement that could not be interpreted as anything but a jab at champion Floyd Patterson's low-keyed nature. "We need more guys to liven it up," Clay added, "and I think I can help." Even more than such boasts from such an upstart as Cassius Clay, the question of Sonny Liston also steadily pressed upon Patterson, all adding to the asterisk. As long as the Liston question lay unresolved in the heavyweight boxing picture, respect for Patterson would always be compromised. On New Year's Day of 1961, the *New York Times* had joked that Liston's management would remain in need of "fumi-

139

gation" all year, leaving Cus D'Amato continually searching for an opponent for his champion. This all left Patterson, as one critic opined, "as unlike Jack Dempsey as Roger Maris is unlike Babe Ruth."[1] For Patterson or Maris, this was a tough image to overcome, and neither ever really did.

The press's earlier accusations of Cus D'Amato ducking the best challengers provided a legacy upon which critics harped as they expressed their frustrations with the perceived riddle of Floyd Patterson. A few were giving Patterson credit for his significant charitable and civil rights efforts, as well as for escaping the undue hold Cus D'Amato had maintained. A critical point, however, could not be overcome. It concerned how Patterson could apparently be easily tagged by an opponent. Pete Rademacher, Roy Harris, Ingemar Johansson, and even Tommy McNeeley had hit Patterson with good shots, and he had gone to the canvas more times than any other heavyweight champion. In late December of 1961, one sports analyst sardonically offered Patterson a Christmas gift — "a gyroscope, to keep him on a constant vertical plane in all future fights." As Patterson had "been tipped horizontally much too often," many were quite fearful of what would happen were a big-time puncher like Sonny Liston to connect but once. Few heavyweight champions were ever held with such unrelenting misgivings. With some, like Jack Sharkey, Tommy Burns, or Primo Carnera, who each held the crown for a very short time, there was not much respect, but there was no controversy or debate over it. With Patterson, there had come the plaudits of being both the youngest champion and the first ever to regain the crown. Few could also deny that he possessed some impressive technical skills and great speed. Paradoxically, because there had been such points of praise, the criticisms may have then been leveled with a certain sense of entitlement.[2]

For several months in early 1962, Patterson relaxed from the public pressures and did some traveling. His younger brother Raymond had become a boxer, and Floyd took some time to help with his training. In February, Ray won the New York Golden Gloves heavyweight title, with Floyd serving as one of his corner men. In March the two went to Egypt for a series of boxing exhibitions in Cairo, and they took in some of the region's sites.[3]

The question of Liston would not go away. The issue of his mob connections prompted some, including officials in the Kennedy administration, to maintain a quiet stance opposing Liston ever getting a shot at the title out of fears that it would facilitate further mob penetration of American sports. Organized crime expert Senator Estes Kefauver felt the same way, and he wrote Patterson advising him not to fight Liston. In their interests of African Americans maintaining the best possible image, the NAACP also counseled Patterson not to make a fight with Liston, as did several state boxing and athletic commissioners. International Olympic Committee president Avery Brundage opined here that "the moral side of the sport program is as or more important than the physical side," adding that in amateur sports there is "a clause to the effect that persons of proven moral failings are not permitted to compete." Harry Falk, California State athletic commissioner, knew the Liston case thoroughly. He emphasized that Liston had had Joseph "Pep" Barone as his manager, and Barone's mob connections had been "pretty well established by the Kefauver Committee." Falk pointed out that while Liston claimed to have bought out Barone, the buy-out was taking place over time, hence Liston was still indebted to the mob. Falk was adamant that Liston would not be given a license to fight in California, adding, however, that if Liston "went out and got a job and behaved in an exemplary manner, he would probably get a license."[4]

Retired baseball executive Branch Rickey also spoke forcibly for the morally indignant in regard to Liston. Rickey held prominence in the sports world and on such questions as this, as he had done so much for racial justice with his leadership role in the integration of Major League Baseball in 1947. In regard to Liston he adamantly exclaimed, "It's plain greed on the part of somebody that brings a character of that type into public view." In view of Patterson possibly getting into the ring with Liston, Rickey added, "I tried to believe I had enough respect for Patterson that he wouldn't get down to that level." Rickey was a pious, ethical gentleman, one who indeed demanded such integrity from those with whom he broke down racial barriers in baseball. The question of why, then, a deeply flawed white man, like a Ty Cobb, could have then been allowed to play (and rage) with complete impunity remained (remains) unanswered. Rickey never commented here. Instead he lamented his ethical stance to be an impossible one to impose with the Liston case, for, apparently unlike baseball, "boxing is sick — a messy business." Still, Rickey could not merely despair and give in, for, he noted: "I don't think any human being gets beyond a state of redemption," adding pointedly, "but I don't think Liston has given any indication he wants to be redeemed." A prominent fight manager of the day, Jack Hurley, agreed with Rickey on the fact that boxing was a messy business. He argued, however, that it was the "free TV fights that have done and are still doing much to cheapen and damage boxing." Considering all this destruction, Hurley concluded that a Liston-Patterson fight could not injure the sport terribly much more. Rickey was less cynical and drew a moral line in the sand, but most other people of prominence, and of commonality, even if they saw Liston as unredeemably evil, felt he should be given a shot, lest Patterson's title be tainted with the idea that the true champion lay beyond the pale. Perhaps in awareness of the general public sentiment, no figure in the Kennedy administration's Justice Department, their other strong stands against the mob notwithstanding, openly spoke out against Liston being given a license to fight. They could argue, of course, that such licensing matters were individual state issues. (Several years later, their federal successors would ignore the states-rights argument and take a markedly different position with regard to Mr. Muhammad Ali.)[5]

John G. Bonoms, a special assistant attorney general for New York State, and a former assistant counsel for Senator Estes Kefauver's committee that investigated organized crime, put a somewhat measured, legal cast on the Liston matter. Bonoms stated that he saw in Liston no "demonstration of any real rehabilitation" and added: "He hasn't gotten rid of his underworld connections." Thus, Bonoms concluded cynically, Liston presents to America "an example of how you can get to be world champion regardless of your personal life — if you have enough gangster support." With that rather harsh indictment, Bonoms nonetheless argued that he "did not think Liston should be barred forever.... He could get rid of his gangster associates and improve his record enough to fight in the future."[6]

While legal minds and moralists conjectured, the basic view among all boxing fans fell largely along lines that the criminal record or the mafia connections of a man did not and should not cloud the question of who is the best fighter in the ring. From Great Britain, Sir David Harrington Angus Douglas, the 12th Marquess of Queensberry, aristocratically sniffed: "I would have rather thought it wasn't all that relevant whether or not Liston was a good character.... If he's a very good boxer, he must be entitled to a fight with Patterson.... After all, if a man breaks the world record for running 100 yards, it doesn't make any difference who he is." Branch Rickey's own protégé, Jackie Robinson, also favored the fight. He expressed disappointment that "Liston's record isn't better." But he recognized that "to prove himself to the public, ... Patterson has to fight him." Robinson then added with optimistic enthusiasm that if the fight did occur, "Patterson would demolish the man." Other prominent African Americans also spoke of someone deserving a chance. Bill Nunn of the *Pittsburgh Courier* wrote that until Patterson "proves he is a better fighter [than Liston] his sincerity must be doubted. The moment of truth is at hand." Baseball star Bill White, later president of the National League, observed: "By what I understand to be the Christian principle, every man should have a chance.... From a sports standpoint, the man deserves a chance if he is a good boxer.... Liston made some of his mistakes when he was a boy, and these should hardly be held against him." Like Jackie Robinson, White was also firm in his belief that "I don't think he [Liston] would beat Patterson, [because] Patterson's faster." (Whether White or Robinson would have felt differently had they believed Liston would win, or if they were, in effect, manufacturing their enthusiasm for Patterson as a consequence of their stance, cannot be determined, as neither publicly commented after the eventual Patterson-Liston fights.) The *Pittsburgh Courier* printed what it purported to be a cross section of man-in-the-street African American opinions over the question: "Should Liston's police record keep him from boxing profession-ally?" The answer was 100 percent "No," Liston deserved a shot at the title.

Already emerging as a noted comedian and ersatz philosopher, Dick Greg-ory took the occasion of the Liston controversy to swipe at Cus D'Amato. While many were obviously concerned with Liston's management, Gregory could not pass up an opportunity slyly to snip at the idea of a white man con-trolling the life of a black boxer. "It certainly isn't up to Patterson's manager," he joked, "to determine whether Liston should be or shouldn't be allowed to fight." Gregory also argued that Liston deserved a chance to fight for the title. Harlem congressman Adam Clayton Powell, also always eager to tweak liberal sentiments, underlined the idea that "in our democracy ... every man should be given a second chance." Liston, he said, deserved that opportunity, adding, "If he doesn't have that chance, you will be sending him back to where he came from." Some could argue, and hindsight would confirm, that even if Liston had the chance, he would still "go back," but even though he did, the ques-tion that could not but dominate the boxing landscape then simply concerned who was the better fighter. In the barber shops and bars of the day, the irony of how in 1962 a good-quality white boxer with a record of some sort of Klan-style violence would have never been denied a title shot was not lost, but no one of prominence would put that in print.[7] In the late 1970s, a South African boxer named Kallie Knoetze ranked in the top ten of the world's heavyweights. Knoetze also had an unsavory past, as he had served in the apartheid-enforc-ing South African police and had once shot and killed a young black protester in Pretoria. Several African American political leaders protested Knoetze get-ting any shot at the title. As with Liston, the protests raged, but no fights were cancelled. Knoetze's star fizzled, as in June of 1979 he lost to a rising Ameri-can fighter named John Tate and never fought a significant bout after that.

With Liston and Patterson, the simple question of who was the better boxer came ever more to dominate the debate. As long as Liston was not under actual indictment or in jail, most believed he should be allowed to fight. Patterson had said he would fight Liston if his connections were above reproach. In May of 1961, Patterson noted Liston "has got[ten] rid of some of the people around him," adding, "next year he should be even cleaner." Against the expressed advice of the NAACP, of Estes Kefauver, and of sev-eral boxing commissioners, Patterson came to an agreement with Liston in 1962. Patterson had told young Howard Cosell in a radio interview that Lis-ton deserved a title shot. In cognizance of Liston's past, Patterson was mag-nanimous, genuinely so given his own boyhood, pointing out that "many of us get off to a bad start in life" and that "Liston has paid for his crimes." Not-ing that he had met Liston at a boxing writers' dinner, Patterson noted "I think he has a lot of good in him." From there he frankly added: "Should he be able to win the championship, these qualities will rise to the surface. I think you would see a completely new and changed Liston." With all the generous talk of second chances and redemption, Liston did nothing here which anyone of the slightest political acumen would have advised. Upon being told of Patterson's ennobling gestures, he simply snorted: "I'd like to run him over with a truck." The question of who was the better human being was and would never be in question. When Patterson retook the crown from Johansson, Patterson had been unnerved by the sight of Johansson out cold on the canvas with his left foot twitching. Reflecting on the hate he had summoned for the fight, Patterson had confessed, "I hope I never have to be that vicious again," later noting while preparing for Liston "I have to build up a viciousness for him. How this feeling will come, I'm not sure." Liston showed everyone quite clearly that he would always be vicious and not lose a second of sleep over any of the consequences from it. For many fans, the smirks engendered by Liston's utterly mean nature reinforced the sense that he was the superior fighter. The fight was on, and there would be no diminution of the social contrasts at play here.[8]

After Patterson's two defeats of Johansson, Sonny Liston loomed as the principal heavyweight contender in 1962. Many boxing pundits and public officials from Cus D'Amato to President John Kennedy advised against the idea of Floyd Patterson fighting Sonny Liston. Keenly concerned with the undue power of the mob, many federal officials felt such a connected figure with an utterly sordid past as Liston did not deserve a title shot. Several NAACP leaders felt exactly the same way. The simpler question of "who's the better fighter?" held the day among the general public, however. Patterson heeded the public pressure and agreed to a bout with Liston. The ambivalence of the situation was reflected in both their faces at the fight's contract-signing ceremony. In the fight, Liston would utterly annihilate Patterson in the first round and do it again in a rematch. ©Bettmann/CORBIS.

As the details for the Patterson-Liston bout were being negotiated in the winter and spring of 1962, a major tragedy struck the boxing world. On March 24, 1962, Emile Griffith knocked out Benny "Kid" Paret in a welterweight championship fight at Madison Square Garden. The two had fought twice before, each winning once. There was bad blood between them. A major factor here involved Paret deriding Griffith's manhood and alluding to his homosexuality, a most taboo topic anywhere in 1962, let alone among professional boxers. In twelfth round of the fight, Griffith cornered Paret and battered him mercilessly. Then and since, many criticized the respected veteran referee Ruby Goldstein for not stopping things sooner. Regardless of possible blame, Paret was knocked unconscious. He had suffered two brain hemorrhages. Comatose, he was rushed directly to a hospital where he was operated on to relieve bleeding and pressure in his brain. The doctors' efforts would prove fruitless, however, as Paret's injuries were too extensive. Paret never regained consciousness, and ten days later he died. Benny Paret's death was by no means the first fatality in professional boxing. Since 1900, an estimated 450 had died in the ring. In 1962 alone, three boxers had died prior to Paret. Paret's death was also not even the first in Madison Square Garden. (Georgie Flores died fighting Roger Donoghue in the Garden in 1951, and Primo Carnera killed Ernie Schaaf there in 1933.) Still, no fight ending in a death had ever been so high profile, and reactions were severe. In Washington, Senator Estes Kefauver reasserted the need for more effective federal control over boxing. In the emotionally trying days immediately after the fight, Paret's manager, Manuel Alfaro, had been criticizing the work of referee Goldstein, and he told of receiving death threats for his perceived insolence. This added to Kefauver's concern about the mob's presence in the sport. The British Broadcasting Company halted all boxing broadcasts, and several newspapers editorialized that something needed to be done about the dangers of the sport. Some began calling for the sport simply to treated like bullfighting or cockfighting and be permanently banned.[9]

The state-by-state structure of boxing authority in the United States made any sort of outright ban highly unlikely, but the talk was widespread. Out in California, for example, a hotly contested race for governor was taking place between incumbent Gov. Edmund G. "Pat" Brown and former Vice President Richard Nixon. Even though the Paret fight had occurred in New York, the tragedy entered the two candidates' cross-fires. Nixon and Brown openly differed on the state issue of capital punishment. Brown was against it, and in that context he was asked about Paret's death. The governor went on the record here, stating that he wanted to outlaw boxing in California. He openly acknowledged that his position would likely gain a poor reception among several groups including "the beer drinkers, the sweatshirt crowd, [and] the minority groups." Always a big fight fan, and equally eager to garner votes from the very groups that Brown enumerated, Richard Nixon opposed any such boxing bans. Whether the fallout from the Paret tragedy was a factor or not, later that autumn, Brown defeated Nixon.

While Californians and others debated, the discussions about boxing's future bristled in earnest back in New York, as Madison Square Garden had been the site of the Paret debacle. Even though they knew it would be a futile gesture, the *New York Times* called for a statewide ban of boxing. No such ban would ever come, but Paret's death would mark the beginning of a decided decline in the previously unquestioned place of New York as the world's center of prizefighting. In the 1930s and since 1945, no city, indeed no combination of any other fight locales equaled the significance New York had held in the nation's (or the world's) fight game. Even before Paret's death, a few changes had already begun. Back in June 1961, the famous Stillman's Gym had announced it was closing, as the property had been purchased for development. In the spring of 1962, scarcely a month after Paret's death, old St. Nicholas Arena on 56th Street also closed its doors. Plans were already in the works for a new Madison Square Garden on 33rd Street to displace the boxing mecca that was the Garden on 78th Street and Eighth Avenue. The harmful mob connection publicity was also not going away. Until the death of Paret, such developments indicated no collective significance. Now they all seemed to be contributing to an unraveling.[10]

The huge image problem that was threatening boxing and impacting New York placed yet more pressure on Patterson to uphold what was left of boxing's decency and respectability, especially given the nature of his next opponent. Patterson, indeed, continued some of his charitable work, making several appearances in early 1962 on behalf of the NAACP and for several New York community centers. Virtually all public attention on Patterson, however, concerned the upcoming bout with Liston. During the negotiations with Liston, there were the usual wranglings over money and location. As matters dragged on, Liston took the opportunity to tweak Patterson's nose, claiming the delays were due to Patterson simply stalling. Here Liston feigned compassion and understanding for Patterson's position, pointing out that he fully understood how a man about to go to the electric chair would always stall for time. It was a nice verbal jab, but many felt the allusion was hardly appropriate given what had just happened to Paret. Few expected little more of Liston anyway. Meanwhile, Liston just smiled about it all.[11]

While the fallout from Paret's death did not lead New York State to banish the sport, it did sour the enthusiasm many New Yorkers had about staging the Patterson-Liston bout. "New York does not need it," pompously proclaimed the *New York Times*. In early April, the paper ran an article listing the toll of boxing deaths—450 since 1900; three others besides Paret already in 1962. On April 27, the New York State Athletic Commission explicitly denied Sonny Liston a license to fight there. Liston's long police record and mobbed-up image were somewhat pompously held to be part of the picture here, but the fallout from Paret's death certainly added pressure to the situation. The *Times* applauded. Had other states followed suit here, the Paret tragedy may have led to a truly significant shift in boxing's future in the United States. But as soon as New York wavered even the slightest bit in its desire to host the Patterson-Liston bout, a slew of other already-interested locales eagerly leapt at the prospect. The Cuban Kid Paret's death was one thing, but hosting a heavyweight championship fight meant status and money. For many chamber of commerce types, that was the long and the short of the debate. Chicago, Baltimore, Las Vegas, Los Angeles, Seattle, Detroit, Philadelphia, Dallas, and Houston all made bids. The New York Commission's noble efforts thus proved pure illusion. Indeed, the futility of the state's posture quickly engendered some guffawing. "New York boxing officials, in a high moment of morality," chuckled Gay Talese, "declared that Liston's police record and table manners are unworthy of Manhattan's Eighth Avenue [cite of Madison Square Garden] standards, and so refused him a license to practice mayhem in this state." Boxing would indeed decline in New York. A heavyweight championship fight would not take place in New York City for five years, when Muhammad Ali met Zora Folley in March 1967. By then, the noble sentiments in the wake of Paret's passing were long gone, and N.Y. boxing writers were now nobly applauding the return of boxing to its rightful headquarters. With New York temporarily out of the picture, the boxing world simply sorted out its many suitors, the temporary hiccough of New York morality apparently having no impact anywhere else. With Patterson's support and Liston's acquiescence, Chicago was ultimately selected as the site for their bout. Negotiations first focused on Soldiers' Field, with the hope of building upon the legacy of the famous Dempsey-Tunney "long-count" fight held there in 1927. The city's Comiskey Park offered a better deal, however. Its management demanded a lower percentage of the gate, so there it would be — Comiskey Park, September 25.[12]

Out in Illinois that summer, the two fighters settled into training camps. Reporters covered their preparations. With the clear noble-evil dichotomy between the two figures, the build-up to the fight came to involve more than the thoughts of traditional boxing writers. To many thoughtful people, the fight symbolized the clash of messages to and images from the nation's African American communities. Neither fighter was cast here as an Uncle Tom. That was not at issue. Patterson was a hero to many involved in the early years of the civil rights movement. He had always appeared altogether civilized, religious, urbane, modest yet intent, everything that civil rights leaders could use as they proclaimed to the nation: we obviously deserve to be treated as the equals of anyone. (Conversely, Sonny Liston obviously did not represent any such example, and they officially deemed him "a poor example for the youth of America.") *Esquire Magazine's* publisher, Arnold Gingrich, noted: "I'm awfully impressed with the way Patterson talks. I've heard Senators who aren't half as good." Poet Marianne Moore proclaimed Patterson's autobiography "a manual for descriptive writing, ... delicately done, ... a model of modesty and tenacity." Various other literati descended upon Chicago to cover the two men and the fight. Author James Baldwin visited Patterson and extolled the champion's nature. "There is," he wrote, "a kind of gentleness and a kind of toughness [in Patterson] I've seen all my life." He gave Patterson copies of two of his books—*Another Country* and *Nobody Knows My Name*. On them, Baldwin inscribed: "For Floyd Patterson: Because we both know whence we come, and have some idea of where we're going." Baldwin's presence appeared to hold much significance. It was as though the great writer from Harlem was saying to all those allegedly chic, street-smart white writers who had been gnashing for years over the riddle of "Freud" Patterson, that he understood Patterson's complexity completely, hence that the goodness he represented was solid and could meet both the challenge to civility as well as the one to boxing posed by the fearsome Sonny Liston.[13]

The major betting lines favored Liston, but *Sports Illustrated* reified liberal hopes with a prediction of a Patterson victory. Whatever perceived weaknesses that had grown about Patterson because of his performances in some prior bouts, *SI* optimistically accounted them as extensions of the quality of his opponents. "Patterson," *SI* opined, "is only as good as he believes his adversary to be." Praising Patterson's speed and versatility as assets Liston neither possessed nor had ever seen in an opponent, the widely popular magazine believed it would be "Patterson in 15." Among former champions, James J. Braddock, Joe Walcott, Ezzard Charles, Rocky Marciano, and Ingemar Johansson all picked Patterson to win the fight. (Charles actually told *Sports Illustrated* that Patterson would win, while predicting a Liston victory to the *Pittsburgh Courier*.) Jack Dempsey, Joe Louis, and Sugar Ray Robinson were not sure. Ben Skelton, a professional sparring partner who had recently worked with both Patterson and Liston also gave Patterson some positive spin. Like Marty Marshall, Skelton was certainly respectful of Liston's power. Referring to Liston's left jab, Skelton could not have been more emphatic: "I've never felt a punch equal to it," he observed, "and that includes Joe Louis.' It is so hard that for a week after being hit with it I was taking pills to kill the pain." But Skelton contrasted how Sonny disdained road work, while Patterson "is a demon for running," so, he predicted, "around the seventh round Sonny is going to run out of leg." Skelton's analysis seemed plausible. Sonny had one style—slugging. Hence if Patterson could mix up his style, he could frustrate Liston, tire Liston, and pile up points. Clearly, Patterson had the skills to do this—a young kid's legs and quickness with a veteran's savvy. But, warned Skelton: "Floyd also has a stubborn pride, and if this pride overrules his good sense and he chooses to stand in the ring and slug it out — then that's it." Others also worried similarly for more technical reasons. Patterson's best weapons were his hooks. To employ them he had to get in close, and that was very risky against a man like Liston. "There is trouble ahead for Patterson," noted the *Pittsburgh Courier*'s Wendell Smith.[14]

Amidst various liberals seeking bases for optimism, James Baldwin's sometimes friend Norman Mailer reflected further on the social implications of the big fight. Touring about the training camps, as well as around the city of Chicago, Mailer noted that "just about every Negro one talked to in Chicago" was for Patterson. It was not, Mailer wrote, "only the grey-haired Negroes with the silver-rimmed glasses and the dignity of the grave, the teachers, the deacons, the welfare workers, the camp directors, the church organists who were for Patterson, ... the word was out — 'You got to stick with the champion.'" Of course, as Mailer himself noted, he was a white man. Hence there was "no need to assume the questions were asked so skillfully or decently that the truth was obliged to appear." Expressing support of Patterson may have been the safe answer — what white liberals wanted to hear. With the memories of the "snaky elegance one finds in ... [a] Sugar Ray Robinson," some like Mailer sensed that beneath the church-goers' support for Patterson lay a sense that beneath it all lay the real truth was that the world of Sonny — the mob, the pimps, the dope dealers, the prostitutes ... was going to take that tightly wound NAACP world of Floyd Patterson, Ralph Bunche, Eleanor Roosevelt, Adlai Stevenson, Jackie Robinson, and Jack Kennedy and tear it apart like some sort of meaningless welfare check that never came close to covering the ever-inflating bills. Floyd Patterson was outwardly a symbol to African Americans, "the Great Black Hope of the Urban League," as Gay Talese called him, whose legacy implied that the white man's middle class security was attainable if one worked hard and played by the rules. Liston symbolized a one-word answer to such noble thoughts, one that resonated with many on the margins — "Bull____!"[15]

Liston appeared to do everything he could to fit the evil-incarnate image everyone held of him. Upon the arrival of a London TV executive who was visiting his Chicago camp, Liston calmly took out a revolver and shot one of his handlers whom he accused of stealing $50 from him. The spurting blood turned out to be ketchup, and the bullets — blanks. Liston greatly enjoyed the stunned looks on his guests' faces. "It's frightening to be in the same room with Liston," nodded writer Bud Schulberg. Liston enjoyed such clippings. Getting close to him was like going to a horror movie. People knew they were going to be scared but somehow they still wanted to explore the dark catacombs of their souls, with the world of boxing seeming an altogether appropriate place for such a sinister exploration.

With his dark, intimidating ways, Sonny Liston represented no direct opposition to African American advancement and civil rights; he just appeared to hold a steady, spiteful sneer at all notions of morality and decency. He embodied all that was evil and fearsome about the parts of the African America that mainstream America tried to ignore, could never forget, and dreaded the thought of their children ever contacting. The dope dealers, the seedy jazz clubs, the pimps, the prostitutes, the loan sharks, the violent criminals — no one needed to use some sort of McCarthyistic label to convey the fear this world posed. It spoke for itself quite simply and effectively. This was a world that always responded to mainstream America with a decided contempt, one that said not only that it didn't want or need any help from or integration with the mainstream, but that it could and, with the slightest opportunity, would yank as much of that safe, pretty world down to its mean level just as fast and hard and brutally as it could. With nineteen criminal arrests and a glower that appeared to spit acid from his eyes, Sonny Liston was every bit the embodiment of all that. He was truly satanic, and that summer in Chicago no description could be too hyperbolic: "the toughest man to hit Chicago since John Dillinger;" wrote one scribe with a smile; "the most frightening fighter," said another, "since Goliath." "Liston," rhapsodized Norman Mailer, "was the secret hero of every man who had ever given mouth to a final curse against the dispositions of the Lord and made a pact with Black Magic. Liston was Faust." For many thoughtful people, Patterson, who certainly came from as tough a background as Sonny, represented a hopeful world that simply had to prove it was the greater force. It just had to. (Please!) Amidst all the prognostications, metaphors, and social commentary, the bookies installed Liston as the favorite. Some said 3:2; others 7:5 and 8:5; the lines held right up to the time of the fight. The wagering was heavy, and the ticket sales were brisk. The Chicago Stadium sold out, and closed circuit television sold 600,000 seats at 247 locations, a record that would stand until Muhammad Ali and Joe Frazier first fought in 1971.[16]

The clash of metaphors, symbols, and cultures inherent in the fight could have yielded several appropriate finishes in the ring. Obviously, if Patterson had won, liberal America, white and black, would have smiled smugly and broadly. Had there been an ebb and flow in the fight over several rounds with each giving and taking something to and from the other, an outcome for either would have been coincidental to the symbolism of their two worlds coming to terms amidst the struggle of two men who came to respect each other in the crucible of a great duel in the ring and embraced thereafter. What happened gave no room for any such reactions and inferences. The bell rang. The two sparred a bit. About six punches were thrown. Liston connected with a right to the head. Patterson went down. He struggled to get up and didn't quite make it. That was it; two minutes and six seconds in the first round.

People were stunned. It all happened so fast and with such brutal decisiveness, "like a man beating the resistance out of a boy in a street fight," wrote one shaken pundit. At the closed-circuit theaters, many had barely settled into their seats. As for the cultural symbolism of the fight, those searching for meaning could only draw the worst. Writer Joyce Carol Oates, herself a great boxing enthusiast, applauded great matches that brought out the souls of opponents in true tests of stamina and skill, but to her such a mismatch as Liston-Patterson made her feel nothing but sheer physical loathing. "Civilization's trajectory," she conjectured, "is to curve back upon itself ... like the mythical snake biting its own tail and take up with passion the outward signs of gestures of 'savagery.'"

If anyone embodied such savage signs and gestures, it was Liston. No matter how others bought or rejected such rhapsodizing, amidst it, Patterson seemed the pathetic, helpless victim. Howard Cosell made Liston chuckle when he fed him a line. Cosell asked him with a smirk, "At what point in the fight did you realize that you had Floyd Patterson beaten?" Some speculated that Liston's baleful stare at Patterson in front of the referee before the opening bell had beaten Floyd right there. Whether or not that was true, the fact that some believed it spoke volumes as to how overwhelming was the sense of Sonny's victory. Novelist Norman Mailer spent the night after the fight drinking steadily. Without sleep, he staggered into a Liston press conference the next morning, blathering loudly that Patterson had actually "won the fight existentially." No one had a clue as to what he meant, not even, indeed especially, Mailer. Some other reporters and several of Liston's people were ready to toss Mailer out of the conference room. Sonny Liston was actually the one who reacted with the most charity here. Mailer was able to get close enough to Liston to whisper to him that he could drum up controversy and yield a rematch which would give him a much, much bigger payday. "Let the bum speak," Liston snorted. Mailer had little to say, of course, but Liston half smiled Mailer's way and nodded, "I like this guy; ... we both came here to make money."[17]

Patterson was not physically hurt. He would eventually be $165,827 richer. This was delayed because of a round of disputes with the IRS. (A young assistant to Attorney General Robert Kennedy, Bob Arum, investigated possible illegal transfers of income. Some had expected Patterson would bank as much as $2 million to $2.5 million.) Patterson left the ring and stayed in the dressing room for a full half hour. Sandra, his mother, and several of his brothers and cousins were with him. As they came out, it was clear that Sandra had been crying. No one from the family had much to say to the press. What was there to say? Back in New York that night, the Yankees had just clinched the pennant. They were celebrating in the locker room when word came in about Patterson losing in the first round. "Oh no," remarked pitcher Whitey Ford,

"That's terrible. This spoils the night for me." As they left the arena, Patterson and his party tried to leave Comiskey Park through the ushers' room. They accidentally locked themselves in and had to hacksaw a padlock on the back door. Patterson donned sunglasses and fake whiskers. He left with the disguise on and drove all the way back to New York. The trip took thirty hours, and it was about as depressing a thirty hour span as anyone could imagine. With the sunglasses and fake whiskers, many wondered the obvious question: who brings a disguise to a championship fight in case of a loss? What do such preparations say about a man's confidence? Patterson had actually packed the same disguise gear for his second and third fights with Johansson and for his Toronto fight with Tommy McNeeley. As Joe Louis once said, "A fighter can't think that way." Promoter Roy Cohn snapped at reporters who asked him about the apparent mismatch. "Why blame me for a bad fight?" Cohn scoffed, pointing at Patterson's dressing room, "How did I know he was going to turn yellow?" Many wondered about Patterson's confidence more generally, but since this was part of a regular set of known habits, others could dismiss the psychological morsel as not terribly important. Still, to the many head scratchers, the issue of "Freud" Patterson now had more evidence to consider. The really damning point here was that it now did not seem to matter so much. Who cares about analyzing a loser? All attention was now on Sonny. Deep down, everyone was still afraid of him. Nevertheless some even tried to make him into a likable hero. When Patterson had tried to see good in Liston, people scoffed.[18]

The night Patterson beat Johansson to recapture the crown, he had reacted in horror when the felled Johansson lay on the canvas with his left leg quivering convulsively. Patterson confessed that he had developed a hatred for Johansson in the year after he had lost the championship to him. After viewing the twitching carcass of Johansson, Patterson resolved never to hate again, and the boxing public and press applauded in solemn satisfaction that the champion was taking the art of championship boxing to a truly higher level. After Liston's victory, many of the same arm-chair boxing experts took such a resolve as proof of the man's lack of championship mettle. Bill Nunn of the *Pittsburgh Courier* had been one of Patterson's strongest supporters. He now wrote of Patterson's "ineptness in attempting to defend his title" and of how many ticket buyers legitimately felt "'taken.'" Others wrote wondering "how Patterson had ever become champion in the first place" or whether a return bout was really necessary. The sporting public is never kind to losers, and in boxing the fair-weather nature of most friendships is probably the cruelest. One reporter cavalierly sniffed at Patterson's vow against hatred as having been "good Dostoevsky, but not reassuring to bettors."[19]

Soon after getting back to New York, Patterson took a get-away trip to Spain. He wore the same fake beard, moustache, and glasses, with which he'd left Chicago. Now he added a hat. As he made his way to the airport, he also limped in order to make himself look older. Writer Gay Talese later learned that Patterson would spend $3000 annually to maintain a set of disguises. Some of this may have stemmed from a desire to avoid attention in general, but shame was certainly a big motive here. At this point, Patterson's depression was enormous, even greater than what followed the loss to Johansson. Now no encounters with the sick and suffering in New York area hospitals would revive him. Perhaps it was because he had lost in such an overwhelmingly disastrous way and because part of him knew, deep down, that he could not beat Liston. He thought of all those months of training, and pondered how it was all a waste given the brevity of the bout. Trying to get away, he could only think of how he could have done this sooner too. "I was alone," he muttered in recollection, when I got to the airport "I didn't care what plane I boarded; I just looked up and saw this sign at the terminal reading 'Madrid,' and so I got on that flight." When he got to Madrid, Patterson registered in a hotel under an assumed name — "Aaron Watson." It was illegal to do that in Spain, as a local identification or a foreign passport was required to register, but Madrid hotel clerks proved to be willing to make allowances if properly paid. The time in Spain was hardly restorative. Still in disguise and under an alias, it was like returning to the Brooklyn subway hole in which he used to hide as a boy. All sense of how he had eclipsed the troubled young lad he had once been was now stripped away. Wiltwyck, Eleanor Roosevelt, President Kennedy, not only did their support no longer matter, he felt he had let them all down. "In the daytime [in Madrid] I wandered around the poorest sections of the city, limping, looking at the people, and the people stared back at me and must have thought I was crazy because I was moving so slow and looked the way I did." It was as though the street kid had to condemn himself to what he had imagined he would turn into if he hadn't gotten off the streets of Bedford-Stuyvesant in the first place. Everything he did seemed perversely calculated to accentuate his depression. He took most of his meals in his hotel. When he went to a restaurant, he ordered soup. "I hate soup," he confessed. "But I thought it was what old people would order. So I ate it. And it was after a week of this [that] I began to actually think I was somebody else." When he later reflected on such behavior, after another ring loss, Patterson mused. "You must wonder what makes a man do things like this. Well I wonder too. And the answer is, I don't know.... I think that within me there is a certain weakness. It is a weakness that exposes itself more when you're alone. I have figured out that part of the reason I do the things I do, and cannot seem to conquer that one word — *myself*— is because I am a coward" (emphasis his).[20] Patterson's autobiography had been entitled *Victory Over Myself*. He seemed to have forsaken everything he had accomplished. As there was not a hint of frivolity in his words, it is difficult to imagine how someone, short of suicide, could be more depressed.

Theorizing about the Liston fight began to grow. Among those who wanted to find an excuse for Patterson, a few could get away with the notion that Liston had simply landed a lucky punch. There had always been the haunting sense that Liston was so much the heavier hitter that Patterson did not stand a chance. The two-minute knockout made that hard to dispute. Some were speculating that Patterson had lost the edge off some of his skills when he asserted some independence from Cus D'Amato. (Before the fight, of course, many of the same reporters were praising Patterson for having separated himself from the complete dictates of Cus.) Patterson now seemed a kind of unsympathetic teacher's pet who'd been unduly elevated by the special treatment and had now gotten a rude awakening from one of the other kids in the class, never so anointed but actually just as, indeed much more sharp. This of course touched on the sensitive point that back when D'Amato called all the shots, he had kept Patterson on top by avoiding the top challengers. As before, these debates went around and around, but as the fight had been such a quick massacre, the discussions now had a distinct hollowness.

The overwhelming nature of Liston's victory quickly embedded itself in the nation's vocabulary. When the stock market dipped on September 26, the *Wall Street Journal* described previous day's gains as "a rally that lasted about as long Floyd Patterson." At the end of September, the Los Angeles Dodgers shortstop Maury Wills bettered Ty Cobb's single season stolen base record. This new record brought to the fore many old stories about Cobb, including his clash with Honus Wagner in the 1909 World Series. Recounting how Cobb had tried in vain to intimidate Wagner, one reporter noted that trying to scare Wagner "was as profitless as Floyd Patterson trying to scare Sonny Liston." In late September, early October, when the Los Angeles Dodgers lost the pennant to the San Francisco Giants, L.A.'s fall from a five and one-half game August lead was called "the Floyd Patterson collapse." L.A.'s collapse included thirty consecutive innings without a run, and their hitting power here was said to have "rated in the same class as Patterson."

In early October, with the year's elections approaching, political commentator Tom Wicker wrote a column in which he pointed out how a certain ability to nuance one's thoughts usually served a candidate well. Politicians, he wrote, "like Floyd Patterson, may be shown that the graceful evasion prolongs a career better than the proffered chin." In a similar spirit, *New York Times* columnist James Reston praised President Kennedy's deftness at picking opponents and issues when he campaigned. "Floyd Patterson," Reston joked, "is no longer heavyweight champion of the world today because he ignored Kennedy's law of prudent selection." Some could have pointed out that when Cus D'Amato was selecting opponents prudently for Patterson, few were praising him. The inconsistencies here were irrelevant, however, as Patterson, the man, was no longer important. He was a symbol, and now a somewhat pathetic one, to be exploited. Patterson's image versus Liston's dirty past was now of little importance. Liston's sordid nature was no less distasteful, but it did not need any contrasts with the image of a "loser."[21]

Patterson, wrote columnist Gay Talese, had been proof that a man could arise out of the slums, succeed as a sportsman, and be a sensitive, intelligent good citizen. His loss to Liston proved to some that in the process of that transformation he had lost some of his hunger and anger. The logic in such analyses was specious, as well as completely circular, but in the sports world pundits always love to make sweeping sociological theories out of the most minimal evidence. Patterson reflected on this point: "It's okay to be the good guy when you're winning. But when you're losing, it is no good being the good guy." A few weeks before Christmas, the Wiltwyck School suddenly found itself in need of more money. Patterson no longer seemed able to raise funds anymore.[22]

For a time the only comfort for Patterson could be found in the fact that he and Liston were slated for a rematch. Patterson did actually take up flying, and that may have given him something in which to absorb himself and help lift the post-fight depression. In any event, he did take lessons and eventually get a pilot's license. Nonetheless, his depression was severe. He could not sustain his attention even to read a book. "I just feel that no writer today has anything for me," he shrugged. "I mean none of them has felt any more deeply than I have, and I have nothing to learn from them." The issue of fighting Liston preoccupied him, just as had the prospect of a rematch after losing to Ingemar Johansson. Among boxing fans and writers, the thought of another Patterson-Liston bout made more than one reporter scoff. "They won't need a stadium for that one," snickered one. "Any room slightly larger than a telephone booth would suffice." When the fight site was being negotiated, one writer mused that "the ideal spot would be Ulan Bator in Outer Mongolia." Former champion Gene Tunney scoffed that the first fight had been "a terrible hoax."

Patterson had indeed actually fallen to number two among the contenders, with Eddie Machen taking the top spot. Meanwhile Cassius Clay, now number seven, was making even more noise. It was here that for the first time reporters heard him pronounce: "I am the greatest." He bragged how he had knocked out Archie Moore in four rounds and predicted he would knock out Liston in eight. In regard to the Liston-Patterson fight, Clay declared it "was an embarrassment to boxing." With a bit of sardonic wit he noted how "the champion of the world should be able to take a beating longer than that." Later he waxed poetic in ways that would soon become one of his famous trademarks:

As the people left the park,
You could hear them say:
Liston will stay king
Until he meets Cassius Clay.

While Cassius Clay may have wanted to, or at least said he wanted to fight Sonny Liston, Liston himself dismissed the idea, spitting: "I don't fight children." There was actually talk of a bout between Clay and Patterson, especially after Clay knocked out Archie Moore in four rounds on November 15. Hindsight may reveal that fighting Clay to have been a reasonable alternative for Patterson, and Patterson was actually offered twice what he would get for his second fight with Liston if he would first fight Clay. There was no chance of this occurring, however. Patterson had one thing on his mind. Clay's next fight would be against a solid journeyman named Doug Jones, and he would barely beat him by a decision, one which many fans and reporters hotly disputed. For a time, Clay's stock dipped a bit, with *Sports Illustrated* headlining, "Cassius Clay turns out to be an illogical contender, ... a clown instead of a contender." Meanwhile, the return-match clause in the original contract between Liston and Patterson was not to be disregarded. Patterson would think of nothing else but fighting Liston. With a seemingly nervous codicil in his thoughts that again sent analysts scratching their heads, Patterson said: "I believe I have a good chance of regaining the title for the second time, although I am by no means cocksure about it." No one else was either.[23]

Some sectors of the New York sports world continued to snort and recoil from boxing. They reminded people of the death of Benny "Kid" Paret. Two other boxing deaths that year — Davey Moore and Ernie Knox — compounded the anger, as did another horrible set of injuries sustained in the ring by the Argentinian heavyweight Alejandro Lavorante, injuries which left him a paraplegic, and dead within a year. Once again, however, the rest of the country's major sports sites proceeded to do anything but extend any moral indignation. Of those that jumped at the chance to hold the next heavyweight championship, Miami Beach, Florida, did the best job this time. The rematch was first set for there in April 1963. Then Liston twisted a knee, swinging a golf club while relaxing after a day's training, thus postponing the bout until June and ruining the Miami Beach plans. After some hand trouble from Patterson, the June date also had to be put off a month. The final arrangements were for July 22 with Las Vegas as the site.[24]

Amidst the preparations for the second Liston fight, the nation's civil rights movement was heating up in several circles. A major crisis erupted in Birmingham, Alabama, with the bombing of an African American Baptist church that May. The resistance of the city's all-white government to bring the church bombers to justice or to do anything that even began to phase out the laws and customs of racial segregation had been growing increasingly ugly. Beyond the church bombing, Birmingham's notorious police chief, "Bull" Connor, employed German shepherd dogs and the city fire department's high pressure hoses to attack demonstrators.

Amidst these troubles, Floyd Patterson joined with former baseball player Jackie Robinson to go to Birmingham and stand with the beleaguered demonstrators. "I have to live with myself [and] look at myself in the mirror each morning," Patterson explained. Recognizing how greater his fortunes were than so many, he affirmed: "Whatever I have to do to relieve my conscience I will do. You have to have respect for yourself.... You have to put first things first." More than anything, Patterson simply wanted to play a part in the movement, noting with sincere modesty, "I'm not a politician, and I'm not a leader. I just like to be an active participant, one of the crowd." Sizing up the situation in Birmingham, Patterson noted almost like he was preparing for a fight, which indeed he was: "I expect to be handled roughly." While Patterson affirmed Martin Luther King's call for non-violence, he did add, "I will protect myself against police dogs." Dr. King's theory of non-violence required often super-human discipline. The slightly less than full nature of Patterson's adherence reflected, in reverse, somewhat the same sort of complexity over which many boxing aficionados had been pondering for years. While in Birmingham, Patterson took part in a protest parade and indeed

Patterson endured many of the indignities of racism that affected all African Americans in the 1950s and 1960s. In his generally quiet manner, Patterson spent a great deal of time and effort in service to the NAACP, CORE, and other organizations in their efforts to combat the many legacies of Jim Crow. Here in 1963, Patterson, second from the left, confers with Ralph Abernathy, Martin Luther King, and baseball great Jackie Robinson as they gathered in Birmingham, Alabama, to confront the city's racial violence. ©Bettmann/CORBIS.

felt the fear of the struggle. "You feel like an animal in the jungle," he noted, adding with, for him, a verbally clumsy touch that likely reflected the anxiety he felt, "It's not like part of the United States." Some may have thought that Liston would never feel such emotions. Others could point out that Liston would never go to Birmingham in the first place — unless someone was paying him.[25]

Amidst the furor over the Birmingham situation and the involvement of people like Patterson and Robinson, voices from a seemingly new political angle among African Americans began to be heard. Theretofore little known outside of African American communities, Nation of Islam leader Malcolm X expressed criticisms of some of the civil rights activities in Birmingham. He criticized, for example, how Birmingham's civil rights leaders, including King, were intentionally using children in the demonstrations to draw sympathetic press and general public attention. Malcolm X made a point here of adding that Jackie Robinson and Floyd Patterson were going down to Birmingham to serve liberal whites' hopes that they can "head the columns away from trouble." These sorts of criticisms were but the beginnings of some serious disputes among 1960s African American activists. From the outset, Patterson knew what the black radical movements were doing, and he would always have nothing to do with figures like Malcolm X and the organizations around him. In that spring he adamantly declared: "I have no respect for the Black Muslims. They're a colored Ku Klux Klan. They're out for revenge more than anything else." Patterson had internalized his Catholicism quite dutifully and sincerely. The Black Muslims represented so much into which he knew he could have fallen from the streets of Brooklyn had but a few circumstances in his life been only slightly different. He saw the moral choices he had made to be the wise ones, and could not see organizations like the Black Muslims as being anything but morally flawed. He would never alter his views here, but Malcolm X's slaps felt like verbal versions of what Sonny had thrown at him several months before. At the time they were but a nuisance, but they were the first wave of an onslaught that would come to hurt at least as much as Liston.

Meanwhile in Birmingham on May 10, about 2,000 demonstrators would turn out to see Patterson and Jackie Robinson speak. Robinson and Patterson exhorted the people not to waver in their commitments to the cause of civil rights. The crowd cheered loudly and warmly. As Malcolm X had criticized, they were indeed meeting on the other side of the city from where most of the violence had been occurring. The wisdom of such decisions, and many more such decisions thereafter, remained up for debate. They were still close to the troubles, and could they have met closer to the site of the bombing and not risked greater violence, with no positive results and quite possibly more deaths and injuries? During the Birmingham riots, President Kennedy expressed fears that the non-violent approach to the civil rights movement could fail and that, if it did, the door could open to such extremist groups as the Black Muslims. Kennedy would not live to see the mixed results that would emerge here in the politics of 1960s African American political activism. And neither he nor anyone else could foresee how the world of boxing would come not merely to reflect but actually contribute to the shaping of this political mix. For the time being, however, such political matters appeared peripheral to boxing. Patterson's involvement seemed aberrational. Over and over, Sonny Liston simply shrugged at repeated questions of politics, of Martin Luther King, or of Malcolm X. He scoffed, "Just stupid questions, that's all."[26]

No matter the words of Malcolm X, Patterson's commitment to the cause of civil rights did not waver. Was Patterson unwittingly abetting a moderate-liberal cause, laced with postures and manipulations? At the very least, the defenders and romanticizers of Malcolm X enjoy(ed) such assertions, then and since. The debates over proper approaches as well as over the sincerity of various parties grew heated and unresolved at the time; historians' ruminations have provided more debate but no resolutions or consensus.

Floyd Patterson's involvement would represent one element in the ways the boxing world would both represent and influence the different elements of African American outlooks in the decade of the 1960s. On the one hand, there was the moderate-liberal Patterson. Meanwhile, the contrasting, non-involvement of Sonny Liston, sneeringly committed to nothing but himself, marked an obvious contrast. It was like the musical tastes of boxing fans shifting from Nat King Cole to Miles Davis. The emergence of a decidedly different voice in this political mix, which had come first with Malcolm X, was initially (and for some permanently) quite a mystery to the nation's political mainstream. In Muhammad Ali, the boxing world would provide a — indeed *the*— major force of visibility and demystification here. The different voices among African Americans would each continue and have influential personifications in politics and in the world of heavyweight boxing. Their relative strengths as fighters would serve the strengths of the various causes they each represented. Indeed as the police dogs and the fire hoses continued to plague demonstrators in Birmingham, Patterson helped out where he could, and the likes of Malcolm X and his select circles continued to take his work on racial issues about as seriously as the boxing public now regarded the former champion as a pugilist. Such political and athletic disregard would only grow.

XI

Four Seconds Longer

Out in Las Vegas, city officials were delighted to host the upcoming heavyweight rematch between Sonny Liston and Floyd Patterson. Amidst the fires, riots, and water hoses of Birmingham and the ever-more racially tense, teeming streets of such neighborhoods as Harlem and Watts, Las Vegas appeared both delightfully and defiantly set apart. Out in the Nevada desert, the crossfires and politics of the civil rights movement had little meaning. Las Vegas was a world unto itself, and it was a world that very much wanted to boost itself in the name of its sole preoccupation — money. A great heavyweight fight would certainly help do that. The last time the state of Nevada had held any such significant sporting event as a championship fight was back in 1912 when Jack Johnson beat up a nobody named Jim Flynn. That bout had been in Reno (Las Vegas was nothing then), and just prior to that fight, Reno had been the site of the famous July 4, 1910, bout when Jack Johnson rudely halted the comeback effort of racist Jim Jeffries. The memory of Jack Johnson, and all the racial terror and tension his presence had unearthed, held a symbolism that served to underscore the fearsome aura that Sonny Liston was bringing back to boxing. Many urban leaders throughout the nation were afraid of such a specter, given the dangers they envisioned it raising in the streets. Las Vegas scions did not object to the image one bit, as long as it made them money.

With champions like Joe Louis and Floyd Patterson, the racially chilling tones that Jack Johnson had laid bare had always been consciously and successfully avoided. With Liston such control seemed to loosen. Jack Johnson had been a symbol of the repression of African Americans, and by the 1960s his plight had certainly come to deserve respect and sympathy. The play *The Great White Hope* would emerge on Broadway just a few years ahead. Johnson's standing in historical memory would then change even more. Meanwhile, the fact of his bad image remained undeniable with the crown sitting with Sonny Liston. Johnson had never been involved with the work of any such contemporaneous civil rights figures as Booker T. Washington, W.E.B. DuBois, or Marcus Garvey, and Liston never lifted a finger to help Roy Wilkins, Martin Luther King, or Malcolm X. Some African American activists may have noted this, but out in the narcissistic gambling mecca of Las Vegas such a figure as Johnson or a man like Liston held a certain swagger among the gamblers, the mafia figures, and the early '60s cool cats who were busy making the city a center of nightclub entertainment, money grubbing, and hedonism. At a certain level, race did not matter among such folks. The issue was simply money. Indeed an entertainer like Sammy Davis, Jr., could perform there with Frank Sinatra and Dean Martin and engender fewer raised eyebrows than he could most anywhere else. The connected Mr. Sinatra insisted on it. The unstated part of this implicit bargain, however, was that the city's absolutely singular priority on money was not to be muddied with any sort of moral appeals, be they about gambling, alcohol, cigar smoking, racial injustice, boxing, or anything else. Indeed while many New York editorialists continued to ponder the morality of boxing, out in Las Vegas no one shed any tears for Benny Paret, Ernie Knox, or Davey Moore. The common attitude there was that they took their chances in the ring just like a gambler does at the Vegas tables. It was all a kind of Faustian bargain that worked perfectly within the confines of Las Vegas, and this was the kind of atmosphere into which a Jack Johnson or a Sonny Liston fit comfortably. Liston thrived there. He gambled, did drugs, smoked big cigars. He would later settle there to live, and die. Soon after the Birmingham riots, when Patterson and Liston arrived in Las Vegas to fight, such questions as those concerning Patterson's work in Alabama, or the umbrage taken by Malcolm X, seemed utterly peripheral, or, as Liston said, "stupid."

There was a reduced, smug sense of mafia-defined reality that the emerging life of Las Vegas imparted that nicely served the sense of Liston as the worthy champion. The mob, as Norman Mailer noted at the first Patterson-Liston fight, "seemed to be for Liston, almost without exception. It was not," Mailer emphasized,

because his prison record stirred some romantic allegiance in them, nothing of service to India, sir, or graduates from the same campus; ... nor was it part necessarily and absolutely of some large syndicated plot to capture and run the Heavyweight Championship of the World so that the filaments of prestige which trail from such a crown would wind back into all the pizza parlors and jukeboxes of the continent.... It's more like the Polish Corridor was to the Nazis...; it's a broken boil. In their mind Patterson was a freak, some sort of vegetarian. It was sickening to see a post of importance held by a freak, or by the manager of a freak.

The limousine-liberal approved values that Patterson had nobly embodied to the likes of John Kennedy and Eleanor Roosevelt were now laughable. Mrs. Roosevelt had passed away, and, to say the least, the mob had never set much store by her example. Kennedy was still alive, but the mob would soon help deal with him too. Patterson did not need to be expunged in any extraordinary way; Liston had done it in a most perfunctorily ordinary way. To the mob, Liston was one of their own, and he had executed the necessary hit with cold perfection. With Liston's victory, moreover, the mob no longer had any major concerns with Cus D'Amato. Now the "silly" rematch was set in an appropriate venue, and this silly little challenger would have the same chance, no matter that Meyer Lansky had insisted that the gaming tables not be rigged, as some sucker at a Las Vegas casino.[1]

Few people thought Patterson had any chance in his rematch with Liston. Norman Mailer smugly described Patterson as "Chaplinesque, simple, sheepish, eloquent in his clumsiness, sad like a clown, his knees looked literally to droop. He would seem the sort of shy, stunned, somewhat dreamy Negro kid who never knew the answer in class." (When one of American liberals' black heroes fails them, those same liberals do indeed quickly revert to racist stereotypes. Then they turn and find some sort of deeper truth in the implicit critiques of liberalism, whose rejection a victorious Patterson had previously rendered noble.) Another journalist wrote of how strikingly "soft, gentle, inert, and vulnerable" was Patterson's hand when one shook it. "It is like shaking hands with an infant or the dead." After his loss to Liston, Patterson had been hurt by such sweeping indictments. When he learned, for example, that the machismo-deluded actor Anthony Quinn had declared that his fight with Liston had been disgraceful *and* that he (Quinn) could have done better, Patterson angrily scoffed:

> People often say that—*they* could have done better! Well I think that if *they* had to fight, *they* couldn't even go through the experience of waiting for the fight to begin. They'd be up the whole night before, and would be drinking, or taking drugs. They'd probably get a heart attack. I'm sure of that. If I was in the ring with Anthony Quinn, I would wear him out without even touching him.

Patterson was doubtlessly right about the lack of appreciation that the snorts of a man like Anthony Quinn represented. Of course, athletes always endure, and usually giggle at the expressions of any such "I can do that" fantasies. Patterson doubtlessly knew that Sonny Liston felt as he did, but for Sonny it was all an entertaining trifle, like watching an opponent getting flustered by a heckler in the crowd.[2]

Sonny Liston's infamously intimidating, scowling manners had not abated, and they continued to impress everyone. Cassius Clay's loquacity was already becoming a benchmark among the press, and reporters began to call upon Liston to make a "Clay Style" prediction. Liston disappointed, as he would not pick a particular round, but he did predict the fight would not go past five. No one disagreed. The oddsmakers' betting line held at 4:1. A few reporters strained for some bases to be optimistic about the former champion's chances. One described him as "calmer and more relaxed than he was last September." Another pointed out that in the prior fight he had stayed in close with Liston. Here "he violated one of the fundamentals of boxing. He should have known better," wrote one reporter. "When anyone clinches with Liston, he should come in close and tie him up or push away fast to get out of range. But Floyd gave him hitting room from up close. This is easily correctable. He won't do it again." The fact of needing to stay away from Liston was obvious but easier said than done. Liston could bore in, and he was so strong that he easily could avoid being tied up, and then hit at close range and inflict a lot of damage.[3]

The fight took place on the night of July 22, and it lasted a full four seconds longer than the first. Patterson did not get on his proverbial bicycle, as many had advised and hoped. Patterson later admitted: "I reasoned that I was almost as strong as Liston and that I could do just as much damage moving forward as he could, so why go backward? I disobeyed my trainer and walked right into Liston." Patterson indeed came directly into Liston, and he paid the price. Liston pummeled him, dropping him quickly. In actual fighting time, the bout was shorter, as Patterson was knocked down three times, and his first two times on the floor took up sixteen seconds. Liston was on top of Patterson the whole time. Whether it was a lesser or worse beating than the first fight was a matter of hair splitting to say the least. Patterson was counted out in two minutes and ten seconds. The first Liston fight had raised a few conjectures about how Patterson could have fought differently. This time there was nothing that anyone in the press, the bars, or the barber shops felt like raising. Cus D'Amato, back in Patterson's corner this time, charged that Liston had fouled Patterson with rabbit and kidney punches, but no one took any serious regard of this. Phrases like "poor Floyd" dotted the newspapers. "Another gross mismatch," lamented one writer. Few saw any reason to be charitable: "Patterson ... had foolishly walked straight into the threshing machine and had been ground into mincemeat for his stupidity." Words like "lucky punch" were nowhere to be found, nor did anyone pen the word "rematch." All significant press attention was on Sonny. The main questions regarding Patterson now concerned whether he was going to retire.[4]

Floyd did not don any fake whiskers and sunglasses after this loss. If he had the press was ready to pounce. Before the press Patterson was somewhat rueful, but he was firm about retirement. His answer was "No." "I'm going back to the bottom and start all over again," he said firmly. "I love boxing and if there was no money in it, I'd stick to it anyway." Patterson's future was completely obscure, however. There was obviously no point in anyone even thinking about him getting a shot at the title. Other fighters would be in Liston's immediate future, one in particular. Cassius Clay was actually at the fight, and he made his presence felt, seeking obviously to boost his candidacy as Liston's next opponent. Liston and his people actually barred Clay from their post-fight dressing room activities with the press. Clay bothered them more than Patterson.[5]

As Patterson contemplated his loss and his future, he again had to face being the butt of various forms of humor and irony. At the end of July, one baseball writer was discussing some of the oddities in the way pitchers can earn or not earn wins. Pitcher X could be leading 6–0, give up five quick runs and leave the game with the bases full. The reliever could come in from there, pitch perfect ball, yet if the score remained 6–5, X would get the win. "It's a system," wrote the *New York Times'* John Drebinger, "that could almost win back Floyd Patterson's title for him." When the price of natural rubber dropped precipitously in the international commodities market that summer, an economic analyst declared that "1963 has treated natural rubber with the same consideration Sonny Liston treated Floyd Patterson." In early August, the National Football League champion Green Bay Packers actually lost in the then annual pre-season game that pitted the defending champions against a squad of college all-stars. "Had Floyd Patterson knocked out Sonny Liston," wrote a shocked reporter, "the surprise would have been no greater." That Christmas, the *Times'* present for Floyd Patterson was "a gyroscope, for staying in a vertical position." Noting that Patterson was trying some skiing that autumn in Sweden, they joked that when Patterson fell down on the slopes, which he reportedly did twelve times on his first day, it was something at which he had already had a lot of practice.[6]

Irritating as such clippings were, back in New York there were real troubles for Patterson, and this time at home. A local appliance serviceman up in Westchester County had been rude and pushy with Sandra. With Patterson away and training so often, Sandra had to call servicemen when some of the household equipment malfunctioned. A dishwasher repairman came and while looking at the dishwasher kept smiling at Sandra and calling her "Baby." The machine kept breaking down every week, and Patterson grew convinced that the serviceman was deliberately leaving the machine in such a state that it would keep malfunctioning so he could keep calling and hitting on Sandy. Patterson was never able to confront the man, but it depressed him greatly that he could not be there for his wife.

An even worse matter concerned his eldest daughter Jeannie. Jeannie was then the only African American girl in her Scarsdale Catholic school's third-grade class. She was the victim of some hateful teasing, and some older boys once crept up to her from behind while she was walking and suddenly lifted up her school uniform dress, obviously a most upsetting thing for any eight-year-old girl. Patterson went to the schoolyard one day and had Jeannie point out who had lifted her dress. The boy to whom she pointed was walking with four others, each about twelve to fourteen years old. The boys shrugged and denied doing anything wrong. One boy said his friend didn't do it but his little brother may have. Patterson knew he was being lied to, but he felt powerless to do anything about it. All he could to do was mildly threaten: "Look, boy, I want you to stop it. I won't tell your mother — that might get you in trouble — but don't do it again, okay?" The boys shrugged, said "okay," and headed up the street. Patterson remembered his own days on the streets of Bed-Sty and knew the boys had obviously "gotten away with it." He may have felt more frustrated here than he did about losing to Liston. This was his daughter, and he could not do anything with the situation to give his daughter some sense of redemption. It hurt a lot, and his panoply of frustrations came together with the depressing sense he frankly expressed — that if it was someone in Sonny Liston's family, the kids would have been far more fearful, knowing that the schoolyard could have easily been littered with limbs. It was hard for Floyd not to feel that the boys got the idea that they could taunt Jeannie because of the loss to Sonny Liston. He deeply felt like a loser.[7]

Sandra wanted Floyd to retire. But there was the mortgage and other bills to pay. Patterson was still only twenty-eight when he lost to Liston the second time, and he still felt he had something to say to the world athletically. Retirement was just not something he seriously contemplated. His heavyweight ranking had fallen to number 9. The question was how, and where, could he get a serious fight for himself that would pay him decent money. Ingemar Johansson and his promoter friend Edwin Ahlquist would come through for him here. The Swedish public had taken a genuine liking to Patterson. The strong aura of sportsmanship that surrounded the three Patterson-Johansson bouts resonated well with the Swedish boxing fans, as did Patterson's gentlemanly nature. The Swedes had no lurid fascination with the blood-sport, mean streets world that surrounded such people as Sonny Liston. "They don't like fighting here," joked Patterson, "but they like me." The Swedes had actually grown a trifle resentful of their own Ingemar, as he officially changed his citizenship to Switzerland in order to escape the high Swedish taxes. In late November, Patterson went to Sweden and found himself greeted as warmly as he ever had. "I completely forgot about my defeat by Liston the moment I landed in Sweden," he nodded with a smile. "Over here, they're still talking about the last fight with Ingemar." Sweden would always be special to Patterson. When he visited a famous Stockholm restaurant, the Operakalleren, he found himself surrounded by a group of well-dressed, elderly ladies. One hugged him and kissed him. One royally kissed his hand, and Floyd kissed her hand in return. He received scores of gifts —

glass vases, poetry, hand-carved kitchen utensils from children. His twenty-ninth birthday, on January 5, 1964, fell just two days before the fight he had scheduled in Sweden, and the Swedes treated it like some sort of national day. Back when he first lost to Johansson, Patterson had received hundreds of letters from Swedish fans wishing him well. After his second loss to Liston he received 2000 letters urging him not to retire. Of the 2000, about 1400 were from Sweden. "Fighting was still in my heart," he said, "but that alone was not enough. I needed support, and I got it from the letters." After so much endlessly depressing news in New York, spending time among the Swedes felt very good. Only the New Yorkers made fun of his skiing mishaps. A Swedish mens wear manufacturer had Patterson pose for some clothing advertisements. As Patterson himself noted, "Where in America would I be asked to model suits?" "I feel a closeness with the Swedish people," he noted with genuine gratitude, "that I have never felt anywhere else.... It's like being in a family."[8]

Ahlquist arranged a fight for Patterson in the Swedish city of Goteborg. They also placed a fight on the undercard for Patterson's younger brother Raymond. (His opponent was a young Swedish fighter named Lars Norling.) Floyd was to fight an Italian contender for the European heavyweight crown named Sante Amonti. The European crown was then vacant, so for Amonti the bout with Patterson held great possibilities for his hoped-for rise up the ladder. He was then ranked number 2 in Europe behind a German named Karl Mildenberger who would later fight Muhammad Ali. For Patterson it would be a respectable payday of $50,000, with the obvious pressure that if he lost there would be no choice but to retire. Less than a week before the fight, Patterson said he would indeed retire if he lost. Some New York and Las Vegas pundits could snicker at the venue. Patterson's traveling so far for a fight venue prompted a *New York Times* comment in a tongue-in-cheek January column of sports predictions for 1964. The *Times* forecast that in the spring "the barnstorming Floyd Patterson [will] climb off the deck to finish off an unknown Nigerian. On the strength of that glittering performance," predicted the sarcastic *Times*, Patterson would sign for a new bout with Liston. The Swedes were never so cynically irreverent, but there was a sad reality in the New York press. A rematch with the champ was certainly a long way off, but Patterson had to start somewhere. Amonti was certainly a relative unknown. Still, he was a legitimate heavyweight in European circles with a record of 50 victories in 57 bouts. For Patterson, now twenty-nine years old just before the fight, a victory was a career do-or-die.[9]

The fight had a gentlemanly aura. In addition to the Swedes' celebrations of Patterson's birthday, Amonti sent him a telegram; Patterson treated him to dinner after the fight. In the fight, Patterson did not look impressive. He won every round, but that said more about Amonti's performance. Patterson's mind wandered during the bout. "When the bell sounded at the start," he confessed, "the memory of those other [two Liston] fights came back to me. I jabbed and backed off, and after the first round had ended I sighed and was relieved." "Ragged" was a word that appeared in several reporters' coverage. "A touch of tiredness," wrote one. It all seemed a touch contrived and sterile, much like the atmosphere in Sweden that shocked American reporters — they were not allowed to smoke in the arena; at a boxing match?! Accustomed to New York and Las Vegas, Americans snorted in disbelief, as they did in the fourth round when Patterson knocked Amonti down and went over to help him up. Even the referee was taken aback. Patterson's explanation was even more befuddling: "I knew I hadn't hit him hard enough to keep him down, so I thought I'd help him up." With Helsinki not too far away, memories of such behavior in Patterson's younger days surfaced here, thoughts reinforced by a couple of wild rights from Patterson that nearly caused him to lose his balance. Patterson won with a TKO in the eighth round. (Ray Patterson lost his bout in six.) While a loss would have caused a little coverage in the press only for his retirement announcement, the victory caused barely a notice.

Patterson stayed in Sweden for a few more weeks, doing some boxing exhibitions for charity. The Swedes loved him for it. Meanwhile, the boxing world had its mind on something else — the upcoming fight between Sonny Liston and Cassius Clay. With his victory over Sonny, Clay, of course, "shook up the world," making fools of all the pundits, oddsmakers, and writers who had given him no chance. Clay had been predicting a victory, but everyone took it as part of his usual extrovert antics. He had bragged that he would be able to protect himself, and here he went out of his way to contrast his tactics with others. "Now you take Floyd Patterson," he quipped. "He was too dumb to back up, but I'm so fast." Patterson was among many whom the new champion would readily insult, and it was just one more in the string of not-so-comic barbs Patterson had had to endure. No one went to Patterson for any rejoinder to Clay. Patterson had to admit: "I'm not looking to get the title back but to fighting Sonny again. Right now I don't deserve the chance. My comeback, if successful, should take a couple of years." If he was being realistic about his future as a boxer, Patterson did celebrate his own spirit, as he forsook those who advised him that he had to cultivate a hatred for Liston in order to get back and beat him. Patterson had traveled that road after losing to Johansson, and he wanted no part of it again. "Hate disorders the mind," Patterson counseled. "I have no feeling toward Liston whatsoever, except I feel sorry for him. He looks like a person who hates. If he does, he must be miserable." After he lost to Clay, Liston began immediately to make hateful noises about getting a rematch. Liston, of course, sought to disparage the new champion. Patterson did enter the picture here, as Liston went out of his way to say that he considered Patterson to be a better fighter than

Clay. Of course, he meant it as a way of insulting Clay. There was no explicit clause calling for a return match between Clay and Liston, so some were speculating that Clay's next opponent could be Patterson. Floyd was not hopeful, however.[10]

While controversies flew over the Clay-Liston fight and over future pairings for the crown, they suddenly paled before the new champion's other announcements. He said his name was now "Cassius X." He was a member of the Black Muslims and a follower of Elijah Muhammad. Most mainstream boxing fans had no real idea what Cassius X was talking about, but, in their ignorance, it scared the hell out of them. From his work with the Southern Christian Leadership Conference, especially during the Birmingham troubles in 1963, Patterson had had some exposure to the Black Muslims, and he did not like them one bit. He had once referred to them as no different than the KKK. When Cassius X announced his new commitment to them, Patterson was angry. From his work with troubled youths, and in general terms, Patterson was extremely concerned with the example that the heavyweight champion sets. When Cassius X announced his allegiance to Elijah Muhammad, Patterson spoke out immediately. The champion's conversion, said Patterson, was "a shocking revelation." "I disagree with the precepts of the Black Muslims," Patterson declared, "just as I disagree with the Ku Klux Klan — in fact so much so, I am willing and desire to fight Cassius X to take the title from the Black Muslim leadership and will do so for no purse whatsoever, whenever and wherever they might desire." Cassius X had declared that the Black Muslims had helped him in his victory over Liston. Patterson retorted: "I give you this opportunity to see what help they can give you in a fight against myself." Contending that the champion "should be a symbol that all Americans can look up to," Patterson conceded: "Cassius, I have admiration for you as a boxer.... However," he added. "I don't honestly believe you know what the Black Muslims portray." Here there may have been a certain condescension in Patterson's reaction. Like many others, Patterson saw the young champion to have been taken in by some in the movement. Patterson felt he knew better. "I am proud to be an American and proud of my people," he confirmed, implying that the new champion had taken on an attitude that looked down on the rest of African Americans that had not joined the Muslims. "No one group of people could make me change my views. Therefore," he concluded, "I challenge you not only for myself, but for all people who think and feel as I do." Patterson was not just hyping here to bring about a shot at the title for himself, and he did not believe that Cassius X was merely hyping about his new religion, even though much else of what he had done had involved a lot of apparent clowning. Patterson sincerely believed that Cassius X had been taken in and brainwashed. In regard to a possible fight, Patterson was *somewhat* firm: "I feel, after having watched some of Clay's fights on film — including the Liston one — that I can beat him. I can be wrong, mind you, but I don't think so."[11]

A New York promoter named Al Bolan took Patterson at his word and offered Cassius X a bout against Patterson with a guarantee for him of $750,000. Patterson would fight for free. Muhammad Ali, his new name as of that point, although the press still incessantly referred to him by his "slave name," rejected the offer. Disdainfully, Ali quipped that the offer was insufficient "for such an international bout." There was a lot of posturing, of course; what made this potential fight any more international than any other and why such a fight of international status (like Patterson's with Amonti?) automatically assumed higher standing were questions that had no logical answers. Ali was just mouthing off, and that was to be expected given both the already well-known nature of the man and the situation. In taking offense, Ali did go beyond his usual hyperbole, however, claiming that Patterson had "attacked my religion." There was some odd exaggeration here, as Ali asserted that in doing so Patterson was "attacking Cairo, Egypt, the holy city of Mecca, Pakistan, Turkey, and 300,000 Muslims in America." The press and general public of the day saw it all as a bunch of typical boxers' nonsense. Few realized or even thought of considering that Ali was in deadly earnest about his new religion. It would take time for the public and press to begin to get that.

Patterson actually understood more than most, and in that regard Ali would not forget the insult. Ali laughed that "a little fellow like that doesn't belong in the ring with me; ... a puny light man who can't take a punch." Later he joked that Patterson was good enough to be a nice sparring partner for him. But Ali was stung by the religious dimensions in Patterson's challenge. At one level he tried to maintain a gracious, lofty air, holding, "I don't want no religious war." But the fighter in Ali could not but come out too. If he fought Patterson, Ali announced, he would let the fight go for a long time. "I'll play with him for ten rounds," Ali boasted. "He has been talking about my religion. I'll just paw him. Then after I beat him, I'll convert him." Few understood the serious edge in Ali's taunts. That understanding would not come for several years. Meanwhile, a bout with Patterson would also have to wait. And in the ensuing time, Ali would not forget the religious level at which Patterson had criticized him.[12]

For his first title defense, Muhammad Ali would consider nothing but a rematch with Sonny Liston. Most boxing fans seemed sure that his victory over Liston had been a fluke, and fears over his new religious and political leanings compounded confused senses that Ali could and should lose his rematch with Liston. Some boxing organization officials were equally confused and angry about Ali's new ways. Using the point that there was no contractual requirement (some argued it was forbidden) for a rematch with Liston, calls grew for other challengers. The managers of heavyweights Eddie Machen,

Zora Folley, and Cleveland Williams, respectively number's 4, 5, and 6 in the heavyweight contender rankings, felt their fighters were worthy of a title shot. Bill Swift, Folley's manager, said the three fighters were "overdue for a break in the heavyweight division," a clear reference to his lingering, angry perception that Cus D'Amato and Patterson had intentionally avoided them during their championship years. "The heavyweight division," Swift opined, "has been a farce long enough — six years with Patterson and now Clay." People like Swift had felt slighted by D'Amato, and, as Muhammad Ali's antics were now utterly incomprehensible to them, they blindly looped all such actions they did not like and could not control. Swift suggested a series of elimination bouts to determine Ali's next challenger.[13]

At the very time Swift was sounding off to the press, Sonny Liston again ran afoul of the law. More stories of shady mob connections and financial disputes were arising. Out in Denver that March, a policeman pulled Liston over for speeding (76 in a 30 mph zone). Liston was intoxicated. He was carrying a concealed pistol, and he threatened to "whip" the police officer who had pulled him over. Liston was having managerial problems as well. Two different management groups each claimed they had legitimate, hence conflicting, representation agreements with him. Despite these events and the further pressure it exerted for him to fight someone else, Muhammad Ali still went forth and ultimately arranged a rematch with Liston. With Ali's focus on Liston, various boxing officials grew even madder at him. Using again the contractual point that no rematch with Liston was required (and possibly forbidden), and driven by their fears, ignorance, and hatred of Ali's religious and political beliefs, the World Boxing Association withdrew their recognition of Ali as champion on September 14. They later sanctioned a series of matches, the ultimate winner of which was Ernie Terrell, to whom they gave recognition as champion. Few others took the WBA seriously here. Ali remained the champion in every major boxing venue and among virtually all serious fans. He would defeat Terrell in 1966.[14]

As the controversies with Muhammad Ali were raging above him, Patterson could do little but shoulder on for himself and arrange other bouts. Some talk came out of Madison Square Garden for Patterson to fight Cleveland Williams, but it did not pan out. Patterson again turned to Sweden for a venue. He was now calling his own shots ever more. The gap that had begun years earlier that began to erode the formerly total control which Cus D'Amato had exercised over Patterson's career became a complete break in June of 1964. That month, Patterson fired D'Amato. His trainer, Dan Florio, became his manager. There was no rancorous spouting off to the press. D'Amato had a stable of others fighters, including José Torres, who would eventually become the light-heavyweight champion (and who would also employ the peek-a-boo style to great success). There was actually more of a falling out here between

Patterson and Torres. When under the common management of D'Amato, the two had been quite close. Now there was a discomfort, and the two basically drifted apart. Both formally and informally, Patterson and Florio's partnership would be a business relationship in which Patterson would exert more control. The choice of again going to Sweden was the first clear example of how Patterson's inclinations would dictate the decisions. Edwin Ahlquist arranged a new bout, this time in the main sports arena of Stockholm on July 5. The fight was to be with Eddie Machen, one of the IBC fighters D'Amato appeared to be ducking when Patterson was the champion. Machen was then the number 4 heavyweight contender; Patterson was then ranked seventh.

Patterson trained in Ronneby, a town in the very south of Sweden, in sight of the Danish coast and Elsinore Castle. Thoughts of Hamlet combined with the years of head scratching over "Freud" Patterson's depressive nature engendered a few shrugs and smirks among the reporters. Some Stockholm fans were a trifle miffed at Floyd's "Greta Garbo" choice of such an isolated training venue. But the local Swedes down in Ronneby were delighted, and they negated the possibility of any Elsinor-type depression tinging the training. They flocked to Patterson's training sessions, and standing-room crowds cheered his every move. Patterson was stoic and focused in his workouts, and he spoke little to the press. Some speculated that without Cus, Floyd was depressing himself, handling too many of his professional and financial details personally. The local Swedes, however, seemed to appreciate his determination; it all seemed perfectly natural to them.[15]

Both the training and the Machen fight came off pretty well for Patterson. In Ronneby he made many local appearances. At one gathering he told the audience that after he retired from boxing he would like to live in Sweden six months out of every year. From the fight, he pocketed $50,000. The same pressure was there as it was when he fought Amonti — a loss would mean he would have to retire. Patterson knew it, and Machen was a lot better a fighter than Amonti. Still, with the losses to Liston and no matter his gently snarling postures about fighting Muhammad Ali, it still appeared that Patterson's future was of no consequence. To many, he was and would never be anything more than a has-been, a curiosity, fighting in far-away venues like Stockholm. Just before the fight, one writer lamented that "once upon a time Patterson and Machen ranked at the top. Now they're just a couple of mixed-up kids journeying along the road to nowhere." (The words "mixed up" were horribly cruel ones for a reporter to use in regard to Machen, as he had just been sidelined for a year with a nervous breakdown, but no one ever said "the sweet science" was ever to be a sweet business.) Patterson won the fight in a twelve-round decision, and the general views of his performance were dotted with words like "dull," "occasional flashes," and "unimpressive." He seemed to let Machen get away when he had him ready to go. Ingemar Johansson was there, and he concluded to Patterson, "You too nice, Floyd." *Sports Illustrated*'s Tex Maule agreed. Patterson, Maule opined, is "still too tender to be a tiger."[16]

Despite those who were pooh-poohing Patterson's performances and venues, after his defeat of Machen, Patterson was named Fighter of the Month both by *Ring Magazine* and by the World Boxing Association. *Ring*'s publisher, the legendary Nat Fleischer, had gone to Stockholm to witness the fight personally, and he lifted Patterson's standing. In *Ring*'s rankings of heavyweight contenders, Patterson suddenly stood at #2. Patterson appeared to be a player again. Serious talk as to his next opponent ran to all the other major contenders as well as to Muhammad Ali. Patterson capitalized on his renewed status as a top contender. "I want to destroy Clay," he told *Sports Illustrated*. Amidst the furor over Ali's new religion and racial outlook, Patterson stepped in as powerfully as he could. Patterson exclaimed that he "can't leave things that way," meaning the title in the hands of a man of the views of Muhammad Ali. "I can't leave people remembering that I lost to a man who quit cold [Liston quit between rounds in his loss to Ali] to another man who's taken the championship that belongs to the whole world and given it to the Black Muslims, who don't want to be part of our world." Whether Ali read the comment directly is not known, but the Muslims definitely read it.[17]

In the fall of 1964, Ali was himself immersed in preparations for his rematch with Sonny Liston. Here a possibility considered for the fight's undercard was a bout between Floyd Patterson and George Chuvalo. Chuvalo was Canada's top fighter and had suddenly emerged as one of the top heavyweight contenders as a result of his surprising November '64 knockout of the highly ranked Doug Jones, a contender who in March 1963 had nearly defeated Ali. The Ali-Liston fight was originally slated for the Boston Garden. Then in mid–November, Ali suffered a hernia and required surgery. Everything had to be cancelled, and the ensuing renegotiations dragged on and on. (With the bad blood and with the fears of the Black Muslims that surrounded Ali, Boston and various other venues backed out, with the rematch finally held in the nowhere site of Lewiston, Maine.)[18]

Amidst the delays and tedious Ali-Liston negotiations Patterson's undercard possibility vanished. But the possibility of fighting Chuvalo did not. Now Patterson did not have to turn to Sweden. Madison Square Garden set up a WBA sanctioned bout between Patterson and Chuvalo as the main event for the evening of February 1, 1965. As the WBA was ineffectually no longer recognizing Ali as the champion, their imprimatur gave the bout a direct link to a sort-of-title, as their plan was to have the winner fight Ernie Terrell for the vacant crown. Even if he was not taking the WBA crown seriously, Patterson had no reason not to accept the offer. Considering his non-status in the fight game after his second loss to Liston, it certainly marked a respectable twenty-month comeback. In December, Patterson went off to Puerto Rico for a tune-up fight with a journeyman named Charley Powell. As with the bouts in Sweden, Patterson would be sacrificing everything in his boxing career if he lost. But he felt he needed the sharpening. It proved a one-sided affair, with Patterson pounding Powell at will for six rounds, stopping him with a right cross that KO'd him. The bout paid him all of $5000, but with the fight Patterson felt he was ready for Chuvalo and for a full reestablishment in the heavyweight picture.[19]

XII

Muhammad and the Rabbit

Rocky Marciano once half-jokingly observed that "if every fight was 45 rounds, George Chuvalo would be the greatest boxer of all time." George Chuvalo was a tough guy in every sense of the term. The big Croatian-Canadian was strong as an ox. He was also quite intelligent, articulate, and well read in such figures as Freud, Jung, and Confucius, but that concerned few fight fans of the day. They just knew that Chuvalo hit very, very hard. His principal weakness was that he could be hit. That seldom mattered, however, because Chuvalo possessed the proverbial granite chin. Superlatives are always difficult in boxing, but among heavyweights Chuvalo may have been the best ever, and without any doubt one of the best ever, at taking a punch. In his entire career, including fights such notables as Doug Jones, Floyd Patterson, Muhammad Ali, and George Foreman, not only did no one ever knock out George Chuvalo, no one ever even knocked him down. He was a bull. While Floyd Patterson was elated in the knowledge that his fight with Chuvalo denoted he was back among the contenders, he also knew he was in for one big fight. Given what Liston had done to him, thoughts certainly flew about the nation's bars and barber shops as to what Chuvalo might do. Patterson took no rest after December's Charley Powell fight. He flew right back to New York and headed up to his camp in Marlboro, N.Y., to resume training. Some reporters were back talking about "Freud" Patterson and his befuddling, reclusive ways, images which were enhanced by contrasts with Chuvalo's outgoing tough-guy personae.

Amidst the pre–Chuvalo fight build-up, Muhammad Ali entered the fray. Ali was always every bit as savvy a showman and publicist as he was a fighter. Even before his first fight with Liston, Ali's antics had grown legendary. At that point some thought he was simply crazy, which was certainly

174

a major part of the unsettling image he wanted to, and likely did, implant in Liston. As Chuvalo and Patterson were preparing to fight one another, Ali was still in recovery from the hernia operation that had caused the postponement of his return bout with Liston. With a bit of time available, Ali signed with the Patterson-Chuvalo fight producers to be one of the television commentators. He used this TV post to justify scouting the two fighters' camps, and here he did much more than scout.[1]

Ali was thinking ahead. He usually did. Fully believing, unlike everyone else, that he would defeat Sonny Liston, Ali thought that the winner of Patterson-Chuvalo, likely Patterson, would be a good fight for him. The more publicity he could draw to the fighters, the bigger the payday would eventually be for all. More than coincidentally, Ali also relished the spotlight and loved pumping up any fight, especially where it would draw attention to himself. As Patterson and Chuvalo were training for their Madison Square Garden bout, Ali was a constant presence among the New York sports media. Cognizant of his media access, Ali dubbed the two fighters with nicknames, a habit for which he would become deliciously notorious. Earlier Ali had famously christened Sonny Liston as "the Bear;" with Patterson and Chuvalo he would further indulge his imagist fancies. Chuvalo had a tendency to windmill his punches. As this reminded Ali of an old homemaker scrubbing at a washboard, he named Chuvalo "the Washerwoman." He visited Chuvalo's camp and brought the big Canadian a gift of a bucket and mop. This caused but a mild stir. A bigger stir occurred when he visited Patterson. One Thursday afternoon, with a press and personal entourage of seventy-five, Ali paid a very noisy call upon Patterson's training camp in Marlboro. He came bearing a gift of a grocery bag full of lettuce and carrots. With a big grin on his face, Ali yelled over and over: "Where's the rabbit?" The lettuce and carrots, he announced, were "rabbit food." Back in November, before Ali's hernia, when the fight with Liston was about to occur in Boston, Ali had already referred to Patterson as "the rabbit," but then it was barely noteworthy. This time, Ali made it stick. With the press gathered at Patterson's camp, Ali kept calling Patterson "the rabbit." When a reporter asked him to explain the nickname, Ali was ready as always. He smiled, rolled his eyes playfully, and declared: "'Cause he's scared, man, scared like a rabbit."[2]

Ali and his entourage went to Patterson's gymnasium and waited for him, making noises to the reporters the whole time. Patterson was upstairs getting dressed and about to come down for some sparring when he heard all the commotion and learned that Muhammad Ali was in the house. Ali was inventing a new tactic here. Patterson later recalled that fighters would do the usual out-staring of one another when taking the referee's instructions, but this new "sort of stuff began when Cassius Clay came into the ring." One of Patterson's seconds advised him to go down there, shake hands, and shrug it

After Muhammad Ali won the heavyweight title from Sonny Liston in 1964 and defeated him in a controversial rematch the following year, his next title defense would come against Floyd Patterson in late 1965. Ali had invented a new level of showmanship in boxing as he hyped his bouts and taunted his opponents with zany antics, jive talkin' and poetry (which some cite as the genesis of rap music). While training, Patterson endured some of the early manifestations of Ali's unique displays and treatment. Here Patterson is attempting to ignore a surprise visit by Ali to his training camp. Ali ranted for over an hour, trashing Patterson endlessly, much to the bewilderment of most observers who had never seen anything like it. Ali definitely succeeded at getting under Patterson's skin. Patterson later responded in the press with taunts of his own, earnestly criticizing Ali's affiliation with the Nation of Islam and conspicuously referring to him as "Cassius Clay." In the fight, Ali absolutely humiliated Patterson, punishing him mercilessly. Later, the two would actually be very good friends. For the rest of his life, Patterson would be the *only* person Ali ever permitted to call him Cassius Clay. ©Bettmann/CORBIS.

all off as an inconsequential stunt. Another was more nervous: "Don't do that; he'll put a carrot in your hand and it'll look bad." Patterson claimed he was not bothered by it all. Amidst the confusion, bursts of laughter from downstairs kept vibrating the floor boards beneath him, and Patterson heard Ali repeatedly roar "Where's the rabbit?" Patterson finally came downstairs, and there was Ali holding up a bunch of lettuce and carrots. Patterson made his away around the room, convivially shaking hands with many in the crowd. Then he turned to Ali, forced a bit of a smile, and extended his right hand. Ali playfully slapped the backside of Patterson's hand. The cameras drew closer. Patterson shrugged and shook his head at Ali's antics. Ali then seized the moment to make a loud speech. "If you can beat the washerwoman you may have a wonderful opportunity to regain your pride and joy, the heavyweight championship." Ali made a point here of being as patronizing and condescending as possible. Meanwhile, Patterson seemed unable to come up with a single word with which to counter, still mired in the personae of that little kid in school afraid to speak up even though he may have had the right answer. With Patterson seemingly stunned, Ali's stream of abuse never let up. He actually grabbed Patterson's arms and shoulders, announcing "I wanna size you up." After this "measurement," Ali snorted: "What makes you think you can beat me?" To the degree the mere talking was boxing, Ali certainly showed everyone at that point that he had the physical edge and then some.

Patterson was angry at the antics. He walked away from Ali and stepped into the ring. There he turned to the throng and began quietly: "Despite the carrots and lettuce, I am glad that the heavyweight champion, Mr. Cassius Clay in here." Hearing Patterson refer to him as "Cassius Clay," Ali began shouting: "That's not my name! Call me by my right name, Muhammad Ali!" Ever so softly and casually, Patterson turned his hand and nodded "Ali." The champ either did not hear it, or pretended not to, and continued to yell: "I want to hear my name!" At this point Patterson's manager, Dan Florio angrily shouted back, "Cassius Clay." Now Ali's dander was up, just as Patterson finally became a trifle playful. He calmly noted to Ali: "The name you were born with *is* Cassius Clay." Ali began waving his fist in the air, screaming back: "Cassius Clay is a slave name. I'm free. You got a slave name. You ain't nuthin' but an Uncle Tom Negro. You Uncle Tom, I'll jump right in there on you now." Patterson looked at him, beckoned him to come forward, and calmly said: "Well, do it." Some people in the crowd applauded. But Ali was never to be shaken verbally. He kept shouting over all others, and several of his Muslim associates melodramatically "held him back" as he made some strenuous gestures trying to get into the ring and go after Patterson.

Dan Florio cancelled the sparring session. Patterson looked disgusted at it all; "ready to bite," according to one reporter. As the training session appeared to break up, Ali then immediately began bragging how he'd told people that Patterson would not spar in front of him and how this was another of his predictions that was proving to be right. Patterson responded by turning back to the ring. He put on his gloves, and sparred a couple of rounds. Reporters noted that he seemed uninspired and mechanical, obviously still a bit psyched out by all the nonsense and abuse from the champ. Ali watched the sparring and, of course, shook his head and mocked: "No match, no match." When Patterson concluded his sparring and left, Ali jumped in the ring and gave a demonstration of shadow boxing, clearly trying to demonstrate who was the superior fighter.[3]

Muhammad Ali was a master showman. Harry Markson, director of boxing for Madison Square Garden, was at the lettuce-and-carrots event. He later said he was "sick at heart [at] Clay's ... racist tirade against Patterson." Then he added: "I can't help but admit it, though, ... the gimmick was what put the [Patterson-Chuvalo] show over the top and gave us a sellout." As a complete extrovert, Ali's taunting and bench jockeying always resonated well with virtually any audience, especially in his youthful days. As with other such extroverts, his antics came, however childishly, straight from the heart and struck people as natural and innocent, no matter any mean overtones, much like children taunting one another in the playground. In regard to any notion that people should be more sensitive about such cruelty, such views were hardly common in 1965, and professional boxing certainly was, and is, the last place anyone would think of asserting such a point. Yet for Patterson, and his troubled background, such playful taunting was indeed hurtful. He always said that words hurt him more than punches. Still, no one could feel terribly sorry for him, as he chose to stay in the boxing business.[4]

The mix of personalities played perfectly into Ali's hands. To the degree that Ali was not just playing, the situation also accommodated him perfectly. Boxers embody that duality which so many possess that involves basic barbaric, violent instincts versus finer notions of civility. For boxers, given the expectations on them to turn their propensities toward extreme violence on and off like a light switch, the divide can be so extreme that it can border on schizophrenia. (For some boxers like Mike Tyson it may more than merely border.) For Patterson, when pressed and goaded as he had been by Ali, there was nowhere to turn, at least within the realm of the law, but into that shy, disturbed self that turned mute with pressure and had turned to boxing as a release. Hence he said little to the taunts of Muhammad Ali and mechanically climbed into the ring.

For the extrovert Ali, the situation was one that was full of fun, and one in which, if civility broke down, he had his newly adopted new religion to defend. (If he had any inner troubles at that point, it concerned the way that Elijah Muhammad and the Nation of Islam were pressuring him to renounce Malcolm X, the only member of the Nation ever to defy their leader.) The incident at Patterson's camp was a wonderful venue for Ali. He could shift back and forth between the frivolous and the serious — the lettuce, the carrots, relative boxing skills, the issues of his religion and his correct name. The flow from one idea to another was seamless. It was one of the reasons that many people of that time did not get it when it came to Ali's composite of clowning, religion, boxing, and politics. His tone and volume were seemingly identical throughout. He effectively clowned so much that many did not, or would not, grasp that some of his antics involved serious business. For Ali there was no proclivity, and no reason, to be introspective or self-analytical here. Explanations did not have any impact on the majority of the day still disposed to see it all as mere clowning. For Patterson there was, in contrast, every such proclivity toward introspection, and this did little to boost his mood or his stature with the press or the boxing public. Even among those who did not like, or feared, Ali, the chief emotion they could feel for Patterson here was not respect but pity.

Elsewhere, Muhammad Ali would continue to disparage Patterson. "A bum," he sniffed, "I wouldn't want to talk about him and make him seem too big." He mocked Patterson's small size and predicted how he would pepper Patterson with quick jabs to the head and fell him with a left uppercut. He demonstrated the scenario to reporters, and with the widest of eyes, followed the slow descent of Patterson to the canvas. Reporters giggled here at Ali's reasonable skills as an actor. Meanwhile, Patterson had to work hard to convince himself that he was a fighter capable of beating Muhammad Ali. Part of this battle was having to overcome the sense that he knew he could never come close to matching Ali in the areas of talk and showmanship. After Ali left his lettuce and carrots (and, amidst snowy conditions, drove his entourage's bus into a ditch on the way back to New York City), Patterson went back to work. He put all the "rabbit" talk out of his mind. Most felt Ali put his little prank aside too. Few then realized how he would resentfully hold onto being called "Cassius Clay." It just appeared to be another of his antics. To most observers, that matter paled before that of Ali calling Patterson a "rabbit" and giving him a bag of carrots and lettuce. For the most part, Patterson did put the insult aside. It was Ali who never forgot.[5]

While Patterson was preparing for Chuvalo, he was also getting his family together for a move back to Long Island. In 1961, amidst the euphoria of having regained the heavyweight title, Patterson had moved his family to the Beech Hill section of Yonkers in New York's Westchester County. From the outset, there had been a string of problems. His neighbor had built a fence to block any view of the Pattersons' house and family. A local appliance serviceman had "hit on" Sandra, and there were the terrible and humiliating experiences his daughter went through at her Catholic school in Scarsdale. It felt like one thing after another, and there definitely appeared to Patterson no sense of any community rallying in sympathy to his situation. Patterson's simultaneously losing twice to Sonny Liston did not help his overall mood here obviously. There seemed no haven from a heartless world in Yonkers. Whether Patterson felt that the anxieties over the bits of racism he and his family endured contributed to his poor showings in the ring, he never said. If he had, it certainly would have been seen as lame. It was more the other way around — the losses in the ring deepened his depression over what was occurring to his family.

Patterson was trying to live the classic American dream. He had risen out of poverty and boot-strapped himself into financial security. He had become a hero in the eyes of liberal leaders, and he had taken his family into the good life in the suburbs. Then the criminal world, represented by Liston, took him down in the ring. When he lost to Liston, President Kennedy threw away the autographed photograph he proudly displayed on his desk that Patterson had given him. And once settled in Westchester County, the Pattersons found themselves suffering various racial stings. The message that

Muhammad Ali, Malcolm X, and others were then spreading against many of the traditional, racially blind tenets of liberalism spoke directly at the idea that blacks like Patterson who sought to make it via the white world's ways were kidding themselves. Were the doors ever really going to be open? After being insulted and angered by Ali and his bag of carrots and lettuce, the significance of the various events from Westchester to the White House had that much more depressing a hue. With his losses to Liston, it seemed as though the mainstream world would indeed not accept him, and because he would not embrace the alternative stance of Muhammad Ali and his cohorts, they heaped ridicule upon him too. There seemed no where to turn.

The village of Scarsdale, New York, had received some bad press as a result of the notoriety of Patterson's experiences there. Various papers and magazines that covered some of the indignities the Pattersons endured had been reporting that the family lived in Scarsdale. Some of the village's residents went to some fastidious efforts to draw the distinction between Scarsdale and Beech Hill, Yonkers, where Patterson actually lived. Beech Hill was in the very northeasternmost corner of Yonkers, and it was serviced by the Scarsdale Post Office, but it was not actually in Scarsdale. Carefully noting this geography, one village resident clacked off a letter to the *New York Times*. "I would have welcomed Mr. Patterson and his family ... had they decided to move here," the writer asserted, adding, "I feel sure that my neighbors would have done the same." Whether that was true, or whether one trashy resident behaving badly would have led other villagers to conclude that, in the interest of ongoing community harmony, it was somehow better to indulge the older neighbor's eccentric ways, thus leaving the Pattersons feeling like outsiders and troublemakers, Patterson did not care to find out. Scarsdale, Beech Hill, Yonkers, to Patterson they all looked alike. He sold his house, and in late January 1965 he moved back to Long Island. Perhaps the adverse publicity over what had occurred in Yonkers-Scarsdale had something to do with it, but the Long Island community of Great Neck went out of its way to welcome their new residents into their $75,000 (1965 value) home in Great Neck Estates. Various community spokesmen and women turned out to greet them. Numerous local merchants sent gifts of welcome. Sandra had no more trouble getting hair appointments. No one harassed her, or her daughters. In such a nice community, the taunts of Muhammad Ali had a little less of a sting. Patterson did not have too much time to enjoy the welcome, however. He was touched and grateful after all he had gone through in Westchester. But the very next day after completing the move, he headed back up to Marlboro (a northern Westchester County community he liked) to train further for his bout with George Chuvalo.[6]

With the publicity that Muhammad Ali had helped generate with his antics, interest in the Patterson-Chuvalo fight shot up. Madison Square Garden was sold out at 18,400. Promoters accommodated additional demand with another 700 standing room tickets. Two hundred ninety applications came forth for press credentials. Sixty-four theaters in forty-four American cities, plus ten more in Canada, broadcast the fight via closed-circuit cable, a very high number for a non-championship bout. The gate would pocket Patterson $140,000 (Chuvalo would get $85,000). It was the richest non-title fight to that point in ring history, with total TV and gate revenues of just under $800,000. The fight would live up to all expectations.

With the memories of the two fights with Liston still on everyone's mind, Patterson needed to show the boxing world that he was not going to fight stupidly and that he could indeed take a punch. Chuvalo had a lot of power, and it made perfect sense for Patterson to dart in and out in the early rounds, hold in the clinches, build up points with effective jabbing, and stay away from Chuvalo's big punches, which would be at their greatest power in the early rounds before any fatigue set in. This was all easier said than done, of course, as Chuvalo anticipated Patterson would be on the move and sought to cut off the ring, trap and maul him every chance he could. The fighting would be intense. There were no lulls. The crowd noise was endless. In the second and fourth rounds, the two fought through the bell.[7]

In the early rounds, Patterson was successful. His quickness indeed dominated. He landed most of the punches. Chuvalo tried to maul, but the referee was quick, too quick to suit Chuvalo and his trainer, to separate the fighters and prevent much heavy pounding in the clinches. When Chuvalo tried to pummel in the clinches, the crowd booed loudly. He landed some heavy shots to Patterson's kidneys. Muhammad Ali repeatedly told the TV audience that Chuvalo's body punches were "dirty." After five rounds, Patterson was up four rounds to one. The crowd was shouting, "Let's go, Floyd!" Then in the sixth and seventh rounds, Chuvalo got in his best licks. Perhaps it was fatigue, but Patterson failed, when drawing close, to get in a few quick punches and then either get away or grab. Chuvalo was thus able to pound away at Patterson's body, including several more shots to the kidneys. In the seventh, he knocked Patterson against the ropes. He appeared to do some real damage and won both rounds unanimously. Dan Florio kept yelling at Patterson to keep his distance. When Patterson finally did so, he retook some of the fight's initiative. He won the next two rounds, although not unanimously. In the ninth, Patterson opened a small cut on Chuvalo's left eye. Chuvalo took the tenth, with the judges split here too, but he got in a powerful shot that wobbled Patterson and shook his mouthpiece out.[8]

Sitting at ringside doing TV commentary, Muhammad Ali, who'd received a shower of cat-calls when introduced before the bout, expressed respect for Patterson. "George Chuvalo is tough," Ali noted, but "Floyd's fighting a smart fight; he's movin'." Ali exclaimed this several times, adding once: "He doesn't look like the old Floyd Patterson I used to know.... I gotta' give him credit. He's a good fighter; he fights hard." After the tenth round, Ali asserted: "I believe Floyd would beat Liston fighting like this.... He's fighting as I did against Sonny Liston. I didn't believe he [Patterson] was this smart." Ali was, of course, concerned about promoting interest in a future fight with Patterson, so his praise may have been a trifle disingenuous. "I'll be ready for the winner," he once blurted out, revealing what was truly on his mind. But Patterson was definitely fighting well. Some said it was his best fight, even better than his second bout with Johansson. The crowd reacted to him. He was, after all, a native New Yorker. To help enhance the sentiment, indeed, Patterson came into the ring that evening wearing a robe bearing the "NY" logo of the New York Yankees. He was no dope. As the final round approached, the fight appeared to be close to all in attendance. Before the start of the twelfth round, with many regarding the decision to be very much up in the air, the New York crowd again began to chant over and over: "Let's go, Floyd!" Patterson needed and got a lift from the crowd's noise and energy. More that a few Canadians were on hand loudly rooting for Chuvalo, but there was no doubt as to who was the Garden favorite. Patterson had always wanted to be and "never had been," as the *New York Times* noted, "a hero in his hometown." He would express gratitude for "the wonderful feeling" the crowd gave him. (In the 1980s, after he had retired from the ring, Patterson ran several marathons. There he experienced the infamous wall about which long distance runners often speak. Patterson encountered it and of it he noted: "The only thing I can compare it to in boxing was when I fought George Chuvalo.... After five rounds I was totally exhausted. I couldn't even hold up my arms. I was so tired I lost the next three or four rounds. But the crowd started cheering me, and I knew I had to do something. Somehow I won the last three rounds.") The crowd chanting for Patterson carried through much of the twelfth, as did some appreciative cheering and applause for both. As before, with all the noise, the two combatants fought through the final bell. It seemed altogether appropriate; it had indeed been one hell of a fight. Everyone felt they'd seen a great bout and certainly gotten their money's worth. When the final bell sounded, Muhammad Ali proclaimed in satisfaction and delight: "A beautiful fight."[9]

Floyd won on all cards, although there were some discernible boos from the crowd when the decision was announced. (As much as New Yorkers, if not more, Canadians are loyal to their own too.) The details of the judging showed how close the fight was. Patterson only won three rounds unanimously; Chuvalo two. With the judges and referee divided over each of the other seven rounds, a slightly different shade of thinking by but one judge here and there could have tipped the balance in either direction. Chuvalo did not criticize the decision. He did later complain about the referee breaking the clinches too quickly, preventing him from doing some damage. As it was, he'd done a great deal. He pounded away at (and behind) Patterson's ribs. In addition to calling the punches "dirty," Muhammad Ali had emphasized that "body punches don't work if you[r opponent is] in shape." Nonetheless, Chuvalo's blows caused such bruising to Patterson's kidneys that he collapsed in the shower after the fight, and for the next month there was blood in his urine![10]

The fight was so impressive that in defeat Chuvalo's status was not hurt in the least. Within a year he would get a shot at Ali. For Patterson both the fight and the praise from Muhammad Ali meant a great deal. After the fight, Ali stepped up to the ring and interviewed Patterson. Patterson was his usual humble self. He complimented Chuvalo, who he said had hit him with some stinging shots. He even went out of his way to affirm that Chuvalo's punches in the clinches were legal. That was disputable. But Patterson was firm in proclaiming that he had proven to the world that he could indeed take a punch, that he did not possess a "China chin." Ali proclaimed to the TV audience: "I didn't believe he [Patterson] was this smart.... I bet on the wrong man." The *New York Times* called it "a magnificent fight." Previously disparaging of Patterson, columnist Arthur Daley nodded that Patterson "looked to be a more complete fighter ... than he had looked to be when he was champion." *Sports Illustrated* was one journal that took exception to the euphoria. They conceded that the fight was exciting but sniffed at it as but "a high-class club fight," adding: "neither man proved he has any business in the top heavyweight class." Patterson, they said, proved he could take a punch from Chuvalo, "but it seems extremely doubtful that he can take the kind of punishment either Clay or Liston is capable of inflicting." *SI*'s judgment may have been more objective, but it was not as important as Muhammad Ali's. At the fight's end, Ali made the big announcement. "Patterson will definitely be a contender for my crown after I take care of my unfinished business with Sonny Liston."[11]

Many viewers guffawed at Ali talking so positively about what he was going to do to Liston, as few believed he would beat Liston when they finally fought again. But for Patterson, the shot to regain the title he had been seeking since 1963 was now at hand. Ali and Liston would of course meet again — that May in Lewiston, Maine, and in one of the weirdest heavyweight championship fights in history, Ali tapped Liston near the ear in very the first round. Liston stumbled or fell, lay on the canvas, and rolled over. Somewhere amidst that, and in spite of Ali yelling at him to get up and fight, Liston either could not or decided not to get up. No one knew what to make of it all. Controversies flew every which way, but the KO stuck, and it left Floyd Patterson with the title shot he so wanted. He was now to fight the most controversial of opponents — there was the way Ali beat Liston; there was Ali's new religion; there was Ali's antics and big mouth. Furthermore, the World Boxing Association, which had removed its recognition of Muhammad Ali as the heavyweight champion, wanted Patterson to fight the winner of an upcoming about between Eddie Machen and Ernie Terrell, with the WBA championship as the reward. (Terrell would win that bout.) It was tempting, but when Ali said he would fight Patterson after beating Liston, that was an offer upon which Patterson could certainly not pass. Even before the Chuvalo fight, he had told several reporters that his goals were to beat Chuvalo, then fight Ali and, if victorious, redeem himself against Liston then retire. It would not quite work out that way, but at this point, amidst the euphoria after the victory over Chuvalo, Patterson was certainly not going to change plans with everything, at long last, seemingly falling back into place.[12]

When Patterson beat Chuvalo, Ali interviewed him, all the while jumping about like the somewhat irritating and always delightful kid he always was. The last time Ali had spoken to Patterson he was up at Floyd's Marlboro training site when he had brought his bag of lettuce and carrots to "the rabbit." Now Ali was thumping Patterson on the back, acting like he was his biggest fan. After some of Patterson's best rounds, Ali had made an approving round thumb and index finger gesture toward Patterson, and this may have been genuine. In large measure, however, his antics were all part of the hyping at which Ali was the undisputed master. When he was haranguing Patterson with the lettuce and carrots it was completely genuine. And when he was congratulating him so profusely after the Chuvalo fight, the feeling was no less so. For Patterson it was like being a kid back in Brooklyn encountering a local playground bully. One day the bully is attacking you; the next time he's your friend. The bully is not a calculating hypocrite. He's just so totally self-absorbed that his needs one moment to the next are all that exist in his frame of reference. As a modus operandi in the world of the fight business, this can be very effective. It certainly was for Ali. And if the outwardly befuddling nature of it was troubling for a sensitive person like Floyd Patterson, so much the better. To the amazement of most reporters, Patterson appeared to respond naively to Ali's show of friendship. "Up in camp he was quite derogatory, but tonight I found him quite warm," Patterson exclaimed. "He came to me and said I'd be the next man — so maybe he does like me a little bit." Ali may have been amazed at this too — amazed mainly that he could so easily gain an important psychological edge.[13]

With Ali's second defeat of Liston, Patterson knew he would be the champ's next opponent. Ostensibly to keep himself sharp, in late May, Patterson still made another friendly hop over to Sweden where he fought a bout against a relatively unknown Texas heavyweight named Tod Herring. (Herring's claim to fame was that he was the Texas heavyweight champion! It smacked a bit of a Roy Harris redo, although Stockholm bore little resemblance to Cut 'n Shoot.) Patterson won with a TKO in the third round. A few were impressed. Most felt the bout was needless. Patterson was loyal to his Swedish friends. They had given him the necessary venues after the Liston losses to open a comeback road. He would never forget that, nor would he ever tire of the warm, race-less environment he always encountered there, one where his quiet ways were altogether normal, "his favorite corner away from home," as one writer put it. As for the bout with Herring, it would not only be quickly forgotten; a few people grew quite tired of it as it took place. Even the Swedish papers guffawed. Noting the willingness of Stockholm fans to turn out for Patterson's bouts, one Swedish editor headlined with a smirk: "Are We That Fond of Floyd?" Another Stockholm writer was struck with the name of Patterson's opponent, as herring (*sill*) was always a popular delicacy in Sweden. Mr. Herring proved indeed to be a bit of a fish, and, noted a Swedish scribe, "This Herring business does not seem very tasty." Patterson explained that, just as he had fought Charley Powell before Chuvalo, he needed such a fight before facing Muhammad Ali. He believed he sharpened the hit-and-run style that he and most others knew he should have used against Liston, and would need against the champ. Against such a *sill* of an opponent, however, few saw any real skill sharpening.[14]

Meanwhile Muhammad Ali, having been so graciously complimentary toward Patterson during and immediately after the Chuvalo fight, quickly returned to his brash, insulting ways. Within hours of the Chuvalo fight, well before the second bout with Liston, Ali was poetically predicting his future: "Right after The Bear, we want The Hare." Ali steadily predicted Liston's fall and disparaged Patterson. "I'm glad the Rabbit won [over Chuvalo]," he chortled, "but it makes no difference, because I'm going to have the crown for the next twenty years. I am the greatest." The "beautiful" fight he saw against Chuvalo suddenly had a different cast for him. Patterson "tried to fight like me against Chuvalo, but he ain't near as fast as me, because they ain't no heavyweight ever lived been as fast me and probably never will be. So I fight 'The Rabbit,' and I think I will beat him pretty quick, because he is not so hard to hit.... I'll have a ball with that Patterson when we fight. I make them so mad, they forget what they doing. And I'll really get him upset, as strange as he is."* Ali was always one to go straight for the psychological jugular. To

---

*The ungrammatical elements in the quotations from Muhammad Ali appeared just this way in Sports Illustrated. Ali was always a thoroughly articulate speaker, but many newspapers and magazines of the era preferred to depict his speech in ways that were a trifle demeaning along racial lines. It was anything but accidental and likely stemmed from a combination of racism, fear, ignorance, and misunderstanding over the particular politics and religion for which Ali stood, and which were then so jarring to the preponderance of white, middle-class journalists and readers. Ridicule had always been a tactic which many Anglos then used against African Americans who intimidated them or generated such acute discomfort as Muhammad Ali first did.

him it made no sense to be in the fight game and behave any other way. It was hard for anyone to disagree here, and if it bothered Patterson, that was his problem.[15]

Patterson got over his injuries from the Chuvalo fight. After a month his urine ceased to show blood, and otherwise he was fine. Patterson thought he had actually injured his hand (a bone separation, he thought, in his left fist) which had first troubled him while fighting Charley Powell. He was claiming that as a result of the feeling in the hand, he was more defensive in the Chuvalo bout than he would have otherwise been. The New York State Athletic Commission supervised a medical inquiry into the matter of Patterson's hand, however, and they concluded the claim of hand injury to be untrue. With that cloud quickly vanishing, Patterson had emerged ever more a bona fide contender. Ali's odd defeat of Liston in May, meanwhile, added to the negative image the champion held in mainstream sports circles. This all served to compound the sense of mission that surrounded Patterson's quest for a shot at Ali's title. Before the Ali–Liston rematch, the often critical Arthur Daley had written: "Patterson [v. Chuvalo] has breathed new life into boxing. It will be up to Clay and Liston to keep from deflating it again."

As Ali's weird victory in Maine then signaled another deflation, many eyes turned to Patterson. Ali's religion and politics were always part of this picture. Robert Lipsyte of the *Times* noted that "since the emergence of Muhammad Ali (Cassius Clay), Patterson has been under continuing pressure from civil rights and religious organizations to return to fighting and take the title away from this non–Christian, racist-oriented black man." Many in the fight game, Lipsyte went on, have "also put pressure on Patterson." The issue here was not any sort of high blown philosophical exception taken with respect to Ali's religion and politics. Rather it was the simple sense that, for whatever reasons, many people were clearly turned off by Ali, even more primally than they were by a miscreant criminal like Liston. For boxing people the unsettling result here was that, with such champions, fights would lose popularity, and this meant that everyone in the game — reporters, corner men, managers, everyone — would be earning less money. It was just that simple and direct, and Patterson then became the man who could save so many from these financial woes. What had happened against Johansson and twice against Sonny Liston, all the anger over D'Amato ducking the best challengers, all the head scratching about general neuroses and the wearing of disguises — that was now ancient history. The matter was simple: Muhammad Ali's impact threatened the stability and financial well being of boxing, and Patterson seemed to be the best man to quash the threat. The concept of "the great white hope" had given way to a "the great mainstream America hope." Some were indeed calling Patterson "the Black White Hope." In an odd, perverse way, this marked some progress in regard to racism. From another standpoint, it simply showed how ignorance and racism in mid–'60s America simply sought any friend as they fixated on targets which hit them at their most primal levels. In the mid–1960s, Muhammad Ali certainly hit middle America as hard as anyone, in or out of sports.[16]

Patterson understood the many pressures here, and he did not shy away from them. With great press attention, and with much popular appeal among the mainstream of white America, Patterson spoke of how "the image of a Black Muslim as the world heavyweight champion disgraces the sport and the nation." (Well aware of the controversial nature of Patterson's words, *Sports Illustrated* printed this sentence on its article's title page in large font, displaying it *in Patterson's own handwriting*, so there would be no question that the words were truly his.) With words that became quite famous, Patterson went on to emphasize, then, how he wanted to "defeat Cassius Clay in order to bring the title back to America." Elsewhere he elaborated about the controversies aroused in the country by the Nation of Islam:

> I have nothing but contempt for the Black Muslims and that for which they stand.... I have the right to call the Black Muslims a menace to the United States and a menace to the Negro race. I have a right to say the Black Muslims stink. I am a Roman Catholic. I do not believe God put us here to hate one another. I believe the Muslim preaching of segregation, hatred, rebellion and violence is wrong. Cassius Clay is disgracing himself and the Negro race.... If I were to support Black Muslims, I might just as well support the Ku Klux Klan.

Generally one to avoid controversy, Patterson could not have hit the issues surrounding Muhammad Ali and the general question of racial radicalism in 1965 more starkly. He spent much of the *Sports Illustrated* article explaining how he believed he could tactically defeat Ali in the ring. Although most did not notice, he also went out of his way to defend Ali against those who had been arguing that his knockout Liston that spring had been a sham. Patterson called the knockout blow "a legitimate, sharp, hard right-hand chop under his left ear." All this discussion, as well as talk of how he could win, were typical pre-fight statements. It was Patterson's words about the Black Muslims that made headlines. "The Black Muslim influence," he declared, "must be removed from boxing."[17]

Ali was blunt and emphatic in response. He had already called Patterson an "Uncle Tom." Now he said something different than his usual jolly prediction of the round in which he would win: "I'm going to whip this man; I'm going to punish him!" The political lines drawn here were absolutely obvious. In 1965, emerging African American radicalism, to the degree it was understood, was very frightening to middle class Americans. Patterson was telling these Americans that he understood their fears and fundamentally agreed with the political and moral commitments that lay beneath them. Boxing was thus presenting a pair of combatants who symbolized the conflicting liberal and radical sensibilities which had emerged among African Americans. Ali had been friends with Malcolm X, but under pressure from Elijah Muhammad he had abandoned Malcolm. Throughout these years, the chief member of Ali's entourage was Herbert Muhammad, Elijah Muhammad's son. What Ali truly felt about the murder of his former friend, Malcolm X, he never made public, but his loyalty to the Black Muslims was then complete. In contrast, Patterson took hold of the situation to cast himself as the man who could save the nation from this evil influence. He would rescue boxing from a sinister force that struck an even more fearful image than had Sonny Liston and his mob connections.[18]

While Ali and the Muslims took offense at Patterson's words, Ali was too much of a showman and businessman to leave it at that. A climate of hatreds, fear, and animosity would not sell tickets. In the same tone that underlay much of his usual clowning, Ali made a point of taking one different sort of exception to Patterson. "Patterson says he's gonna bring the title back to America." Ali quipped. "If you don't believe the title already is in America, just see whom I pay taxes to." Ali's tone here may have been as light as it was when he was smiling and spouting off his poetry. Still, the overall tone of the situation remained very tense. Elsewhere, indeed, Ali emphasized, "What do you mean 'Bring it back to America!' Floyd, I'm the heavyweight champion of the world, and I'm an American. I stand for the people, the black people, the poor people, the poor people in the ghettos, both black and white." Patterson's words cut at the heart of the social-religious movement to which Ali had devoted himself with a sincerity few at the time fully realized.

Elsewhere Ali went about steadily disparaging Patterson. He told reporters that in most respects it would be more of a challenge for him to fight Chuvalo. Patterson, he shrugged, would be easier to knock out. Here Ali added a little poetic jab in regard to Patterson's many knockdowns. He mocked poetically: "The rabbit has a bad habit." In the summer of 1965, a few others in boxing were indeed nervously looking past Patterson for some sort of significant challenge to Ali. Ernie Terrell was one major contender. The World Boxing Association was still touting him as the real champion, although few took it seriously, and, indeed, the WBA relented as in September it announced it would recognize the winner of Patterson v. Ali as champion. At this time a few in the press began speculating about other opponents. Some began asserting that Ali could even fight the giant basketball star Wilt Chamberlain. (Having been fired by Patterson, Cus D'Amato was actually the first to offer Chamberlain a contract and manage him as a professional boxer. D'Amato was also making efforts to take over the management of Sonny Liston and help him make a comeback.) Speculations about Chamberlain fighting Ali would go on for almost two years.[19] Nothing ever came of it but one entertaining ABC–TV confrontation between Ali and Chamberlain in 1966. (Ali told Wilt that he would have to shave before getting in the ring with him: "I ain't fightin' no billy goat!") The fact that there was thought given to the idea of Wilt Chamberlain fighting Muhammad Ali was indicative of how far many would look to find someone who could dethrone the man who confronted mainstream America at so primal a level as Ali did. And it was in view of this challenge that Patterson became a kind of poster boy for those who clung to middle American values against an onslaught they did not fully understand but greatly feared.

In early September, Ali and Patterson agreed to a fight. On September 14, the two actually appeared together before the press in New York, and they were largely civil. Ali pumped up the situation, holding forth about Patterson, "He's fast, he's determined, and he knows it's do or die. This is the type of man who might whup me." Always full of games, Ali wanted to build up expectations with the obvious goal of increasing gate and revenues. He earnestly pronounced at this point: "Patterson is no longer the Rabbit." It was fairly effective staging. If Ali continued to declare that Patterson was not a worthy challenger, many fans would not see the bout as worthy of serious attention, or money. As they appeared together, Ali sat close to Patterson at times. There he appeared to rest his head on Patterson's shoulder, close his eyes, and whisper things in his ear. It was all good posturing to signify that Ali liked Patterson and respected him as an equal. He did add, however, that he preferred to sit rather than stand with Patterson, because a standing side-by-side contrast would reveal how much smaller Patterson was and then "they wouldn't bet on Patterson." Ali announced, to the surprise of many, "I'm no longer loud and boastful; I'm humble and quiet. I'm more like Floyd Patterson." Not a soul believed him. Later, Patterson admitted that between the times Ali was screaming and bragging to the press, he had leaned over to Floyd to keep him in the event, whispering: "You want to make some money, don't you, Floyd? You want to make lots of money, don't you." Everyone definitely believed that.

Patterson quietly smiled through it all. It seemed for the moment that the ill will between the two was a myth. Ali even joked in regard to the stories which were flying about to the effect that he was going to put a clause into the fight contract that if Patterson lost he would have to join the Muslims. "That was just humor," Ali intoned. Here Patterson smiled. Then Patterson touched on the serious issues each had previously raised. He mentioned to Ali the point that he had indeed given credit to the Nation of Islam for his victories over Liston. Ali returned fire, asking Patterson to confirm that he had indeed said that, "being a Catholic," he wanted "to take the title away from the Muslims." Patterson freely acknowledged he had said this and reemphasized to Ali how he "gave credit to the Muslims for your title." Still apparently playful, Ali snapped: "Do you think it's wrong for a man to submit himself to God?" Patterson said it certainly was not wrong, and jabbed back to Ali: "Aren't you proud of your country?" Ali confirmed he was proud of the nation, but asked Patterson: "Aren't you ashamed of 310 years without getting paid, with getting shot down [asking] for a cup of coffee." The tone was definitely growing more tense. Then Ali challenged Patterson to promise that if he lost, Patterson "would have to spend three days with him, going to a mosque and meeting with other Muslims." Patterson responded that he would not need three days and challenged Ali to spend 24 hours with him if he lost. Ali immediately agreed, jumped up, gave Patterson a hug, and announced loudly to the press: "Let the world hear it. If Floyd wins, I spend 24 hours with him. If I win, he spends 24 hours with me." It all seemed basically gentlemanly and fun. No one realized how Ali's extrovert nature continued to belie a steely commitment to his new religion. Nor could they grasp how this commitment resolved him to give anyone like Patterson, who questioned the nature, the ethics, and the politics of his newly adopted culture, the deepest possible lesson he could give in boxing, politics, and religion. The press conference may have been fun, but Ali had a serious side that could not be shaken. Drew "Bundini" Brown had been Ali's trainer from 1962 to 1965, but he had been forced out of Ali's camp because, according to Brown, he refused to join the Muslims. He sounded a warning to Patterson that applied to such meetings as the funny New York press gathering. "Pay no attention to any conversations, friendly or otherwise," Brown warned. "Get your business taken care of and get back to your camp."[20]

Back in training camp that fall, Patterson did have one major tragedy. On October 4, his head trainer, Dominick "Dan" Florio suddenly took ill. He was rushed to Mary Immaculate Hospital in Queens, and within a week he died. Patterson had not been as close to or as dependent on Florio as he had been with Cus D'Amato, and the other trainers in his camp, led by Buster Watson, would carry on with the preparations for the upcoming bout as scheduled. Patterson was moved by Florio's passing, of course. Florio had been honest and loyal to him. He had never stolen, as many managers and trainers in the fight game do, and he had given Patterson the room to manage himself, the very thing Patterson wanted and needed after the early years of extreme control from D'Amato. Florio's passing was a rude shock, but one which Patterson had to and did bear.[21]

No matter the mutually beneficial performances before the press, the gaps between Floyd Patterson and Muhammad Ali in sensibility, religion, politics, and personality were each wide and unbridgeable. That was one of the appeals of boxing. All such matters only add to the hype, and here the politics gave especially poignant dimensions. To many mainstream observers of the day, the Black Muslims simply appeared to be a hate group, nothing more. Patterson assuaged some of their fears. Ali had chided Patterson for disparaging the Muslim faith. Later he elaborated:

> I kept my peace until you made the statement that you wanted to bring the title back to America. You let whites goad you into attacking me because I'd become a follower of the Honorable Elijah Muhammad, this black man who preached unity and progress, who had taken thousands of hopeless addicts off the streets and changed their lives, gave them purpose and programs.... All the white press was backing you, all the Catholics, all the Protestants. And even though Sonny Liston had destroyed you twice, they revived you just so you could get to me. The only reason they gave you a title fight was they wanted to see you perform a miracle. They wanted to see a nice Catholic boy defeat a Black Muslim.

As the religious issues grew hotter, Patterson attempted to clarify himself: "Some believe I'm against the whole Black Muslim movement, but," he insisted, "I'm not. I'm against their insistence on segregation of blacks and whites. I'm for integration, something [for which] the Negro has been fighting for centuries. I'm not against their religion." Patterson could have caused Ali some discomfort here by alluding to and emphasizing the views to which Malcolm X came at the end of his life, views that rejected the racial separation on which Elijah Muhammad insisted. It may have been an effective rhetorical ploy, but Patterson did not touch on this. Patterson recalled how President Kennedy and others like Ralph Bunche had previously implored him to defeat Liston because of all the evil he represented. Now Patterson felt he was on an even more important such good v. evil crusade, and in his sense of mission he brought some along with him. *Sports Illustrated* noted Patterson's sense of mission and his popularity here, but they did so with a grim codicil: "The fact that Patterson represents the majority of Negroes and that he has done nothing to discredit himself (except that he can't fight) is causing a lot of people to make small speculations on him." The bigger speculations of the heart were on Ali, especially among the black youth of the nation. Patterson just did not appear cool. Ali did, and his reflection several years later perhaps summarized it most neatly: "Floyd was a good boy, but I'm a bad nigger."[22]

Just before the fight, Patterson appeared self-assured and "grim to the point of surliness," as one writer saw it. He was, however, knocked down by one of his sparring partners during training, and this engendered some concern. Patterson continued to be generous in his comments about "Cassius Clay," but he continually called him "Clay." Asked about Ali's insults, he smiled, "That's part of Clay's pattern, and I've grown accustomed to it. If he said nothing about me, then perhaps I'd be worried. Sometimes I get the idea that Mr. Clay is trying to convince himself more than me." Patterson made believers out of a few reporters. Maybe their desire to see Ali and the Black Muslims lose was overweening, but various writers strained to show how Patterson would be a stronger opponent for Ali than Liston had been. They emphasized how Patterson would show Ali new boxing skills. "The relatively inexperienced and still amateurish Clay never has met a man with the rounded skills and ring guile of Patterson," wrote one hopefully. Liston supposedly "had the mobility of a fire hydrant, [and] Patterson won't be a standing target for Clay." Cus D'Amato emphasized, in an optimistic tone, that "Clay has never fought anyone with Floyd's ability to put punches together — true combinations — and against this kind of pressure," D'Amato predicted, "he will find it difficult to defend with his hands down." "Patterson," wrote another, "is not obsessed by the chilling terrors awakened in his too vivid imagination by the frightening figure of Liston." Patterson "is enough of a craftsman to have the wherewithal to put the silencer on the loudmouth braggart from Louisville." Folks were indeed trying hard to convince themselves that Patterson could "bring the title back to America." With unwitting irony, Cus D'Amato even went so far to point out that Patterson, even though a "smaller, inferior force," could beat "a superior one," he conjectured, "as Rommel did in Africa to the British"(!). The racism inherent in the reference to the Nazis' hero, Field Marshal Rommel, as well as the fact of Rommel's ultimate fate in Africa and elsewhere was somehow overlooked here. To an Ali supporter, then and since, the strains in such parallels were rather amusing. Patterson as "the Erwin Rommel of boxing" who could bring "the title back to America?" Ali never offered a comment. He always got along with Cus D'Amato anyway.[23]

Whether Patterson had genuinely convinced some of the boxing press or whether Ali's politics, religion, and antics had left them desperately wanting to be convinced, all the arguments led interest in the fight to grow quite nicely. The Las Vegas Convention Center sold out, with ringside seats going for $100. Thirty-two theaters around the U.S. and Canada brought another 750,000 paying customers to the fight. Television outlets in Europe were televising the bout. The Convention Center received press applications from many parts of the world, including thirty-two from Sweden, fifteen from Great Britain, and three from Japan, whose sports press had never before shown any interest in heavyweight prizefighting. The betting parlors of Las Vegas had Ali a 3–1 favorite. But the betting was heavy. People were taking the fight seriously, and interest was wide. Revenues from the fight would total just over $3.8 million.[24]

From the very opening of the fight, all the hoopla proved for naught. From the first round, Ali was in complete command. There was no aspect of the fight that Ali did not dominate. Ali was stronger as well as quicker. He hit harder; his defense was better; his reach was longer; and he was psychologically in complete control. The crowd was completely for Patterson, but it made no difference. They had roundly booed Ali during the introductions, but this made absolutely no impact on the champion. Before the opening bell, as the two stood with the referee in the center of the ring, Ali looked down intently upon Patterson and began to taunt him, calling him "the American white hope." As they stood at the center, the three inch height difference between the two was striking, and from the outset of the fight it was even more so. Patterson looked stiff and halting, Ali loose and confident. No matter the relative attributes of foot speed and power in his prior fights, Patterson had always been the fighter with the fastest hands. With Ali he did not even have that edge, and in addition to his superior hand speed, Ali had greater reach. From the outset, he showed that at will he could snap Patterson with his left jab or right lead. Patterson, meanwhile, could not get close enough to land a good punch, and he never did. Ali kept just the right distance and was virtually untouchable throughout every round. In the few times Patterson was able to get inside, Ali quickly tied him up. Truly remarkable, given that Patterson did indeed have fast hands, was the fact that virtually every time Patterson threw a significant punch, especially one of his hooks, Ali quickly shot his head back, always just enough to make Patterson miss. Ali never flinched at fake punches either, he was just that much quicker in response to any shot Patterson could offer. Patterson missed and missed, and this wore him down as much as any of Ali's successive blows. The crowd cheered at anything that hinted of a Patterson punch landing, and the strained nature of this only served to heighten the psychological as well as physical victory that Ali was enjoying.

By the fourth round, Patterson's footwork was slowing. Meanwhile, Ali did not seem the least bit fatigued. Indeed he continued to talk and taunt Patterson, as well as hit him. "Come on, America; come on, White America!" Referee Harry Krause even warned Ali to "stop the chatter," but Ali would never stop for long. Patterson later said he could not make out what Ali was saying, but, he confessed, "I was disgusted that I couldn't do anything about it." Somewhere in the fourth or fifth round, one of Patterson's lunging left hooks missed and the rotating force of the punch badly strained one of Patterson's back muscles. Some said he may have herniated a disc. After the fight, one diagnosis declared he had slightly rotated the fifth lumbar vertebrae. In any case, Patterson endured back spasms the rest of the evening. Patterson's doctor, Michael Blatt said it was a pre-fight back injury. If there was a pre-fight injury, there could be no excuse, as Patterson could have then legitimately put off the bout. Dr. Blatt said he had urged Patterson to do just that.

Patterson had always had a problematic back. As far back as 1952, when he first trained and fought as an amateur, he experienced some pain. For many years he slept on a hard board. In addition to Dr. Blatt, Patterson had hired a chiropractor, Reginald Gold, a man who had been with him as far back as the third Johansson bout. According to Gold's nomenclature, Patterson suffered from subluxation, which he said was a slight rotation of the fifth lumbar vertebra. Several missed hooks, he said, could have severely aggravated this. "The pain was so bad," Patterson later acknowledged, "that it was the first time in a fight I was begging to be knocked out.... But," he added, "I could not take a dive."

With his back hurting badly, Patterson seemed to cringe more and more, and this made him look even more meek and submissive. By the sixth round bell, Patterson was only able to walk out from his corner. Ali had promised to "punish" Patterson, and he did just that, especially in the sixth. He peppered Patterson with every sort of left and right jab, lead, hook, and uppercut. Amidst the onslaught, Patterson gave out for a moment as he collapsed onto one knee. This counted as a knockdown, and Patterson took an eight count. Showing not a hint of mercy, Ali came back and poured it on even more. Patterson had but to hold onto a hope of landing one of his hooks, and everyone in Las Vegas and in the closed circuit theaters around the country knew there was absolutely no chance of that. Ali was easily winning virtually every round, and he appeared to be loving every minute of it. The two judges actually gave Patterson the first round, and the referee gave Patterson the eleventh round, even though he would soon stop the fight. Otherwise, Ali won every round on every card with the exception of one judge calling but one of the rounds even.

At the bell ending the eighth round, Patterson nearly collapsed. His corner men then began lifting him up to stretch out his back, trying to relieve some of the muscle spasms. Chiropractor Reginald Gold later stated that this lifting probably aggravated matters and that he could have manipulated Patterson between rounds and given him relief. As Gold was not an official corner man, such an intervention would have led to an immediate disqualification. Patterson could have quit, as Sonny Liston had against Ali the year before. He kept going, however, and Ali never let up. As the pathos of the fight grew, the crowd was booing and yelling, but now they were yelling at Ali to end it all with a knockout. Even more, they were yelling at referee Harry Krause to put a stop to it. It was not just Patterson's back that was troubling him. Ali's blows had caused a blood clot in Patterson's left eye. This limited his vision. "If Clay had realized this," Patterson later admitted, "he could have hit me all night long with right hands." Ali pretty much did this anyway.

By the tenth round, Patterson's helplessness was total. He slogged through the round, with Ali making sure to land a series of combinations right before the bell. In the eleventh Floyd looked even more helpless. Before the twelfth, the official fight doctor was called to Patterson's corner. Patterson said he could continue, and the doctor let him do it. At the bell, Patterson was terribly wobbly. Ali continued to peck away. His trainer, Angelo Dundee, was fully aware of what his man was doing. He even yelled at Ali in disgust, "Knock him out for Christ's sake!" (Ali had long severed that allegiance.) The crowd was booing ever more loudly, and finally, at 2:18 of the twelfth round, Harry Krause mercifully stopped the fight.[25]

With the long awaited end, the crowd booed even more. In his post-fight interviews, Ali was outwardly gracious. He expressed surprise that Patterson could take so many punches. "He's a real man," Ali commented, "I hit him but he didn't go down.... I have two swollen hands to show for it." He looked at Patterson and acknowledged: "You wouldn't fall. You kept taking it.... You took everything I threw.... You were good. You had guts and heart. You were better than those egging you on." The "eggers" were Ali's real enemy. Ali mocked the fans. "Too many people cheered me tonight," he scoffed. "There weren't enough boos." He later reflected, "I didn't see myself hitting Floyd Patterson. I was fighting the white reporters behind him, the Jimmy Cannons, and the white celebrities, the Frank Sinatras, the Joey Bishops, the Arch Wards, the Dick Youngs." In this mood Ali also patronized Patterson. In reference to the "white hope" label, Ali said, "I won't let your Negro beat me!" He mocked Patterson, snorting that he was deserving of "honors and medals [given] the spot you was on." Referring to all the things Patterson had said about him and the Muslims, Ali acknowledged, as he had promised: "I gave him a wuppin'.... It was no contest. Get me a contender." *Life Magazine* called the whole thing a "Sickening Spectacle in the Ring."[26]

It was with the Patterson fight that some reporters began to clack out words to the effect that Ali might indeed be as great a boxer as he had been claiming he was. Generally, however, the boxing press and public were still in deep states of denial and fear about Ali, "the giant they love to hate," as *Sports Illustrated* put it. In 1965, mainstream America did not know how to take, let along honestly dialogue with, Ali and the Black Muslims. They were, as yet, completely beyond the pale of comprehension. As fear was then the emotion still driving the general public, press reactions which focused dismissively on Ali's cruelty resonated best among the mainstream. A vicious, sickeningly cruel man need not be comprehended at any other level, and words to this effect could be easily found. Referee Harry Krause said he certainly felt it was Ali's intention not to knock Patterson out but to punish him. Tennis star Arthur Ashe, although a great admirer of Ali, actually confessed to have been pained by the cruelty Ali showed in the bout. Even Joe Louis declared, "Clay is selfish — and cruel." (Within a year, watching Ali defeat but have trouble with the German heavyweight Karl Mildenberger, Louis would turn around and opine that Ali lacked the necessary killer instinct.) Of course, loads of television and newspaper staffers echoed the same sorts of lines about "cruelty." "They talked about how cruel I was," Ali wrote. "The trouble was they [Jimmy Cannon, Dick Young, Frank Sinatra] wanted to see something cruel happen to me."

Ali's savage defeat of Patterson in the ring could not have made mainstream America madder. To add to this, after the fight Ali offered Patterson a copy of Elijah Muhammad's book *A Message to the Black Man of America*. Most white viewers had barely heard of Elijah Muhammad and knew nothing of his book or the issues it encompassed. To them Ali's offering was simply unsportsmanlike taunting. If Ali was to be the champion, people solemnly believed, he needed to act properly, indeed, like Patterson, "a tiger in the ring and a pussycat outside the ring," as Eldridge Cleaver would mockingly write. Mainstream Americans were mad enough when a criminal like Sonny Liston confronted their sensibilities. But Liston had merely been a singular figure of evil, directly attached to no political agenda. Ali's impropriety was no less defiant, and it contained a most threatening political message. As it seemed no one could beat him, mainstream American hysteria could only grow. In 1965, any such notions as diversity and tolerance were hardly part of the political lexicon.

The more Ali would win, the more he would generate anger. "I was talking back," he reflected,

> I was saying, "I am America." Only I'm the part you won't recognize. But get used to me. Black, confident, cocky; my name, not yours; my religion, not yours; my goals, my own — get used to me! I can make it without your approval! I won't let you beat me.

Already extremely angry with Ali, older mainstream America had dearly hoped that Patterson could silence him. As he could not, the mainstream could now find less and less of a mere boxing vocabulary with which to vent itself. There was so much more at stake here than mere boxing rankings. Eldridge Cleaver would write that Ali's title defense against Patterson reflected

> the consolidation of certain psychic gains of the Negro revolution. The white hope for a Patterson victory was, in essence, a counterrevolutionary desire to force the Negro, now in rebellion and personified ... by Ali, back into his "place," while the black hope was to see Uncle Tom defeated, to be given symbolic proof of the victory of the autonomous Negro over the subordinate Negro.

Cleaver and the other leaders of the Black Panthers had anything but affection for the Black Muslims. They considered them racists, and they greatly despised the way that Muhammad Ali, under pressure from Elijah Muhammad, had distanced himself from Malcolm X. But at the time Ali triumphed over Patterson, all such notions as the racist ideology of the Muslims, and the resulting divisions among African Americans and their various leaders, paled before the perception that, as Cleaver put it, "Ali was more in harmony with the furious psychic stance of the Negro today, while Patterson was an anachronism light years behind." The Ali-Patterson bout came to encapsulate so much more than a mere matter of who was the better fighter (as though anyone ever really wondered about that in the first place). "For there to be so deep an uproar over Muhammad Ali," Cleaver noted, "should indicate that there is something much more serious than a boxing title at stake, something cutting right to the center of the madness of our time."[27] With the issues here indeed so greatly transcending the narrow confines of sports, the emotions of older white Americans could only grow ever more raw. The millions of haters would seek any means necessary to get back at the man they so despised. They would eventually get him, but paradoxically it only drove Ali's fame to greater levels.

As for Patterson, many commentators were quite demeaning. All memories of his working with CORE, with Jackie Robinson, and with Martin Luther King now conveniently faded. The Uncle Tom image stuck, as did the pathetic image of him seemingly cowering in the ring before the punishment from Ali. While Patterson insisted on not using his back trouble as an explanation or excuse for his poor performance in the ring, many did. Here Muhammad Ali himself commented that he believed Patterson's back was hurt, but he noted that Floyd "don't want to publicize it. He's a man." Others were not so generous, however. Pooh-poohing the matter of Patterson's back, referee Harry Krause openly disparaged Patterson. "I don't think the back injury made much difference," he scoffed. "Patterson looked bad even in the first two rounds — like an old woman." Others said Patterson was "hypnotized then pulverized." It was hard to find any sort of silver lining. Some reporters extolled Patterson's courage and "high valor." Even with such praise, however, reporters had to admit they were praising the man and not the fighter. As one wrote, "Patterson has the flaming courage of a lion, ... but the fighting equipment of a rabbit." Frank Sinatra, who had befriended Patterson when he had become champion, proved the completely egotistical fairweather friend many would know him always to be in many contexts. Patterson went to see him the day after the fight, and Sinatra turned his back on him, barely uttering a word. Patterson almost wept. The rude incident implied that Ali was right — that the Frank Sinatras of the white world did not really embrace Patterson. They simply wanted to find anyone who could beat the hated Ali, and once a black man failed to perform for them as they desired, he was just an utterly worthless _____. Behavior like Frank Sinatra's fed the logic of the appeal to black men of such ideologically varied radicals as Eldridge Cleaver and Elijah Muhammad. Yet at this point African Americans abandoned Patterson just as obnoxiously as Frank Sinatra. "Patterson," as Cleaver noted, "was the symbolic spearhead of a counterrevolutionary host, leader of the mythical legions of faithful darkies who inhabit the white imagination." Angry African Americans, Cleaver then noted, heaped "cold, deadly hatred and contempt upon Patterson and the boot-licking art of the puppet in the style of his image."

If there was a quality challenger to Muhammad Ali out there, and the American mainstream desperately wanted to find one, people now knew Patterson was certainly not it. In January, Ali admitted that he had carried Patterson in their fight. All charges of Ali's cruelty, bad sportsmanship, and taunting, while they certainly magnified the hatred people felt for the champion and all that he represented, could generate no greater levels of respect for Patterson. Some of the reporters who had let themselves go out on a limb and wishfully say that Patterson *could* beat Ali were now sneering at the fight as a "horrible mismatch." For Patterson, the main thing that would grow here was pity. As Patterson had said after losing to Johansson, "I hate pity." Patterson told his fans, "I wish I could have given you a better fight." Acknowledging that he could make no excuses for his performance, he concluded: "I will just say I am sorry," adding: "I can do much, much better. That I know."[28]

Patterson may have known this, but he was the only one of any significance in the fight game who did. When he had lost to Liston, matters seemed over, yet he had climbed his way back to the top of the contender list and made believers out of at least a few along the way, although the desperation of so many to find someone who could possibly beat the hated Ali did not hurt here. In December of 1965, however, Patterson was just a month shy of his thirty-first birthday, while Muhammad Ali was only twenty-three. In the two to three years in which some sort of comeback could conceivably occur, Patterson's skills could easily begin to show some deterioration while the champion's would likely sharpen. How could Patterson hope to climb back into such a picture against a much younger champion who had shown himself to be so superior, as well as against the constant waves of strong newcomers? If Patterson kept fighting, his career appeared to be one doomed to that of an obscure has-been, laden with the political disdain of an emerging new age whose confident, youthful leaders were content smugly to dismiss any who appeared to represent the ways of the past.

XIII

Nowhere to Go

After the loss to Muhammad Ali, Patterson's spirit may have been crushed, but at least he and his family were in good financial shape. Floyd had made $350,000 from the bout. (Ali made $700,000.) With his very personable nature, Patterson could have likely retired at that point and gained a lucrative position as a television fight commentator. In those very years of the mid–1960s, ABC Sports paid the likeable and reasonably well-known professional bowler, Billy Wehlu, $10,000 per Saturday for his expert commentaries on the network's coverage of the Pro-Bowlers' Tour. Patterson was a vastly more prominent sports figure than Wehlu, and boxing certainly commanded at least as much of the sports public's attention as pro bowling, so such a nice salary per broadcast, possibly as often one or two times a month, was more than plausible. Sandra definitely wanted Floyd to retire and do such safe work. She was greatly distressed by the devastating manner of her husband's loss to Muhammad Ali and felt it was long past time for him to give up the brutal game.

In 1965, lots of other signs could also be interpreted to point to retirement for Floyd. In the summer, for example, the *New York Times* ran a short Sunday sports article about athletes who have that certain something — animal magnetism, charisma — the words varied, but whatever that elusive "it" was, certain ones have it, said the *Times*, while others, though quality sportsmen, somehow come up short. In baseball, for example, the *Times* named Willy Mays as one who had "it," and Mickey Mantle as one who did not. In basketball Bill Russell had "it"; Wilt Chamberlain did not. Arnold Palmer was the obvious example in golf compared with the likes of Jack Nicklaus and Ben Hogan. When they turned to boxing, the *Times* pointed to a man like Sugar Ray Robinson as having that certain quality. (Muhammad Ali was conspicuously absent from their discussion here.) Who did the *Times* cite as the best lackluster example in contrast to Sugar Ray — Floyd Patterson.[1] No one argued with the characterization.

"Boring" was no more admirable a trait than was the stolidity that Patterson represented next to Muhammad Ali's outgoing dash. Ali may have cast many fearsome images with his political and religious affiliations, but these attributes were beginning to resonate positively among people, especially among the younger generations. Here the hazy sense of Patterson being less than Ali in political sentiment galvanized with the obvious comparison of their relative strengths in the ring. Even among those for whom Ali's religion and politics continued to be negatives, they could never offset the obvious point that he was the superior fighter. Patterson was a lesser athletic light, and in an age increasingly obsessed with image, Patterson and the mainstream politics he represented just did not look cool. The heavyweight division and the broader forces of history had merged at various times in the past, notably in the days of Jack Johnson and of Joe Louis. Because Muhammad Ali was, without any doubt, the best boxer of his era, he helped the politics that surrounded him assume an ever increasing aura of coolness, a matter of which several figures in the federal government were beginning nervously to take note. Among certain trendy, chic crowds of the mid and late 1960s not only was conservative "out," being considered a mere liberal was uncool too. Hindsight may reveal different perspectives on the legitimacy of many of the allegedly radical ways of the 1960s, the fact that many of the history textbooks are being written by children of that time who may still romanticize some aspects of the era's radicalism notwithstanding. Muhammad Ali himself would come completely to abandon the Black Muslims and embrace a more traditional form of Islam. But amidst the heating months of the mid–1960s, Ali was proud of his religious and political affiliations. As he cast a radically non-conformist image that was decidedly "in," many wanted somehow to win such a status for themselves. The "good boy scout" image that Patterson had held to sports fans of the late '50s and early '60s now held absolutely no sway with any who wanted to be considered cool. Even though one's athleticism has nothing to do with the legitimacy of one's politics, the fact that Ali was the best and Patterson had been beaten greatly reinforced this general public sense of Ali being politically interesting and Patterson, to the extent anyone thought about him anymore, being every bit the Uncle Tom that the loquacious Ali had dubbed him. In any kind of schoolyard, barber shop, or barroom venue, anyone who spoke words to the effect that "Patterson may not be as good a fighter as Ali, but the ways of his good Christian life and traditional liberal politics are still better models for the nation and its youth" would have been considered laughably pathetic.

To a generation of a self-consciously New Age, Patterson's heyday in the late '50s and early '60s seemed not of the immediate past but a distant memory, more part of the eras of Joe Louis and Rocky Marciano. The emerging "New" Left of the mid and late 1960s was full of people who prided themselves, as their proudly chosen adjective implied, that they were freshly different and tied to no legacy. Among their symbols and leaders from the Port Huron Statement, to the Beatles, to Stokely Carmichael, to H. Rap Brown and the Black Panthers, all seemed to disregard not only the traditionalists, but also the leftists and non-conformists of the past. All were uninstructive and irrelevant. As much as any figure in any of these movements, as much as any figure of the age, Muhammad Ali embodied this "New" outlook. His fighting style, especially with his hands held so daringly low, appeared not just to break all the rules but successfully mock them. His religion and politics were also a complete challenge to any prior orthodoxy. And because he was such a success in the ring, his influence in the country, and not just in sports, was remarkably striking.

Such a combination of athleticism and charisma was altogether unprecedented. As his image took on a life that encompassed so much beyond just its own athletic sphere, the opponents within Ali's true back yard of boxing thus seemed to be left utterly in the dust, and no one was dusted here more than such a solid citizen as Floyd Patterson. In contrast to Ali's hands held low, Patterson's peek-a-boo defense posture represented the uptight defensiveness of un-cool elders. No matter how noble had been Patterson's rise out of poverty, through the Wiltwyck School, and up the social-economic ladder had earlier appeared, there no longer seemed anything socially instructive about his life. Roy Wilkins, then the long-time national director of the NAACP, had similarly done enormous work on behalf of African Americans and other minorities. Yet with many crude verbal swipes, a new generation of African American leaders cast him off. Historians of African America have since given Wilkins great respect for his work, but any chroniclers of the 1960s have also to note the fact of how cruelly such people as Wilkins were sneered at by the emerging hep youth culture of Anglo and African American activists. Tinges of self-absorption and immaturity (as well as pseudo-euphoric drugs) doubtlessly infected their many movements and activities, but the legacy of a man like Wilkins did not resonate one iota among the millions of would-be hipsters of the day. In such a sea change of cultural images and superficialities, it was impossible for Patterson not to feel cruelly cast off. It was as though the world had told him ever since his first day at Wiltwyck that if he played by the rules, as hard as that may be, he would be rewarded. Patterson did as he had been told, and now that same world, to the extent they paid a man like Patterson any heed, was snorting and laughing at him like he was an overly trusting soul who had been the victim of a slick scam.

Earlier that summer 1965, *New York Times* reporter Gay Talese published a book in which he utilized a theme the novelist Ernest Hemingway once employed about people who "take that extra step, climb too high, lean too far, go too fast, get too grabby with the gods." Hemingway had called them "overreachers," a term that became the title of Talese's book. In his discussions, Talese offered Floyd Patterson as one of his prime examples. (Others included such lesser-lights as Broadway and Hollywood director Joshua Logan and a gambler and mafia figure, Frank Costello.) Talese's characterization was hardly the kind of publicity Patterson wanted, but, like the charge of not having any of Sugar Ray Robinson's charisma, it certainly made sense among the reading public. After the Ali bout, that image of a charismaless overreacher seemed both apt and complete. "He's a drowning man," said Ali's trainer Angelo Dundee. He had apparently gone beyond his depth, and the superior Ali had oh so casually dunked him.[2]

In the wake of the Ali fight, former light heavyweight champion Tommy Loughran commented about Patterson's career. Patterson, Loughran lamented, had once been "so lithe, so supple, and ... punched with such power." Then, according to Loughran, "something happened." Patterson, he felt, had become "a deliberate puncher," contending this declension had stemmed from "all that unneeded muscle and weight." Loughran had been a light heavyweight. As he had been content to keep himself just a shade light of the heavyweight division, he may have been overly disposed to see the illogic of "going up" as Patterson had. Still, with Patterson's record of regularly hitting the deck, and given especially what had happened with heavier punchers like Johansson, Liston, and Ali, Loughran's analysis made some sense. No one could deny that Cus D'Amato's program of weight gain for Patterson had put him into some money fights of which Loughran could have never dreamed. But now it all seemed over. At one level it may indeed have been a mistake not to remain a light heavyweight. Patterson had the hand speed and the general boxing skills to be one of the greatest in that division. Aside from Ali, who was better in every respect, it was the only big sluggers who always put Patterson down. Such figures rarely lie below the heavyweight division. Still, it was impossible for anyone not to recognize that Patterson had indeed been the heavyweight champion and thus enjoyed a level of financial and general public success that never comes to any light heavyweight. No matter how people felt about such analyses, at the end of 1965 the issue seemed settled: Patterson's best days were obviously behind him. He had succeeded, but his overreach had caught up with him. Had Patterson chosen to retire after the Ali debacle, all the pundits in the papers, bars, and barber shops would have regarded the move as entirely fitting.[3]

Reflecting on the Ali fight, Patterson had steadfastly refused to make his back problem an excuse for his performance, but he did let it gnaw at him mentally. If while fighting Clay, he thought, the devil had come by and said, "I'll make your back better if you let me blind you in one eye, flatten your nose, take away all your teeth, and give you a cauliflower ear," I'd have made the deal gladly. I wouldn't need a disguise then, would I? ... if I could have said the hell with my back and fought my fight. [As it was] I couldn't think about throwing punches. My mind was back there [on his back spasms].

Clearly, Patterson was (and he was the only one who was) thinking that, under only slightly different circumstances, he could have beaten Ali. It was in this frame of mind that he considered the retirement issue that made such sense to so many. "*Quit?*" he asked

Can you picture *me* sitting in a corner? As long as I could stand there on two legs and every once in a while throw *one* punch.... [Against Ali] I just wanted one more chance, a little more time. Maybe if the referee had waited. [emphases his]

Fretting this way about the loss to Ali, he seemed to be delusional, as well as a little disassociative. Here, however, he did recognize his own tendencies, but the delusions did not abate: "'A little more.' 'One more time.' These are favorite phrases of mine," he nodded. "Clay; I'm faster than he is. I didn't prove it, but a fighter has a way of knowing." Patterson certainly knew of aging fighters tragically kidding themselves about how they could still do it, but clearly he could not help himself. "When I think about retiring," he reflected:

my feet get very hot. I get chills. No more gym. No more road-work.... I say to myself, "You know, Floyd, you're not going to live forever." Why always one more time? Why? [Because] I enjoy training more than anything else. Walking in the country. Wipe that out of my life? I could build a gym in my home, but it's not the same. I don't train to keep my body in shape, I train to have my body beaten. I've got to retire sooner or later, but I prefer later.

Patterson's thoughts clearly meandered, and as they did, he exemplified some of that "Freud" Patterson who had baffled so many for so long. Could anyone have imagined Muhammad Ali or Sugar Ray Robinson saying they train "to have their bodies beaten?" Beyond this, Patterson was obviously fixating on certain points. He still thought he could beat Muhammad Ali. He still he thought he had some good fights in his future. And even if he lost, the training still captivated him. He clearly enjoyed the life in his training camp. But there was a darkness in the way that he was drawn to the ascetic, monkish style on which he insisted. At some level he was still running away from reality, like that disturbed little boy hiding and finding some sort of tranquility in the filthy, dank janitor's ante-room of a subway stop. Training camp was the only place he apparently felt the comfort of that solitude he never stopped seeking, and which he mistakenly defined as peace.

For anyone who saw such issues and problems in Patterson at this point, the question was whether he *or she* could possibly get through to him and convince him that it was still the right time to hang it up. The answer was apparently "no," because when it was clear that Floyd was not going to retire, Sandra filed for divorce. Enjoying his "training more than anything else," Patterson did not contest the divorce in any way, so they split. Sandy took the children and moved to Springfield, Massachusetts. Patterson always paid support without fail. He sold the newly purchased family house in Great Neck and made his spartan training camp in Marlboro, New York, his new permanent residence. Angelo Dundee had said that Floyd was "drowning." The metaphor may have been a trifle strained, but he was willingly cutting off his life from a lot of healthy air, preferring the claustrophobic world of his own making, as well as a new level of financial austerity, in Marlboro. "I live up here," he half-mused. "I don't even have a home in New York [City] any more.... Box 213, Marlboro, N.Y., that's my address." Then he added cryptically, "I go into New York once a week to try to bandage the parts of my life that other people may have wounded, that's all I'll say about it.... I don't stay overnight. Down and back the same day." The strain was there;

Patterson and his wife Sandra after his second defeat of Ingemar Johansson in 1961. Sandra enjoyed the good life with the money that Floyd made from boxing, but after he lost the title and then failed badly against Muhammad Ali, she grew increasingly upset with the idea of her husband continuing to fight. Sandra urged Floyd to retire. Floyd would not, however, and she eventually divorced him. ©Bettmann/CORBIS.

indeed less than three weeks after Sandy had filed for divorce, someone broke into the home of Patterson's brother Raymond and stole the gold and diamond crown that Cus D'Amato had made for Floyd back in 1959. The crown was worth $35,000, and Patterson had not insured it. The sense of being victimized when down here only reinforced the general sense of him as a loser.[4]

While Patterson's non-retirement cost him everything in regard to his personal life, the rest of the boxing world barely took notice. In 1966, Muhammad Ali was the champion, and he, his political and religious controversies, and his future opponents occupied everyone's attention. Patterson was a nobody.[5] If Patterson had complained about the obscurity, no one would have cared, but Patterson liked living and training in isolation anyway. To some extent he felt some liberation. He missed Sandy and the children, of course, but the rest of his world took on a simpler, happier cast. In camp, and in his big fights with Liston and Ali, Patterson had maintained eight full-time people in his retinue. For him that was a lot. As he noted, "they only added to the confusion." With a touch of bitterness, Patterson went on: "Each one worried about his cut. Was he getting enough? Was the next guy getting more? One guy made $250,000 in five years. Then, when he thought I was washed up, he sued me because he didn't think he got enough." Now that he was less of a contender, Patterson noted with a rueful smile here: "Well, the rats left the sinking ship." He maintained the barest of retinue and definitely preferred it that way.[6]

Amidst his relative obscurity, Patterson made one move in 1966 that garnered some significant public attention. The Ali fight had been in November of 1965, and after that Patterson did not have another fight for over ten months. He trained steadily, but he also took the time, with the help of an amanuensis, writer Gay Talese, to write a magazine article in defense and praise of Muhammad Ali. *Esquire Magazine* picked it up. The article was not a mere post-fight rationalization or a Pollyanna call for friendship. Neither *Esquire* nor any other major publication would have taken any paean of that sort seriously. Patterson took on Ali's many critics. Patterson noted Ali to be so much more fulsome a human being than the mere antics for which he was celebrated and mocked in the press. Ali, said Patterson, was a most thoughtful and sincere man. He defended both Ali's rights and the sincerity of his increasingly famous opposition to the Vietnam War and the military draft, even though Floyd disagreed with him here. Pressures were already coming to bear on Ali for his outspoken politics. Several key state boxing commissions, including New York and Illinois, were preventing him from boxing there. Indeed, after the Patterson fight, Ali's next four title defenses of 1966, against George Chuvalo, Henry Cooper, Brian London, and Karl Mildenberger, each occurred outside the United States. Political troubles dogged the staging of any fights in the U.S. A planned bout with Ernie Terrell could find no site in the country, and when it finally found a stage in Toronto, Terrell pulled out because the rewards were too slim. George Chuvalo replaced him. When Ali fought in Toronto, as well as in London and Frankfurt, many American closed-circuit television theater operators also boycotted the bouts.[7] The politics surrounding all this would come to a head in April 1967, when Ali refused the draft and had his title stripped. But as the troubles were heating up in August of 1966, Patterson spoke firmly in Ali's defense.

It would be grossly cynical, and flatly wrong, to say that Patterson was just trying to get on Ali's good side after the things he had said about the Black Muslims the year before in *Sports Illustrated*. Patterson was an ardent believer in free speech and he resolutely defended Ali's rights. Additionally, he fully knew and tried to persuade people that Ali's religious convictions were sincere and deserved to be respected like any others. In 1966, few were willing to speak out in defense of Ali as Patterson did. Some fighters like Ezzard Charles continued to take him a trifle lightly, as "just a big joking kid." Jim Braddock was like most middle–Americans of the day. He praised Ali's ring skills but firmly believed he should keep his mouth shut when it came to all matters of politics and religion. (Sonny Liston was asked to comment about Ali, and he snapped at the reporter: "I have no feeling for him. [Then suddenly he thundered:] Say, listen, how'd you get my phone number?") Patterson was very much on his own here, and he was quite sincere. There was a glaring problem in the public perception of the article, however. Patterson entitled the article, "In Defense of Cassius Clay." Some took that as a signal that the whole thing had an ironic edge and that Patterson was still willing to taunt Ali. Others sniffed that it showed that the old-fashioned Uncle Tom still "didn't get" Muhammad Ali. In the article, Patterson did point out that Ali had flown to Chicago to be photographed with him for the magazine cover and that he'd asked Ali, "It's all right if I call you Cassius, isn't it?" Ali, said Patterson, "smiled and said, 'Any time, Floyd.'" No such facts did anything to move those who were predisposed to side with Ali here.[8]

When the article came out, another *New York Times* reporter, Arthur Daley, asked Ali about it. Ali shrugged, "It was nice, but he insists on calling me Cassius Clay." It was always hard to know when Ali was acting. Patterson felt that the Nation of Islam had deeply frightened Ali with their then recent murder of his friend Malcolm X, hence he believed Ali felt he needed always to posture when it came to defending his still-newly adopted name and identity. (Later, after Ali had left the Nation of Islam, Floyd Patterson would be the *only* person, anywhere, whom Ali ever permitted to call him "Cassius Clay," and this remained the case for the rest of Patterson's life.) At the time, Ali may have been going along with whatever Patterson wanted to do in the context of the article, with the hopes that future money-making fights could ensue. Ali was then in a financial bind. He always had high entourage expenses and taxes. Additionally, he had just been divorced and was dealing with many legal troubles because of the growing selective service issues he was facing.[9]

While Ali was off fighting a series of new opponents in 1966, Patterson once again began to rebuild his career. His standing as a heavyweight contender in *Ring Magazine* had fallen to #9. In September of 1966 he flew to London to face British heavyweight Henry Cooper. Just as when Patterson fought Eddie Machen after losing to Liston, critics scoffed at the bout as a meaningless match between two obvious second-raters. Earlier that year, Cooper had already been beaten by Ali in a bloody bout; Ali had opened a cut over Cooper's left eye that bled profusely, causing the referee to stop the bout. If Patterson beat such a man, what would it prove? In reference to that and to Patterson's back problem when he fought Ali, critics were sneering at the fight as "a one-eyed man versus a cripple." If Patterson lost, it would again prove that he should retire, and Patterson promised to do just that if Cooper beat him. It proved no contest. "Patterson," noted *Sports Illustrated*, "looked remarkably like the exciting, decisive Patterson of seven or eight years ago, not the confused, limited Patterson who was stopped twice by Sonny Liston and once by Cassius Clay." Patterson was in complete control for the first three rounds. In the fourth, Patterson floored Cooper. Cooper rose at the count of nine, and Patterson promptly finished him off with a combination of hooks to the head. (Then, as with others, he went to Cooper's side and tried to help him up.)

At the very least, Patterson did prove that his back was not bothering him. Patterson said that Ernie Fowler, one of his few loyal seconds in his old entourage, had spotted how his right hand work had grown weak, how he had begun to bring his right foot too far forward, and stood too flat-footed. Now, he said, "I feel happy and satisfied for the first time in a long while." Patterson may have been blowing smoke, but some verification here actually came from Muhammad Ali. ABC Television broadcast highlights of the fight on their Saturday *Wide World of Sports* program. Ali was called in to offer comments and analysis with Howard Cosell. "I figured Cooper would beat Floyd," Ali confessed. As he watched the fight film, Ali did laugh when Patterson tried to help the fallen Cooper get to his feet, but otherwise he was impressed. "Hmmm," he mused, "Floyd's comin' back.... He looks impressive." Whether Ali was sincerely impressed or just pumping up the financial picture of a possible fight in the future, was a debatable matter. He could have easily been doing both, of course. Regardless, he was leaving the door open to Floyd to keep trying. Patterson told the press after the victory, "I felt different, more capable. I was thinking in the ring for the first time in years.... I hope I am one step closer to Cassius Clay." Was he again trying from afar to goad Ali here, or did he still just not get it? Opinions varied. Still, the win was a good step back into championship contention.[10]

The Cooper victory was indeed encouraging, but for Patterson there remained a long way to go. When the *New York Times* reviewed the 1966 year in sports, a mention of Patterson was immediately followed by a parenthetical "remember him?" He was far off the radar when it came to every pundit's thoughts about the heavyweight division. Ali had run through some European fighters in 1966 — Cooper, Brian London, and Karl Mildenberger. Then he beat the well-regarded Cleveland Williams in what many regard as his best fight. His next bout with Ernie Terrell brought back some of the memories of Patterson, but not in a very complimentary way. Before to the fight, Terrell went out of his way to show disrespect to Ali, calling him "Cassius Clay" to his face. Patterson had gotten Ali's dander up with that, and Terrell did it even more: "You['re] acting just like an old Uncle Tom, another Floyd Patterson," Ali yelled at him (and actually slapped him), "and I'm going to punish you." He sure did. He tortured Terrell, and, as he pecked and pounded away, Ali famously kept yelling "What's my name?" Among many fans, the memories of the Patterson bout resurfaced. Some actually called Terrell's loss a "Floyd Patterson humiliation."[11] These memories and images brought back on Ali much of the hatreds and fears which he had endured after humiliating Patterson. When confronted with the charge of brutality, Ali logically commented that such have always been the ways of boxing: "I'm out to be cruel; that's what the fight game is all about." He may have been right, but it was not logic but political-religious ignorance and fear that were the forces driving much of the sporting public's opinions.

People were irrationally lusting for any excuse to hate Muhammad Ali. This was not the kind of image Ali wanted, and, by implication, it was not doing much for the previously humiliated Patterson either. A sometimes (and mediocre) poet of boxing, Bernie Glickman, commented in early 1967, "I still say, that Clay's the second most overrated fighter in the world. Floyd Patterson's the first."[12] Glickman had been an associate of Ernie Terrell. As Ali had pasted his friend, and as Patterson and D'Amato had seemingly ducked Terrell seven and eight years before, Glickman's judgment was hardly objective. But in early 1967 it was clear that the mainstream American public's general opinion of Muhammad Ali remained extremely hostile. Ali's religious and political leanings had never wavered, and he had conspicuously spoken out against the Vietnam War in a manner and with a visibility that was quite unusual (and gutsy) in 1966 and 1967. ("I ain't got no quarrel with them Viet Cong; no Viet Cong ever called me 'nigger.'") Posterity has praised Ali for his stand against the war and for his courage in taking it. At the time, however, middle America generally hated him for it. Patterson's defense of Ali in *Esquire* was of little help. Likely, it only diminished Patterson.

After beating Cooper, Patterson began sending out feelers for new challenges in late 1966. He negotiated with the young 1964 Olympic heavyweight champion, Joe Frazier. But Frazier's people wanted to wait until the next summer, and Patterson wanted to fight as soon as possible. Germany's Karl Mildenberger had given Ali a tough battle in the summer, and Patterson nearly settled with him for a bout in December, but the deal fell through. Thad Spencer was another young rising heavyweight, and Patterson's people opened negotiations, nearly settling on a fight to take place in San Francisco, but Spencer's manager had an inkling he would land a deal to fight Ali, so he withdrew. Patterson, of course, hoped for another shot at Ali too, and there were rumors that the two would fight in Japan (or possibly tour the Far East together, giving exhibitions), but the details for either proved too complex to work out. Patterson settled for a February 13 bout with a nobody from Florida named Willie Johnson. Here Patterson fought at just over 200 pounds, his heaviest fighting weight ever. To the writers in attendance, he seemed a little slow, but he knocked out Johnson in the third round, so it was no setback to his reputation. The next month he fought another nobody, a Pittsburgh truck driver named Bill McMurray, winning that one with a KO in the first round. As with Johnson, a loss here would have ended Patterson's career. That risk was always there. Meanwhile he needed fights to keep sharp, and he needed the money. He wanted Ali.[13]

When Muhammad Ali fought Ernie Terrell in Houston in February of 1967, Zora Folley was introduced among the boxing dignitaries before the fight, and the TV announcers declared him Ali's next logical opponent, assuming a victory over Terrell. That is what occurred. Amidst this, Ali had hardly become one bit more liked by the establishment of professional boxing, but here money ruled. The Folley fight was the first heavyweight championship bout in New York since Patterson fought Johansson. The death of Benny Paret had soured some of the New York cognoscenti, and some of these feelings remained. Indeed after Muhammad Ali's humiliation of Terrell in their Houston meeting in February, the *New York Times* once again pompously called for an outlawing of the sport. A much more intense feeling among New Yorkers, however, concerned the fact that other rising fight venues like Las Vegas and Miami Beach had been stealing NYC's thunder, and money. With the opening of the new (actually the third) Madison Square Garden on 33rd Street, the hope for a return of championship boxing to its rightful place dominated all other New Yorkers' priorities. And when an Ali-Folley fight was arranged for MSG in March, the various obstacles Ali had been encountering as he sought bouts in the U.S. subsided for the moment. Ali easily defeated Folley, his sixth successful title defense since beating Patterson in November of 1965, and with the defeat of Folley, the question emerged as to whom Ali could now fight. No one could accuse him of ducking any challengers. He had convincingly beaten everyone.[14]

In 1967 there were some rising young heavyweights like Jerry Quarry,

Manuel Ramos, and Joe Frazier, but they did not yet appear to be ready for a fight with a man like Muhammad Ali. Whether it was the sense of gratitude over the *Esquire* piece, the sense that his back spasms had indeed compromised his 1965 challenge, the belief that he had made a good showing against Cooper, or the simple sense that there was no one else to fight, on April 4, Muhammad Ali agreed to fight Floyd Patterson. The bout was set for Las Vegas (after unsuccessful efforts to stage it in Detroit), April 25. Both fighters were ready; neither needed a lot of preparation time. So there it was; Floyd had that new chance for which he had been yearning, a desire which had cost him his marriage. Now he could prove that he had the skills of which he believed unfortunate circumstances had previously deprived him the fullest use when he'd fought Liston and Ali. For a week, Patterson was training hard and felt euphoric. He was in shape. His personal life was in order. His retinue was as trim as he was. This time, he believed, he would win or at least make a damn good show of it.

Then the roof fell in. While the Nevada State Athletic Commission had previously approved the Ali–Patterson bout, on April 11, they suddenly reversed themselves. The commission admitted that they were acting at the direct request of Nevada's governor Paul Laxalt, who had personally paid them a visit. Laxalt pompously claimed that staging the bout "would give Nevada a black eye." "If Clay carries Patterson and knocks him out," Laxalt opined, "it will only be a repeat of their previous fight. If Patterson should win, eyebrows would be raised all over the world." Laxalt's motives here were not sports minded; they were obviously political. Were the bout between two fighters without any political elements in the picture, the whole matter would have been celebrated like any other Las Vegas fight — with the sole concern being the excitement and the money it would bring into the state. Laxalt pontificated that his decision was rooted in Nevada's effort to upgrade athletics, hence that an Ali–Patterson fight would be mark a "step backward." No one, then or since, ever found any public statements, bureaucratic memoranda, or anything else which noted any efforts or campaigns from Laxalt's office, or from anyone else in the Nevada government, to upgrade the state's athletics, whatever that meant anyway. Laxalt had never been an athlete of any note, but he was a politician. His verbiage belied the motives of other politicians that would fully reveal themselves over the next weeks.[15]

Patterson's victory over Bill McMurray in March had taken place in Pittsburgh. The city had just constructed a new indoor sports arena, and the city's leaders very much wanted to show it off to the world. They never got a chance. When Laxalt killed the Patterson-Ali fight in Las Vegas, Patterson's and Ali's representatives contacted Pittsburgh officials. Laxalt telephoned Pennsylvania governor Raymond P. Shafer, however. The papers reported that Laxalt had told Shafer that the previous Ali-Patterson bout in Las Vegas had not been a good bout. It was hard for anyone to believe that such issues as standards of sporting quality were central in the discussions between two state governors. The point was obvious — the political word was out. Ali was about to be forced to face the military draft. In March the U.S. Selective Service Commission had upgraded his draft status to 1A. A day of reckoning was soon to come, and no rematch with Patterson was to cloud the picture. Governor Shafer followed Laxalt's lead and insisted that the Pennsylvania Athletic Commission ban the Pittsburgh bout. Shafer got his way. Patterson's and Ali's negotiators then put out desperate feelers to have the bout in Albuquerque or Atlanta. In each case, the state's respective governors, David Cargo and Lester Maddox, intervened directly. (Ali's manager, Herbert Muhammad, nodded when he learned of the Atlanta decision going to the desk of Governor Maddox. Muhammad smiled ruefully: "I understand he's kind of anti–Negro.") A political gang-up had killed the bout; no one would touch it. On April 28, three days after he was to have fought Patterson, Muhammad Ali was called for, and he refused, induction into the United States Army. Within twenty-four hours, the World Boxing Association, some forty state athletic commissions moving in concert, and individual state commissions in New York, Texas, and California each rushed to strip Ali of his heavyweight crown.[16] Muhammad Ali had tweaked the noses of virtually every political, religious, television, and sporting leader in the nation. He was not the least bit naive about what could happen to him. When they lowered the boom on him, he took it stoically. The rest of the nation, and the world, would eventually give him full respect for his convictions, for his willingness to take what came by not deviating from them, as well as for his boxing skills. For the time, however, the leaders from Lyndon Johnson and J. Edgar Hoover to Paul Laxalt, Raymond Shafer, and Lester Maddox all smirked; at last they'd gotten their most hated _____.

The boxing world had never experienced a situation like this. As talk among the boxing authorities clumsily groped about looking for a sense of how to proceed, talk naturally focused on what boxers could, through some means, become the new champion. Patterson's name was on most lists here. For Patterson, the question in the short run was what he should do to be prepared for whatever may come.

XIV

California Rules

In April 1967, with Muhammad Ali out of the heavyweight title picture indefinitely (the refusal of any state to give him a license would last three years and seven months), Patterson realized he would likely have some chance in the emerging new championship picture. Unlike other fighters like Ernie Terrell who may have relished in Ali's legal plight, Patterson did not gloat one bit. Nonetheless, he recognized that important bouts would be in the offing, and that he had to stay sharp. Having fought two non-entities that year, Willie Johnson and Bill McMurray, Patterson remained determined to find a better challenge. Efforts failed to land a bout with Karl Mildenberger, Thad Spencer, Joe Frazier, or Ali. Less than a week after Ali's draft refusal, on May 4, Patterson signed to fight a young Southern California prospect named Jerry Quarry.

Just four days after the Quarry signing, a new promotion company called Sports Action, Inc., proposed the organization and financing of an elimination tournament to determine a successor to Muhammad Ali. There would be eight fighters, hence four fights, followed by two semi-finals between the winners, and then a championship bout. The original eight fighters for the proposed tournament were Thad Spencer, Ernie Terrell, Oscar Bonavena, Karl Mildenberger, Jimmy Ellis, Joe Frazier, Jerry Quarry, and Floyd Patterson. Negotiations began immediately. Within two days, however, Joe Frazier's manager, Yancey Durham, pulled his man out of the tournament, claiming he wanted more money. Sports Action was offering $50,000 to each fighter in the first round, with subsequent purses to be determined. Durham had an independent course in mind for young Frazier, one that would ultimately prove successful. The Sports Action tournament organizers moved ahead. They found a journeyman Philadelphia fighter named Leotis Martin to take

Frazier's place. Had some other sports promotion corporation lured Frazier and one or two other top heavyweights into a different elimination, the whole emerging championship process may have been upset. But, with the sufficient financial offerings, the other fighters did not bolt, and the Sports Action tournament, minus Frazier, went ahead.

Several other fighters could raise legitimate "what about me" questions about the Sports Action tournament. George Chuvalo, Zora Folley, Manuel Ramos, and the still active Sonny Liston were contenders who ranked as highly as the likes of Leotis Martin and Jimmy Ellis. There was also a new huge heavyweight making his mark named Buster Mathis. Some rumors were flying that the leadership of Sports Action, Inc., was made up of the white remnants of an older, more interracial group, Main Bout, Inc., which had handled the ancillary rights of Muhammad Ali. Adding to the racial edge of these rumors, some of Sports Action's people had allegedly confronted the arguments that Ali was still the champ and that the tournament was then a farce with a jocular, "Cassius who?" Political controversies surrounded Sports Action's tournament, no doubt, but it was hard to make charges of racism stick, given their invitation to Frazier, their inclusions of Patterson, Terrell, Ellis, Spencer, and Martin, and their exclusion of Chuvalo. More importantly, with no other emerging means of determining a heavyweight successor, with Sports Action's money on the table, and with television contracts quickly signed, the tournament quickly implanted itself in the minds of the press and public, and events moved forward. For Patterson, it was not as direct a shot at the title as the April contract to fight Ali had given him. He still had a chance, however, and the tournament money would be respectable. Meanwhile, he had his separate bout with Quarry for which to prepare.[1]

Jerry Quarry was a big white guy, and that was important to a lot of the day's boxing fans who were still angry with and bewildered by Muhammad Ali. Since the retirement of Rocky Marciano, the heavyweight division had not seen any white Americans contend for the crown in any significant way. By 1967, national sensitivities about race had begun to improve, so with Quarry there were no flagrantly racist statements about a "great white hope," as Jack London had famously raised about Jim Jeffries when he fought Jack Johnson some sixty years before. Still, the idea, indeed the hope, of a white American taking back the championship brought smiles to the faces of more than a few boxing fans, even if they had to be a little quiet about it. Even *Sports Illustrated*, hardly a Southern Democrat publication, wrote of Quarry, in not too terribly veiled language. "Boxing," they opined, "needs him desperately." Quarry was, himself, quite open about what he knew he had to offer in view of his race. "I'm the only one who can really help boxing," he frankly asserted. "Boxing needs a white heavyweight champion to replace Cassius Clay. It's an extra incentive for me." To some degree, Quarry was thinking strictly in a marketing and not in a racial or racist context. Still, the words certainly stung a lot of people. Ironically, Quarry was emerging here as a contender at the very time that the play *The Great White Hope* by Howard Sackler, subsequently a famous movie, was about to open and make a reasonable run on Broadway. With the play and then the movie, the vicious nature of the world that had surrounded Jack Johnson began significantly to penetrate the historical knowledge of a broad range of Americans. This would hardly be enough, however, to counter any quasi, let alone fully racist desires for a man like Jerry Quarry to gain the title. His whiteness remained very much an issue as he emerged in the heavyweight picture in the late 1960s and early 1970s.[2]

Quarry appeared to have all the right skills. He was big and stocky, seemed able to take a punch, had reasonable hand speed, and he had a big right hand. He had been on the way up for several years. When he signed to fight Patterson his record stood at 23-1-3. Patterson knew not to take Quarry lightly. As he was already prepared to fight Ali, he simply needed to maintain the ascetic training regimen that he loved anyway. The fight would take place in Los Angeles on June 9. Patterson came in at 194 pounds, nearly 10 pounds lighter than he had been in February and March when he sluggishly beat Willie Johnson and Bill McMurray. Quarry was a native Southern Californian, and the crowd was very much in his corner. Sonny Liston was on hand, as was Joe Frazier, and they were actually among the few who were not rooting for Quarry. Quarry's vaunted right hand showed itself in the second round, as he knocked Patterson down twice. Anticipating an upset, the crowd was screaming madly, but Patterson survived the round and regrouped. In the fourth, Patterson opened a significant cut over Quarry's right eye. For the rest of the fight, Quarry bled all over his face, giving the already savage bout an even more grim quality. From there the two went at it fiercely. Three times they fought through the bell, and the referee had to strain to stop them. In the seventh round, Patterson got even with Quarry when he knocked him down. Quarry's people claimed he was stumbling at the moment of the punch, but the referee did rule it a knockdown.

The fight went the distance. Most of the pundits from the East who had gone out to cover the fight felt Patterson had gotten the better of it. One judge gave the edge to Quarry. The referee and the other judge ruled the fight dead even. Under California's system, the majority ruled, and the bout was officially a draw. The partisan California crowd booed loudly. Patterson stood, jaw agape at the decision, so sure was he that he had won. Many criticized the peculiarity of the California scoring system. It had indeed benefited Quarry. In the California system, the winner of a round, with a good knockdown, could receive as many as five points, with the loser getting zero. (Conceivably, then, in a 10 round fight, someone could decisively win two rounds, lose all of the other eight, and win the bout 10–8.) When he knocked Patterson down in the second round, Quarry got the maximum points, hence a 5–0 boost. To the spectrum of reporters on hand, Patterson won either six or seven of the other rounds. The standard ten-point must system of New York and many other venues would thus have yielded Patterson a clear decision, even with Quarry winning the second round decisively. No reporter on hand felt Quarry had drawn even with Patterson, neither did Joe Frazier.[3]

Patterson had been introduced to the crowd as "the most congenial of heavyweights." His congeniality was tested with the news of the decision, but he did little but shrug. "The officials saw it as a draw. That's good enough for me," he said. "We gave the people a good fight. They got their money's worth, didn't they?" Besides, he emphasized with finality, "nobody got hurt."

Ties do little for the spirit, and the Quarry-Patterson tie had little to no impact on the boxing rankings. Both Quarry and Patterson were in the new elimination tournament, and winning there was all that mattered for either man. After the Quarry fight, Patterson took a few weeks off. The USO organized a tour for him to visit the troops at several bases in Vietnam. Patterson may have wanted to offset some potential grumblings resulting from his *Esquire* "Defense of Cassius Clay." More deeply, Patterson felt for the troops, no matter anyone's opinion of the geo-politics of the war. So he went, avoiding a lot of fanfare just as he did when he worked for CORE, and lent what boosts to morale that he could. When Patterson returned from Vietnam, he discovered that the random draw of the elimination tournament had left him in an interesting spot. The first round of the tournament pitted Thad Spencer first fighting Ernie Terrell and Jimmy Ellis against Leotis Martin. Karl Mildenberger would later fight against Oscar Bonavena, and the final bout had Jerry Quarry once again fighting Floyd Patterson. Now the debatable June draw with Quarry was irrelevant. In August, Ellis and Spencer each won, Spencer's victory somewhat of a surprise. (Ironically, Terrell had originally drawn Ellis for the first round, and he had indignantly protested that fighting the lowly ranked Ellis was "demeaning," so the tournament officials accommodated Terrell, and changed his pairing to Spencer. Spencer won, and Terrell never contended again.)[4] In September, Bonavena outslugged Mildenberger, leaving only Patterson to fight Quarry to determine the fourth semi-finalist. The fight would be on October 28, again in Los Angeles.

Patterson was positive before the bout. He snorted a bit at those who were asking what he, at age thirty-two, was trying to prove. "I don't fight to try to prove anything," he nodded softly. "I'm not fighting for any reason than that I like fighting. Not the adrenalin, really. But the smell of the gym, the living in seclusion, all the things that go into it.... If I can find something as exciting and intriguing as boxing, I'd hang 'em up, but I don't know anything else that is. Maybe it's the suspense." When fighters have repeatedly to justify staying in the game, no matter their stated reasons, it means that many think it is time for them to get out. Patterson was not entertaining such notions, however. Nor did he even promise, as he had before several then recent bouts, to retire if he lost. "I choose to block that out," he eagerly said this time. "It helps you to think positively." Patterson acknowledged Quarry's punching power, judging it to be "in a class with Ingemar Johansson and Sonny Liston." He believed Quarry had shown weaknesses in the clinches when they fought in June, and expressed the belief that he would be improved there this time. Still he believed, he was "the better man" and that he would emerge victorious, adding graciously, in contrast to so many others involved with the elimination tournament: "If I won the tournament, I would only consider myself to be partly the champion, with Clay." It was gracious, but the name to which he referred was still what it was.[5]

"I'm a slow starter," Patterson once conceded, and that would be in evidence this night against Quarry. At the outset, Quarry took the initiative, as the bigger puncher usually will. The first round held fairly even, but Quarry was the aggressor in the second. At the end of the second round, Quarry connected. He caught Patterson on the jaw with a chopping right, and Patterson went down. He was back up instantly and showed no sign of being hurt, but the knockdown helped Quarry pile up some points under the peculiar California scoring system. The same thing occurred in the fourth round. Patterson was floored by a Quarry right. One writer said "it looked like a slip, ... but it was a knockdown, if not a very good one." Again, Patterson was up quickly, but Quarry was building a lead. In the sixth, another Quarry right connected, this time to Patterson's midsection. He did not go down, but he sagged under the blow, and the crowd and the judges knew it. From the seventh round on, however, Patterson's conditioning revealed itself. He still seemed fresh, and the more ponderous Quarry appeared to tire. Patterson's jab and uppercut began to land again and again. From the tenth through the final twelfth round, Patterson was in command, connecting with hard body shots and left hooks.

At the final bell, the crowd was abuzz, as the decision was very much in doubt. *Sports Illustrated*'s reporter believed that two rounds had been even, with Patterson winning six of the other ten. Most agreed, and, as in the June bout, Patterson would have won under most scoring systems. With the discretion allowed judges in the event of knockdowns, Quarry had a possible edge, and it proved decisive. The referee ruled the bout a draw. The two judges, however, gave Quarry extra points for the knockdowns, and these gave Quarry the decision. At the Los Angeles Olympic Auditorium, as it was built and first held fights during the Depression, fans had a tradition of throwing money after a good fight. (It was how Depression-era boxers made a little extra cash.) That tradition continued into prosperous times, but on this

After losing to Muhammad Ali in 1965, Patterson continued to fight and again rose in rank among the contenders. Ali and Patterson had signed to fight again in 1967, but Ali was stripped of his title for refusing the U.S. military draft. In a tournament to determine Ali's successor, Patterson fought Jerry Quarry in Los Angeles, having just fought him to a debatable draw earlier that spring of 1967. Peculiarities in the California scoring system yielded Quarry the decision. ©Bettmann/CORBIS.

night, even with their own Southern California boy getting the decision, the crowd did not throw a dime; indeed they began to hurl cups and cups of beer, none of which anyone in the ring found the slightest bit refreshing. Boos echoed all over the place. As Quarry left for the locker room, a fellow Southern Californian, sounding more like a New Yorker in both tone and loyalty, snarled at him: "You lost, Quarry; you lost, and you know it. You got a pass, you bum. You didn't deserve this fight."

Patterson had indeed gotten a raw deal. The odd California system was the key here. Patterson had clearly not been hurt by either knockdown. Nevertheless, one of the judges ("who," wrote *Sports Illustrated*, "should have two weeks rest and no visitors") actually gave Quarry three points for the weaker second knockdown. "One wonders," scoffed *SI*, "what he would have given Quarry if Patterson had had to crawl back to his corner." If Quarry had been given but one point for each of his knockdowns, as he certainly should have, Patterson would have won the fight. The California crowd booed. Apparently even the white hope elements in the crowd were not at all happy with the decision. Californians wanted their man to win, but backing into a victory as Quarry apparently had hardly gave them anything about which to brag. Those anxiously waiting for a true champion to emerge from white America were, as *SI* complained, "still waiting."[6]

As for Patterson the questions about his future came forth once more.

With the Quarry defeat, he was not bitter. He took it philosophically: "I feel discouraged, sure," he shrugged, "but I can't say the decision was unjust. I didn't count the punches I landed, or the ones that Jerry landed." "Retirement?" was a question he encountered over and over. Patterson would not commit here. As Joe Frazier had boycotted the tournament and was seeking a path to the top on his own, a Frazier-Patterson bout was obvious, tempting, and potentially lucrative. The often critical Arthur Daley of the *New York Times* noted generously that "time has not eroded his [Patterson's] skills to any measurable extent." Given who was left in the tournament, Daley shrugged that Joe "Frazier, [Buster] Mathis, and Patterson form a far more appealing stockpile of talent than Spencer, Ellis, Bonavena, and Quarry."[7] Everyone was looking for something to bring a sense of liveliness and legitimacy back to the heavyweight division. As long as Muhammad Ali was out of the picture, this was not emerging too quickly.

XV

Robbed in Stockholm

With Patterson on the sidelines, the Sports Action elimination tournament went ahead to find a "logical successor" to the politically dethroned Muhammad Ali. In the final-four round, Jerry Quarry defeated Thad Spencer, and Jimmy Ellis beat Oscar Bonavena. This set up a finale between Quarry and Ellis, with the bout to be held on April 27, 1968. Since the point when they had organized their tournament in the late spring of 1967, Sports Action's managers had felt a smug sense that they held a kind of majestic control over the boxing world. This sense suddenly suffered a jolt, however, as a counter effort finally emerged against them. Edwin B. Dooley, chairman of the New York State Athletic Commission set up a separate venue. No one had appointed Sports Action the arbiter of the heavyweight championship. There was no one who could. It was a matter of free enterprise — and politics. Edwin Dooley was the man who had moved so swiftly to take away Ali's crown when Ali refused the draft. Seeing (or wanting to see) himself and his New York Commission as the epicenter of the boxing universe, Dooley was angry about the Sports Action Tournament, in part because Sports Action displayed a *chutzpah* he felt only he could wield from New York and even more because of the fact that Sports Action had excluded New York City as one of its fight sites.

Dooley was one of the many New York leaders who were all trying to put the state and city back on top as the world's top boxing location. The fallout from boxing deaths like "Kid" Paret's and the righteous indignation of the *New York Times* and others against boxing had faded, but the damage had been done, and the resurrection of the "Old" Madison Square Garden–era supremacy was not so easily achieved. Patterson, Liston, and Ali had all fought their major bouts elsewhere. From 1961 to 1968, Las Vegas, Miami, and Houston each had a stronger claim than New York as the nation's and world's boxing center. The "New" Madison Square Garden on 33rd Street was certainly pursuing high-profile fight card. Still, to that point their only big heavyweight night had been in March of '67 when Ali fought Zora Folley. And the significance of that fight proved not terribly great, as immediately afterward arose Ali's military draft issue, the abrupt stripping of his title, and the Sports Action elimination tournament which held its fights elsewhere.

While some certainly considered the Sports Action tournament to involve a certain amount of inflated self-promotion, Dooley's countermove revealed an element of equally self-inflated hype, one of classically provincial, New York-centered vintage. On January 5, 1968, Dooley announced that on March 4, Joe Frazier would fight a big but not highly ranked heavyweight named Buster Mathis.[1] Frazier was certainly a contender on the way up, as was Mathis, though to a far less obvious degree. Dooley arbitrarily and arrogantly declared here, with the full approval of Joe Frazier's manager, Yancey Durham, that this fight was "for the heavyweight championship of the world," recognized as such by Dooley and the New York State Athletic Commission. Each American state's athletic commission could, and can, do as it pleased, so there was nothing illegal or unethical here, just a whole lot of NYC presumptuousness. Dooley and the New York sports press proceeded to advertise the bout like mad. When weather permitted, Joe Frazier did some late winter public training outdoors in Times Square. New Yorkers eagerly bought into the event and all its hype, as all their venues were the obvious ones to score residual financial gains. In the March fight, Mathis put up a good struggle, but Frazier soundly beat the never-distinguished Mathis, and the victory indeed gained him NYAC recognition as heavyweight champion. Soon thereafter, Maine, Massachusetts, and Illinois added their official imprimaturs. Pennsylvania did so a bit later. There had been talk of having Frazier or Mathis fight Patterson before such a championship bout. The New York managers could also have added any such well regarded contenders as George Chuvalo and Manuel Ramos (or even Sonny Liston) to their list and had their own elimination tournament. It may have been a more effective approach, but they were basically betting on Frazier. Neither Frazier's people nor Mathis's had felt it was necessary to fight a man like Patterson (or Chuvalo or Ramos). They believed the ballyhoo of the sanction of the New York Athletic Commission after one victory would be sufficient. It was all indeed a classically *sui generis* New York phenomenon, but Joe Frazier now possessed a crown of some sort.

With Edwin Dooley and the NYAC having their boasts, the New York press chortled, and Joe Frazier indeed appeared to many to be the best new heavyweight out there. With the competition of the NYAC looming, Ellis and Quarry subsequently fought their championship bout in April. Ellis won. His victory left an odd taste in a lot of mouths, and not just because of the competing specter of "Smokin' Joe" Frazier. Some said the fight was dull. Ali fans loved the fact that the winning Ellis had previously been Muhammad Ali's sparring partner and a regular on the under cards of many of Ali's bouts. He still lived in a $75-a-month apartment in Louisville, Kentucky. Ellis's victory thus did little to convey, and a certain amount to detract from, any sense of a great or "logical successor" to Ali's crown coming from the Sports Action tournament. Making Ali's sparring partner the new champion only reinforced the sense of who remained the true champion.[2] Nevertheless, Ellis was now officially regarded as the heavyweight champion in forty-five states. Meanwhile, *Ring Magazine* recognized neither Ellis nor Frazier. They still said the champion was Muhammad Ali. The trouble was that *Ring* had no authority to issue boxing licenses. Ali could not get any state license. Some resourceful promoters attempted to arrange charity bouts but were refused. They even approached the leaders of some Indian reservations, where state authorities had no jurisdiction, but this also came to naught. With the federal government having confiscated Ali's passport, foreign venues were out for him too.[3] The Feds had their victory, or so they thought.

Many fans and pundits naturally wanted Ellis immediately to set up a fight with Frazier. But some of Ellis's handlers, as well as scions from Sports Action, remembered all too well that Joe Frazier's managers had snubbed and jeopardized the credibility of their elimination tournament and that Edwin Dooley and his New York friends had been using Joe Frazier to steal their thunder. Why should their man get first shot at Ellis? One answer here was obvious — because Frazier was the top contender. But such logical thoughts as "fighting the top contender" do not always dictate the events of boxing, especially when politics and personal rivalries are at stake. Cus D'Amato's earlier management of Patterson had proven that several times. Amidst the political jockeying here, Frazier's people were able to underscore their rival claims in another subtle way, as that winter and spring they signed to have Frazier do a TV commercial for Personna razor blades in which Frazier snarled with a smile: "If Personna can shave me easy, it can shave you real easy; 'cause my beard is tougher than your beard!" It may not have sold many more razor blades, but the symbolism for Frazier's stronger claim to the crown was obvious.

In 1968, New York City was making a come back. The city had been feeling itself down for many years. Inflation, various public workers' strikes, rampant crime, smut, and racial tensions all fed the image around the country of a sin city that could no longer function as rationally and intelligently as it once had. The sports world had reflected this discomforting, embarrassing slide. New York's hold on boxing had been receding for years. In football, the Giants, so preeminent in the '50s and early '60s, had fallen on hard times. The Knicks and the Rangers had each been jokes for many seasons, and, most famously, the mighty Yankees, often the champion and almost always at least a powerful contender from 1920 to 1964, had fallen into embarrassing mediocrity. Now, however, the Mets, the Knicks, and the Jets were beginning to show some spunk with new sensations like Tom Seaver, Bill Bradley, and Joe Namath. Even if he was still officially fighting out of his native Philadelphia, Joe Frazier was their eager counterpart in boxing, and New Yorkers rallied around them all in a kind of "We're back" self-absorbed congratulations.

With stars like Namath, Seaver, Bradley, and Frazier, the question was whether the combination of skills and hype could carry the day. For Frazier and his supporters the problem was that, at least in the short run, it was clear that Ellis's management wanted to snub New York's heavyweight champion. Ellis and his people could do so, but they would still have to maintain credibility by fighting someone else of good standing. The question was to whom could they turn as a worthy challenger to Ellis? Here there was some talk of Sonny Liston, for example, as Liston had been seeking to make a comeback, fighting and defeating journeymen since 1966. Given the raw deal some had cried about the Patterson-Quarry bouts, there was another obvious answer here, and it was the same person that some of Joe Frazier's and Madison Square Garden's managers had as they thought about a opponents for Frazier if they could not get Ellis — Floyd Patterson.[4]

Some of New York's hype over Joe Frazier as the real champion had a decidedly political cast. This was only natural, given the circumstances involving the stripping of the championship from Muhammad Ali. It was obviously not within the nature of the culture of the boxing world for anyone to contend for the crown in a modest, polite manner. Thus he who presumed to contend for the crown which had been stripped from Muhammad Ali would likely act disdainfully of the fate to which Ali had fallen. Frazier's camp certainly showed this. Frazier's seconds always snarlingly referred to Ali as "Cassius Clay." One would have been booted out of camp if any respectful referrals were uttered. Frazier's manager, Yancey Durham, sometimes simply referred Ali as "that big mouth." In addition to such insults, time was not being at all kind to Ali here. He would eventually win his fight against the U.S. government and the Selective Service Commission, but that would take over three years, and in that considerable stretch of time his skills would not grow as they would have for any great athlete in his mid-twenties who maintained a regimen of steady training and regular bouts. Kept out of the ring, Ali's visibility would by no means vanish, but it would dim. It was simply hard to keep the same old story in the public's mind. Words began to appear in the papers like "no one man is greater than the whole boxing world" and "the fight game is not standing still, not even for Cassius Marcellus Clay."[5] As the debates over this or that other champion began to rage, Ali's place diminished further.

While many were beginning to overlook Muhammad Ali, among the emerging political radicals of the day respect for Ali not only never diminished, it actually increased. Indeed 1968 was the point when many of these radical figures were coming fully to the fore. In the spring of 1968, for example, Black Panther leader Eldridge Cleaver published his famous work *Soul on Ice.* While in subsequent times many of his views have become virtual clichés, the ideas he expressed were then remarkably refreshing, as well as quite threatening to many mainstream Americans. Muhammad Ali was the premier figure among those who came across to Cleaver as true heroes, not merely because of his supreme boxing skills, but because of the ways he combined his supreme athleticism with a defiant scorning of any sort of cooperation with the principal institutions of white-dominated America and because he showed others that such an alternative path was not only possible but better. Others who Cleaver felt had, in contrast, allowed themselves to be manipulated by whites, engendered his ire. Here Cleaver pointedly named Floyd Patterson as an example. The concurrent popularity on Broadway of Howard Sackler's *The Great White Hope* underscored the radical chic at play here. Patterson was indeed seen to have been at the time he fought Ali as a whites' hope. While Cleaver did not comment directly, as the matter arose after he wrote the book, but the boxing world's question of Ellis v. Frazier could have been cast here as another clear example of white-led organizations, like Sports Action, Inc., and the New York State Athletic Commission, using black people as pawns in one of their many financial power games, with the obvious answer to "who's the champ?" being: "Neither; Ali," thus revealing the false choice at hand foisted by the white money makers.[6]

While the sensibilities of many sports fans since the 1970s have idolized Muhammad Ali (and presumed he had always been respected), before then Ali had been roundly resented by most of the nation's established sports and journalistic leaders. The youth of America, as well as of the rest of the world, became fans of Ali much earlier, with very much the same generational patterns of support and anger on hand as were emerging with regard to civil rights issues and the Vietnam War. To the elders, a man like Ali was a buffoon, a miscreant, a religious oddity, a law breaker (and, to more than a few, simply a _____). As late as 1967, Jack Olsen, an editor and writer for *Sports Illustrated*, wrote a book, *Black is Best: The Riddle of Cassius Clay.* Olsen tried to solve "the riddle" explain to mainstream America that Ali simply went against all the unwritten rules. The old ideals of the nation hailed the humble champion who expressed kind thoughts about his opponents and somehow protected the public from the sport's bloody brutality. When Ali beat the likes of Floyd Patterson and Ernie Terrell, writers were virtually apoplectic over his apparent cruelty. One of Olsen's points was that such older ideals were exactly what prior champions like Joe Louis, Joe Walcott, Rocky Marciano, and Floyd Patterson had embodied. Patterson, indeed, wrote one reporter in this context, "came nearest to the Joe Palooka ideal." Ali represented and indeed led the fact that a new age had come forth, one whose sensibilities greatly negated many old ideals. Olsen was trying to reconcile the public to the new ways, but he was not terribly successful. In 1968, middle America still did not get Muhammad Ali, and thus hated and feared him.[7]

Such analyses of the sports world that radicals like Eldridge Cleaver posited were being extended by such other emerging social critics as sociologist Harry Edwards, who was then quietly assembling a concerted effort to stage a racially-based boycott of the upcoming summer Olympics. Edwards and others wanted black athletes to use their preeminence in sports for "higher purposes" and utilize, even sacrifice, some of their athletic fame in order to bring decidedly stronger attention onto the plight of the average black man and woman in America (as well as, laughed some cynics, to exploit famous black athletes to bring stronger attention and wealth onto such theretofore unknown and poorly paid sociologists and intellectuals as Harry Edwards).[8] In the spring of 1968, the emerging radicalism among African Americans took a quantum leap as politics boiled over into chaos. The Vietnam War was growing ever more divisive. In Vietnam, the Tet Offensive scared and changed many who had previously supported President Johnson's policies. Eugene McCarthy offered effective challenges to Johnson in the early presidential primaries. Anti-war demonstrations on college campuses and elsewhere were growing larger and more edgy and violent. The civil rights movements also took on more extreme ways. In the late winter of 1968, an ongoing set of demonstrations in Washington, D.C., called Resurrection City attempted to expose the plight of African Americans to be not just a matter of political rights but one of economically-based concerns too. Martin Luther King himself was turning his attention more in the direction of economic rather than purely political rights and justice. And in April of 1968, most significantly, as this more radical phase was just beginning to unfold, King was murdered in Memphis, and the nation's cities erupted in violence. Dr. King had never deviated from his principles of non-violence, and it remained a hotly debatable point as to whether a more radically economic focus in the civil rights movement would be able to accommodate those principles. But with King's murder, that point was moot. In the immediate aftermath of King's death, with violence breaking out all over the country, the ideas of some radicals, including Eldridge Cleaver and Stokley Charmichael, who had each actually been harshly critical of King, resonated (some would say paradoxically) among so many who were now oh so frustrated with the ongoing patterns of racial discrimination and hardship.

It would take a long time, and many may argue that the process is still going on, for people to sort out the varying utilities of different outlooks and tactics that African American activists considered, especially in the wake of the death of Martin Luther King. In the short run, amidst the paroxysms of violence in American cities, about the only point of unity came when the world stopped for Dr. King's funeral. At his funeral, in addition to the thousands of everyday people, came dignitaries from the government, from the clergy, from the diplomatic corps, and from public life in general. Among the public figures only two came from the world of sports. One was Jackie Robinson. The other was Floyd Patterson.[9]

Just as they had demeaned Martin Luther King before he died, some of the leaders of increasingly radical African American politics had disparaged Patterson and the ways he allegedly represented, forgetting perhaps the work he had done against segregation in Alabama and Mississippi. As with most politicians everywhere, it is always easy for activists to pick out certain images which seem to strike resounding chords with constituents as illustrative of what is not desired. By 1968, Floyd Patterson had become such a symbol and target. The completely coincidental fact that he was not as good a boxer as Muhammad Ali meshed conveniently with the idea that Ali's prowess in the ring rendered his political views all the more resounding. As Patterson was the loser in the ring, it was then easy, even natural perhaps, for African Americans as well as for whites who were trying to posture themselves as cool, to toss Patterson away as an antiquated Uncle Tom. It was like actor Anthony Quinn's snorts, after Patterson's first loss to Johansson, that he could have fought better than Patterson. Facts never matter much amidst such self-deceiving image construction, be it in Hollywood, in politics, or in sports. Patterson had been going through this for years, and in 1968, with radicalism so in, what presence he had left in the public mind had little content but that of a meekling. Throughout such crossfires, Patterson had never altered his ways. His Christian principles always guided him, and King's principles of non-violence, passé as they may have become in certain chic and angry circles, were always his — except in the ring. Patterson was terribly shaken by King's death, but he knew that resorting to any anger or violence would have betrayed the man he so loved and grieved.

The death of Martin Luther King made many political issues in such connected but lesser areas as sports take on a diminished status for a time in 1968. The Quarry-Ellis bout came just weeks after King's murder, and this added to the unheralded standing of Ellis's title with the public. As the traumas of 1968 continued, with further violence in cities, more killings in and divisiveness over Vietnam, the murder of Robert Kennedy, and the riots in Chicago in August during the Democratic convention, a sense grew that traditional liberal answers were no longer legitimate or useful in regard to the pressing questions of the day. Ali continued to be lionized by the burgeoning political left, and his example of someone who put his principles above any expediencies that may have served his athletic profession and fame inspired others. That October two American sprinters at the Mexico City Olympics, Tommy Smith and John Carlos, who had finished first and third in the 200 meters, famously stood with heads down and black-gloved clenched fists raised during the medal ceremony. They were banned from the rest of the Olympics as a punishment, and they were not only unfazed but took it proudly, as they, like Ali, to whom they explicitly referred, put racial politics ahead of personal glory. For openly political reasons, several prominent college basketball players, including Lew Alcindor, soon to take the name Kareem Abdul-Jabbar, boycotted the Olympics altogether.

Such seemingly daring views and actions resonated among many of the nation's youth, black and white. Sports events of the era whose outcomes challenged established patterns seemed to imply a certain spirit of the age that further reified broader challenges that were occurring in American society and politics. The 1968 New York Jets Super Bowl victory over Baltimore in January 1969 was one such event, as was the '69 Mets World Series victory, albeit that some of the hype the media attached to the victory stemmed from the New York provincialism of so much of the day's media. Still, the stock market rose with both events, and both implied that those who bucked the establishment could win. The world of boxing then seemed to be frozen amidst other sports venues yielding positive symbols to some of the nation's political activists of the heady, narcissistic era of the late 1960s. As long as Muhammad Ali was not allowed to fight, the contenders for the crown, even Joe Frazier, who most felt to be the best of the rest, appeared to be condemned to shadow boxing.

In 1968, the forty-five state (and World Boxing Association) champion Jimmy Ellis could have gathered much publicity if he had elected immediately to fight five-state champion Joe Frazier. But for the moment intra-boxing politics would not let that occur. Even when that match occurred a year later, with Frazier winning convincingly, there remained the obvious question of "What about Ali?" And the fact that Frazier later beat Ali still led many to ask what would have happened if Ali had not endured his enforced exile and fought Frazier earlier and in full prime. In the summer of 1968, amidst a somewhat self-imposed no man's land, Ellis and his handlers then sought a title defense. On July 1, 1968, Ellis agreed to a fight — with Floyd Patterson.[10]

Having endured the questionable draw and loss to Jerry Quarry, and with the fact that Ali had agreed to fight Patterson just before he had been stripped of his title, Patterson still certainly remained a legitimate contender. No one could accuse Ellis of loading up on some chump here. Patterson was thirty-three, but his previous three fights had been good enough to earn Ali's respect. Meanwhile, the venue was intriguing. After all the furor over Ellis and Frazier being recognized by different states as the champion, where would the

Jimmy Ellis, 1968. When Muhammad Ali was stripped of his title in 1967, an eight-man elimination tournament ensued to determine his successor as champion. Ellis, a former Ali sparring partner, was the surprise winner. His first title defense would come against Patterson. In 1968, the two squared off in Stockholm, Sweden. Patterson appeared to win in the eyes of virtually all fans and reporters. The referee saw it differently, however, and under Swedish rules, the ref was the sole judge. Ellis kept his title, subsequently losing it to Joe Frazier. Swedish newspapers declared that Floyd had been "*Bortdömd*" ("Robbed"). ©*The Ring*.

Patterson-Ellis fight take place? The answer was: Sweden. Las Vegas and Stockholm had each sought the bout. Ingemar Johansson's former manager, Edwin Ahlquist, now managing the boxing career of Floyd's younger brother Raymond, put together the best package. Patterson would get $60,000 plus 20 percent of the gate receipts; Ellis was guaranteed $125,000. Ray Patterson would fight on the under card.[11]

Patterson had been busy after the Quarry fights, but a bit less with boxing. He had actually done a bit of acting. That summer he had signed with CBS television to play a leading guest role in an episode of the popular Western series of the late '60s, *The Wild, Wild West*. The episode involved a politically poignant scenario, as Patterson played the role of the leader of a group of African American homesteaders who were being unfairly pushed off their land by unscrupulous white businessmen. The episode even had a good fight scene in which, to the nervous displeasure of some of the stunt men, Patterson threw his own punches. A stand-in took Patterson's place, however, when one punch sent him flying through a window.[12] The acting was fun, and profitable, but for Patterson, when the negotiations over the Ellis fight solidified, it was back to training in earnest.

Patterson had strong ties in Sweden. Ellis had been to Sweden once before. In 1965 he went there on an exhibition tour with Muhammad Ali. He and Ali had quickly learned then just how popular Patterson was over there. Ali had boxed an exhibition with Ellis and then sat before a throng of Swedish reporters and fans. The consensus was that Ali had boxed badly. Always the quick-witted extrovert, Ali responded to the charges of a "bad show" by asking if it was true that "Floyd Patterson is a great man in Sweden." A loud chorus of "*Jah*'s" ensued, and to that Ali smiled and retorted: "I did not show my best tonight because then you might not bet on him [Patterson] when we fight." With that Ali won some of the crowd, but "Floyd," which was all anyone in Sweden needed to utter in reference to Patterson, remained their established hero. In a little park in Stockholm, the *Kungstradgarden*, the government erected a statue of him. After Patterson and Sandra had divorced, Patterson had met and married a Swedish woman, Janet. She and their 13-month-old daughter were in Sweden with him that summer. Floyd's brother Raymond had expatriated and became a Swedish citizen in August 1968. When Ellis returned to Sweden to fight Patterson, few could even identify him. Some asked him for autographs, but, as Ellis quickly discovered, they were doing so thinking he was Floyd.[13]

Although Patterson was immensely popular in Sweden, few gave him much of a chance against Ellis. Many reporters emphasized that Patterson was now 33 years old, while Ellis, at 28, seemed to be at his peak. Oddsmakers in London set Ellis as an 11–5 favorite. People expected Ellis to be a loud-mouth like Ali, but Ellis was never a braggart. He expressed respect for Floyd. Asked for Ali-like predictions, he merely said he was confident he would win. Meanwhile, Patterson also expressed confidence in himself. Asked if he would retire in the event of a loss, he replied: "I never think of defeat." This comforted some who remembered the fake moustache and whiskers.[14]

By 1968, the nation of Sweden had developed a new image in the American press and public. With the Vietnam War raging, some young American men deserted from the service and were able to find friendly asylum in Sweden. Numerous draft dodgers went to Sweden as well. Many of these young Americans escaping from the American military were on hand in Stockholm at the time of the Patterson-Ellis bout. Reporters noted their presence, especially with their then shockingly long hair and bedraggled appearance, acutely enhanced by their open consumption of significant quantities of hashish. As that lifestyle contrasted so strikingly with the fighting trim of the two boxers, the imagery resonated in favor or against neither. Patterson was a good Catholic, Ellis a good Baptist. Neither had made any expressions about the war. Ali was the obvious hero of the anti-war Americans in Sweden, and his popularity carried over to no one else in any significant way. Still amidst the deserters and draft dodgers, a victory by either fighter implied the approval of the anti-establishment, something that lent a touch of politically- charged compensation for the fact that neither had been given the respect from the sport's mainstream each felt he was due.

Swedish boxing rules had one odd feature. They did not use fight judges. As in the U.S. the referee controlled matters in the ring, of course, but in Sweden he was also the sole arbiter of the bout if there was no knockout (and in a technical sense, he controlled that too). The referee for the Ellis-Patterson bout was Harold Valen, a native of Brooklyn. No one questioned his objectivity, and during the bout he appeared to do his job perfectly well. In the fight Patterson seemed to land the better shots. He broke Ellis's nose in the second round and cut Ellis above his right eye, a gash that would require seven stitches. He appeared to knock down Ellis in the fourteenth round, but it was ruled a slip. A few times Patterson missed with wild hooks and long left jabs. Ellis, however, was always a skillful and graceful defensive fighter, and he successfully evaded much of Patterson's offense. It was not just the partisan Swedish crowd, but most of the reporters (and American television fans) who felt that Patterson had the edge throughout the fight. From the standpoint of Ellis, the best that could be said was that the fight was fairly even and that he clearly won the fifteenth round. Otherwise, when the fight ended, most felt Patterson had gained himself a share of the crown once again. Virtually everyone was then absolutely stunned when the referee awarded the fight to Ellis. The next day the chief Stockholm paper, the *Dagens Nyheter*, simply headlined, not merely on its sports page, but on the very front page: "*Floyd Bortdömd*" ("Floyd Robbed").[15]

The Swedish fans were outraged by the decision. Their usual stoic reserve went out the window. Many Swedes spoke English. They began chanting, and the rest of the fans quickly caught on and joined: "Floyd Champ! Floyd Champ!" As always, there was nothing anybody could do, however. Fourteen months later, the Swedish Parliament voted to outlaw professional boxing, despite the presence of Ingemar Johansson at the debate. Thereafter anyone taking part in, promoting, or financially backing prize fighting in Sweden was liable to a fine or imprisonment. The move showed the outrage, but with the Patterson-Ellis fight the referee's decision was final. The victory did little to the already minimal luster that tinged Ellis's hold on the heavyweight championship in the minds of boxing fans. By the autumn of 1968, Joe Frazier held the greatest respect among the heavys. Meanwhile, new figures like

Olympic champion George Foreman were emerging on the scene. As Foreman was conspicuously managed by Cus D'Amato, the sense of the turning
history pages shunting Patterson to the past grew all the more poignant.[16] Five
months after the Stockholm bout, when Joe Frazier soundly knocked out
Jimmy Ellis, the boxing world felt that a legitimate champion had finally
come forth. The specter of Ali still lurked, of course, but no other boxer held
any competing stature.

As for Patterson, the loss in Sweden appeared to seal his fate. He would
have fought Muhammad Ali in the spring of 1967 if the government had not
intervened in Ali's career. That summer he had suffered the two bad decisions with Jerry Quarry, the second one costing him his chance in the Sports
Action tournament. Then he was robbed by a referee in Stockholm. Had he
been awarded the fight over Ellis, few may have given him much of a chance
against Joe Frazier, who would have obviously been his next opponent. Still,
he had come agonizingly close to regaining some share of the title. If some
felt his earlier holding of the title had been a trifle flukey, given the various
opponents D'Amato had selected and avoided ten years before, there was an
awfully cruel compensation in what befell Patterson in 1967 and 1968. Regardless of sympathies, everyone appeared to shrug and assume Floyd would now
retire.

As always, Patterson was altogether, some felt overly, gentlemanly about
the Ellis fight and the controversial decision. Immediately after the bout, Patterson did not appear before the press, which everyone found highly unusual
for him. Asked later about the referee's judgment, he noted perfunctorily: "It's
hard to say when you're in there.... The referee decides. I have nothing to say
about the decision. I do not wish to detract from Jimmy's fight." Asked about
Ellis's second round broken nose, Patterson was irritated by rumors that he
had butted Ellis, but then he told everyone, "I'm sorry I busted his nose."
The boxing public again shook its head. What other boxer ever said such a
thing? The gentlemanly character of the man, which such a writer as Jack
Olsen had tried to raise as an example of pre–Ali, pre–'60s cultural ideals,
appeared once again to turn neurotically beyond reason. Here Floyd's strong
links to Sweden seemed especially poignant. Reporters on hand for the fight
were busy noting the Bergmannesque melancholy of their Swedish hosts. "We
think too much," explained one Swede, "We sit in the parks all day and think
too much." One American draft dodger shrugged about his adopted people:
"No soul. The people are nice, but completely spiritless. It makes you sad
just being around them."[17] Such national characterizations may have been
simplistic and harsh, but they resonated among reporters trying to put a kind
of epitaph on the career of Floyd Patterson.

Patterson's wounded, introspective nature appeared to have meaning to
the apparently depressive, introspective Swedes. The enigmatic nature of the

boy who hid in janitor's closets in the New York subway was otherwise fascinating only when he was the champion. Now that he was out of the championship picture, it seemed a kind note on which to leave him — at home among a people who appeared to share his sensibilities. He is, wrote one scribe, "no longer ... engaged in lonely struggle with himself, no longer the kind of person who could get so tormented that he would have to get out of bed and write his thoughts down or go to the gym and 3 o'clock in the morning and work out.... Behind him — at long last — is a career that helped him conquer ignorance and a weird childhood, a career that was often shattered and derided, and finally one that was at once sad, unbelievably comic and altogether unreal."[18] There was a clear bond for Floyd with the people of Sweden, but it would not prove to be the sanctuary that would yet keep him out of the fight game. For Floyd there would be a few more flickers of light, more bases for derision, and developments that would be quite sad, not at all comic, and all too real.

XVI

Just One More Shot

With the painful loss to Jimmy Ellis, Patterson dropped out of the public eye. "He must have retired" seemed the obvious conclusion. Back in New York, he was invisible. Patterson's first public appearance after the Ellis fight was obscure. It was on Long Island, where he refereed some intramural fights among fraternity students at C.W. Post College, a charity occasion, with ticket sales going to the aid of the U.S. Olympic Fund. As the program also included such former boxing stars as Willie Pepp, Tony Zale, and Joey Giardello, the sense that Patterson had now retired from the ring seemed ever more underscored. Two weeks later he joined a similar group of former champion boxers, including Jack Dempsey and Ray Robinson, in a Salute to Boxing parade in Times Square. This time, some active fighters were there as well, including Joe Frazier, but the sense of Patterson as a ring memory remained nonetheless. In late December 1969, the *New York Times*' Dave Anderson explicitly referred to Patterson as "apparently retired." Patterson's 1968 appearance on CBS television's *The Wild, Wild West* had prompted a similar guest shot in 1970 on the NBC program *Daniel Boone*. Some speculated here that Patterson was indeed out of boxing, having fun, and making extra cash with TV acting.[1]

In June 1970, Madison Square Garden held a ceremony (and a fight between Mac Foster and Jerry Quarry) to honor Jack Dempsey on the occasion of his 75th birthday. Various former champions were on hand—Gene Tunney, Georges Charpentier, Jack Sharkey, James J. Braddock, Dick Tiger, as well as Joe Frazier. Each received a warm greeting from the crowd. Aside from the applause for Dempsey himself, the Garden crowd's loudest ovation went to Floyd Patterson. The same thing would happen in August of 1970 when Patterson was introduced to the Garden crowd before a fight between

232

George Chuvalo and young George Foreman. These warm receptions underscored what many in Madison Square Garden's management well knew — that Patterson was still immensely popular in New York and that it would make financial sense to woo him into coming back and fighting once again. Here the New York pundits speculated about a return bout with Sonny Liston. They also considered pushing a rematch with Ellis, something many certainly thought to be appropriate, given the referee's ridiculous decision in Sweden. In either case, the motive was obvious — money. Ring justice, an aging fighter's safety — that was all secondary.

While Patterson was still considered good gate among New York fight organizers, nothing seemed to happen. In February 1970, amidst the coverage of the Garden's Jimmy Ellis–Joe Frazier bout, columnist Dave Anderson wrote "even though Patterson is now 35 years old, his mystique makes him the best box-office attraction of the possible challengers." At that very time, Madison Square Garden's chief fight maker, Teddy Brenner, said that he was indeed trying to induce Patterson to fight Joe Frazier, claiming he could guarantee Patterson $250,000. Nothing came forth. Earlier in 1969, when Muhammad Ali was still out of the championship picture, Brenner had also claimed that he had been close to setting up a "foursome" for the Garden, with Frazier fighting Jerry Quarry, Patterson rematching Ellis, and the two winners subsequently squaring off. Again, nothing materialized. Here Brenner lamented that it was Patterson who had "pulled out because he did not want to fight Frazier." All these stories underscored the point that, while there had been no formal announcement, the assumption of Patterson's retirement seemed pretty clear.[2]

Patterson did indeed appear to go into hiding, not that such behavior marked anything unusual from him. Aside from his little New York–area appearances at a few fights and fetes, he seemed content to live with his new wife, Janet, and their two young daughters. He bought property, an old chicken farm, north of the city in the town of New Paltz. There Patterson did set up a boxing ring for himself, however, and quietly continued a steady training regimen. This may have been out of simple love of conditioning, however, something that would stay with Patterson for the rest of his life. Patterson never did make any explicit announcement of retirement. Later, in July 1970, however, after he had committed to another fight, he outlined to a reporter: "Before I lost to Ellis, I dropped a decision to Jerry Quarry, and before that I had drawn with Quarry, so I felt that with three [non-wins] in a row I'd had it and decided to quit." At that very point, however, Patterson said a matter had arisen concerning the death of his friend Al Bolan, a man with whom he had worked for six years in the lining up of bouts. Bolan passed away in September of 1969, leaving a widow and five children, and Patterson decided then to set up a bout to help Bolan's family. At the end of January 1970, he announced that on April 1, he would fight the #2 ranked light heavyweight in the world, a fighter named Mark Tessman. So the talk of retirement ceased. Amidst training in March, however, Patterson accidentally cut himself as he brushed his hand against a broken porcelain handle while showering. The cut was serious. It severed an artery in the index finger of his left hand and forced the bout with Tessman to be postponed. Some scheduling difficulties with Tessman then ensued, causing the fight ultimately to be cancelled. Patterson still wanted to help the Bolan family, and with the taste of training for an actual bout back in his system, he arranged in July 1970 for another bout to take place that September. The fight was to be against a relative unknown named Charlie "Devil" Green.[3]

There seemed no glaring pathos in Patterson's announcement of a comeback. He made it clear that he did not want anyone to label him as somehow "new" or "different." He did not appear to make any great brags, pathetic or otherwise, about what he could do. He simply said he was feeling good mentally, which he asserted was "the real key to my success." He assured people that his previously cut hand was fine, and he was frank about the point that he needed to measure himself after being out of the ring since 1968. "I'm just interested again," he said. "This fight with Green," he genuinely nodded, "will be a test for me. I don't know what I have left, if anything. It's not easy to be out of the game for two years, although I have been training diligently every day I can." Patterson acknowledged the obvious, that Charlie Green, with a mere record to that point of 13 and 6, was no towering figure. Patterson even used this fact to jab a bit at a major heavyweight. "Green isn't a Cassius Clay," he smiled; "he's not a — what's the champion's name? [pause] He's not a Joe Frazier. But he's the type of guy who would show me where I am." Patterson also told one reporter, however, "I know I'll have to fight my way back into the picture. I hope I can, but we'll see what happens."

The thought of getting "back into the picture" was thus remaining a bit on his mind. Like so many aging boxers, Patterson was still, deep down, dreaming of great things. Most people in their 30s dream of such things, for in most walks of life such an age is young. The trouble for athletes, and for boxers especially, is that such dreaming can not only be delusional but highly dangerous. Most figured Patterson did not need the money. He seemed to be fighting for the pleasure and contentment that it brought him. "It's a strange way of finding pleasure," wrote Arthur Daley, "but Patterson always was a strange one."[4]

As the Green fight approached, some of the old head-scratching reappeared from some of Floyd's statements. "I don't like to watch fights," Patterson confessed. "I don't like to see blood, for one thing. It's different when I bleed, that doesn't bother me because I can't see it." Sizing up the new champion, Joe Frazier, and the appeal of his personality in comparison with past champions, one writer wrote of Patterson as "too complex, too fine in his sensibilities, too rich in his neuroses." When Patterson was champion, such matters were interesting, if frustrating. After he had lost but was contending, they were irritating, or a trifle funny. By this point, it was like discussions of the eccentricities of a family's oldest dog. Within this, the notion that Patterson was beginning some sort of comeback did anything but fire anyone's imagination. As he prepared for Green, Patterson would once again be a recluse from reporters during his training. This time, however, few appeared to care. And once again, Patterson said he would retire if he lost.[5]

Oddsmakers favored Patterson 2-to-1. Madison Square Garden did sell a respectable total of 10,000 tickets. The New York fight managers were indeed right: they could still make money off a Floyd Patterson fight. A big plus for the business of the fight was that ABC chose to televise it. September 1970 was the very time that ABC television began its *Monday Night Football* telecasts. The network's chief officers had no idea whether the weeknight televising of major sports would draw viewers. It had rarely been attempted, but ABC was going to try it, and here they were interested in testing the potential of other sports' appeals for broadcasts on weekday evenings. Years ago the old *Fight of the Week* program had been a staple, but it was on Friday night and in an era before television had advanced to more sophisticated levels of programming and marketing. In 1970, not everyone was sure the weeknight televising of sports would work. Football on Monday night would, of course, prove a winner. Boxing would not, but not because of the Patterson-Green bout. Here the fans and sponsors got their money's worth.

The bout prompted some minor stirs. With the relatively new political movement then called Women's Lib, Charlie Green's wife, Winona, raised a few traditionalists' eyebrows when she served in her husband's corner. She was the first woman to be a licensed as a second at a Garden fight. More controversy concerned the referee. The ref originally named for the bout, Davey Feld, had limited experience, and both Patterson's and Green's handlers said they did not want him. Some said Patterson threatened to stay in his locker room unless Feld was replaced. The memory of the ridiculous refereeing in the Ellis fight in Stockholm may have made the prospect of an undependable ref especially upsetting to Patterson and his people. With the objections, and fearing the fan reactions if Patterson was indeed going to refuse to come out of his locker room, the NYAC turned to another man. Davey Feld, nonetheless, actually appeared at ringside and seemed to try to enter the ring just after the two fighters had come into the arena. Feld claimed he merely went to the ring apron to try to make eye contact with Patterson. Apparently, he did not believe Patterson had really objected, suspecting that he had instead been stabbed in the back by some NYAC official due to some sort of petty commission politics. Whatever his beliefs and explanations, Feld's appearing at ringside was certainly a bizarre act, and immediately upon his arrival on the ring apron, two policemen immediately grabbed him. Several others bodily removed him from the Garden, one actually holding him in a choke hold. The New York Athletic Commission suspended Feld's referee's license. Patterson and Green then got down to business.

In the actual fight, Green appeared to have a lot of savvy and seemed to hold the upper hand in the early rounds. In the first round, maintaining the bizarre tone established with would-be referee Feld's physical removal, Green actually wrestled Patterson to the canvas on two occasions. At the end of the fourth round, he stunned Patterson with a hard right and kept up the barrage after the bell. In the fifth round, Green opened a cut over Patterson's left eye. A few weeks before, Patterson had suffered a small cut while sparring, and it had not healed as fully as he had believed, so the cut was less a consequence of Green's work than the fans and viewers believed. With all such wildness in and around the bout, the Garden crowd was definitely into it, and many began to think this was, at last, the end for Patterson. Throughout the clamor Patterson held to his fight plans, however. He methodically wore Green down. By the fifth round, Green appeared to tire. He began to hold his left a little lower, and Patterson steadily pecked away with greater and greater success. The tide inexorably turned, and the crowd could sense it. In the tenth, Patterson connected with a powerful left hook in the ribs that shook Green badly. Barely able to breathe, Green went down. While struggling to get up, his eyes appeared to stare eerily in two different directions. ABC highlighted this in both stop action and slow motion. Green did not beat the count, and the crowd roared for Patterson.

Patterson's 1965 victory over Chuvalo had been an exciting fight, but it some consigned it as essentially a mere club fight between two well-matched men, neither of whom would ever again seriously contend for the crown. While such a characterization had been a trifle debatable, there was no doubt of it here with Green. Patterson later admitted, "My performance was terrible. I saw openings, but my reflexes lagged so far behind I couldn't take advantage of them." The fight had some excitement, but it took Patterson nowhere. Green never amounted to anything. For Patterson it may have been nice to hear the crowd roar once more, but for a 35-year-old it was a heck of a way to pocket $35,000. Harry Markson, director of boxing at Madison Square Garden, did not care; the Garden's gate totaled $72,985. He soon began working on Patterson to fight Ellis again (which never materialized) and actually worked out an agreement for Patterson to fight the Argentinean Oscar Bonavena. Charlie Green faded into obscurity, fell into the drug world of Harlem, where, in 1983, he shot five people, killing two, and spent the rest of his life in jail.[6]

While Patterson's reappearance in the Garden was a blip on the boxing world's radar, the big news of 1970 involved Muhammad Ali regaining his license to box. The draft issue was now falling behind him, and he was able to think about the heavyweight crown again. With Joe Frazier otherwise the undisputed champion, Ali began to prepare to fight him. Rather than fight Frazier straight away, Ali staged two prep fights. He first beat Jerry Quarry. Then in December 1970, he beat Oscar Bonavena. This fight would affect Patterson. Bonavena had originally scheduled for himself two fights. The first was the one with Ali in early December 1970. The second was to be with Floyd Patterson on January 22, 1971, both at Madison Square Garden. The Ali-Bonavena fight proved to be a grueling 15-rounder, with Bonavena losing in the last round. Bonavena's countrymen still cheered him heartily when he returned home, and amidst the hoopla of his homecoming in Buenos Aires, Bonavena proudly announced that he was still going to fight Patterson in January. Four days later, however, Bonavena's doctor, Roberto Paladino, advised him to postpone the Patterson bout because of his general exhaustion and malaise from the difficult encounter with Ali. It made sense, and no one accused Bonavena of ducking. Originally, the Patterson-Bonavena fight was rescheduled for February 12. A hand injury and a subsequent wrist break to Bonavena caused further suspensions. As often occurs in such situations, inevitable complications in everyone's training and schedules made any rescheduling of a Patterson-Bonavena fight increasingly difficult. They would fight, but not for a full year.[7]

Fight organizers at places like Madison Square Garden obviously cared not one whit about the long-term health of the fighters they wanted. Patterson's age, Bonavena fighting two big bouts in less than seven weeks, it did not matter to them. The fight game was all about money, first and last. Fighters were like pieces of meat to be used for whatever purposes possible. If anyone needed to be reminded of just how sinister and dangerous the game of fighting could be here, it was in January 1971, just before the date when Patterson was to have first fought Bonavena, that the papers suddenly announced that Sonny Liston had died in Las Vegas, with apparent quantities of heroin and foul play suspected. As with the premature deaths of other boxers, like Benny Paret, the boxing world stopped for a moment, paid respects, and returned to its sweet, cool, dirty business. Patterson admitted that he had often dreamed of getting a rematch with Liston. He never got a chance.[8]

Upon learning of the first delay in the Bonavena fight, and not knowing, of course, that the fight would be ultimately cancelled that year, Patterson went ahead and scheduled a tune-up fight for himself in Miami Beach against a virtual amateur named Levi Forte. That week in January in Miami, the National Football League's American Conference championship game was to be played with the defending Super Bowl champion Baltimore Colts meeting the Miami Dolphins. The game was slated for January 17, and the

Patterson-Forte fight was arranged for January 15 as part of the week's festiv-
ities. Were it not for that context, there would have been little to no interest
in the bout. Forte was thirty years old and had not fought in thirteen months.
He was working in Miami as a bellhop at the Fontainebleau Hotel. To that
point he had a most undistinguished record of 19–20, but, his one claim to
fame, he had lasted a full ten rounds against the young, undefeated George
Foreman.

Muhammad Ali's handler, Angelo Dundee, had a part in the management
of Forte, and, not coincidentally, Dundee's brother Chris promoted the Miami
fight. Angelo tried to pump the fight, claiming Forte was "better than his
record." Dundee had said the same things about Brian London when he fought
Patterson in 1959. Few paid much heed this time either. Patterson faced very
few press questions about Forte, but he did have to contend with inquiries
about why he did not retire, especially since he had apparently come to fighting bouts at such a low level. To this he snapped somewhat defensively: "The
more people tell me to retire, the more determined I become to prove them
wrong." Fighting Levi Forte would not prove much. In just the second round,
Patterson knocked Forte down three times. With the third knockdown the referee ended the fight with Forte pathetically draped on the ropes. After the fight,
Forte told reporters that Patterson was always his idol. To that Angelo Dundee
sniffed, "Levi should have admired him more from afar." The Miami fans, all
4000 of them, did give Patterson standing ovations both before and after the
bout, but they seemed more for the memory of the man's prior greatness than
for anything about the evening's bout. Since Patterson was still thinking that
he soon had his upcoming meeting with Oscar Bonavena, he did not have to
face too many post-fight "why's" from reporters. Patterson expressed the sense
that he had improved since the Charlie Green fight, but was that saying much?
As no fight with Bonavena jelled in the immediate future, it all proved to be
an unhelpful tune-up for nothing, and Patterson pocketed all of $10,000.[9]

When Muhammad Ali beat Oscar Bonavena that December, the bruising fight not only ruined the immediate possibility of Patterson fighting
Bonavena, it also proved circuitously to ruin the chances Patterson had built
up in his mind of fighting someday for the title. Patterson believed that if he
could beat Bonavena he "should get another title shot."[10] Then the Bonavena
arrangements fell through. Meanwhile, Muhammad Ali's victory over
Bonavena left him ready to fight Joe Frazier. The prospect of the Ali-Frazier
match-up completely dwarfed everything else in the boxing game, and the
rest of the entire sports world at that time. Madison Square Garden would
land the bout on March 8, 1971, and as the preparations and press build-up
gathered momentum, all other heavyweight fighters and their designs were
left in the dust. Patterson's utterly faint hopes of another title appeared gone.
Now thirty-six, he appeared ever more a has-been.

With the boxing public's eyes fixed on Muhammad Ali and Joe Frazier, Patterson did what he could to stay alive as a boxer, hoping against hope that he could get one more good shot. While Madison Square Garden officials had wanted and got him to fight Charlie Green, no one in Manhattan seemed the slightest bit interested any more. Patterson would not quit, however. He turned to the minor circuits. In the early days of the twentieth century, when a poorly paid major league baseball player had had his day in the big leagues and had to keep playing to make money for himself and his family, he would return to the minors. A common term for an ex-big leaguer doing this was "on the way down." This certainly seemed an appropriate label for Patterson.

From March to August of 1971, Patterson would fight four times against low- and middle-level boxers before middle sized crowds in Philadelphia, Cleveland, Erie, Pennsylvania, and Buffalo. His opponents were a group of nobodies named Roger Russell, Terry Daniels, Charley Polite, and Vic Brown. Russell had been an impressive 10-1-1 as a light heavyweight. Then he moved up to the heavyweight division, and from there his record was a poor 1-7-1, with his last seven fights being those losses. Polite was but an ex-tennis star in Erie, Pennsylvania. Vic Brown was a local Buffalo boxer who had sparred for Joe Frazier. Patterson beat Russell on a TKO in the ninth round (despite Russell having knocked him through the ropes in the third). Patterson handily won over Polite and Daniels. He got a "near shutout" win with the judges over Brown. Throughout the fights, the local reporters gave kindly, sympathetic note to how Patterson "showed some flashes of old form." As some of the local reporters were meeting the former champion for the first time, many were personally impressed and noted, in contrast with so many other fighters, "his sincerity, cooperation, and dedication to the battered, shaky, and seedy fight game." It may have been nice for more people to know, first-hand, what a good man Floyd Patterson was, but Patterson was not fighting for personal public relations. He hardly needed it. The money was not anything great either — $15,000 in Cleveland, $10,000 in Philadelphia, less in Erie and Buffalo. It was quite a come down from the $600,000 he made fighting Johansson, and various newspapermen noted this. Patterson was still somehow holding onto the idea that he could keep winning and figure once again into the championship picture. "As long as I can see progress," he nodded after the Russell fight, "I'll continue to try to prove that I can get back what I lost." In Erie he asserted that a victory over Vic Brown would get him a fight against young George Foreman. In Buffalo he actually claimed: "I feel I haven't hit my prime yet as a fighter. They're talking of Clay and myself in November." It was getting embarrassing. Had something happened to the man's mind?[11]

Amidst the low-level fights, Patterson liked his little farm up in New Paltz. Through the rest of the summer of 1971 he kept his training regimen going. In November, three months after beating Brown, he did get another fight, but it was definitely not with anyone like Muhammad Ali. He flew out to Portland, Oregon, for a fight with somebody named Charlie "Emperor" Harris (8-12-1). Patterson had not been in the Northwest since 1957 when he fought Pete Rademacher. Still, the fans and reporters remembered him fondly as he had given the region a big fight, and they responded to Patterson with the same warmth and respect as had people in the other small venues that year. Harris proved no challenge. In the fourth round, Patterson knocked him through the ropes. The crowd pushed Harris back into the ring, reminding some of the famous Dempsey-Firpo bout of 1923. But Patterson then KO'd him in the sixth. While in Portland, Patterson stayed at the home of Dick Wagner, the tough middleweight Patterson twice fought at Eastern Parkway way back in 1953. It had been eighteen years! The reunion and their Thanksgiving dinner was each a joy for both men, but the contrast of Wagner, now comfortable and safe, watching Patterson still taking tough shots in the ring made many sigh sadly.[12]

Remarkably, after messing around in such Palookavilles as Erie, Buffalo, and Portland, Patterson was able to get a fight he truly wanted. He would get his shot at Oscar Bonavena, in Madison Square Garden. It was a full year late, after the various injuries and cancellations, but the fight came on February 11, 1972. "Can Floyd still fight," asked the *New York Daily News*, "or is he just star gazing?" The oddsmakers were certainly not optimistic. They made Bonavena a 7:5 favorite. Bonavana chided Patterson as he signed the fight contract before the press. Floyd was absent, and Bonavena looked around to make sure. After all, he joked, "maybe he [is here and] has a moustache and a beard on." Fighters will often "dis" one another before a bout, and Patterson's vulnerable spots were always easy targets. The question was whether a 37-year-old man could teach the younger braggart a lesson. Patterson told the press that a victory would boost him back on top and get him another shot at Ali or Frazier. While noting pridefully how he loved keeping himself in shape at all times, Patterson postured that he had undertrained for his last New York fight against Charlie Green and that his reflexes were much sharper now. "Believe it or not," he bragged, "I feel better than I did five years ago." Floyd's brags were typical of the man. In his defensiveness, he always gave his detractors a base to respond, and many, indeed, did not believe him.

Just before the Bonavena fight, on February 8, 1972, Floyd's father, Thomas Patterson, died in a Bronx hospital. He had been in declining health for some time and had recently undergone two operations to try to sustain his life. The fight with Bonavena was slated for February 11. In 1971, injuries had led Bonavena to cancel his fight with Patterson four times. Now the possibility of a cancellation fell into Patterson's lap, and certainly no one would have chided him for pulling out under such circumstances. But Patterson decided to go ahead with the fight as planned. The completely dollar-conscious Garden handlers were happy. The Garden was a near sell-out. Whether it was the grief or his age, no one knew, but Patterson started badly. For the first five rounds, the 7:5 betting line in favor of Bonavena looked good. Floyd appeared to have little. In the fourth round, he went down, later claiming it was a slip. Most reporters' cards had Floyd down four rounds to one. Then Bonavena appeared to tire. He could not put any more good combinations together, and Floyd's excellent conditioning shone through. He took the offensive and kept it. By the ninth, the New York crowd was keyed up, yelling "Floyd! Floyd!" When the tenth round ended, Patterson had won it on all cards. A few were cynical enough to claim that Patterson won on sympathy over his advanced age and his father's passing. The majority were not quite so disrespectful. His victory was legitimate, but everyone wondered where it could possibly take him.[13]

After the fight, Patterson offered some odd excuses for his poor showing in the early rounds. "I couldn't get started," he panned. "I just could not get the momentum of my punches working. Maybe it was a lack of interest." No one knew what "getting the momentum of my punches working" actually met, and the notion of a "lack of interest" seemed even more strange, but fighters and other sports figures, always peppered by reporters, often come up with verbiage that has no real meaning. Various people like Muhammad Ali and Casey Stengel could always make their nonsense entertaining. Patterson was never terribly adept here. Given his age, it now seemed even more pathetic, especially since Patterson continued to make noises about once again contending for the crown. Considering possible opponents for Joe Frazier, the *New York Times* snorted here about "such [a] shopworn figure as Floyd Patterson." The boxing business never leaves much room for kindness, and Patterson's title hopes did seem delusional, not to mention a little dangerous.[14]

Throughout 1971, Patterson had repeatedly said that if he could beat Bonavena, he wanted a shot at Muhammad Ali, four full years now after their rematch had originally been contracted. It was in March of 1971 that Ali lost to Joe Frazier. This left Ali in an abeyance that would take a few years to resolve. Joe Frazier would not give Ali an immediate rematch, fighting a couple of easy bouts against Terry Daniels and Ron Stander, then giving young George Foreman a shot in January 1973. Here Foreman would surprisingly annihilate Frazier. Twenty-one months later, Foreman would finally give Ali the shot he wanted, and in the famous "Rumble in the Jungle," Ali KO'd Foreman to regain the title. This would all take years to play out. In the meantime, Ali had to keep himself sharp. After losing to Frazier, Ali would fight fourteen times before going to Africa and beating Foreman, the fourteenth being a revenge victory over Joe Frazier.

During this active hiatus between his championships, Ali fought a bunch of nobodies like Jurgen Blin, Al Lewis, and Rudi Lubbers. He beat some reputable boxers like Buster Mathis, Jimmy Ellis, George Chuvalo, and Jerry Quarry. He lost to, and then beat a then unknown youngster named Kenny Norton. And it was during this string that he signed to meet Floyd Patterson, with the fight originally slated for Madison Square Garden on August 28, 1972. This was something Patterson had wanted since 1965 when he was utterly humiliated in Las Vegas, fighting Ali with his bad back. He had nearly gotten the rematch in 1967, but then Ali's encounter with the Selective Service Commission intervened. When Ali came back in 1970 and 1971 he used other stepping stones than Patterson — Quarry and Bonavena — to get to Frazier. Now Ali was an ex-champion, still seeking a title shot.

Patterson was delighted. The Bonavena fight had netted him $60,000 against 30 percent of the gate. This time he would get $125,000 v. 25 percent, with Ali getting $250,000 v. 35 percent. As usual, in the pre-fight Floyd was a gentleman, praising Ali, saying "he didn't look like he lost anything [from his enforced layoff from the ring due to the draft]. His combinations are just as fast [as ever]." Meanwhile, Ali was markedly different in tone compared with his 1965 anger. He was now sincere in his praise for Patterson. Ali had gone through a genuine change of heart from his famous disrespectful bravado of previous days. About Patterson, Ali nodded with a smile: "He's such a nice fella, talking so softly while I'm hollering." Most remarkably, Ali conceded: "He still says 'Clay,' but I can't even get mad at him, he's so nice. Everybody else calls me 'Muhammad' and he calls me 'Clay.' He's the only one who can get away with it." This would indeed remain the case with Ali. No one else would dare call Ali "Cassius Clay." He never forgave those who had done so, like Ernie Terrell, and held even more anger at those who continued to do so, especially Joe Frazier and his camp followers. But Floyd Patterson had a special place in Ali's heart and mind. Others who fancied themselves as radicals may have enjoyed lionizing Ali while laughingly dismissing Patterson as an "Uncle Tom." But Ali knew more than the mere ideologues of his time, including some of the Black Muslims who remained around him. He was more than a symbol of radicalism and of the Nation of Islam, a group he would eventually abandon, and it was within that human dimension that he confounded many ideologically-driven sycophants by openly respecting and befriending Patterson.

In the spring and summer of 1972, knowing the possibility of an Ali fight was before him, Patterson sealed himself off at his home in New Paltz and engaged in his usual rigorous training regimen. He made but one public appearance in May — on behalf of a 12-year-old boy from his Weschester neighborhood, David Ingraham. Ingraham had earlier enjoyed coming by Patterson's farm to watch him train. Then he was suddenly stricken with bone

cancer and had to have a leg surgically removed. As Ingraham was still a growing adolescent, the replacing prosthesis had to be continuously adjusted and
changed, and the medical bills from all this were staggering, more than his
family could afford. Patterson set up an exhibition bout with Charlie Harris,
against whom he had just fought out in Portland, Oregon. They sold 3000
tickets for a three-rounder, with all the money going to Ingraham's family to
pay their medical bills. It was not much of fight, but pugilism was a minor
part of the picture here.[15] Eldridge Cleaver and others may have chicly dismissed Patterson, but Muhammad Ali knew better.

As a tune-up for his big fight with Ali, Patterson set up a ten-round bout
in July against an unheralded Puerto Rican named Pedro Agosto. The fight
would be local, at the Singer Bowl in Flushing Meadows, Queens. Patterson
wanted a rehearsal, but Agosto, as most reporters saw it, was "no test" and
"proved of little value as an opponent." Patterson battered Agosto for the first
five rounds, and in the sixth he opened a nasty cut over Agosto's left eye. With
that, the referee stopped the bout. The inconsequential fight date did mark
the twentieth anniversary of Patterson's Olympic gold medal. Twenty years is
a long career in any sport, and no sport is more physically taxing than boxing. It was impossible for anyone not to wonder why Floyd was still fighting.
Johansson had long retired in comfort. Sonny Liston was dead. That August,
Eddie Machen died — of an apparent suicide. The sense of a boxer's mortal-
ity was certainly strong. Why was Patterson still out there? He did not apparently need the money. His expressions of love for and indebtedness to the
fight game were banalities. What was he doing? "All those years, all those
punches," wondered Red Smith. Was Patterson still engaged in some sort of
psychological hiding, now from the feared emptiness of retirement?[16]

Due to a scheduling need from the Ali camp, the Patterson-Ali bout was
put off to September 20. Madison Square Garden did their usual hyping, and
to some good effect. None less than President Richard Nixon put in a request
for a videotape. He was definitely for Patterson, and on August 8 he hosted
Patterson on a visit to the White House, Patterson's second presidential visit.
Not many boxers ever did that. In 1972, Richard Nixon had not altered his
politics or his disdain for what Muhammad Ali had done and come to symbolize so dramatically in the late 1960s. The country had shifted, however.
By the summer of 1972, the intense feelings about Vietnam had reduced significantly. J. Edgar Hoover was dead. Disenchantment with the war was no
longer the least bit radical, and Muhammad Ali ceased to present any threat
to many popular sensibilities. Ali had stood by his principles, paid a big price,
and much of the public now respected him for his willingness to stand unwa-
veringly for his beliefs and take the consequences. Amidst this, Patterson had
so faded that he no longer symbolized anything much to the boxing public
but an aging ex-champ. Still, the Garden knew they had a money-maker, not

anything like what they would have had when Ali and Patterson contracted back in 1967, but one that would generate good profits. As the fight approached, no great controversies brewed between Ali and Patterson, even though Patterson did indeed refer to him several times as "Cassius Clay." Ali was again firm here; he knew Patterson did not mean anything disrespectful, and he confirmed to the press: "He's the only man who can get away with calling me Mr. Clay." As for Patterson's feelings, they too had mellowed from the criticisms he had previously raised about Ali's affiliations. "I've gotten older," Patterson told the public, "I've got no ill-feelings against Clay and the Black Muslims. He respects me, and I respect him." Patterson, concluded the *New York Daily News* in its pre-fight write-up, is "a complex man ... no longer complex. He no longer thinks dark thoughts. At long last, [he] has made peace with himself." The Garden may have preferred a little controversy, but they were not going to get it. They would have to be content with the legacy and stature of the two, and with the questions of what Ali had left as he hoped to regain the title from Joe Frazier. The Garden management guarded their investment in the evening by co-featuring a lightweight bout between champion Roberto Duran and former champion Carlos Ortiz. Duran would withdraw, and another former champion, Kenny Buchanan, took his place. Whether or not the extra pairing was needed, the evening was a success. The Garden sold 17,378 tickets, netting $512,361.[17]

With the mild build-up, the night had a few exciting moments. The biggest came before the fight when Joe Frazier was introduced to the crowd. As he came into the ring, Ali feigned a "let-me-at-him!" set of shouts and gestures and let himself be restrained by his seconds. Few were moved one way or the other by the old act. Patterson shrugged at it all. No one gave him much of a chance. Ali actually had a thirty pound advantage over him, 218 to 188. When all the hoopla with Frazier ended, Patterson went to work, and he first looked pretty good. He won the first two rounds. Ali won the third, although barely. Then Patterson regained the upper hand in the fourth and fifth. The crowd was stirring, as an upset seemed possible. After the fifth round, Ali's long-time manager, Angelo Dundee, yelled at his fighter, telling him he was down and that he had better go to work. Ali did just that. He *was* the better fighter, and everyone knew it. He had been disinterestedly toying in the early rounds. After the fifth, Ali took his game up a notch and began snapping off leads at Patterson at will. He clearly gained the upper hand in the sixth round, and Patterson quickly looked markedly overmatched. The new fight balance remained in the seventh, and in that round Ali opened a serious cut over Patterson's left eye. Patterson's eye swelled and bled. He wobbled, throwing some desperate left hooks to try to interrupt Ali's assault. It did not work, and by the end of the round, Patterson went to his corner half blinded. "I'd been hit in the eye," Patterson recalled, "but I wasn't aware of it because there was no pain. I blew my nose, because my nose was running. No air came out of my nose. Instead, I blew my left eye out. I could have killed myself." Referee Arthur Mercante saw this, went to the corner, as did the NYAC's attending doctor, A. Harry Kleiman. Kleiman inspected the eye. He told Mercante to stop the fight, and Mercante did just that. No one in either corner or anywhere in the Garden disagreed with the decision, not even Patterson.[18]

It was an OK fight for the fans. Ali's quest for the crown would go on, and the same question came back for Patterson, now with more force than ever. Is this finally it for you? The answer would still not yet be "yes." Patterson came back to the Garden the next day for a press conference, with a patch over his left eye and a cut that had taken seven stitches. He spoke wistfully of a rematch. Red Smith of the *New York Times* shrugged at this. With the obvious point in mind that no one could suggest anything about retirement that Patterson had not heard a thousand times before, Smith sniffed: "Unsolicited advice is an impertinence." Who indeed could possibly tell Patterson anything here? Within two months, he actually received an offer to fight an unknown New Jersey boxer named Chuck Wepner (a big bumbling white guy who would later fight Ali, sort-of knock him down once, and inspire the movie *Rocky*). The offer was for all of $15,000. Patterson turned it down. It *was* actually over. There was no big announcement. Boxing fans everywhere pretty much shrugged to the effect that it was long overdue.[19]

XVII

Contentment

For any great athlete, the adjustment to retirement is never easy. There are the normal psychological matters of feeling at loose ends. Further, with the ego so wrapped up in the achievements, with all the positive memories, and with the natural tendency to repress any bad memories, so many aging athletes believe they can still perform. They often make errors as a result. In many sports this can lead to humiliation. In boxing it can sadly be that and much, much more. With all the psychological struggles of his early life, Patterson was actually able to handle these obstacles fairly well. Eleven years after the second fight with Ali, Patterson reflected the emotional ups and downs he experienced when facing the fact that his ring career was over: "You don't accept it," he noted. "You attribute poor performances to not training hard." This kind of thinking can be seductive, he recognized, because "in some cases you're right. [But] in many cases you're wrong." The recognition that his days in the ring were in the past "came in very, very small doses. I could not accept it right away — the fact that you'll never climb in to the ring again.... I missed the sacrificing, the excitement, the challenge. It was hard to settle into a life of quietness. But it was inevitable. I realized, you can't fight the inevitable." While he was honest about the anguish, he made no reminiscences that showed the potentially deadly signs of looking back that would goad him into trying that one more time. Perhaps most significant here was the fact that Patterson continued to stay in top physical shape. In one sense this may have kept boxing hopes alive for Patterson, but it also kept his mind and body sharper, preventing any depression from growing unduly. Perhaps because of his physical conditioning, several months into his retirement, some papers were still mentioning Patterson as a contender. Still thinking Patterson was active, Red Smith of the *New York Times* sneeringly referred to

Floyd here as "a senior citizen." Patterson made no efforts to respond here. He was content.[1]

Just seven months after the last Ali fight, Patterson began making appearances as a fight announcer. A new cable television network called Home Box Office was in its infancy, first broadcasting largely in eastern Pennsylvania and New Jersey. HBO's executives decided that the fights were a good venue to pursue to attract viewers, and they hired Patterson to be one of their commentators, co-chairing with the legendary fight announcer Don Dunphy. Critics gave Patterson good marks for his work. "They make a good team," noted Red Smith, "Dunphy has always been the best fight reporter on the air, and the self-effacing Patterson sounds fairly comfortable in his role as the newest of sport's golden voices. Face to face," noted Smith, "Floyd is often hesitant in speech and almost inaudible, but boxing has been his world for 27 of his 38 years. To him it is the best of worlds. Here he is sure of himself. His hamfat content zero." Patterson obviously knew the fight game, and he indeed proved discerning and articulate, especially when analyzing the tactical reasons for a particular fighter getting into trouble and what adjustments he could make (circle to his right, hold his left higher, aim for the body) to alter his predicament. Patterson even showed some instincts for political subtlety. At the end of one fight, for example, Dunphy left his seat to go into the ring and interview the winner, leaving Patterson alone at the microphone. Patterson carried on without hesitation under potentially awkward circumstances. "Here's a very interesting thing most of the viewers may not know," he quipped in an outwardly jovial tone. "Harold Valen, the referee, is the same man who refereed my fight in Sweden. He was the only judge, and I believe I lost that on a decision." No fight fan could doubt that Patterson remembered Valen, Jimmy Ellis, and Sweden all too well, but his understated tincture was perfect for the cool medium of HBO television. Patterson knew better than to use the air as a forum for expressions of resentment or editorializing. It would have served no purpose, and it was not in his nature anyway. He was a good, smooth announcer. (When Valen, himself a former boxer, passed away at the end of 1991, having suffered from dementia pugilistica, Patterson offered no comment.)[2]

Patterson's microphone work also appealed to the general nature of boxing fans in the early 1970s when he covered some Olympic-level amateur exhibitions that pitted American fighters against Russians. It was at the 1972 Olympics that American boxers, as well as other U.S. athletes, most famously the basketball team, endured the results of some obvious fixing and meddling by Russian and East Bloc authorities. In some subsequent international boxing exhibitions, highly prejudiced refereeing and judging continued to be in evidence. In December and January of 1974 and 1975, the Soviet boxing team toured the U.S. against a group of American Olympic hopefuls. In one match,

in Madison Square Garden, American Eddie Davis thoroughly beat his opponent, Oleg Karatayev, having him on the verge of a KO on several occasions
in just two rounds. Nonetheless, the judges inexplicably awarded the fight to
Karatayev. When the decision was read to the New York crowd, cups of beer
began flying into the ring and a chorus of chants, that sounded to one reporter
somewhat like "*Bolshoi*," could be heard throughout the forum. (Few knew
so many New York fight fans spoke Russian, or why they were chanting about
the decision being "great.") While many journalists and television commentators tried to be diplomatic in such situations, Patterson was honest and
blunt. "You can hardly blame the fans for reacting like this," he noted unhesi-
tatingly. "If we're going to cater to the Russians like this, why bother to hold
such bouts? Are we so concerned with the Russians that we have to take decisions away from our boys?" The HBO network was then still focused on places
like Wilkes-Barre, Scranton, Bethlehem, and Allentown, and the plain-folk
fight fans out there appreciated the refreshing candor.[3]

Patterson was also clear headed and direct in some truly important ways.
In early November of 1974, a bout of racial violence broke out in New York's
Westchester County. It was in the early 1970s that African Americans were
moving in significant numbers into some previously all-white Westchester
communities. Floyd had moved there over a decade earlier, and the move had
not been altogether smooth. Some Westchester towns remained exclusively
white, however, and this resulted in contrasts that would be in stark evidence
when various area high schools contested one another in sports. A November '74 football game between White Plains High School and Newburgh Free
Academy was one such example. Tensions were palpable from the outset, and
fights broke out between black and white students. For the next week, the
two schools were kept closed as authorities thought that having school would
too easily facilitate further plans for attacks and retributions. Meanwhile, violence and vandalism erupted anyway among the young people with more time
on their hands. The trouble spread throughout Newburgh and into Beacon,
a nearby community just across the Hudson River. Newburgh police imposed
an 8:00 P.M. curfew for all residents. The town lay just a few miles south of
Patterson's home in New Paltz, and amidst the tensions, Patterson drove down
there and spoke in Newburgh's City Hall to a meeting composed largely of
African American teenagers. Pollyanna calls for good behavior were not going
to make any impact, and Patterson well knew it. He spoke thoughtfully, and
honestly from the heart. "If someone hit me," he confessed, "I'd hit him back
because that's my instinct. But," he noted, "if I thought about it, I would
take him to court instead." The youth assembled chuckled and nodded sardonically. No one can say how many violent incidents Patterson may have
forestalled (nor, for that matter, can one definitely say he prevented any), but
he was acting in accord with the principles of non-violence he had learned

with Jackie Robinson from Dr. Martin Luther King, yet expressing them in a way that was genuinely from his soul. It resonated with those he wanted to reach, and the violence in Newburgh did soon abate.[4]

While Patterson could be blunt with regard to the Russian team and deeply sensitive with violent youths in Newburgh, he could be more purely diplomatic, as well as fun-loving. In 1975 he made an appearance in Rochester for a fund raiser on behalf of the New York Republican party. (The previous year, he had campaigned for Democratic gubernatorial candidate Hugh Carey.) Before 1500 paying fans, with none less than Jersey Joe Walcott serving as the referee, Patterson stepped into the ring against the New York State Republican chairman, Richard Rosenbaum. The fans obviously expected a merely staged fight, but they actually got a bit more of the real thing than they anticipated. Rosenbaum had done a little amateur boxing at Hobart College in upstate N.Y. He had been Hobart's intramural heavyweight champion, but obviously no one expected him to match legitimately with such a figure as Floyd Patterson. As they boxed, Rosenbaum first landed a couple of shots to Patterson's midsection, and towards the end of the second round he may have been stupidly allowing himself to feel a bit cocky. Then, as Rosenbaum aggressively strode forward, Patterson casually threw a left hook that caught Rosenbaum squarely in the right eye. Rosenbaum immediately went rubbery-legged, and Walcott quickly stopped the fight. Patterson felt terribly about the blow, and he apologized profusely. Rosenbaum maintained his political poise and commented that he should have known better since Patterson had previously campaigned for Democrat Hugh Carey. It was a good one liner. For the next week Rosenbaum sported a huge black eye. Still, it did not hurt his political stature when he told people he got his shiner while fighting Floyd Patterson.[5]

Patterson would involve himself in other political campaigns. In 1981, he was openly supportive of New York City mayor Ed Koch's bid for reelection. "He's down to earth," Patterson extolled. "He's like the average worker." Koch won. Patterson's support of Democratic governor Hugh Carey served him well, for in February of 1976, Carey appointed Patterson to the New York State Athletic Commission, to oversee all professional boxing matters in the state. Such incidents, like the 1970 Davey Feld refereeing brouhaha, which had occurred when Patterson fought Charlie Green, had reflected badly on the New York boxing administration. Putting Patterson on the Athletic Commission was a savvy move. Patterson obviously knew the whole fight game inside and out. He could provide intelligent guidance, and his presence would certainly lend an excellent image to the organization. Patterson first worked on the commission with James Farley, Jr. When Farley left in 1977 (under suspicion of kickbacks), Patterson's new chief commission colleague was a young man named Mario Cuomo.[6]

Through his work with the NYAC, as well as by the simple virtue of living near New York City, Patterson was generally "where the action is" in the N.Y. boxing world for much of the remainder of his life. In 1983, Mayor Koch put him on a five-member City Sports Commission that advised the city government on details about many events, safety issues, celebrations, and festivals. He was on hand for many of the big fights over the next twenty years in Madison Square Garden, and he made appearances at scores of public gatherings. In 1974, in the events leading up to the famous Muhammad Ali–George Foreman fight, Patterson was on hand at the Waldorf-Astoria for a New York Boxing Writers Dinner where Ali and Foreman tangled in front of the podium and Foreman ripped Ali's suit. In 1976, Patterson was in Yankee Stadium, and witnessed the pre-fight South Bronx riots, for the third Muhammad Ali–Kenny Norton fight. He saw future heavyweight contender Gerry Cooney fight when Cooney was still but a touted nineteen-year-old amateur in the New York Golden Gloves.[7]

When Ali fought Earnie Shavers in 1977, Ali was up to his old antics, taunting Shavers with a special nickname ("The Acorn"). In his capacity as an official of the NYAC, Patterson was on hand at the weigh in. Ali's antics could have brought back the bitter 1965 memories of "The Rabbit" and the humiliation in Las Vegas, but Patterson appeared honestly to enjoy it all. He had clearly put past troubles behind him, and it was no mere act. When controversial fight decisions inevitably arose in New York, Patterson could be counted on as a firm voice of reason and experience from the NYAC. In January 1978, for example, welterweight Wilfred Benitez beat Bruce Curry despite Curry knocking Benitez down three times. Curry's people were in an uproar. Patterson could only say that the NYAC could not alter a decision but could do something about the officials. Since he had obviously been a victim of some bad decisions, Patterson's voice could resonate among the angry, just as it did among the youths of Newburgh. With everyone fully acknowledging how deeply Patterson was devoted to the principle of fair judging, he was able to make other changes. It was Patterson who was able to appoint the first women as fight judges in New York. Eva Shain, for example, was one of three judges at Madison Square Garden in 1977 when Muhammad Ali fought Earnie Shavers. With judging, Patterson simply knew not to care about the issue of gender. Knowledge and fairness were everything to him. He told Shain to forget about any of the hoopla over her or over the personalities of the two fighters. Stick to the business at hand, Patterson told her: "It's just two fighters in there." Shain did so, and she established a fine reputation for herself, not because of her gender but simply because she did her job well. Shain would judge several of Mike Tyson's championship bouts in the 1980s. While supporting women like Eva Shain as boxing judges, Patterson was, however, always dead-set against women being allowed to box. "I have always respected women and have been a supporter of women's lib," Patterson said in 1978, "but in the boxing ring, no. I can't stand to see women cutting each other up and spilling blood in the ring."[8] When promoters like Don King began to recruit such people as the daughters of Joe Frazier and Muhammad Ali and fans bought tickets to see them box, there was nothing a man like Patterson could do about it.

While on the NYAC Patterson took on even tougher matters than bad referee decisions. In November of 1979, a middleweight named Willie Classen was badly hurt in a fight at Madison Square Garden. He had suffered a sub-dural hematoma and brain stem failure. It was Benny "Kid" Paret all over again. Classen was carried out of the ring in a coma, and he never came out of it. In five days he was dead. Patterson helped sit in vigil at the hospital and kept Classen's wife company during the ordeal. Few people showed such a capacity for empathy. On another occasion in February, 1982, Patterson's old adversary Thomas "Hurricane" Jackson was struck by a motorist. Patterson immediately went to see him in the hospital. A week later, Jackson died from his injuries, and Patterson sat with Jackson's family through the funeral.[9]

With such tragedies as Classen's death and with his complete knowledge of the dangers of the fight game, Patterson used his position on the NYAC to advocate strongly for reforms. He advocated more extensive eye examinations for fighters before each bout and for generally tougher medical standards. He opposed several efforts to create federal commissions to oversee the sport, preferring the idea of the existing state commissions coordinate with one another to toughen and regularize standards. Promoter Don King was also against the federalization of control, leading many to think that a federal commission must be a good idea. But Patterson disagreed, likely not because he merely wanted to guard the bureaucratic purview that he and the NYAC held, and certainly not because he was guided in any way by the thoughts of Don King. When another boxing death occurred in November of 1982, and on television no less (a Korean lightweight named Duk-Koo Kim died when fighting Ohioan Ray Mancini), more calls for tighter regulation of the sport ensued. This time Patterson stepped forward in favor of greater federal control. Here he was concerned that efforts could grow to ban the sport, and he urged that it not be, emphasizing how it was a "way out" of poverty for him and continued to be for many others. "If it wasn't for boxing," he proclaimed, "I would probably be behind bars or dead."[10]

In the early 1980s, Patterson tried to push for the requirement of a safer boxing glove, one which more fully took the thumb out of use. General traditionalism and conservatism among fighters and trainers, and the fact that the gloves required that boxers' hands be taped differently, first blunted the success of Patterson's efforts here. As Patterson's term on the NYAC was extended, his efforts for boxing safety would continue. Thumbless gloves would ultimately be mandatory in New York, and, according to the *New York Times*, Patterson was the man "most responsible" for this.[11]

In addition to his work with the New York Athletic Commission, Patterson kept his boxing presence pleasantly alive through coaching. In 1972 he founded the Huguenot Boxing Club in Esopus, right next to the site of the Wiltwyck School. In 1979 he helped train and coach a team of young boxers from the Hudson Valley Region. In 1984 he coached the New Paltz Boxing Club. Working with young people always brought Patterson some of his greatest joys: "I have found contentment," he acknowledged. Some may have wished to consign this to a mere matter of positive sublimation from his own troubles, but whatever the roots, Patterson was very effective in his work here, especially in the most important area of providing young boys' lives with structure, direction, and discipline. The Hudson Valley group competed locally and in some regional tournaments like the Empire State Games. On another occasion, Patterson's coaching took on much higher-level venues. In 1980, the Olympic Games fell into controversy. The games that year were set for Moscow, but President Jimmy Carter took the U.S. out of the games because of the Soviets' invasion of Afghanistan. Many American allies joined in an international boycott of Moscow. Patterson actually participated, however. He did it by coaching the Swedish boxing team. In 1984 he also traveled to Africa to give talks and boxing clinics to Olympic hopefuls in Zambia, Zimbabwe, and Nigeria.[12]

Another international venue and controversy that involved Patterson once again concerned broadcasting. In the late 1970s and 1980s international pressures began to affect the sports world in regard to anything connected to the nation of South Africa and its ongoing regime of apartheid. Some wanted a ban on any sort of economic or journalistic commerce with the nation as long as apartheid was in force. Others supported ongoing interaction, with a justification that friendly contact could be a basis for the exertion of pressure on the regime to reform its ways. During the final days of apartheid and since its end in the early 1990s, historians and journalists have all debated whether commerce or non-commerce was, or would have been, the better policy. While the system of apartheid remained in place, the debates over proper courses of action were often quite intense.

Boxing was one of the highly visible components in the arguments here, as questions raged over whether bouts should be broadcast from South Africa and whether various white South African fighters deserved to be given opportunities to fight against major contenders. In the early 1980s, two South African heavyweights — Kallie Knoetze and Gerrie Coetzee — ranked in the world's top ten, and the question of whether they should be granted the right to fight other top opponents drew a great deal of controversy. (Knoetze's visibility held a special obnoxiousness, as he had served as a South African police officer and had, claiming self-defense, shot and killed a South African youth during an anti-apartheid demonstration.) Amidst the debates, those who wanted non-commerce rarely won their point, although they were able to get a number of American institutions, notably some private schools and universities, to divest South African components from their investment portfolios. Patterson played a minor role in these debates, as he chose to go to South Africa and do fight broadcasts for a South African radio station. He may have irritated some on the political right when he went to the Moscow Olympics as the coach of the Swedish boxing team. It was barely eight weeks later, October 1980, that he then went to South Africa to cover a fight between Coetzee and American Mike Weaver. (Weaver won.) He returned there the next March to cover another fight. Patterson could always perplex some of the political activists that surrounded the sports scene. And his helping Sweden, going to Moscow, and then going to South Africa presented a befuddling composite. Patterson never offered any comment. He likely felt that the fighters deserved a chance to rise as high in the rankings as their ability would take them regardless of their nationalities and that he would accept engagements from South African radio stations as long as he was not breaking the law in doing so. After all, he had always defended Muhammad Ali against political persecution and, against Cus D'Amato's advice, he had been willing to give Sonny Liston a chance, police record and all.[13]

While Patterson thus continued on his own political paths, he continued quietly to make appearance after appearance on behalf of worthy charities, causes, and people. It was a cliché, but Patterson meant it when he said he "wanted to give something back to the sport that's been so good to me." When Patterson was boxing, people wrote with a decided tone of frustration of how he had "the instincts of a fighter and the compassion of a priest." Now such a view showed no contradiction. Responding to the years of head scratching among the many "wise" ring pundits over Floyd's gentlemanly ways, his daughter Jennifer put it simply: "The problem with my father," she smiled, "is that other men just never measure up." In 1986, Patterson and his son were driving on the New York State Thruway. He saw a car overturned in a ditch. He pulled off the road, ran to the car, reached through an open window, and held a three-year-old boy, Colin DeVries, eighteen inches above a pool of muddy water until the paramedics arrived. The driver, the boy's grandmother, died in the accident. Patterson and the boy regularly stayed in touch thereafter.

In 1995 Patterson donated a gift of boxing lessons to the highest bidder for a Franciscan Sisters of the Poor Foundation auction party to assist people with AIDS and H.I.V. In 1991 he donated a pair of autographed boxing trunks to an auction to help restore a performing arts center in nearby Nyack, NY. (A blouse donated by pop-star Madonna garnered more money.) In 1984 in Baltimore, at age forty-nine, Patterson climbed back into the boxing ring to do some exhibition boxing for the city's Catholic charity society, St. Vincent de Paul. While Patterson obviously implied no come-back by his actions here, he was not lacking in good physical conditioning when making such appearances, for through his forties and into his fifties Patterson had kept up a rigorous physical training regimen. He sparred on TV as late as 1994. He had always found contentment in the solitude of training. His example was also a good motivator for the many young people he regularly trained in New Paltz. In the previous October, indeed, Patterson had run in and completed the New York City Marathon, and it was the third marathon he had finished that year. His best time was an impressive three hours and thirty-one minutes. While in his forties, he ran three other marathons as well. (Hitting the proverbial runner's wall at the twenty-mile mark, he noted, reminded him of his fight with George Chuvalo.) "When I get up in the morning and I run and I work out in the gym," he reflected, "it puts me on a physical high that is so good I don't need any other drug. That's what boxing did for me, and for hundreds of kids that I've trained. It steered them off alcohol and drugs and put them on a path of physical fitness for the rest of their lives." In September 1995, Central Park staged the first Floyd Patterson Challenge, a five-kilometer race, with entry fees going to charity. In November of '84 the Norwegian Cruise Lines contracted with Patterson to join some other prominent athletes to take part in a Caribbean Cruise for Fitness. The liner sold out.

In addition to ongoing athletic achievements, Patterson also kept in the public eye with some small acting parts. He did television advertisements for Old Spice cologne, and he accepted a part opposite his old friend James Cagney in a TV movie called *Terrible Joe Moran*. Cagney, then 84, portrayed an aging boxer, confined to a wheelchair. (It would be Cagney's final acting role.) Floyd Patterson played the part of a former opponent, as did Art Carney, while New York mayor Ed Koch appeared as an old promoter — an all-star cast of a different sort. In the movie, Patterson and Cagney portrayed former ring enemies who had become close friends, and that was very much how Patterson regarded all the boxers he had once opposed. All the tauntings from Ali and his associates were completely in the past as far as Patterson was concerned.

Patterson and Ingemar Johansson also remained close. They appeared on television together several times. In 1990 they traveled together to Helsinki to be honorary guests of the nation of Finland for their national boxing championships, with the event held in the same hall where Patterson had won his middleweight gold medal in 1952. In 1992, the Finish government invited Patterson and his adopted son back for a celebration of the fiftieth anniversary of his medal. In 1987, Swedish film maker Lasse Hallstrom premiered his movie *My Life as a Dog*. The film portrayed the boyhood of Ingemar Johansson and ended with his KO of Floyd Patterson. Patterson happily attended the New York premier. In 1988, professional ice hockey players from the United States and Sweden set up a nation v. nation exhibition game. At a time before the Winter Olympics allowed professionals to play on their national teams, this was a rare opportunity for professionals to play one another for national honor. To add to the rivalry and good sportsmanship in the situation, Patterson and Johansson were invited to be honorary opposing advisors and coaches, along with tennis stars John McEnroe and Mats Wilander. Patterson and Johansson would continue to see one another at public occasions, and the warmth of their friendship never failed to radiate.[14]

Throughout his retirement years, Patterson's fight legacy would still be a touchstone of futility for some grim sports events. In 1984, for example, when the defending Super Bowl champion Oakland Raiders lost to the Seattle Seahawks in the following year's NFL playoffs, they played poorly, so poorly indeed that, in the words of one writer, they showed little "hope of putting up a better title defense than Floyd Patterson did against Sonny Liston." When the Buffalo Bills lost their third straight Super Bowl in 1994, a Buffalo reporter suggested that the players "don false whiskers, phony glasses" as Floyd Patterson did when "he was knocked cuckoo by Liston." When the New York Nets outclassed the Knicks in the 2004 NBA playoffs, the lopsided nature of the games reminded a reporter of the way Ali once humiliated Patterson. Such memories would never go away, but Floyd remained a respected popular figure, especially in his native New York area. He was enshrined into several halls of fame: the Olympic Hall of Fame, the New York Sports Hall of Fame, and, in 1991, the International Boxing Hall of Fame, boxing's version of Cooperstown. When he threw out the first pitch at opening day in Yankee Stadium in April of 1984, reporters noted that his introduction "prompted almost as much applause as Yogi Berra['s] did a few minutes earlier." Patterson made some appearances at Catskill area summer clubs, touring the traditional Borscht Circuit. A school near his home in New Paltz, Marist College of Poughkeepsie, NY, asked him to appear at its 1988 graduation. He had done much laudable work in the local area for the mentally retarded and with the Floyd Patterson Children's Fund. The students loved him, and he spoke to them from the heart as to the ways they, as the fortunate ones in the land, should give back as best they can. As is normal in such situations, Patterson received a doctorate of humane letters. Although the degree was purely honorary, it was certainly another extraordinary mark of contrast from the streets of Bedford-Stuyvesant and the dingy ante-rooms of the High Street subway stop.[15]

Patterson's good name continued to hold cache in politics. In May of 1984, he joined with a group known as Athletes for Reagan-Bush, whose ros-

ter, beyond Patterson, included boxers Joe Frazier, Rocky Graziano, Joey Giardello, as well as numerous former stars from baseball and football including
Roger Maris, Don Newcomb, Bart Starr, Andy Robustelli, Chuck Bednarik,
Carl Eller, and Willie Davis. Davis had been one of the National Football
League's players who had stood defiantly in support of Muhammad Ali when
he refused the draft in 1967. By 1984, the tone of politics and sports had
changed markedly, and Davis's support of Reagan was one of many indica-
tions here. Even more stark in this regard was a campaign billboard which
appeared that fall in New York, New Jersey, Pennsylvania, Ohio, and Michigan. The billboard showed President Reagan standing with three boxers over
a caption which stated: "We're voting for this man." The three boxers were
none other than Joe Frazier, Floyd Patterson, *and* Muhammad Ali. Patterson
put in several appearances on behalf of Reagan in 1984. The following year
he was a conspicuous presence at an evening at the New York Hilton sponsored by a group of black Republicans to honor former President Richard
Nixon. (Muhammad Ali did not join Patterson on that one.) In 1992, Patterson attended Ali's fiftieth birthday celebration. Together they attended a
ceremony commemorating the twenty-fifth anniversary of Martin Luther
King's murder. When Ali fought Larry Holmes at the very end of his career,

In retirement, Patterson was often a conspicuous political celebrity in his native New
York. He worked with and supported various figures, Democratic and Republican,
including Ed Koch, Mario Cuomo, Hugh Carey, and George Pataki. On several occasions he served on and chaired the New York State Athletic Commission. Here he
meets with former President Richard Nixon at a fundraiser in 1985. While vice president, Nixon had been a big Patterson fan. During the evening in 1960 when Patterson regained the heavyweight crown, Nixon interrupted a White House meeting to
get all the details of Patterson's victory. ©Jacques M. Chenet/CORBIS.

he did state that Patterson was a superior boxer to Holmes. Throughout the years, Ali was always happy to let Patterson, and *only* Patterson, call him "Cassius Clay."[16]

Patterson's work as a coach and trainer of young boxers was always rewarding to him. Patterson's own children never showed much interest in boxing, and Floyd never pushed it. "I would never encourage anyone to box who didn't want very much to do it. That could lead to serious injury. I myself wanted it very much." He simply told his own children, "find something you like, and do your best at it." His children pursued other sports and activities. With boxing, noted his son, Eric, "You have to give up your private life. I would go out to dinner with my father and people would flock for his autograph. It got me angry." Eric was keen on baseball; another daughter pursued acting. Most of all, with their father's keen approval, they pursued their education, all successfully.[17]

Even though his children did not take part in boxing, many young boys did, and they came to Patterson's training camp in New Paltz. With the legacy of Johansson very much alive, some Swedish fighters came, including a lightweight silver medalist from the '88 Olympics, George Cramne. Another who achieved some prominence was a middleweight named Danny Chapman. Yet another was a shy kid named Tracy Harris. Tracy was a troubled boy who never knew his biological father. He wandered into Patterson's gym one day. He was eleven years old, almost exactly the same age Patterson was when he went off to the Wiltwyck School. Tracy was a complete loner in the gym, and Patterson quickly befriended him. "Tracy came off and on to the gym for about a month," Patterson recalled. "He sat and watched. He never said anything. One day I said to him, 'Would you like to try it?' He said, 'Yeah,' and I got him some shoes and trunks and gloves." He showed some aptitude and, with Patterson's attention, became a daily visitor to the gym. He was also often reluctant to go home at the end of the day's training. Sensing a need, Patterson offered to pay Tracy to stay and help with chores like mowing and weeding. Tracy eagerly took up the offer and quickly befriended the family.

With Mrs. Annie Harris's approval, Patterson let Tracy stay one night in the bedroom space above Patterson's gym. The next day, Patterson went off to California for two weeks, and when he returned his wife told him, with a smile and a shrug, that Tracy was still staying in the little room above the gym. Patterson looked into Tracy's home situation and discovered that his mother had been abandoned by her husband, had her hands full with four younger boys, and had been laid off her job as a nurse's assistant at a local hospital. Patterson also learned that Tracy had been getting into trouble at school and had been stealing, not candy or trinkets, but disposable diapers for his mother and his baby brothers. The parallels with what he had faced as a boy back on the streets of Brooklyn were all too obvious, and Patterson believed he could provide some stability in Tracy's life, just as the Wiltwyck School had provided him. With Mrs. Harris's approval, Tracy continued to live at the Pattersons' home and work diligently on his boxing and schooling. His behavior straightened out. He graduated from New Paltz High School, and he showed both the talent and dedication needed to become a good fighter.

In 1978, when Tracy was thirteen, his mother had decided that she was going to relocate back to her original home in Alabama. Tracy protested as he did not want to give up the boxing world with Patterson to which he had grown so terribly attached and in which he was showing such promise. Fortunately for Tracy, his mother agreed that he could stay with Patterson. A year later, when Tracy was fourteen, again with no objections from Mrs. Harris, Patterson officially adopted Tracy as his son. Mrs. Harris wanted her son to be able to use every opportunity that befell him. Meanwhile, Patterson said, "I wanted Tracy to be my son, because it felt like he already was my son." The familial love was genuine and wonderful for both. Tracy also flourished as a boxer. Patterson said he recognized Tracy's ability "right from the start." Tracy never developed the bulk that Patterson had and "filled out" only to the super-bantamweight division, whose maximum weight is 125 pounds. "I don't worry about following in my father's footsteps," Tracy acknowledged. "They're too big for me to fit in." Within his bantam division, nonetheless, Tracy Harris-Patterson became a major figure in the late 1980s and early 1990s, and his adopted patrimony prompted further journalistic note.

When Tracy made his professional debut in June, 1985, Patterson was in his corner. "*I'm* nervous," nodded Patterson (emphasis his). "I think I'm more nervous than I was for any of my fights." Tracy won that night, and he reeled off a string of twenty consecutive victories before his first loss. By the end of 1992, he had accumulated a record of 45–2 and won the WBC super bantamweight title after defeating Thierry Jacob of France; "the proudest moment of my life," Floyd proclaimed. Just as Floyd's first child was born the day he beat Archie Moore, just three days after Tracy beat Jacob, his wife gave birth to a daughter.

While establishing a strong reputation for himself as a bantamweight, Tracy Patterson was always identified in the press and Floyd Patterson's son. Tracy did not seem to mind. "I'll always be known Floyd's kid," he smiled, adding, "and what's wrong with that? He's a great man to be the son of." As with Cus, some criticized Floyd for bringing Tracy along too slowly, but it was hard to argue with the results. As Floyd did with Cus, Tracy eventually broke with Floyd, in May 1994, and continued his career on his own. Floyd understood. Even more than Floyd did with Cus, Tracy would later reconcile with his father. "Titles go away," said Tracy. "When you build a relationship, that's forever." The reconciliation meant a great deal to both men. Tracy

Floyd Patterson, where he was always happiest, on his own, training hard. In retirement he maintained a strong conditioning regimen, keeping himself in top shape.
He hit the bags, sparred, lifted weights, and ran several marathons. He also trained
many fighters, including a youngster, Tracy, whom he would adopt. With Floyd in
his corner, Tracy Patterson would become boxing's super-featherweight champion.
© *The Ring.*

was with Patterson the night on the New York Thruway when he saved young
Colin DeVries from drowning. While Tracy had been proud of his adopted
father in many, many respects, the saving of Colin was always greatest thing
in his mind. Tracy Patterson later took the super-featherweight championship
and finished his career with an admirable record of 63-8-2.[18]

In addition to his dedicated work with his adopted son, Patterson made a small dent as a trainer in the heavyweight division in the 1990s as he helped train the contender Donovan "Razor" Ruddock. On several occasions, Patterson had noted that since his time, boxers had shown less and less ability at defense (as well as more and more of a preoccupation with money). With Ruddock he tried to hone the young fighter's defensive skills, and let others deal with money matters. With Patterson, Ruddock would be a strong heavyweight contender, defeating such notables as Mike Weaver, Michael Dokes, and Greg Page. But in 1991 he was twice knocked out by the strongest fighter of that era, Mike Tyson. Here, noted a reporter, "Ruddock showed little of Patterson's influence."[19]

Mike Tyson was indeed the absolute brute of the boxing world in the late 1980s and early 1990s. His notoriety actually recalled to many reporters some of Patterson's glory, as he and Tyson were the "bookend" champions of the career of Cus D'Amato. Patterson was D'Amato's first great fighter; Tyson was his last. Each at times used the peek-a-boo style. Floyd had also been the youngest to win the title, five weeks shy of his twenty-second birthday, and it was Tyson who took that honor from him, winning the title at the age of twenty years and four months. In the late 1980s, as Tyson was easily knocking out all his opponents, some began to guffaw at the unworthy quality of his opposition, much as the press had done to D'Amato and Patterson thirty years earlier. Among Tyson's opponents was the journeyman Peter McNeeley, who happened to be the son of another journeyman, Tommy McNeeley, whom Patterson had fought in 1961. Patterson knocked Tommy McNeeley down eight times; Tyson knocked Peter McNeeley out in eighty-nine seconds. Over the charges of light opponents, Patterson himself spoke out in Tyson's defense: "Tyson's a great fighter, no doubt about that. Unfortunately, there's no competition around for him to prove it." Tyson, Patterson asserted, likely recalling the charges he once endured, is ducking no one.

Many saw the sad, self-destructive cycles into which Tyson's career would degenerate tracing themselves to the point when Cus D'Amato died in November 1985. Patterson concurred. If Cus was still alive," he noted in 1992, "I don't think any of the things you've been reading about Tyson would have happened." To many, including Patterson, the simultaneous rise in the influence around Tyson of Don King and his associates seemed especially corrosive too. Patterson noted how, after D'Amato died, Tyson's new people made a point of telling him to avoid contact with Patterson. When D'Amato died, Patterson acknowledged, indeed, "there will never be another manager or person who cared about his fighters the way Cus did. Cus," Patterson noted reverently, "cared more about his fighters than money. He gave money away like it was just giving somebody a drink of water. He wasn't a greedy person. His main concern was his fighters." Frankly believing he was a good trainer of fighters, like Tracy, Patterson emphasized nonetheless, "Good as I am, I could never touch Cus." Few could, indeed, and counterfactually Tyson's career sadly showed this. Reflecting on his own career, in cognizance of the criticisms so many had raised of D'Amato and of the ways he had broken from the paths D'Amato thought wisest, Patterson ruefully acknowledged, "It turned out that whatever Cus said, worked out to be true." Patterson, along with José Torres, another D'Amato champion, were pallbearers at D'Amato's funeral. The two, without Tyson, were also present in 1993 for the dedication ceremony when the section of 14th Street at Irving Place, where Cus's gym had stood, was renamed "Cus D'Amato Way."[20]

Patterson was a conspicuous presence amidst the sad infirmities and deaths of various notables with whom his career had crossed paths. He sat with José Torres and Muhammad Ali at the funeral of Howard Cosell in 1995. He was a pallbearer at the 1986 funeral of his old friend Jimmy Cagney, along with Mayor Ed Koch and dancer Mikhail Baryshnikov. Cagney was eighty-six when he died, so his passing lent feelings of loss but not tragedy. But for Patterson the pain of the moment was doubly heavy, as just two days before one of his younger brothers, who was partially disabled, had suddenly died of a heart attack, alone in his Bronx apartment at age thirty-seven. In addition to the loss of his little brother, the sad declines and the premature deaths of various boxers were especially poignant for Patterson. Liston had died young, and mysteriously, as had Eddie Machen. Various fighters showed signs of precipitous decline and dementia, and they did so in ways that were sadly not in line with medical norms. Joe Louis grew to be a pathetic figure by the time of his death in 1981, just a month shy of seventy-seven. Louis's decline was a source of discomfort for many boxing fans, and in the 1980s this public anxiety would grow with the increasingly noticeable physical failings of Muhammad Ali. Patterson was as pained as anyone about this. "Of all the heavyweight champions I've ever known," he noted, "none could take a punch like Ali," adding poignantly, "I guess sometimes that can be bad." Bad and then some, to say the least.

In 1999, Patterson's old nemesis Jerry Quarry died. As with Ali's infirmities, Quarry's passing was due to dementia pugilistica. Few knew until the time of his death that Quarry had been a completely mute invalid for the last two years of his life. Quarry's brain, said his neuro-psychologist, "looks like the inside of a grapefruit that has been dropped dozens of times." His family decided to remove the life-support systems that were sustaining him. All such evidence of so many boxers' fates was clear and, to many, the conclusion was obvious — boxing was too dangerous to be allowed to continue. Ali's decline, particularly, prompted the rise of abolitionists, as they began calling themselves, content, as the label implied, to live with the notion that most may at first view them as a silly moralistic enclave of naive, well-meaning do-gooders but who, like their nineteenth-century predecessors, were willing to be patient and win their righteous battle in the end. In addition to point about the physical dangers of boxing, one of the abolitionist arguments concerned the criminal elements and the evil people they bring to the fore as a result of their undue influence. Here some abolitionists did explicitly note, with begrudging respect and a touch of lament, that the fine example of such a man as Floyd Patterson undercuts some of the strength of that part of their arguments. Patterson, while acknowledging that boxing indeed had bad influences against which there had to be steady guardianship, maintained that it still marked a way out of poverty and misery for many like himself and his adopted son. For many years, furthermore, Patterson emphasized, in contrast to the physical declines of such figures as Ali, that mentally he felt absolutely sharp.[21]

The impeccable reputation of Patterson's integrity both as a fighter and, even more, as a man continued to make him a valuable figure for political candidates to court, especially in New York. He supported George Pataki in his successful bid for the New York governorship in 1994, and the following year Pataki saw fit to reappoint Patterson to the New York State Athletic Commission, this time as the head commissioner, with a salary of $76,421. As he had when first on the commission back in the late 1970s, Patterson's appearance and good name held considerable sway. After he was confirmed by the state Senate, every senator in the room, plus all their staffers then present lined up to have their picture taken with him. Patterson's office pressed for maximum attention to be given to safety issues, as well as for yet another rebirth in the status of Madison Square Garden as a boxing mecca. He voiced support on behalf of retired fighters who faced financial difficulties. He had seen with great sadness the financial fates of such greats as Joe Louis and Sugar Ray Robinson. Patterson did not want ex-fighters to "have to walk the streets.... What I want to do," he proclaimed, "is see to it that when a fighter retires, whether he makes it to the top or doesn't, that he has something. That's the thing I'm after more than anything else."

When an Oklahoma heavyweight named Tommy Morrison, grand-nephew of actor John Wayne, tested positively for HIV in 1996, a major scare shot through the boxing world. Here Patterson, as state athletic commissioner, caused a stir when he mumbled: "I fought twenty-three years. There was no AIDS. I just heard of AIDS a few weeks ago." His office later clarified that he had just heard about AIDS in the context of Morrison's condition. Patterson's office strongly advocated AIDS testing for all fighters. Patterson also "vehemently opposed" some of the new-fangled forms of combat-entertainment like Extreme Fighting. As before, his advocacy drew support, and no one could doubt his sincerity or the depth of knowledge and experience which lay in back of his advocacy. At several public appearances,

Patterson's outwardly excellent physical condition had prompted some to comment that he still looked "fit enough to climb back in the ring." "If he has an ounce more fat than he did when he was heavyweight champion of the world," wrote the *Chicago Tribune* admiringly in 1989, "it does not show." In 1996, an Albany reporter declared, "at sixty-one he looks remarkably like he did in a bygone era of sweeping tail fins and black-and-white TV sets."

In August of 1998, however, such matters of Floyd Patterson's physical appearance took a violent turn for the worse. His confused 1996 statement about AIDS may have been a sign here. While testifying in Albany with respect to some athletic issues, Patterson found himself embarrassingly unable to remember the names of some of his fellow commissioners. He resigned from the commission the very next day. He knew what was occurring. It had already begun, but he and his friends had kept it quiet. Some reporters were instantly writing that this had been a problem for some years, and that his work with the NYAC had been largely that of a figurehead. Mrs. Patterson first emphatically denied rumors that her husband often appeared lost and confused. Even less convincingly, Governor Pataki claimed to have been "unaware" of Patterson's condition. People understood Mrs. Patterson's response. Governor Pataki was another matter. "The shame is not on Floyd Patterson," wrote the *New York Daily News*. "Governor Pataki hired a man who, sadly was not fit for the job. Pataki does not deserve another chance to pick a chairperson who must make decisions in a life-or-death sport. Neither do the Democrats." (Pataki was a Republican.) Pataki, charged the *Daily News*, "willfully exploited Patterson's reputation." Patterson's startling dementia was the very thing about which the abolitionists had been harping, despite the nobility of Patterson previously speaking to the contrary. Patterson was suffering from increasingly severe memory loss. As for many fighters, the problem would only grow, and it would be unremitting and irreversible.[22]

In retirement from the commission, and with his failing faculties, Patterson continued to work with kids interested in boxing. The state of New York gave him a $30,000 annual salary to counsel and work with troubled boys and girls through the State Office of Child and Family Services. Just two months after he resigned from the NYAC his adopted son, Tracy, reconciled with him. He continued to make some public appearances. Increasingly, however, with the dementia, he went into relative seclusion. He never moved out of the comfortable home he had built in New Paltz, and there he would remain. He never suffered from the financial depravities that sadly afflict so many ex-fighters, but his mind simply faded. By 2000, Patterson could not remember who he had first beaten for the championship or even the name of his wife.[23]

While forms of political advocacy are not the acceptable norm in the context of biographical writing, the issue which the abolitionists raise about boxing must be given some respect. The American Medical Association called for a ban of boxing in 1986. In addition to Patterson, Ingemar Johansson started showing dementia by mid–2003, and the examples of Joe Louis, Jerry Quarry, Muhammad Ali, and dozens more are truly tragic.[24] Short of an outright federal ban, which is highly unlikely, given the state-level control which remains over boxing in the United States, and with the examples of cockfighting and bullfighting notwithstanding, there is another, perhaps more realistic possibility. At the end of the nineteenth century, many boxing fans and pundits were arguing that the introduction of the required use of boxing gloves would sissify and ultimately kill the manly sport. The shift from bare knuckles to gloves certainly did not destroy "the sweet science." As that fact is undeniable, why, then, could states not begin to require the use of the very headgear which boxers always use in practice and which amateurs regularly use in tournaments? Such a reform would not completely end injuries any more than did the shift from bare knuckles to gloves, but deaths, injuries, and later-in-life brain deterioration could be greatly ameliorated, as they were with the turn to gloves. The actual institution of such an innovation would be no problem, for the equipment already exists. The sport would likely suffer no more than did ice hockey (or football in the 1930s) when it phased in the required use of helmets. The sad cases of the brains of people like Floyd Patterson, Jerry Quarry, Ingemar Johansson, Joe Louis, and Muhammad Ali serve as most compelling evidence here. In boxing, headgear should be as mandatory as gloves. Boxing trainers already know this since they require it in practice.

Shut away in New Paltz, Patterson's brain never regenerated. Prostate cancer also emerged, and in some ways Patterson's mental afflictions made that malady less difficult to bear. At the beginning of May in 2006, he had grown so weak of both mind and body that he had to be hospitalized. Soon thereafter, his wife took him back to New Paltz so he could die at home. The end came on May 11, 2006. He was 71. He is buried at New Paltz Rural Cemetery in New Paltz, Ulster County, New York.

Muhammad Ali once said that Sonny Liston and George Foreman were the hardest punchers he ever faced, and Joe Frazier was his toughest opponent. But when considering which of his opponents had the greatest boxing skills, he did not hesitate when he named Floyd Patterson. When Marvin Hagler and Mike Tyson were each beginning to make their mark as professionals, each kept a picture of Patterson on their training room walls for inspiration. Patterson can certainly not be named as one of the truly outstanding boxers of all time, at the level of Muhammad Ali, Joe Louis, Sugar Ray Robinson, or Willie Pepp. But because he fought in an era of some of the truly great heavyweights like Liston, Frazier, and of course Muhammad Ali, fans can often fail to grasp the excellence of his boxing skills. Similarly, because of the undeniable greatness of Muhammad Ali as a personality as well as a boxer, the political stances Ali took in the 1960s acquired an added element of coolness among fans, especially the young. Various Ali opponents, including Patterson and Frazier, then gained Uncle Tom reputations directly as a result of Ali's very effective propagandizing when he fought them. Frazier was one who resented this deeply. Patterson did too, and both could easily show why the Ali-driven images of them were false. Over the passage of decades, the rift between the political worlds of mainstream America and that which Ali once represented has ceased to be such the yawning chasm that appeared to be the case in the mid–1960s. Much of '60s radicalism either became more mainstream or faded into irrelevance. Ali himself, while never leaving the Muslim faith, completely abandoned the Nation of Islam and its racially divisive politics. Neither Patterson's Christian faith nor his commitment to justice ever wavered. The '60s era, radical-chic driven coloring and miscasting of such figures as Frazier, and, even more, Patterson has still lingered in boxing memory, however. Not only do many boxing fans fail to grasp the quality of the skills that Patterson had, and which Ali acknowledged, they also overlook the significant political work he quietly accomplished amidst the turbulent days of the civil rights movement. The fact that Ali has since distanced himself from the African American organizations to which his allegiance first caused such controversy underscores the view that Patterson and other more mainstream African Americans had expressed sensibilities and outlooks worthy of respect all along. The vast array of humane work that Patterson continued to do in retirement on behalf of the disadvantaged speaks quite nobly to the same point. He was indeed a good boxer — and a very good man. In 1998, sensitive to the fact that the public remembered his losses at least as much as his victories, Patterson told an interviewer, "If I hold the record for going down, I also hold the record for getting up," adding with his ever so slightly wry smile: "I hope fight historians take that into consideration."[25]

Chapter Notes

I. I Never Seemed Not Scared

1. Floyd Patterson, *Victory Over Myself* (New York: Bernard Geis Associates, 1962), p. 11; Gay Talese, "Portrait of the Ascetic Champ," *New York Times*, Magazine Section, March 5, 1961, pp. 102.

2. Patterson, *Victory*, p. 12; Floyd Patterson, "Out of the Night," *Sports Illustrated*, vol. 16, no. 63, May 28, 1962, p. 72; Gay Talese, "The Loser," *Esquire Magazine*, vol. 61, no. 5, March 1964, p. 142.

3. Patterson, "Out of the Night," pp. 72–75; Patterson, *Victory*, p.11; Jack Newcombe, *Floyd Patterson: Heavyweight King* (New York: Bartholomew House, 1961), pp. 5–8.

4. Patterson, *Victory*, p.8; Gilbert Rogin, "The Invisible Champion," *Sports Illustrated*, vol. 14, no. 55, January 16, 1961, p. 58.

5. Gilbert Rogin, "Invisible Champion," pp. 72, 75; Patterson, *Victory*, pp. 6, 8–10, 14–15, 17; Gay Talese, "Portrait of the Ascetic Champ," p. 34; *New York Times*, January 30, 1962, p. 28; Norman Mailer, "Ten Thousand Words a Minute," *Esquire*, vol. 59, no. 6, February 1963, p. 112; Talese, "The Loser," p. 142.

6. Patterson, *Victory*, p. 20; Talese, "The Loser," p. 143.

7. Patterson, *Victory*, p. 23.

8. Patterson, *Victory*, p. 24–25; Patterson, "Out of the Night," pp. 75, 77; *New York Times*, July 5, 1961, p. 37; May 5, 1969, p. 59.

9. Talese, "Portrait of the Ascetic Champ," p. 102; Patterson, *Victory*, pp. 28–29; Patterson, "Out of the Night," p. 77.

10. Patterson, *Victory*, pp. 31–32; Talese, "Portrait of the Ascetic Champ," p. 102; Newcombe, *Patterson*, pp. 14–18.

11. Rogin, "The Invisible Champion," p. 54; *Pittsburgh Courier*, vol. 1, issue 48, March 4, 1961, p. 4; Patterson, *Victory*, pp. 26–27, 32.

II. I Didn't Know Where I Was or What I Was Doing

1. Patterson, *Victory*, pp. 36–37.

2. Ibid., pp. 37–39; Gilbert Rogin, "The Invisible Champion," *Sports Illustrated*, vol. 14, no. 55, January 16, 1961, p. 54.

3. Patterson, *Victory*, pp. 37–38; Floyd Patterson, "Out of the Night," *Sports Illustrated*, vol. 16, no. 63, May 28, 1962, pp. 77–78; *New York Times*, November 14, 1981, p. 15; Newcombe, *Patterson*, pp. 18–20.

4. Norman Mailer, "Ten Thousand Words a Minute," *Esquire*, vol. 59, no. 6, February 1963, p. 114; Patterson, *Victory*, pp. 37–38; Patterson, "Out of the Night," *Sports Illustrated*, vol. 16, no. 63, May 28, 1962, pp. 77–78; Newcombe, *Patterson*, pp. 21–22; *Pittsburgh Courier*, vol. 1, issue 10, June 11, 1960, p. 26; *New York Times*, December 25, 1954, p. 15; October 29, 1993, section B, p. 7.

5. Patterson, *Victory*, pp. 42–44; Patterson, "Out of the Night," p. 78–79; "Champ for Tomorrow," *Look Magazine*, vol. 17, no. 25, August 11, 1953, p. 49.

6. *New York Times*, February 20, 1951, p. 31; Patterson, *Victory*, pp. 46–47; Gay Talese, "The Loser," *Esquire Magazine*, vol. 61, no. 5, March, 1964, p. 141.

7. *New York Times*, March 1, 1951, p. 34; March 29, 1951, p. 45; April 11, 1951, p. 49; Patterson, *Victory*, pp. 47–48.

8. *New York Times*, February 19, 1952, p. 34; March 6, 1952, p. 34; March 25, 1952, p. 34; April 9, 1952, p. 37; April 10, 1952, p. 42; Newcombe, *Patterson*, pp. 22–24.

9. Patterson, *Victory*, pp. 50–55, 59; Patterson, "Out of the Night," pp. 79–80; Mailer, "Ten Thousand Words a Minute," p. 112; Gilbert Rogin, "Meeting in Miami," *Sports Illustrated*, vol. 14, no. 56, March 13, 1961, p. 17.

10. Patterson, *Victory*, pp. 50–55, 59; Patterson, "Out of the Night," pp. 79–80; Newcombe, *Patterson*, p. 61.

11. Patterson, *Victory*, p. 61.

12. *London Sunday Telegraph*, July 19, 1992, p. 25.

13. Patterson, "Out of the Night," pp. 80–82; Patterson, *Victory*, p. 60, 62–65; *New York Times*, April 10, 1952, p. 42; May 28, 1952, p. 38; June 19, 1952, p. 36; *Providence Journal*, June 8, 1989, section Z, p. 1; "Champ for Tomorrow," *Look Magazine*, vol. 17, no. 25, August 11, 1953, p. 49; A.J. Liebling, "Wunderkind," *New Yorker*, vol. 30, no. 40, November 6, 1954, pp. 152–55.

14. Liebling, "Wunderkind," p. 152.

15. Ibid.; Jack Newcombe, *Floyd Patterson: An Original Life Story* (New York: Bartholomew House, Sport Magazine Library, 1961), pp. 23–25

16. Rogin, "The Invisible Champion," p. 53; Patterson, *Victory*, p. 67; Newcombe, *Patterson*, p. 26; Liebling, "Wunderkind," pp. 152.

17. Liebling, "Wunderkind," p. 152.

18. Ibid., p. 153; Patterson, *Victory*, pp. 69–70.

19. *New York Times*, December 25, 1954, p. 15.

20. Patterson, "Out of the Night," p. 82; Newcombe, *Patterson*, p. 25; *New York Times*, August 1, 1952, p. 10.

21. Patterson, "Out of the Night," p. 82; *New York Times*, August 2, 1952, p. 8.

22. Patterson, *Victory*, p. 70; Patterson, "Out of the Night," pp. 82, 84; *New York Times*, August 3, 1952, p. S3.

23. Patterson, "Out of the Night," p. 84; Liebling, "Wunderkind," p. 153.

24. *New York Times*, August 8, 1952, p. 13; *New York Herald Tribune*, August 8, 1952, p. 15; Patterson, *Victory*, p. 68.

25. Patterson, *Victory*, p. 71; Newcombe, *Patterson*, pp. 27–29; *New York Times*, June 14, 1961, p. 21.

III. He'll Be the Champ

1. Floyd Patterson, "Out of the Night," *Sports Illustrated*, vol. 16, no. 63, May 28, 1962, p. 84; Patterson, *Victory Over Myself*, p. 71; "Champ for Tomorrow," *Look Magazine*, vol. 17, no. 25, August 11, 1953, p. 49.

2. Patterson, "Out of the Night," p. 84; Patterson, *Victory*, pp. 73–75; Newcombe, *Patterson*, pp. 34–35; *New York Journal-American*, September 12, 1952, p. 11.

3. Floyd Patterson, "How I Lost the Title," *Sports Illustrated*, vol. 16, no. 64, June 4, 1962, p. 31; Patterson, *Victory*, pp. 75–76; "Champ for Tomorrow," *Look Magazine*, vol. 17, no. 25, August 11, 1953, p. 49; *New York Times*, September 13, 1952, p. 13; *New York Daily News*, September 13, 1952, p. 27.

4. A.J. Liebling, "Wunderkind," *The New Yorker*, vol. 30, no. 40, November 6, 1954, pp. 154–55; "Boxing's Last Gentleman," *The New Yorker*, vol. 71, no. 22, July 31, 1995, p. 29; *Long Island Newsday*, June 6, 1993, p. 12; *New York Times*, April 13, 1953, p. 37; February 15, 1954, p. 30; June 19, 1993, p. 10; January 9, 2000, p. 30.

5. *Washington Star*, March 29, 1954, p. A15; Newcombe, *Patterson*, p. 32.

6. Norman Mailer, "Ten Thousand Words a Minute," *Esquire*, vol. 59, no. 6, February 1963, p. 112; *New York Times*, October 7, 1952, p. 37; October 31, 1952, p. 34; November 1, 1952, p. 25; December 29, 1952, p. 24; December 30, 1952, p. 25; August 11, 1967, section S, p. 28; *New York Daily News*, December 30, 1952, p. 39; Patterson, *Victory*, p. 84.

7. *New York Times*, January 29, 1953, p. 34; *New York Daily News*, January 28, 1953, section 3, page 1; *Pittsburgh Courier*, vol. 1, issue 36, December 10, 1960, p. 3; Patterson, *Victory*, pp. 85–87; Joyce Carol Oates, *On Boxing* p. 80; "Champ for Tomorrow," *Look Magazine*, vol. 17, no. 25, August 11, 1953, p. 49.

8. Mailer, "Ten Thousand Words a Minute," p. 115; Patterson, "How I Lost the Title," p. 31; Patterson, *Victory*, p. 79.

9. W.C. Heinz, "The Tenderhearted Champ," *Saturday Evening Post*, vol. 230, no. 51, July 27, 1957, p. 99; Patterson, *Victory*, pp. 86, 103; *Los Angeles Times*, January 10, 1991, p. 1; Liebling, "Wunderkind," p. 160.

10. Quoted in Liebling, "Wunderkind," p. 160.

11. *New York Times*, April 14, 1953, p. 32; "Champ for Tomorrow," *Look Magazine*, vol. 17, no. 25, August 11, 1953, p. 49; Gay Talese, "The Loser," *Esquire Magazine*, vol. 61, no. 5, p. 70; Newcombe, *Patterson*, pp. 40–41; Patterson, *Victory*, p. 88.

12. *New York Daily News*, October 20, 1953, p. 58; *New York Times*, October 20, 1953, p. 36

13. *New York Daily News*, December 15, 1953, p. 88; *New York Times*, December 15, 1953, p. 58; *Pittsburgh Courier*, vol. 1, issue 10, June 11, 1960, p. 26; Patterson, *Victory*, pp. 88–89; Mailer, "Ten Thousand Words a Minute," p. 111.

14. *New York Times*, January 14, 1954, p. 36; January 15, 1954, p. 25; Patterson, *Victory*, p. 91.

15. *New York Times*, December 19, 1953, p. 21; Newcombe, *Patterson*, pp. 43–44; Patterson, *Victory*, pp. 89–90.

16. *New York Times*, February 16, 1954, p. 31; *New York Daily News*, February 16, 1954, p. 48.

17. *New York Daily News*, March 31, 1954, p. 79; *Washington Post*, March 30, 1954, p. 20, March 31, 1954, p. 41; *Washington Star*, March 30, 1954, p. A17, 19; Patterson, *Victory*, pp. 144–46.

18. *Washington Star*, March 29, 1954, p. A15; March 31, 1954, p. C1.

19. *New York Daily News*, April 20, 1954, p. 64; May 11, 1954, p. 52; *New York Times*, April 20, 1954, p. 39; May 11, 1954, p. 32.

20. *New York Times*, June 7, 1954, p. 29; *New York Mirror*, June 7, 1954, p. 37; Patterson, *Victory*, pp. 93–94.

21. *New York Mirror*, June 9, 1954, p. 46; *New York Daily News*, August 3, 1954, p. 44; *New York Times*, June 8, 1954, p. 30; August 3, 1954, p. 22; Newcombe, *Patterson*, pp. 46–48; Patterson, *Victory*, pp. 95–96; Liebling, "Wunderkind," pp. 155–56.

22. Patterson, *Victory*, p. 96; Patterson, "How I Lost the Title," p. 32; Liebling, "Wunderkind," *New Yorker*, vol. 30, no. 40, November 6, 1954, pp. 155–56; *New York Times*, June 8, 1954, p. 30; *New York Daily News*, August 3, 1954, p. 44.

23. Heinz, "The Tenderhearted Champ," *Saturday Evening Post*, vol. 230, no. 51, July 27, 1957, p. 99; Patterson, *Victory*, pp. 97–98; *New York Times*, July 12, 1954, p. 24; July 13, 1954, p. 26; *New York Daily News*, July 13, 1954, p. 52.

24. *New York Times*, August 3, 1954, p. 22; *New York Daily News*, August 3, 1954, p. 44; Patterson, *Victory*, p. 98.

25. *New York Times*, September 25, 1954, p. 20; October 12, 1954, p. 33; *New York Daily News*, October 12, 1954, p. 54; Patterson, *Victory*, p. 100.

26. Liebling, "Wunderkind," *New Yorker*, vol. 30, no. 40, November 6, 1954, pp.155; *New York Times*, October 22, 1954, p. 32–33.

27. Liebling, "Wunderkind," pp.151, 158–161; Patterson, *Victory*, p. 101; *New York Times*, October 23, 1954, p. 19; *New York Daily News*, October 23, 1954, p. 26.

28. *New York Times*, November 19, 1954, p. 31; November 20, 1954, p. 14; November 23, 1954, p. 28; *New York Daily News*, November 20, 1954, p. 26; Newcombe, *Patterson*, pp. 50–52, 59; Patterson, *Victory*, pp. 101–103.

29. *New York Times*, December 25, 1954, p. 15; December 27, 1954, p. 24.

30. Ibid., January 2, 1955, p. 56; January 3, 1955, p. 31; January 4, 1955, p. 27; January 7, 1955, p. 25; January 8, 1955, p. 17; *New York Daily News*, January 7, 1955, p. 67; January 8, 1955, p. 24; Patterson, *Victory*, pp. 106–107.

31. *New York Daily News*, January 18, 1955,

p. 52; *New York Times*, January 18, 1955, p. 36; Newcombe, *Patterson*, pp. 54–55; Patterson, *Victory*, p. 108; Liebling, "Wunderkind," pp.156–61; A.J. Liebling, "Starting All Over Again," *The New Yorker*, vol. 39, August 10, 1963, p. 62.

32. "Champ for Tomorrow," *Look Magazine*, vol. 17, no. 25, August 11, 1953, p. 49; "The Next Champ," *Time Magazine*, vol. 67, no. 88, February 6, 1956, p. 44.

IV. Champ

1. *San Francisco Chronicle*, March 16, 1955, section H, p. 3; March 17, 1955, section H, pp. 1, 3; *New York Times*, June 24, 1955, p. 26; Paul O'Neil, "Meet The Next Heavyweight Champion," *Sports Illustrated*, vol. 4, no. 5, January 30, 1956, p. 53.

2. "The Next Champ," *Time Magazine*, vol. 67, no. 88, February 6, 1956, p. 44; *New York Times*, May 18, 1955, p. 39; June 5, 1955, section S, p. 8; Patterson, *Victory*, p. 112.

3. *New York Times*, July 1, 1955, p. 19; July 6, 1955, p. 32, July 7, 1955, p. 31; *New York Daily News*, July 6, 1955, p. 79; Newcombe, *Patterson*, p. 64; Patterson, *Victory*, p. 113.

4. *San Francisco Chronicle*, September 28, 1955, section H, p. 4; September30, 1955, section H, p. 1; October 1, 1955, section H, p. 4; *New York Times*, October 29, 1955, p. 15.

5. *Los Angeles Times*, October 13, 1955, section 4, p. 1; December 8, 1955, section 4, pp. 1, 3; *New York Times*, December 9, 1955, p. 39.

6. *New York Times Sunday Magazine*, December 25, 1955, p. 10; January 30, 1956, p. 33; March 13, 1956, p. 59; March 14, 1956, p. 43; April 11, 1956, p. 52; Patterson, *Victory*, p. 115; Paul O'Neal, "Meet the Next Heavyweight Champion," p. 19.

7. Patterson, *Victory*, p. 116–117, 119.

8. Ibid., p. 130; Newcombe, *Patterson*, pp. 65–66; *New York Times*, April 28, 1956, pp. 1, 13.

9. *New York Times*, May 10, 1956, p. 39; May 18, 1956, p. 29; June 1, 1956, p. 18; June 8, 1956, p. 41; Patterson, *Victory*, pp. 109–111, 133.

10. *New York Times*, June 5, 1956, p. 46; June 6, 1956, p. 44; June 8, 1956, p. 41.

11. *Newsweek*, vol. 47, no. 28, June 18, 1956, p. 106; Patterson, *Victory*, pp. 134–35; *Time*, vol. 67, no. 89, June 18, 1956, p. 59; *New York Times*, June 9, 1956, p. 21.

12. *New York Times*, June 6, 1956, p. 44; June 9, 1956, p. 21; June 10, 1956, p. 180.

13. O'Neil, "Meet the Next Heavyweight Champion," p. 21; *Sports Illustrated*, vol. 16, June 4, 1962, p. 32; *New York Times*, June 10, 1956, p. 62; August 10, 1956, p. 28; Patterson, *Victory*, pp. 127–28.

14. *Time*, vol. 67, no. 89, June 18, 1956, p.

59; *New York Times*, June 9, 1956, p. 21, June 10, 1956, p. 187.

15. *New York Times*, June 12, 1956, p. 42; June 28, 1956, p. 38;

16. Ibid., July 27, 1956, p. 15; August 4, 1956, p. 26; August 12, 1956, p. 161; August 14, 1956, p. 28; September 12, 1956, p. 46; October 16, 1956, p. 54; Patterson, *Victory*, p. 138.

17. *New York Times*, October 19, 1956, p. 53; October 26, 1956, p. 48; November 6, 1956, p. 50; November 28, 1956, p. 59; November 30, 1956, p. 42; Newcombe, *Patterson*, p. 75; Patterson, *Victory*, pp. 135–39, 141.

18. Norman Mailer, "Ten Thousand Words a Minute," *Esquire*, vol. 59, no. 6, February 1963, p. 112; *New York Times*, November 29, 1956, p. 71; December 1, 1956, p. 24; Patterson, *Victory*, pp. 139–40.

19. *Newsweek*, vol. 48, no. 29, December 10, 1956, p. 53; *New York Times*, December 1, 1956, p. 24; Patterson, *Victory*, pp. 140–41.

20. *New York Times*, December 1, 1956, p. 24; "Youngest Champ of the Heavyweights," *Life Magazine*, vol. 41, no. 11, December 10, 1956, p. 55.

V. Frustrations on Top

1. *New York Times*, December 12, 1956, p. 69; December 13, p. 53; December 16, sect. S, p. 2; December 23, pp. 85–86; January 15, 1957, p. 49; January 22, p. 49; January 25, p. 25.

2. Ibid., December 17, 1956, p. 46; July 30, 1957, p. 27.

3. Patterson, *Victory*, pp. 146–48, 151; Newcombe, *Patterson*, p. 81; Floyd Patterson, "How I Lost the Title," *Sports Illustrated*, vol. 16, no. 64, June 4, 1962, p. 32.

4. *New York Times*, January 24, 1957, p. 49; January 27, p. 28; February 17, sect. S, p. 2; April 18, p. 40.

5. Ibid,. December 2, 1956, section S, pp. 1, 7; July 30, 1957, p. 27.

6. Ibid., December 18, 1956, p. 53.

7. Ibid., May 7, 1957, p. 44; May 9, p. 54, May 16, p. 53; *Pittsburgh Courier*, vol. 1, issue 27, October 8, 1960, p. 25.

8. *New York Times*, December 28, 1956, p. 31; February 3, 1957, p. 163.

9. Ibid., December 3, 1956, p. 52; December 25, p. 32; December 29, p. 23; January 22, 1957, p. 48; February 17, 1957, section S, p. 8; Patterson, *Victory*, pp. 157–58.

10. Gay Talese, "Portrait of the Ascetic Champ," *New York Times Magazine*, March 5, 1961, p. 34; Gilbert Rogin, "Meeting in Miami," *Sports Illustrated*, vol. 14, no. 56, March 13, 1961, p. 17; *New York Times*, February 4, 1992, section B, p. 7.

11. *New York Times*, May 18, 1957, p. 13; May 25, p. 33, June 2, p. 194; June 30, p. 142; July 28, p. 137.

12. Ibid., June 4, 1957, p. 57; June 29, p. 29; July 24, p. 18; July 28, p. 137; July 29, p. 25; July 30, p. 27.

13. Ibid., July 21, 1957, section S, p. 11; July 27, p. 26; Newcombe, *Patterson*, p. 84; Patterson, *Victory*, pp. 162–63.

14. *New York Times*, July 30, 1957, p. 1, 27; July 31, pp. 18, 19; August 1, p. 35, 40; August 13, p. 45; November 14, p. 54; November 16, p. 23; February 15, 1982, section D, p. 7; February 18, section A, p. 25; Patterson, *Victory*, pp. 158–60.

15. *New York Times*, July 30, 1957, p. 27.

16. See, for example, Joseph Horowitz, *The Ivory Trade: Music and the Business of Music at the Van Cliburn International Piano Competition* (New York: Summit Books, 1990), pp. 21–31.

17. *Seattle Post-Intelligencer*, August 15, 1957, p. 29; August 16, p. 29; August 17, pp. 7, 29, August 18, p. 29; *New York Times*, June 23, 1957, p. 174; June 29, p. 29; July 29, p. 25; August 18, section S, p. 12; August 22, p. 34; *Los Angeles Times*, April 21, 1985, p. 15.

18. *New York Times*, August 6, 1957, p. 48.

19. Ibid., July 28, 1957, p. 137; August 6, p. 48; Aug, 15, p. 25; August 21, p. 35.

20. *Seattle Post-Intelligencer*, August 21, 1957, pp. 21, 23; August 22, pp. 18,19; *New York Times*, July 14, p. 150; August 6, p. 48; August 18, section S, p. 12; August 25, p. 181.

21. *Seattle Post-Intelligencer*, August 20, 1957, p. 23; August 23, pp 24–25; Newcombe, *Patterson*, pp. 56–57, 91–96; Patterson, *Victory*, pp. 160–62; *Seattle Daily Times*, August 16, p. 22; August 17, p. 6; August 18, p. 51; August 20, p. 22 August 22, p. 24; August 23, p. 22; February 5, 1994, section B, p. 1; *New York Times*, August 21, 1957, p. 36; August 23, pp. 1, 13; August 24, p. 9; December 22, p. 103; June 29, 1958, section S, p. 3; August 12, p. 36.

22. Mailer, "Ten Thousand Words a Minute," *Esquire*, vol. 59, no. 6, February 1963, p. 112; *Los Angeles Times*, November 15, 1986, p. 3; *Minneapolis Star and Tribune*, November 30, 1986, p. 5; *New York Times*, December 1, 1957, p. 242; December 22, p. 99; December 25, p. 39; January 5, 1958, section S, p. 2; January 21, p. 38;

23. Tom Donelson, "Pete Rademacher Revisted," www.insideboxing.com/columnist/tom, August 27, 2004; *New York Times*, May 22, 1958, p. 20; June 26, p. 37; July 26, p. 7; August 12, p. 36; Patterson, *Victory*, p. 168; *Los Angeles Times*, April 21, 1985, p. 15; August 9, 1987, p. 4; *Seattle Times*, July 12, 1987, section D, p. 6.

24. *New York Times*, January 26, 1958, section S, p. 6; January 28, p. 33; February 20, p. 22; February 21, p. 30; August 13, p. 30; Patterson, *Victory*, p. 168.

25. *New York Times*, February 26, 1958, p. 33; March 13, p. 35; March 14, p. 35; March 26, p. 50; April 11, p. 32; April 22, p. 41; June 15, section S, p. 5; Patterson, *Victory*, p. 143.

26. *New York Times*, June 27, 1958, p. 32; July 22, p. 33; Patterson, *Victory*, p. 168.

27. *New York Times*, April 21, 1958, p. 30; April 22, p. 41; May 30, p. 19; June 2, p. 31; June 18, p. 42; June 29, section S, p. 3; July 17, p. 24; July 22, p. 33.

28. *New York Times*, July 11, 1958, p. 19; July 31, p. 29; November 30, section S, p. 84; Newcombe, *Patterson*, pp. 97–102; Patterson, *Victory*, pp. 152, 170.

29. *New York Times*, July 1, 1958, p. 42; August 1, p. 16; August 14, p. 34; August 15, p. 29; August 16, p. 9; August 18, p. 26; August 20, p. 31; September 3, p. 44; Patterson, *Victory*, p. 170.

30. *Los Angeles Times*, August 16, 1958, section 2, p. 1; August 17, sect. 3, pp. 1, 5; August 18, sect. 4, pp. 1–4; August 19, p. 1, sect. 4, pp. 1, 4; *New York Times*, August 19, 1958, pp. 1, 32; August 20, p. 31; August 22, p. 19; *Pittsburgh Courier*, vol. 51, issue 7, February 13, 1960, p. 25; Patterson, *Victory*, pp. 170–72.

31. *New York Times*, September 24, 1958, p. 30; Patterson, *Victory*, p. 174.

VI. Ingemar

1. *New York Times*, January 4, 1959, section S, p. 5; January 14, p. 31; January 16, p. 19; January 20, p. 45; Newcombe, *Patterson*, p. 111.

2. *Life Magazine*, vol. 14, no. 6, April 27, 1959, pp. 66–68.

3. Gilbert Rogin, "The Invisible Champion," *Sports Illustrated*, vol. 14, no. 55, January 16, 1961, pp. 53, 57; Newcombe, *Patterson*, pp. 106–07.

4. *New York Times*, October 10, 1958, p. 40; November 25, p. 44, 45; November 27, p. 56; January 4, 1959, section S, p. 5; January 14, p. 31; January 15, p. 42; January 16, p. 19; January 19, p. 32; January 20, p. 45; April 26, section S, p. 2.

5. Floyd Patterson, "How I Lost the Title," *Sports Illustrated*, vol. 16, no. 64, June 4, 1962, p. 33; *New York Times*, January 21, 1959, p. 35; January 23, p. 31; January 24, p. 15; January 27, p. 37; January 28, p. 27; January 30, 1959, p. 21.

6. *New York Times*, February 4, 1959, p. 41; February 5, p. 37; February 15, section S, p. 3; February 17, p. 39; March 11, pp. 1, 45; March 29, section S, p. 13; April 3, p. 31.

7. *New York Times*, March 16, 1959, p. 41; March 20, p. 35; March 22, section S, p. 2; March 26, p. 38; March 27, p. 27; April 2, p. 38; April 16, 44; *London Independent*. January 5, 1997, p. 26; *Chicago Tribune*, July 19, 1986, p. 2;

Pittsburgh Courier, vol. 51, issue 7, February 13, 1960, p. 25; Patterson, *Victory*, p. 174.

8. *New York Times*, April 7, 1959, p. 43; Patterson, *Victory*, pp. 175–76.

9. Patterson, "How I Lost the Title," pp. 32–3; *New York Times*, April 15, p. 42; April 27, p. 32; April 28, p. 42; Newcombe, *Patterson*, pp. 113–14.

10. *Indianapolis Star*, April 26, section 4, p. 2; April 29, p. 27; *New York Times*, October 29, 1993, section B, p. 7.

11. *Indianapolis Star*, April 25, 1959, p. 18; April 27, p. 22; April 28, p. 27; April 29, p. 27; May 1, p. 1; May 2, pp. 1, 14; *Indianapolis News*, May 1, pp. 1, 27; *New York Times*, March 26, 1959, p. 38; April 2, p. 38; April 7, p. 43; April 16, p. 44; April 17, p. 31; April 24, p. 35; April 26, section S, p. 2; Patterson, *Victory*, pp. 175–76.

12. Rogin, "The Invisible Champion," p. 52; *Indianapolis Star*, May 2, 1959, pp. 1, 14; *Indianapolis News*, May 2, p. 1; *New York Times*, May 1, p. 21; May 2, p. 15; May 3, section S, pp. 1, 2; Patterson, *Victory*, p. 177; Floyd Patterson, "Back on Top of the World," *Sports Illustrated*, vol. 16, no. 65, June 11, 1962, p. 40; Newcombe, *Patterson*, pp. 110–11.

13. *New York Times*, April 16, 1959, p. 44; April 28, p. 42, May 3, section S, p. 2; May 15, p. 37; June 13, p. 15; June 14, section S, p. 7; June 18, p. 38; June 19, p. 18; Newcombe, *Patterson*, pp. 138; Patterson, *Victory*, p. 180.

14. *Stockholm Expressen*, June 11, 1959, p. 8; A.J. Liebling, "A Blow for Austerity," *The New Yorker*, vol. 44, no. 36, July 9, 1960, p. 66; *New York Times*, June 21, section S, p. 2; June 22, p. 32;

15. *Life Magazine*, vol. 46, no. 15, May 11, 1959, pp. 42–3; *Saturday Evening Post*, June 20, 1959, p. ; *New York Times*, June 25, 1959, p. 33; June 28, section E, p. 2.

16. *New York Times*, June 21, 1959, sect. S, p. 3, *New York Times Sunday Magazine*, p. 20; May 13, 1979, section S, p. 3.

17. *New York Times*, June 25, 1959, p. 33; Gay Talese, "Portrait of the Ascetic Champ," *New York Times Magazine*, March 5, 1961, p. 34.

18. *New York Times*, May 14, 1959, p. 46; May 22, p. 19; May 23, p. 21; May 25, p. 42, May 27, p. 40, May 29, p. 19; May 30, p. 11; June 2, pp. 38, 46; June 5, p.21; June 10, pp. 44, 45; June 23, p. 26; June 26, 1959, p. 17.

19. Patterson, "How I Lost the Title," p. 34; *Pittsburgh Courier*, vol. 1, issue 8, p. 25; *New York Times*, June 11, 1959, p. 67; June 26, p. 17; June 27, p. 14; Patterson, *Victory*, pp. 183–85.

20. *New York Times*, June 27, 1959, pp. 1, 14.

21. *Los Angeles Times*, July 26, 1998, p. 1; Newcombe, *Patterson*, pp. 117–19; Patterson, *Victory*, pp. 186–87; Patterson, "How I Lost the Title," p. 39.

VII. It's Never Been Done

1. *Pittsburgh Courier*, vol. 51, issue 47, November 21, 1959, p. 25; vol. 51, issue 1, January 2, 1960, p. 25; vol. 51, issue 7, February 13, p. 25; vol. 1, issue 9, June 4, 1960, p. 4; *New York Times*, June 25, 1959, p. 33; June 27, p. 1; June 28, section E, p. 2; section S, p. 2; July 1, p. 36; July 6, p. 32; April 4, 1991, section D, p. 3; Newcombe, *Patterson*, p. 114; Floyd Patterson, "How I Lost the Title," *Sports Illustrated*, vol. 16, no. 64, June 4, 1962, p. 40; Patterson, *Victory*, p. 188.

2. *Newsweek*, vol. 55, no. 33, June 20, 1960, p. 76; Patterson, *Victory*, pp. 198, 203.

3. *Pittsburgh Courier*, vol. 1, issue 9, June 4, 1960, p. 4; *New York Times*, June 29, 1959, p. 38; July 5, section S, p. 3; August 2, section S, p. 12; April 10, 1960, section S, p. 2; Patterson, *Victory*, pp. 190–92.

4. *Life Magazine*, vol. 48, no. 18, June 20, 1960, p. 94; *New York Times*, July 5, 1959, section S, p. 3; *Pittsburgh Courier*, vol. 51, issue 47, November 21, 1959, p. 25; Talese, "The Loser," *Esquire Magazine*, vol. 61, no. 5, p. 141; Patterson, *Victory*, pp. 193, 219–20.

5. Talese, "The Loser," p. 142; *New York Times*, July 17, 1959, p. 17; July 26, section S, p. 3; August 1, 1959, p. 11; August 4, p. 21; August 5, p. 21, August 6, p. 21; August 7, p. 16; August 8, p. 12; August 9, section S, pp. 1, 3, 5; August 11, p. 30; August 12, p. 1, 22; August 13, pp. 7, 22, 32, 33; August 14, p. 15.

6. Norman Mailer, "Ten Thousand Words a Minute," *Esquire*, vol. 59, no. 6, February 1963, p. 113; *New York Times*, August 18, 1959, p. 34; August 21, p. 15; August 22, p. 12; August 25, p. 1, 6; August 26, p. 1, 34; August 29, p. 9; September 2, p. 21; September 15, p. 49; September 16, p. 51; September 17, p. 51; September 18, p. 37; November 7, p. 20; November 13, p. 35; November 24, p. 47; November 25, p. 34; June 13, 1960, p. 37; June 16, p. 42; June 19, section X, p. 11; July 29, 1992, section D, p. 19; Patterson, *Victory*, pp. 201–02; Floyd Patterson, "Back on Top of the World," *Sports Illustrated*, vol. 16, no. 65, June 11, 1962, p. 45.

7. *New York Times*, August 11, 1959, p. 30; Aug.14, p. 15; August 19, p. 21; August 23, section S, pp. 1, 12; August 24, p. 25; August 25, p. 38; August 26, p. 34; September 29, p. 50; October 1, p. 44; October 16, p. 35; October 30, p. 20; November 6, p. 37; November 13, p. 35; December 12, p. 29.

8. *New York Times*, December 19, 1959, p. 23; December 21, p. 36; December 22, p. 45; December 23, p. 31; December 24, p. 25; December 25, p. 28; December 26, p. 11; December 29, p. 30; December 30, p. 26; April 22, p. 35.

9. Mailer, "Ten Thousand Words a Minute," p. 112; A.J. Liebling, "Starting All Over Again," *The New Yorker*, vol. 39, August 10, 1963, p. 65;

Pittsburgh Courier, vol. 51, issue 47, November 21, 1959, p. 25; vol. 51, issue 1, January 2, 1960, p. 25; vol. 1, issue 5, May 7, p. 25; *New York Times*, September 18, 1959, p. 37; September 22, p. 49; September 30, p. 46; October 8, p. 51; October 14, p. 54; October 20, p. 49; October 24, p. 16; October 28, p. 45; November 6, p. 37; November 10, p. 63; November 11, p. 43; November 18, p. 51; November 19, p. 57; November 20, p. 38; November 21, p. 19; November 24, p. 47; December 8, p. 62; December 12, p. 29; December 13, section S, p. 3; December 17, p. 54; December 20, section S, p. 3; January 12, 1960, p. 24; February 9, p. 37; February 11, p. 42; April 8, p. 20; Patterson, *Victory*, pp. 208–09, 214–16; Patterson, "Back on Top of the World," p. 42.

10. Mailer, "Ten Thousand Words a Minute," p. 113; *New York Times*, December 31, 1959, p. 17; January 26, 1960, p. 37; February 3, p. 39; February 5, p. 33; February 22, p. 23; March 12, p. 18; April 1, p. 43; April 22, p. 35; May 18, p. 51.

11. *New York Times*, April 10, 1960, section S, p. 2; Patterson, *Victory*, p. 193–95, 200–01, 207, 218.

12. *Life Magazine*, vol. 48, no. 18, June 20, 1960, p. 93; *New York Times*, May 6, 1960, p. 35; May 9, p. 35; May 11, p. 47; May 12, p. 46; May 13, p. 41; May 15, section S, p. 14; June 5, section S, p. 2, June 6, p. 40; June 14, p. 46; June 15, p. 51; June 17, p. 27; June 22, p. 38; July 31, section S, p. 2; January 15, 1961, section S, p. 2; *Pittsburgh Courier*, vol. 51, issue 7, February 13, p. 25; Patterson, *Victory*, pp. 212–13.

13. *Pittsburgh Courier*, vol. 1, issue 8, May 28, 1960, p. 25; *New York Times*, May 17, p. 47; May 18, p. 54; May 19, p. 48; May 22, section S, p. 2, May 25, p. 46.

14. *Newsweek*, vol. 55, no. 33, June 20, 1960, p. 77; *New York Times*, June 21, 1959, section S, p. 3.

15. *Pittsburgh Courier*, vol. 1, issue 4, April 30, 1960, p. 23; vol. 1, issue 5, May 7, p. 25; vol. 1, issue 9, June 4, p. 4; vol. 1, issue 10, June 11, pp. 26, 27; vol. 1, issue 11, June 18, p. 25.

16. *Newsweek*, vol. 55, no. 33, June 20, 1960, pp. 77–78; *New York Times*, May 24, 1960, p. 47; June 10, p. 27; June 14, p. 46; June 15, p. 51; June 16, p. 42.

17. Patterson, *Victory*, pp. 204–06; *Life Magazine*, vol. 50, no 20, March 10, 1961, p. 34.

18. Gay Talese, "Portrait of the Ascetic Champ," *New York Times Magazine*, March 5, 1961, p. 105.

19. *Newsweek*, vol. 55, no. 33, June 20, 1960, pp. 77–78; *Newsweek*, vol. 56, no. 34, July 4, 1960, pp. 80–81 *Life Magazine*, vol. 48, no. 18, June 20, 1960, p. 94; *New York Times*, June 21, 1960, p. 36; June 22, p. 38; A.J. Liebling, "A Blow for Austerity," *The New Yorker*, vol. 36, no.

44, July 9, 1960, pp. 77–8; Patterson, *Victory*, pp. 224–26; Patterson, "Back on Top of the World," pp. 47, 49.

20. Gay Talese, "The Loser," pp. 141–42; Liebling, "A Blow for Austerity," p. 79; *New York Times*, June 21, 1960, pp. 36, 37; Patterson, *Victory*, p. 227; Patterson, "Back on Top of the World," p. 50.

21. *New York Times*, June 21, 1960, pp. 36, 37, 67; July 22, p. 19; Patterson, *Victory*, p. 229, 231.

VIII. On Top of the Boxing World

1. *Pittsburgh Courier*, vol. 1, issue 13, July 2, 1960, pp. 25, 27.

2. Ibid., vol. 1, issue 11, May 19, 1960, p. 26; vol. 1, issue 27, October 8, p. 25.

3. Gilbert Rogin, "The Invisible Champion," *Sports Illustrated*, vol. 14, no. 55, January 16, 1961, p. 55; Gilbert Rogin, "Meeting in Miami," *Sports Illustrated*, vol. 14, no. 56, March 13, 1961, p. 17; *New York Times*, July 31, 1960, section S, p. 2; July 3, 1988, section S, p. 4; *Pittsburgh Courier*, vol. 1, issue 10, June 11, 1960, p. 26; Gay Talese, "Portrait of the Ascetic Champ," *New York Times*, Magazine Section, March 5, 1961, pp. 34, 102.

4. *Life Magazine*, vol. 49, no. 19, August 8, 1960, pp. 90, 93–4; *New York Times*, June 23, 1960, p. 26; June 25, p. 23; June 27, p. 18; June 29, p. 38; July 21, p. 22; July 22, p. 19; July 31, section S, p. 2; *Pittsburgh Courier*, vol. 1, issue 13, July 2, 1960, p. 27; vol. 1, issue 17, July 30, pp. 2, 26; Patterson, *Victory*, p. 244.

5. *New York Times*, July 28, 1960, p. 23; July 31, section S, p. 2; *Pittsburgh Courier*, vol. 1, issue 30, October 29, 1960, p. 7.

6. *Pittsburgh Courier*, vol. 1, issue 10, June 11, 1960, p. 26; Rogin, "The Invisible Champion," p. 55; Talese, "Portrait of the Ascetic Champ," p. 102; *Long Island Newsday*, October 2, 1994, section A, p. 36; *New York Times*, June 26, 1960, p. 33; November 16, p. 43; December 1, p. 31; December 30, p. 23.

7. Patterson, *Victory*, pp. 152, 162–166.

8. *Pittsburgh Courier*, vol. 1, issue 10, June 11, 1960, p. 26.

9. Interview with Thomas Gaither, former CORE activist, Slippery Rock, Pennsylvania, August 22, 2006.

10. *New York Times*, June 26, 1960, section S, pp. 1, 5; July 7, p. 38; July 13, p. 43; July 17, p. 145; July 23, p. 13; August 3, p. 21; August 4, p. 21; *Pittsburgh Courier*, vol. 1, issue 19, August 13, 1960, p. 26.

11. Talese, "Portrait of the Ascetic Champ," p. 102; *Pittsburgh Courier*, vol. 1, issue 28, October 15, 1960, p. 22.

12. Ibid.; *New York Times*, May 1, 1960, p.

128; August 14, section S, p. 11; August 20, p. 14; October 4, p. 52.

13. *New York Times*, September 7, 1960, pp. 50–51; May 14, 1961, section S, p. 2.

14. Talese, "Portrait of the Ascetic Champ," *New York Times Magazine*, March 5, 1961, p. 34.

15. *New York Times*, August 4, 1960, p. 21; August 19, p. 17; November 4, p. 43; November 15, p. 50; December 14, p. 54; December 19, p. 38; December 22, p. 30; Dec., 23, p. 23; December 28, p. 32; December 29, p. 30; December 30, p. 23; January 4, 1961, p. 37; January 11, p. 30; Jan.18, 1961, p. 41; January 19, p. 34 January 20, p. 35; January 27, p. 26; January 29, section S, p. 5.

16. *New York Times*, December 25, section S, p. 5; December 28, p. 32; December 29, p. 30; December 30, p. 23; January 4, 1961, p. 37.

17. *New York Times*, August 16, 1960, p. 36; September 22, p. 23; January 15, 1961, section S, p. 2.

18. Rogin, "Meeting in Miami," *Sports Illustrated*, vol. 14, no. 56, March 13, 1961, p. 19; *Pittsburgh Courier*, vol. 1, issue 34, November 26, 1960, p. 22; *New York Times*, December 30, 1960, p. 23; December 31, p. 14; January 22, 1961, section S, p. 2; February 1, p. 41; February 5, section S, p. 14; February 6, p. 29; February 7, p. 44; May 14, section S, p. 2.

19. *New York Times*, February 14, 1961, p. 47; February 15, p. 43; March 1, p. 37; March 3, p. 22; March 10, p. 35.

20. Rogin, "Meeting in Miami," p. 17; *Pittsburgh Courier*, vol. 1, issue 42, January 21, 1961, p. 22; *New York Times*, February 26, 1961, section S, p. 2; February 27, p. 31; March 2, p. 22; March 7, p. 44; March 8, p. 40; March 9, p. 33; March 10, p. 35; March 11, p. 16; March 13, p. 37; March 14, p. 38.

21. Talese, "Portrait of the Ascetic Champ," p. 102; *Life Magazine*, vol. 50, no. 20, March 10, 1961, p. 34; *Pittsburgh Courier*, vol. 1, issue 27, October 8, 1960, p. 25; vol. 1, issue 40, January 7, 1961, p. 29; vol. 1, issue 43, January 28, p. 27; vol. 1, issue 46, February 18, p. 27; vol. 1, issue 49, March 11, p. 30; Gilbert Rogin, "The Drama in Miami," *Sports Illustrated*, vol. 14, no. 58, March 20, 1961, p. 18; Rogin, "Meeting in Miami," p. 18; *New York Times*, March 14, 1961, p. 38.

22. *Life Magazine*, vol. 50, no. 21, March 24, 1961, p. 20; Rogin, "The Drama in Miami," pp. 18–19; *New York Times*, March 14, 1961, pp. 1, 38–39.

23. A.J. Liebling, "A Space Filled In," *The New Yorker*, vol. 37, no. 45, March 25, 1961, pp. 156–58; Rogin, "The Drama in Miami," pp. 18–19; *New York Times*, March 14, 1961, pp. 1, 38–39.

24. Rogin, "The Drama in Miami," pp. 19–20; *Life Magazine*, vol. 50, no. 21, March 24,

1961, p. 24; *New York Times*, March 3, 1961, p. 22; March 10, p. 35; March 14, pp. 38–39; March 15, p. 46; March 16, p. 49; March 24, p. 39; March 25, p. 20; March 30, p. 34; March 31, p. 31; April 1, p. 12; May 26, p. 41; September 19, p. 41; December 15, p. 51; *Pittsburgh Courier*, vol. 2, issue 41, January 13, 1962, p. 1.

IX. Sonny

1. Patterson-Johansson III, Fight Film, ESPN-Classic, 2005.
2. Norman Mailer, "Ten Thousand Words a Minute," *Esquire*, vol. 59, no. 6, February 1963, p. 115; *New York Times*, April 26, 1960, p. 44.
3. Patterson-Johansson III, Fight Film, ESPN-Classic, 2005; *New York Times Sunday Magazine*, March 5, 1961, p. 34; *Pittsburgh Courier*, vol. 2, issue 1, April 8, 1961, p. 9.
4. Gilbert Rogin, "The Drama in Miami," *Sports Illustrated*, vol. 14, no. 58, March 20, 1961, pp. 19–20; Gilbert Rogin, "'The Floyd Patterson I Know I Am,'" *Sports Illustrated*, vol. 14, no. 59, March 27, 1961, pp. 28, 33; *Life Magazine*, vol. 50, no. 21, March 24, 1961, p. 24.
5. *New York Times*, March 15, 1961, p. 46.
6. *New York Times*, June 13, 1960, p. 37; June 16, p. 42; June 19, p. X11; December 7, p. 61; March 30, 1961, p. 34; March 31, p. 31; April 1, p. 12; May 1, p. 40; June 3, p. 16; June 9, p. 66; June 10, p. 13; June 22, p. 18.
7. *New York Times*, March 14, 1961, p. 39.
8. Robert H. Boyle, "Will Floyd Fight Sonny?" *Sports Illustrated*, vol. 16, no. 61, February 12, 1962, pp. 8, 10–12; *Pittsburgh Courier*, vol. 1, issue 15, July 16, 1960, p. 25; vol. 1, issue 51, March 25, 1961, p. 31; vol. 2, issue 4, April 29, p. 23; *New York Times*, April 15, 1961, p. 16; April 16, section S, p. 6; April 20, p. 43; May 9, p. 52; May 11, p. 47.
9. *Newsweek*, vol. 57, no. 36, March 27, 1961, p. 65; *New York Times*, June 12, 1960, p. 216; June 22, p. 38; June 23, p. 26; March 17, 1961, p. 37; April 15, p. 16; April 16, section S, p. 6; April 20, p. 43.
10. *New York Times*, June 15, 1961, p. 59; July 2, section S, p 4; August 2, p. 21; August 3, p. 19; September 29, p. 42.
11. *New York Times*, July 15, 1961, p. 13; July 21, p. 17; October 11, p. 57; May 17, 1962, p. 18.
12. *Pittsburgh Courier*, vol. 1, issue 48, March 4, 1961, p. 4; vol. 2, issue 4, April 29, p. 8; vol. 2, issue 6, May 13, p. 32; vol. 2, issue 11, June 17, p. 18; *New York Times*, March 14, p. 38; April 21, p. 37; October 14, p. 16; February 26, 1962, p. 21; July 21, p. 10.
13. *Pittsburgh Courier*, vol. 3, issue 14, July 7, 1962, p. 1; *New York Times*, June 27, 1962, p. 37; July 31, p. 55; *Long Island Newsday*, March 21, 1991, p. 25.

14. *New York Times*, January 18, 1961, p. 35; February 24, p. 33; January 24, 1962, p. 10; May 10, p. 43; May 11, p. 27; June 11 1968, p. 42.
15. *Pittsburgh Courier*, vol. 2, issue 18, August 5, 1961, p. 32; *Ring Magazine*, November 1961, cover.
16. *New York Times*, April 5, 1961, p. 43; April 11, p. 46; April 23, p. 197; May 2, p. 46; May 3, p. 44; May 6, p. 35; May 11, p. 47; May 26, p. 41; June 22, p. 37; June 28, p. 31; July 2, section S, pp. 1, 6; *Pittsburgh Courier*, vol. 2, issue 3, April 22, 1961, p. 32; vol. 2, issue 4, April 29, p. 22; vol. 2, issue 11, July 11, p. 28; vol. 3, issue 1, April 7, 1962, p. 31.
17. *Pittsburgh Courier*, vol. 2, issue 14, July 8, 1961, p. 28; vol. 2, issue 15, July 15, p. 20; vol. 2, issue 18, August 5, pp. 30, 32; vol. 2, issue 26, September 30, p. 31; vol. 2, issue 28, October 14, p. 27; *New York Times*, July 7, 1961, p. 21; July 23, section S, p. 1; July 27, p. 28; August 29, p. 38; September 16, p. 14; September 22, p. 39; September 29, p. 42; October 4, p. 58; October 11, p. 57; October 17, p. 50; October 18, p. 59; October 21, p. 16; October 28, p. 16.
18. Rex MacLeod, "A Hysterical Calm Grips Toronto," *Sports Illustrated*, vol. 15, no. 59, December 4, 1961, pp. 62–3; Martin Kane, "Floyd Yawns While Sonny Signs," *Sports Illustrated*, vol. 16, no. 62, March 26, 1962, p. 18; *New York Times*, November 2, p. 46; November 22, p. 41; December 5, p. 54.
19. Gilbert Rogin, "A Mild Champion Beats an Inferior Brawler," *Sports Illustrated*, vol. 15, no. 60, December 11, 1961, p. 25; Norman Mailer, "Ten Thousand Words a Minute," *Esquire*, vol. 59, no. 6, February 1963, p. 112; *Newsweek*, vol. 58, no. 37, December 18, 1961, p. 71; *New York Times Sunday Magazine*, November 19, 1961, p. 107; *New York Times*, November 29, p. 50; December 1, p. 43; December 3, section S, p. 1; December 5, pp. 1, 54–55; December 6, p. 62.
20. *Pittsburgh Courier*, vol. 2, issue 37, December 16, 1961, p. 28; *New York Times*, December 6, 1961, p. 62; December 7, p. 61.
21. *New York Times*, December 7, 1961, p. 61; December 10, section S, p. 7; December 24, section S, pp. 3, 4.
22. *New York Times*, January 11, 1962, p. 53; January 13, p. 17; *Los Angeles Times*, July 26, 1998, p.1.
23. Patterson, *Victory Over Myself*, p. 27.

X. Sunglasses and Fake Whiskers

1. *New York Times*, January 1, 1961, section S, p. 2; December 25, p. 29.
2. *Pittsburgh Courier*, vol. 2, issue 37, December 16, 1961, p. 29; *New York Times*, Feb-

ruary 6, 1962, p. 54; February 7, p. 60; July 20, p. 16.

3. *New York Times*, March 18, 1962, p. 191.

4. Robert H. Boyle, "Will Floyd Fight Sonny?" *Sports Illustrated*, vol. 16, no. 61, February 12, 1962, p. 11; Robert H. Boyle and Morton Sharnik, "The Heavyweight Muddle," *Sports Illustrated*, vol. 18, no. 67, March 25, 1963, p. 15.

5. Boyle, "Will Floyd Fight Sonny?" pp. 10–11.

6. Ibid., p. 10.

7. Ibid., pp. 8, 10–12; *Pittsburgh Courier*, vol. 2, issue 37, December 16, 1961, p. 29; vol. 3, issue 12, June 23, 1962, p. 2.

8. Boyle and Sharnik, "The Heavyweight Muddle," p. 15; *Newsweek*, vol. 56, no. 35, November 28, 1960, p. 85; *New York Times*, March 15, 1961, p. 46; May 6, p. 35; January 23, 1962, p. 58; February 20, p. 57; March 18, p. 191; March 19, p. 41; March 23, p. 45; March 27, p. 60; *Pittsburgh Courier*, vol. 3, issue 14, July 14, 1962, p. 20.

9. *New York Times*, March 25, 1962, pp. 201, 203; March 26, p. 40; March 27, pp. 30, 57, 61; March 28, p. 42; March 29, pp. 32, 38; March 30, p. 67; April 1, p. 186; April 2, p. 38; April 3, pp. 1, 6; April 5, p. 52.

10. *Wall Street Journal*, April 26, 1962, p. 16; *New York Times*, June 14, 1961, p. 21; March 27, 1962, p. 30, March 29, p. 32; May 13, section S, p. 7; May 29, p. 50.

11. *Pittsburgh Courier*, vol. 2, issue 42, January 20, 1962, p. 13; vol. 2, issue 44, February 3, p. 13; vol. 2, issue 49, March 10, p. 30; *New York Times*, April 18, 1962, p. 64.

12. *New York Times*, April 3, 1961, p. 41; April 13, p. 48; April 17, p. 60; April 21, p. 16; April 28, p. 18, 27; April 29, p. 185; May 1, p. 45; May 2, p. 36; May 24, p. 42; June 1, p. 20; June 24, *Book Review*, p. 22.

13. David Remnick, *King of the World: Muhammad Ali and the Rise of An American Hero* (New York: Random House, 1998), p. 4; *New York Times*, July 19, 1962, p. 31; September 20, p. 39; November 15, p. 39; December 2, p. 478.

14. "The Pick: Patterson," *Sports Illustrated*, vol. 17, no. 66, September 24, 1962, p. 9; *Jet Magazine*, vol. 22, no. 23, September 27, 1962, pp. 56–57; "A Sparring Partner Looks Them Over," *Sports Illustrated*, vol. 17, no. 66, September 24, 1962, p. 26; *Pittsburgh Courier*, vol. 3, issue 12, June 23, 1962, p. 22; vol. 3, issue 15, July 14, p. 20; vol. 3, issue 21, August 25, p. 20.

15. Norman Mailer, "Ten Thousand Words a Minute," *Esquire*, vol. 59, no. 6, February, 1963, p. 114; Gay Talese, "The Loser," *Esquire Magazine*, vol. 61, no. 5, March 1964, p. 139.

16. Mailer, "Ten Thousand Words a Minute," p. 115; Martin Kane, "Floyd Yawns While Sonny Signs," *Sports Illustrated*, vol. 16, no. 62, March 26, 1962, p. 18; Budd Schulberg, *Loser*

and Still Champion: Muhammad Ali. (Garden City, NY: Doubleday, 1972), p. 84; *New York Times*, July 27, 1962, p. 19; September 19, p. 48; September 21, p. 21; September 23, p. 200; September 25, p. 42; March 8, 1971, p. 47; *Pittsburgh Courier*, vol. 3, issue 24, September 15, 1962, pp. 18, 19; Nick Tosches, *The Devil and Sonny Liston* (Boston: Little, Brown, 2000).

17. Norman Mailer, "Ten Thousand Words a Minute," pp. 119–120; A.J. Liebling, "Starting All Over Again," *New Yorker*, vol. 39, no. 47, August 10, 1963, pp. 62–3; Joyce Carol Oates, *On Boxing*, p. 74; *New York Times*, September 26, 1962, pp. 1, 42.

18. Talese, "The Loser," p. 140; Liebling, "Starting All Over Again," p. 63; *Pittsburgh Courier*, vol. 3, issue 26, September 29, 1962, p. 20; vol. 3, issue 27, October 6, pp. 11, 18; *San Francisco Chronicle*, August 10, 1986, p. 5; *USA Today*, April 6, 1987, p. 3; *New York Times*, September 26, 1962, pp. 42, 43, 46; September 27, p. 60; September 28, p. 39; September 29, p. 25; January 2, 1963, p. 10; February 16, 1963, p. 14; April 13, 1981, section C, p. 12.

19. Liebling, "Starting All Over Again," *The New Yorker*, vol. 39, no. 47, August 10, 1963, p. 63; *Pittsburgh Courier*, vol. 3, issue 25, September 22, 1962, p. 19; vol. 3, issue 27, October 6, p. 19; vol. 3, issue 28, October 13, pp. 18, 20.

20. Talese, "The Loser," pp. 140–41; *New York Times*, April 14, 1965, p. 43; Joyce Carol Oates and Daniel Halpern, *Reading the Fights* (New York: Henry Holt, 1988), pp. 114–16.

21. *Pittsburgh Courier*, vol. 3, issue 10, June 9, 1962, p.24; *Wall Street Journal*, September 27, 1962, p. 3; *New York Times*, September 27, 1962, pp. 60, 66; October 1, pp. 40, 42; October 2, p. 48; October 3, p. 51; October 7, section E, p. 5; October 10, p. 63; October 14, p. 88.

22. Talese, "The Loser," p. 139; *New York Times*, December 2, 1962, p. 134.

23. Talese, "The Loser," pp. 65, 68, 139–40; Boyle and Sharnik, "The Heavyweight Muddle," pp. 13–14; *New York Times*, September 27, 1962, pp. 59, 60; October 5, p. 54; October 23, p. 61; November 6, p. 43; November 13, p. 49; November 17, p. 19; December 9, p. 134; April 4, 1963, p. 60; July 22, p. 40.

24. Liebling, "Starting All Over Again," p. 62; Boyle and Sharnik, "The Heavyweight Muddle," pp. 13–14; *New York Times*, November 7, 1962, p. 67; November 9, p. 34; January 10, 1963, p. 16; March 5, p. 16; April 23, p. 44; April 25, p. 29; May 3, p. 23; May 4, p. 15; October 24, p. 41.

25. Liebling, "Starting All Over Again," p. 63; Gilbert Rogin, "Live With Myself," *Sports Illustrated*, vol. 19, no. 68, August 5, 1963, p. 27; *New York Times*, May 10, 1963, p. 35.

26. Mailer, "Ten Thousand Words a Minute," p. 113; Rogin, "Live With Myself," p. 27;

New York Times, May 10, 1963, pp. 1–2, 14; May 11, p. 9; May 12, section E, p. 1; May 14, p. 27; May 15, p. 26.

XI. Four Seconds Longer

1. Norman Mailer, "Ten Thousand Words a Minute," *Esquire*, vol. 59, no. 6, February, 1963, p. 111.
2. Ibid.; Gilbert Rogin, "The Invisible Champion," *Sports Illustrated*, vol. 14, no. 55, January 16, 1961, p. 50; Gay Talese, "The Loser," *Esquire Magazine*, vol. 61, no. 5, March 1964, p. 140.
3. *New York Times*, July 3, 1963, p. 22; July 17, p. 46; July 18, p. 20; July 21, p. 119–120; July 22, p. 40.
4. A.J. Liebling, "Starting All Over Again," *The New Yorker*, vol. 39, August 10, 1963, p. 68; Patterson, "Cassius Clay Must Be Beaten," *Sports Illustrated*, vol. 23, no. 78, October 11, 1965, p. 98; *New York Times*, July 23, 1963, pp. 1, 22, 23; July 25, p. 41; November 16, p. 44.
5. Liebling, "Starting All Over Again," p. 69; *New York Times*, July 23, 1963, p. 23; July 25, p. 41.
6. *New York Times*, July 31, 1963, p. 48; August 4, p. 139; September 1, section F, p. 1; December 1, p. 263; December 5, p. 39.
7. Talese, "The Loser," pp. 139–140;
8. John Lovesey, "A Continental Comeback," *Sports Illustrated*, vol. 20, no. 69, January 20, 1964, pp. 44–5.
9. Lovesey, "A Continental Comeback," p. 46; *New York Times*, August 18, 1963, p. 157; August 24, p. 37; November 13, p. 70; November 28, p. 89; January 1, 1964, p. 19; January 2, p. 37; January 3, p. 17; January 4, p. 17; January 5, section S, p. 2; January 6, p. 36; January 7, p. 27.
10. Lovesey, "A Continental Comeback," pp. 44–5; *New York Times*, February 23, 1964, section S, p. 2; February 27, p. 34.
11. *New York Times*, March 8, 1964, section S, pp. 1, 6; March 22, section S, pp. 1, 8.
12. *New York Times*, March 9, 1964, p. 39; March 16, p. 45; March 17, p. 41; March 24, p. 41; November 3, p. 40.
13. *New York Times*, March 10, 1964, p. 48; March 13, p. 24;
14. *New York Times*, February 28, 1964, p. 22; March 12, p. 45; March 31, p. 42; August 30, section S, p. 7.
15. "Goodbye, Cus," *Sports Illustrated*, vol. 20, no. 70; p. 14; Tex Maule, "A Fight in Sweden Between Boxing's Forgotten Men," *Sports Illustrated*, vol. 21, no. 71, June 6, 1964, p. 50; Tex Maule, "Still Too Tender to Be a Tiger," *Sports Illustrated*, vol. 21, no. 72, June 13, 1964, pp. 20–21; *New York Times*, March 26, 1964,

p. 44; April 7, p. 40; May 25, p. 50; May 28, p. 47.
16. Maule, "A Fight in Sweden," p. 50; Maule, "Still Too Tender to Be a Tiger," pp. 20–21; Floyd Patterson, "Cassius Clay Must Be Beaten," p. 98; *New York Times*, June 7, 1964, section S, p. 6; June 28, section S, p. 7; July 2, p. 38; July 5, section S, p. 6; July 6, p. 22.
17. Maule, "Still Too Tender to Be a Tiger," p. 20; Floyd Patterson with Milton Gross, "I Want to Destroy Clay," *Sports Illustrated*, vol. 21, no. 73; pp. 43, 61;
18. *New York Times*, November 15, 1964, section S, p. 1; December 1, p. 55; January 20, 1965, p. 55.
19. *New York Times*, July 11, 1964, p. 18; August 5, p. 25; August 11, p. 42; August 19, p. 42; November 15, section S, pp. 1–2; November 22, section S, p. 2; December 12, p. 38; December 13, section S, pp. 1, 5; December 14, p. 52.

XII. Muhammad and the Rabbit

1. Gilbert Rogin, "The Croatian Candidate," *Sports Illustrated*, vol. 22, no. 74, February 1, 1965, pp. 54, 56; *New York Times*, January 18, 1965, p. 23
2. *New York Times*, November 13, 1964, p. 44; January 22, 1965, p. 25.
3. "While Ali Babbled," *Newsweek*, vol. 65, no. 39, February 15, 1965, p. 60; *London Independent*, March 5, 1995, p. 9; *Manchester Guardian*, August 29, 1998, p. 1; *New York Times*, January 22, 1965, p. 25.
4. *New York Times*, February 4, 1965, p. 40.
5. *New York Times*, January 14, 1965, p. 20; February 4, p. 40; March 24, p. 41.
6. *New York Times*, April 18, 1964, p. 18; June 7, Real Estate Section, p. 24; January 15, 1965, p. 26; January 26, p. 46; February 7, section S, p. 2.
7. *New York Times*, January 27, 1965, p. 39; January 28, p. 26; January 29, p. 15; January 30, p. 22; January 31, section S, p. 2; February 2, 1965, p. 36; February 3, p. 38.
8. ESPN-Classic Broadcast; *New York Times*, February 2, 1965, p. 36; Tex Maule, "Okay — But Don't Bring on Clay," *Sports Illustrated*, vol. 22, no. 75, February 8, 1965, p. 18.
9. Floyd Patterson, "Cassius Clay Must Be Beaten," *Sports Illustrated*, vol. 23, no. 78, November 11, 1965, p. 83; ESPN-Classic Broadcast; *New York Times*, February 2, 1965, p. 36; February 3, p. 38; October 5, 1983, section B, p. 10.
10. ESPN-Classic Broadcast; *Ottawa Citizen*, April 23, 1988, section F, p. 1; *New York Times*, February 2, 1965, p. 36.
11. Maule, "Okay — But Don't Bring on Clay," pp. 18–19; "While Ali Babbled," p. 60;

ESPN-Classic Broadcast; *New York Times*, February 3, 1965, p. 38.

12. *New York Times*, January 15, 1965, p. 26; February 5, p. 26; March 5, p. 23; March 6, p. 1.

13. ESPN-Classic Broadcast; "While Ali Babbled," p. 60.

14. *Stockholm Idrottsbladet*, May 15, 1965, *Stockholm Afonbladet*, May 15, 1965, quoted in *Sports Illustrated*, vol. 22, no. 77, May 24, 1965, pp. 72–73; *New York Times*, May 14, 1965, p. 29; May 15, p. 24.

15. *New York Times*, February 2, 1965, p. 36; May 24, p. 40; Ted Maule, "The Baddest of All Looks Over the Universe," *Sports Illustrated*, vol. 22, no. 76, February 8, 1965, pp. 21–22.

16. *New York Times*, February 3, 1965, p. 38; February 6, p. 19; February 7, section S, pp. 1–2.

17. Patterson, "Cassius Clay Must Be Beaten," pp. 79, 93, 98; see also *Washington Post*, May 12, 2006, p. E01; Jeffrey Sammons, *Beyond the Ring* (Urbana: University of Illinois Press, 1988), pp. 197–99, 204.

18. Ibid.; Martin Kane, "The Greatest Meets the Grimmest," *Sports Illustrated*, vol. 23, no. 81, November 15, 1965, p. 38; *New York Times*, November 3, 1965, p. 54.

19. *New York Times*, May 25, 1965, p. 49; May 28, p. 22; August 18, p. 28; October 18, p. 48; October 29, p. 55; November 3, p. 54; November 17, p. 57; November 20, p. 39; November 22, p. 52; November 23, p. 55; September 28, 1975, p. 201; Muhammad Ali, *The Greatest: My Own Story* (New York: Random House, 1975), p. 133.

20. Drew Brown, "Floyd, Fight Like He Slapped Your Mother," *Life Magazine*, vol. 59, no. 22, November 19, 1955, p. 122; Patterson, "In Defense of Cassius Clay," *Esquire*, vol. 66, no. 7, August 1966, p. 57; *New York Times*, September 14, 1965, p. 33; September 15, p. 51.

21. *New York Times*, October 12, 1965, p. 48.

22. *New York Times*, November 19, 1965, p. 49; January 8, 1976, p. 51; Gilbert Rogin, "Rabbit Hunt in Vegas," *Sports Illustrated*, vol. 23, no. 80, November 22, 1965, p. 37; Ali, *The Greatest*, p. 133.

23. Kane, "The Greatest Meets the Grimmest," p. 36; Rogin, "Rabbit Hunt in Vegas," pp. 37–8; *New York Times*, November 22, 1965, pp. 52–53.

24. Rogin, "Rabbit Hunt in Vegas," p. 37; Kane, "The Greatest Meets the Grimmest," p. 38; "The 400 Blows," *Newsweek*, vol. 66, no. 93, December 6, 1965, p. 64; *New York Times*, October 19, 1965, p. 54; November 16, p. 64; November 21, section S, p. 3.

25. ESPN-Classic Broadcast; *Life Magazine*, vol. 59, no. 23, December 3, 1965, p. 42; "The 400 Blows," *Newsweek*, vol. 66, no. 93, December 6, 1965, p. 64; Patterson, "In Defense of Cassius Clay," p. 57; Gilbert Rogin, "Champion as Long as He Wants," *Sports Illustrated*, vol. 23, no. 79, November 29, 1965, pp. 22–4; Gilbert Rogin, "Not a Great Fight, But It Was a Real One," *Sports Illustrated*, vol. 23, no. 82, December 6, 1965, p. 41; *New York Times*, November 23, 1965, pp. 1, 54; April 27, 1968, p. 31; September 28, 1975, p. 201; November 16, 1981, section C, p. 4; October 31, 1985, section B, p. 17.

26. ESPN-Classic Broadcast; *Life Magazine*, vol. 59, no. 23, December 3, 1965, p. 42; Rogin, "Champion as Long as He Wants," November 29, 1965, p. 24; *New York Times*, November 23, 1965, pp. 54–55; November 24, p. 42.

27. Gilbert Rogin, "The Giant They Love to Hate," *Sports Illustrated*, vol. 23, no. 82, December 6, 1965, p. 40; "The 400 Blows," *Newsweek*, p. 64; ESPN-Classic Broadcast; A&E Broadcast, "Biography: Muhammad Ali," October 8, 1991; Eldridge Cleaver, *Soul on Ice* (New York: McGraw-Hill, 1968), pp. 91–94.

28. Rogin, "Champion as Long as He Wants," pp. 22, 24; *New York Times*, November 23, 1965, p. 55; November 25, p. 68; January 14, 1966, p. 49; January 21, p. 53; "The 400 Blows," *Newsweek*, p. 64; Rogin, "The Giant They Love to Hate," p. 40; Cleaver, *Soul on Ice*, pp. 91–2.

XIII. Nowhere to Go

1. *New York Times*, August 1, 1965, section S, p. 5.

2. Gay Talese, *The Overreachers* (New York: Harper and Row, 1965), *passim.*; *New York Times*, June 27, 1965, *Book Review*, p. 22.

3. "The 400 Blows," *Newsweek*, vol. 66, no. 93, December 6, 1965, p. 64; Gilbert Rogin, "Rabbit Hunt in Vegas," *Sports Illustrated*, vol. 23, no. 80, November 22, 1965, p. 37.

4. Gilbert Rogin, "The Giant They Love to Hate," *Sports Illustrated*, vol. 23, no. 82, December 6, 1965, pp. 45, 106; *New York Times*, August 24, 1966, p. 26; September 14, p. 38; February 7, 1967, p. 47.

5. *New York Times*, January 14, 1966, p. 49.

6. *Sports Illustrated*, vol. 25, no. 83, October 10, 1966, p. 18.

7. *New York Times*, February 3, 1967, p. 22.

8. Floyd Patterson, "In Defense of Cassius Clay," *Esquire*, vol. 66, no. 7, August, 1966, pp. 55–58; *New York Times*, July 21, 1966, p. 51; July 22, p. 46.

9. *New York Times*, August 4, 1966, p. 53.

10. *Sports Illustrated*, vol. 25, no. 83, October 10, 1966, p. 18; *New York Times*, September 20, 1966, p. 54; September 21, p. 55; September 24, p. 25.

11. *New York Times*, December 29, 1966, p. 38; February 4, 1967, p. 19.

12. *New York Times*, February 3, 1967, p. 22.

13. *New York Times*, January 29, 1967, pp. 1, 6; January 11, p. 62; February 7, p. 47; February 14, pp. 50, 52; March 31, p. 44.

14. *New York Times*, February 8, 1967, p. 30; March 19, 1967, section S, p. 4; March 20, p. 38; March 21, p. 1; March 22, p. 51.

15. *New York Times*, March 31, 1967, p. 44; April 4, p. 51; April 5, p. 53; April 6, p. 52; April 12, p. 55.

16. *New York Times*, March 31, 1967, p. 44; April 13, p. 56; April 14, p. 44; April 15, p. 23; April 29, p. 12; April 30, p. 201.

XIV. California Rules

1. *New York Times*, May 5, 1967, p. 43; May 9, p. 80; May 11, p. 64; October 28, section S, p. 24.

2. Mark Kram, "They're Still Waiting for Jerry," *Sports Illustrated*, vol. 27, no. 84, November 6, 1967, p. 22; Howard Sackler, *The Great White Hope* (New York: Dial Press, 1968), *passim.*; *New York Times*, February 2, 1968, p. 43.

3. Kram, "Still Waiting for Jerry," p. 22; *New York Times*, June 10, 1967, section S, p. 40; June 11, p. 210

4. *New York Times*, June 11, 1967, p. 210; June 23, p. 48; April 29, 1968, p. 54.

5. *New York Times*, October 27, 1967, p. 59; October 28, section S, p. 24.

6. Kram, "Still Waiting for Jerry," p. 22; *New York Times*, October 29, 1967, section S, pp. 1–2; April 27, 1968, p. 31.

7. *New York Times*, October 30, 1967, p. 66; October 31, p. 50.

XV. Robbed in Stockholm

1. *New York Times*, January 6, 1968, p. 32

2. *New York Times*, April 30, 1968, p. 55; September 13, p. 57.

3. Peter Wood, "Return of Muhammad Ali, a/k/a Cassius Marcellus Clay Jr.," *New York Times Sunday Magazine*, November 30, 1969, p. 116.

4. *New York Times*, March 16, 1968, p. 24; April 28, section S, p. 7.

5. *New York Times*, April 30, 1968, p. 55.

6. Eldridge Cleaver, *Soul on Ice*, (New York: McGraw-Hill, 1968), *passim.*; see also *New York Times Book Review*, March 13, 1968, p. 45; *New York Times*, September 21, p. 38.

7. Jack Olsen, *Black Is Best: The Riddle of Cassius Clay* (New York: Putnam's, 1967), *passim.*; *New York Times*, February 10, 1967, p. 33.

8. Harry Edwards, Arnold Hano, "The Black Rebel Who 'Whitelists' the Olympics," *New York Times Sunday Magazine*, May 12, 1968, pp. 32, 39–46.

9. *New York Times*, April 10, 1968, p. 34.

10. *New York Times*, July 2, 1968, p. 45.

11. *New York Times*, May 5, 1968, section S, p. 6; August 9, p. 38; August 27, p. 50; August 29, p. 51.

12. *New York Times*, August 9, 1968, p. 38.

13. *New York Times*, August 29, 1968, p. 51; September 13, p. 57; September 12, p. 64; September 16, p. 64.

14. *New York Times*, August 29, 1968, p. 51; September 14, p. 23;

15. Stockholm *Dagens Nyheter*, September 15, 1968, p. 1; Mark Kram, "Hashup and Hashish in Sweden," *Sports Illustrated*, vol. 24, no. 85, September 23, 1968, p. 26; *New York Times*, September 16, 1968, p. 64.

16. Stockholm *Dagens Nyheter*, September 15, 1968, p. 1; Kram, "Hashup and Hashish in Sweden," pp. 26–27; *New York Times*, October 28, 1968, p. 59; November 28, 1969, p. 54.

17. Kram, "Hashup and Hashish in Sweden," pp. 26–27; *New York Times*, September 16, 1968, p. 64.

18. Ibid.

XVI. Just One More Shot

1. *New York Times*, October 2, 1968, p. 46; October 17, p. 60; June 11, 1970, p. 91; Mark Kram, "Hashup and Hashish in Sweden," *Sports Illustrated*, vol. 24, no. 85, September 23, 1968, p. 27.

2. *New York Times*, February 10, 1970, p. 54; June 18, p. 75; June 19, p. 63; August 2, p. 132; August 5, p. 27.

3. *New York Times*, February 1, 1970, section S, p. 14; March 18, p. 84; July 23, p. 38; September 6, p. 122.

4. *New York Times*, July 23, 1970, p. 38; August 18, p. 42; September 15, p. 56..

5. *New York Times*, February 19, 1970, p. 67; August 18, p. 42; September 6, p. 122; September 15, p. 56.

6. *New York Times*, September 1, 1970, p. 40; Sept. 16, p. 57; September 23, p. 57; November 3, p. 46; May 15, 1971, p. 45; September 20, 1983, section B, p. 5; *New York Daily News*, February 11, 1972, p. 112.

7. *New York Times*, December 11, 1970, p. 72; December 14, p. 70; December 17, p. 66; January 5, 1971, p. 45; January 7, pp. 38, 44; January 20, p. 27; May 16, p. 31.

8. *Miami Herald*, January 14, 1971, p. D1; *New York Times*, January 7, 1971, p. 38.

9. *Miami Herald*, January 15, 1971, p. D3; January 16, pp. D1, 2; *New York Times*, January 15, p. 68; January 16, p. 22.

10. *New York Times*, January 15, 1971, p. 68

11. *Philadelphia Inquirer*, March 28, 1971, section 3, p. 5; March 29, p. 12; *Cleveland Plain*

Dealer, May 23, section C, p. 2; May 25, section D, p. 1; May 26, section E, p. 1; May 27, section F, p. 1; *Erie Daily Times,* July 16, p. 15; July 17, p. 12; July 18, section D, p. 1; *Buffalo Evening News,* August 21, section C, p. 1; August 23, p. 32; *New York Times,* March 18, 1971, p. 52; March 30, p. 29; May 26, p. 28; May 27, p. 49; May 28, p. 26; July 18, section S, p. 13; August 22, section S, p. 6.

12. *Oregon Journal,* November 22, 1971, section III, p. 1; November 24, section III, pp. 1, 3.

13. *New York Daily News,* February 11, 1972, p. 112; February 12, pp. 18, 28; *New York Times,* December 15, 1971, p. 77; January 16, 1972, section S, p. 2; January 26, p. 19; February 3, p. 39; February 9, p. 29; February 11, p. 44; February 12, pp. 21, 23; February 13, section S, p. 5.

14. *New York Times,* February 12, 1972, p. 23; February 18, p. 54.

15. *New York Times,* May 14, 1972, section S, p. 8.

16. *New York Daily News,* July 15, 1972, p. 31; *New York Times,* June 30, 1972, p. 40; July 14, p. 22; July 15, pp. 15–16; July 17, p. 35; August 8, p. 36; September 20, 1972, p. 53.

17. *New York Daily News,* September 19, 1972, p. 89; September 21, p. 129; *New York Times,* August 9, 1972, p. 12, 44; August 14, p. 37; September 19, p. 111; September 12, p. 38; September 20, pp. 53, 55.

18. *New York Daily News,* September 21, 1972, p. 129; September 22, p. 81; *New York Times,* September 21, pp. 59–60; *Albany Times-Union,* May 26, 1996, section B, p. 1.

19. *New York Times,* September 22, 1972, pp. 49, 51; November 22, p. 20.

XVII. Contentment

1. *Los Angeles Times,* February 5, 1987, p. 15; *New York Times,* March 19, 1973, p. 49; November 1, 1983, section B, p. 8.

2. *Long Island Newsday,* December 31, 1991, p. 115; *New York Times,* April 25, 1973, p. 49; May 25, p. 76.

3. *New York Times,* January 28, 1975, p. 21.

4. *New York Times,* November 9, 1974, p. 35.

5. *New York Times,* April 8, 1975, p. 79.

6. *New York Times,* February 27, 1976, pp. 48, 60; November 3, 1981, section B, p. 3; April 25, 1977, p. 58; May 29, p. 127.

7. *New York Times,* June 19, 1973, p. 45; June 23, 1974, p. 203; June 24, 1974, p. 35; March 30, 1976, p. 36; August 28, p. 37; August 17, 1979, section C, p. 21; July 1, 1982, section B, p. 7; July 28, 1983, section B, p. 4; September 16, section C, p. 13; July 28, 1984, p. 27; September 26, section B, p. 13; October 10, section B, p. 12; June 9, 1986, section B, p. 3.

8. *Chicago Tribune,* June 30, 1988, p. 2; *New York Daily News,* June 24, 2003, p. 27; *New York Times,* September 29, 1977, p. 60; January 31, 1978, p. 21.

9. *New York Times,* November 29, 1979, section D, p. 17; February 15, 1982, section D, p. 7; February 19, section A, p. 25.

10. *Los Angeles Times,* July 26, 1998, p. 1; *New York Times,* March 26, 1978, section S, p. 8; March 21, 1979, section B, p. 10; March 30, section B, p. 6; February 3, 1983, section B, p. 11; February 6, section S, p. 2; February 16, section A, p. 26; February 20, section S, p. 4.

11. *New York Times,* November 9, 1981, section C, p. 2; January 28, 1982, section D, p. 19; January 31, p. 200; January 21, 1983, section A, p. 19; July 24, *Sunday Magazine,* p. 50; September 26, 1984, section B, p. 13; November 16, section B, p. 8; May 1, 1987, section S, p. 7; *Wall Street Journal,* October 13, 1982, p. 1.

12. *New York Times,* August 18, 1979, p. 16; July 10, 1980, section B, p. 23; April 13, 1984, section A, p. 28; April 15, section CN, pp. 10, 18; *Modern Maturity,* vol. 41, issue 1, January-February 1998, p. 60.

13. *New York Times,* October 26, 1980, section S, pp. 1, 3; April 1, 1981, section B, pp. 11, 13.

14. *Toronto Star,* March 27, 1988, section H, p. 4; *Boston Globe,* October 24, 1983, p. 1; *Chicago Sun-Times* August 30, 1985, p. 87; *Buffalo News,* August 24, 1998, section S, p. 6; *Seattle Times,* November 2, 1986, section D, p. 5; March 11, 1990, section C, p. 10; September 23, 1995, section B, p. 7; *San Francisco Chronicle,* August 15, 1992, section D, p. 5; *Los Angeles Times,* October 26, 1986, p. 1; July 26, 1998, p. 1; *Long Island Newsday,* June 28, 1992, p. 22; *USA Today,* March 4, 1994, section C, p. 3; *New York Times,* October 24, 1983, section C, p.1; March 8, 1984, section D, p. 26; March 20, section C, p. 21; March 27, section C, p. 20; July 15, p. 34; April 13, 1984, section A, p. 28; September 30, p. XX3; March 24, 1987, section C, p. 14; May 1, section C, p. 16; March 14, 1988, section C, p. 2; April 28, 1991, p. 56; November 7, 1993, section S, p. 13; March 19, 1995, p. 55.

15. *Boston Globe,* December 23, 1984, p. 39; *USA Today,* May 25, 1988, section C, p. 10; July 17, 1987, section C, p. 2; June 7, 1991, section C, p. 13; *Houston Chronicle,* May 19, 1988, p. 3; *Buffalo News,* January 28, 1994, section C, p. 5; May 10, 1992, section F, p. 3; *Houston Chronicle,* July 18, 1987, p. 3; *Chicago Sun-Times,* July 17, 1987, p. 95; July 19, p. 96; *Chicago Tribune,* July 17, 1987, pp. 2–3; *San Francisco Chronicle,* June 10, 1991, section C, p. 6; *Tulsa World,* March 13, 1996, section B, p. 7; *New York Daily News,* April 21, 2004, p. 54; *Long Island Newsday,* February 6, 1991, p. 139; *New York Times,* April 11, 1984, section B, p. 14; July 1, 1984, p. XX36; July 8,

1984, p. XX41; January 27, 1985. p. 38; May 19, 1988, section D, p. 27; http://library.marist.edu/archives/Circle/1988/1988_5_5.pdf.

16. *Long Island Newsday*, September 4, 1991, p. 13; April 5, 1993, p. 7; *Los Angeles Times*, February 29, 1992, p. 15; *Buffalo News*, April 5, 1993, section A, p. 5; *New York Times*, May 23, 1984, section B, p. 14; May 24, section B, p. 14; October 26, section A, p. 29; October 31, section A, p. 20; October 18, 1985, section A, p. 27.

17. *Boston Globe*, May 26, 1984, p. 1.

18. *Ebony*, vol. 42, issue 5, March 1987, p. 46; *USA Today*, January 4, 1989, section C, p. 4; June 23, 1992, section C, p. 2; July 10, 1995, section C, p. 3; *Omaha World-Herald*, April 1, 1988, p. 1; *Chicago Tribune*, October 26, 1988, p. 2; June 24, 1992, pp. 3, 6; *Seattle Times*, November 10, 1990, section B, p. 2; *St. Louis Post-Dispatch*, June 25, 1992, section D, p. 2; *Los Angeles Times*, June 24, 1992, p. 10; July 5, p. 2; December 20, 1997, p. 9; *Long Island Newsday*, June 28, 1992, p. 22; *New York Daily News*, July 12, 1998, p. 98; *New York Times*, April 13, 1984, section A, p. 28; June 23, 1985, section S, pp. 1, 7; October 19, 1988, section B, p. 13; February 11, 1991, section C, p. 2; March 13, 1993, p. 31; December 16, 1995, p. 35; *Sports Illustrated*, vol. 78, issue 11, March 22, 1993, pp. 70–71.

19. *Boston Globe*, April 12, 1992, p. 50; November 1, p. 58; *Houston Chronicle*, June 17, 1989, p. 12; January 12, 1992, p. 13; February 17, p. 2; *Buffalo News*, February 17, 1992, section B, p. 2; *Los Angeles Times*, February 17, 1992, p. 3; *Toronto Star*, February 15, 1992, section B, p. 10; February 17, 1992, section D, p. 10; September 22, section D, p. 5; *New York Times*, January 9, 1992, section B, p. 17; February 16, section S, p. 8; February 17, 1992, section C, p. 2.

20. *San Francisco Chronicle*, November 2, 1985, p. 44; August 19, 1995, section B, p. 1; *Boston Globe*, August 15, 1995, p. 53; August 18, p. 87; *Chicago Sun-Times*, November 13, 1985, p. 35; *Chicago Tribune*, November 5, 1985, p. 4; November 6, p. 2; August 16, 1995, p. 3; *Los Angeles Times*, November 6, 1985, p. 3; February 13, 1992, p. 1; May 25, 1995, p. 3; *Toronto Star*, February 23, 1987, section D, p. 4; June 27, 1988, section B, p. 1; *Seattle Post-Intelligencer*, February 12, 1992, section D, p. 5; *USA Today*, June 29, 1988, section C, p. 3; *New York Times*, November 5, 1985, section B, p. 8; November 7, 1985, section B, p. 23; February 12, 1995, p. CY2.

21. *Chicago Sun-Times*, April 6, 1986, p. 6; July 17, 1987, p. 97; *Chicago Tribune*, July 17, 1987, p. 2; January 4, 1999, p. 2; January 10, p. 8; *Los Angeles Times*, April 1, 1986, p. 1; April 2, p. 18; January 4, 1999, p. 6; *London Daily Mirror*, February 16, 1996, p. 50; *New York Times*, September 23, 1984, section S, p. 11; April 2, 1986, section B, p. 1; May 1, 1987, section S, p. 7; September 9, 1988, section A, p. 25; January 11, 1989, section S, p. 6; May 26, 1995, section B, p. 5; January 5, 1999, section A, p. 15.

22. *Sports Illustrated*, vol. 85, issue 21, November 18, 1996, p. 4; vol. 88, issue 15, April 13, 1998, p. 17; *Chicago Tribune*, May 16, 1989, p. 1; July 28, 1996, p. 2; April 2, 1998, p. 1; *Chicago Sun-Times*, February 15, 1996, p. 90; February 16, p. 107; *USA Today*, September 14, 1988, section C, p. 2; June 20, 1995, section C, p. 2; February 15, 1996, section A, p. 10; *Jet*, vol. 55, no. 5, October 31, 1988, p. 47; vol. 88, no. 9, July 10, 1995, p. 47; April 15, 1996, section C, p. 13; *Long Island Newsday*, June 20, 1995, section A, p. 52; February 15, 1996, section A, p. 106; *St. Louis Post-Dispatch*, September 10, 1995, p. 7; *Minneapolis Star-Tribune*, February 7, 1996, section C, p. 2; *Buffalo News*, February 7, 1993, section D, p. 2; February 7, 1996, section D, p. 2; *Albany Times-Union*, May 26, 1996, section B, p. 1; October 30, 1996, section C, p. 2; *Pittsburgh Post-Gazette*, July 14, 1996, section E, p. 1; *New York Daily News*, April 2, 1998, pp. 23, 93; April 6, p. 8; March 17, 1999, p. 65; March 19, p. 91; *New York Times*, August 11, 1994, section B, p. 4; January 17, 1995, p. 33; January 20, section B, p. 16; January 26, section S, p. 9; June 28, section B, p. 15; September 20, section B, p. 17; November 15, section B, pp. 1, 7; December 15, section B, p. 15; February 7, 1996, section B, p. 11; February 13, section B, p. 9; February 15, section B, pp. 17, 23; February 7, 1997, section B, pp. 1, 4; April 2, 1998, section C, p. 6; April 5, section S, pp. 7, 8; June 1, section C, p. 6.

23. *New York Times*, April 19, 1988, section B, p. 11; *Los Angeles Times*, July 26, 1998, p. 1; *Las Vegas Review*, June 14, 1999, section C, p. 1; *New York Daily News*, May 24, 1998, p. 114; July 12, p. 98.

24. *London Daily Mirror*, July 9, 2003, p. 42.

25. *Jet Magazine*, vol. 93, issue 21, April 20, 1998, p. 46; *New York Times*, March 22, 1987, p. 279; June 15, 1988, section B, p. 14.

Bibliography

Ali, Muhammad, with Richard Durham. *The Greatest: My Own Story.* London: Hart-Davis, MacGibbon, 1976.

Anderson, Dave. *In the Corner: Great Boxing Trainers Talk About Their Art.* New York: William Morrow, 1991.

Anderson, Terry H. *The Sixties.* 3rd ed. New York: Pearson Longman, 2007.

Antsey, Robert Graham. *Muhammad Ali: Shaking Up the World.* Sardis, BC: West Coast Paradise Publishers, 2001.

Anthony, Gene. *Magic of the Sixties.* Layton, UT: Gibbs Smith, 2004.

Ashe, Arthur. *A Hard Road to Glory — Boxing: the African American Athlete in Boxing.* New York: Amistad Publishing, 1993.

Barbour, James, and Fred Warner. *Liebling at The New Yorker: Uncollected Essays.* Albuquerque: University of New Mexico Press, 1994.

Bloom, Alexander, ed. *Long Time Gone: Sixties America Then and Now.* New York: Oxford University Press, 2001.

Brenner, Teddy. *Only the Ring Was Square.* Englewood Cliffs, NJ: Prentice-Hall, 1981.

Burner, David. *Making Peace with the 60s.* Princeton, NJ: Princeton University Press, 1996.

Cassidy, Robert. *Muhammad Ali: The Greatest of All Time.* Lincolnwood, Ill.: Publications International, 1999.

Chalmers, David Mark. *And the Crooked Places Made Straight: The Struggle for Social Change in the 1960s.* 2nd ed. Baltimore: Johns Hopkins University Press, 1996.

Cleaver, Eldridge. *Soul on Ice.* New York: McGraw-Hill, 1968.

Collier, Peter, and David Horowitz. *Second Thoughts: Former Radicals Look Back at the Sixties.* Lanham, MD: Madison Books, 1989.

Cosell, Howard. *Cosell.* Chicago: Playboy Press, 1973.

Cotrell, John. *Man of Destiny: The Story of Muhammad Ali.* London: Muller Publishers, 1967.

Dennis, Felix. *Muhammad Ali: The Glory Years.* New York: Miramax Books, 2003.

Early, Gerald Lyn. *The Culture of Bruising: Essays on Prizefighting, Literature, and Modern American Culture.* Hopewell, NJ: Ecco Press, 1994.

_____. *This Is Where I Came In: Black America in the 1960s.* Lincoln: University of Nebraska Press, 2003.

_____, ed. *The Muhammad Ali Reader.* Hopewell, NJ: Ecco Press, 1998.

Edmonds, Anthony O. *Muhammad Ali: A Biography.* Westport, CT: Greenwood Press, 2006.

Edwards, Audrey. *Muhammad Ali: The People's Champ.* Boston: Little, Brown, 1977.

Farber, David. *The Sixties: From Memory to History.* Chapel Hill: University of North Carolina Press, 1994.

Fischer, Klaus P. *America in White, Black, and Gray: The Stormy 1960s.* New York: Continuum International Publishing Group, 2006.

Fleischer, Nat. *Fifty Years at Ringside.* New York: Greenwood Press, 1969.

Fried, Ronald K. *Corner Men, Great Boxing Trainers.* New York: Four Walls, Eight Windows, 1991.

Gitlin, Todd. *The Sixties: Years of Hope, Days of Rage.* New York: Bantam Books, 1987.

Gorn, Elliott, ed. *Muhammad Ali: The People's Champ.* Urbana: University of Illinois Press, 1995.

Hauser, Thomas. *A Beautiful Sickness: Reflections on the Sweet Science.* Fayetteville: University of Arkansas Press, 2001.

_____. *The Lost Legacy of Muhammad Ali.* Wilmington, DE: SPORTClassic Books, 2005.

_____. *Muhammad Ali: His Life and Times.* New York: Simon and Schuster, 1991.

Heale, M.J. *The Sixties in America: History, Politics, and Protest.* Chicago: Fitzroy Dearborn Publishers, 2001.

Isserman, Maurice, and Michael Kazin. *America Divided: The Civil War of the 1960s.* New York: Oxford University Press, 2000.

Kaplan, Hank. *Boxing—This Is It!* Palm Springs, CA: ETC Publications, 1985.

Knight, Douglas M. *Street of Dreams: The Nature and Legacy of the 1960s.* Durham, NC: Duke University Press, 1989.

Korn, Henry. *Muhammad Ali Retrospective.* New York: Assembling Press, 1976.

Lasch, Christopher. *The Culture of Narcissism: American Life in an Age of Diminishing Expectations.* New York: Warner Books, 1979.

Lemert, Charles C. *Muhammad Ali: Trickster in the Culture of Irony.* Cambridge, UK: Polity Press, 2003.

Liebling, A.J. *A Neutral Corner: Boxing Essays.* New York: Simon and Schuster, 1992.

_____. *The Sweet Science.* Westport, CT: Greenwood Press, 1973.

Mailer, Norman. *The Fight.* Boston: Little, Brown, 1975.

Marsqusee, Mike. *Redemption Song: Muhammad Ali and the Spirit of the Sixties.* New York: Verso Publishers, 2005.

Matusow, Allen J. *The Unraveling of America: A History of Liberalism in the 1960s.* New York: Harper and Row, 1984.

McWilliams, John C. *The 1960s Cultural Revolution.* Westport, CT: Greenwood Press, 2000.

Miller, Douglas T. *On Our Own: Americans in the 1960s.* Lexington, MA: D.C. Heath, 1996.

Morgan, Edward P. *The 60s Experience: Hard Lessons About Modern America.* Philadelphia: Temple University Press, 1991.

Myers, Walter Dean. *The Greatest: Muhammad Ali.* New York: Scholastic Press, 2001.

New Jersey State Commission of Investigation. *Organized Crime in Boxing: Final Report of the State of New Jersey Commission of Investigation.* Trenton, NJ: The Commission, 1985.

Newcomb, Jack. *Floyd Patterson: Heavyweight King.* New York: Bartholomew House, 1961.

Oates, Joyce Carol. *On Boxing.* Garden City, NY: Dolphin/Doubleday, 1987.

Olsen, Jack. *Black is Best: The Riddle of Cassius Clay.* New York: Putnam, 1967.

_____. *Cassius Clay: A Biography.* London: Pelham Publishers, 1967.

Patterson, Floyd, with Milton Gross. *Victory Over Myself.* New York: Random House, 1962.

Plimpton, George. *Shadow Box.* New York: Lyons & Burford, 1993.

Remnick, David. *King of the World: Muhammad Ali and the Rise of an American Hero.* New York: Random House, 1998.

Riccella, Christopher. *Muhammad Ali.* Los Angeles: Melrose Square Publishing, 1991.

Sammons, Jeffrey T. *Beyond the Ring: The Role of Boxing in American Society.* Urbana: University of Illinois Press, 1988.

Sanford, Harry. *Stand Up and Fight: The Fight Game and the Men Who Make It.* New York: Exposition Press, 1962.

Schulberg, Budd. *Loser and Still Champion: Muhammad Ali.* Garden City, NY: Doubleday, 1972.

_____. *Sparring with Hemingway: and Other Legends of the Fight Game.* Chicago: I.R. Dee, 1995.

Schulian, John. *Writers' Fighters and Other Sweet Scientists.* Kansas City, KS: Andrews and McMeel, 1983.

Seltzer, Robert. *Inside Boxing*. New York: MetroBooks, 2000.
Steigerwald, David. *The Sixties and the End of Modern America*. New York: St. Martin's Press, 1995.
Stern, Jane. *Sixties People*. New York: Knopf, 1990.
Stravinsky, John. *Muhammad Ali*. New York: Park Lane Press, 1997.
Sugar, Bert Randolph. *One Hundred Years of Boxing*. New York: Routledge Press, 1982.
_____. *Bert Sugar on Boxing: The Best of the Sport's Most Notable Writer*. Guilford, CT: Lyons Press, 2003.
Torres, José. *Sting Like a Bee: The Muhammad Ali Story*. Chicago: Contemporary Books, 2002.
Tosches, Nick. *The Devil and Sonny Liston*. Boston: Little, Brown, 2000.

Newspapers

Albany Times Union
Boston Globe
Buffalo News
Chicago Sun Times
Chicago Tribune
Cleveland Plain Dealer
Erie Daily Times
Houston Chronicle
Indianapolis Star
London Daily Mirror
London Independent
London Sun Telegraph
Long Island Newsday
Los Angeles Times

Manchester Guardian
Miami Herald
Minneapolis Star and Tribune
Pittsburgh Courier
New York Daily News
New York Herald Tribune
New York Journal American
New York Mirror
New York Times
Omaha World Journal
Oregon Journal
Philadelphia Inquirer
San Francisco Chronicle
Seattle Post Intelligencer

Seattle Times
Stockholm Afonbladet
Stockholm Dagens Nyhter
Stockholm Expressen
Stockholm Idrottsbladet
St. Louis Post-Dispatch
Toronto Star
Tulsa World
USA Today
Wall Street Journal
Washington Post
Washington Star

Magazines

Better Homes & Gardens 37: 60–1, June, 1959

Ebony 18: November 1962
        33: November 1977
        42: March 1987

Esquire 61: March 1964
        59: February 1963
        66: August 1966
        78: December 1972

Jet 70: April 21, 1986
        71: March 2, 1987

Life 41: December 10, 1956
        43: September 2, 1957
        43: August 12, 1957
        45: September 1, 1958
        46: May 11, 1959
        46: April 27, 1959
        47: July 6, 1959
        48: June 20, 1960
        49: August 8, 1960
        50: March 10, 1961
        50: March 24, 1961
        59: November 19, 1965

        59: December 3, 1965
        73: September 22, 1972

Look 17: August 11, 1953
        23: June 23, 1959

Nation 191: July 9, 1960

Newsweek 47: June 18, 1956
        48: December 10, 1956
        50: September 16, 1957
        53: May 11, 1959
        54: November 9, 1959
        55: June 20, 1960
        56: July 4, 1960
        56: November 28, 1960
        56: July 4, 1960
        57: March 21, 1961
        57: March 27, 1961
        58: December 18, 1961
        63: January 20, 1964
        65: February 15, 1965
        66: December 6, 1965
        80: October 2, 1972
        101: March 21, 1983

Reporter 16: January 10, 1957

Saturday Evening Post 230: July 27, 1957
        231: February 28, 1959
        237: June 27, 1964

Sport 68: June 1979

Sports Illustrated 14: January 16, 1961
        14: March 13, 1961
        14: March 27, 1961
        14: March 20, 1961
        15: December 4, 1961
        16: December 12, 1962
        16: March 26, 1962
        16: May 28, 1962
        16: June 4, 1962
        16: June 11, 1962
        17: September 24, 1962
        18: March 25, 1963
        19: August 5, 1963
        20: January 20, 1964
        20: June 1, 1964
        21: July 6, 1964
        21: July 13, 1964
        21: October 19, 1964
        22: February 1, 1965

        22: February 8, 1965
        22: February 15, 1965
        22: May 24, 1965
        23: October 11, 1965
        23: November 29, 1965
        23: November 22, 1965
        23: November 15, 1965
        23: December 6, 1965
        25: October 10, 1966
        27: November 6, 1967
        29: September 23, 1968
        37: October 2, 1972

The New Yorker 30: November 6, 1954
        33: September 21, 1957
        35: July 11, 1959
        35: May 23, 1959
        36: July 9, 1960
        37: March 25, 1961
        38: October 6, 1962
        39: August 10, 1963

Time 67: February 6, 1956
      67: June 18, 1956
      75: May 23, 1960
      76: July 4, 1960
      86: December 3, 1965

Index

7-24-09 4